The
WORLD GUIDE
for the
JEWISH TRAVELER

The
WORLD GUIDE
for the
JEWISH TRAVELER

Warren Freedman

E. P. DUTTON, INC.
NEW YORK

Editor: Sandra W. Soule
Production Editor: Randy Ladenheim
Copyeditor: Leni Grossman
Design: Stanley S. Drate

Published in the United States by E. P. Dutton, Inc.,
2 Park Avenue, New York, N.Y. 10016

Library of Congress Catalog Card Number: 83-72937

ISBN: 0-525-48095-1

Published simultaneously in Canada by Fitzhenry & Whiteside Limited, Toronto

10 9 8 7 6 5 4 3 2 1

First Edition

CONTENTS

v

PREFACE

This up-to-date volume embraces more than 100 countries and regions of Europe, Asia, Africa, North America, South America, Australia, and New Zealand.

The author and his family have visited nearly every place described, have met with fellow Jews, and have diligently searched out Jewish places of interest. We have formed friendships with rabbis, synagogue presidents, leaders of local Jewish community organizations, as well as ordinary lay Jews. This volume is dedicated to the concept that "the sun never sets on the Jewish community." Our emphasis is on the necessity for the survival of the Jewish community in the Diaspora and in the State of Israel. *The People of Israel live!* There is and always will be a basic interdependence of the Diaspora with the State of Israel, i.e., a lifeline for mutual survival. The poet Judah Halevi wrote in his *Cuzari* (c. 1135), "The Jewish people in the Diaspora is a body without a head or heart. . . . Indeed, it is not even a body but scattered bones." But these "scattered bones" are today vital to the survival of Israel, for they furnish nutriment to the body itself, the State of Israel.

According to recent publications, the world Jewish population is approximately 14,527,150—an increase of about 250,000 since 1976. The increase in Jewish population is *not* traceable to the United States where the Jewish population of about 6 million is virtually constant: Jews comprise 2.7 percent of the population of the United States. The largest number of Jews outside the United States are found in Israel (3,884,000); the Soviet Union (2,630,000); France (650,000); Great Britain (410,000); Canada (310,000); Argentina (300,000); Brazil (150,000); and South Africa (120,000). Approximately 47 percent of world Jewry is found in North America, Central America, and South America; 30 percent in Europe; and about 21 percent in Asia, including Israel, Iran (80,000), and India (fewer than 8,000). The 5,000 Jews in New Zealand and 100,000 in Australia constitute less than 1 percent of world Jewry. However, in Africa are found 1.5 percent of the world Jewry: Ethiopia (22,000), Morocco (20,000), Tunisia (7,000), and Zimbabwe (about 2,000). Population figures for European countries include Austria (13,000),

Belgium (41,000), Bulgaria (7,000), Czechoslovakia (12,000), Denmark (7,500), Germany (38,000), Greece (6,000), Hungary (80,000), Ireland (2,000), Italy (40,000), the Netherlands (30,000), Poland (6,000), Romania (45,000), Spain (12,000), Sweden (17,000), Switzerland (21,000), Turkey (24,000), and Yugoslavia (6,000). Estimated Jewish populations in the Americas, excluding the half million Jews in Brazil and Argentina, include Uruguay (50,000), Mexico (40,000), Chile (30,000), Venezuela (20,000), Colombia (12,000), and Peru (5,200).

A word about the mystery of the Lost Ten Tribes of Israel who were dispersed by the Assyrian deportations of 740–700 B.C.: certain peoples like the Mormons, the Karaites, the Khazars, the Tat Jews of Russia, the Persians, the Afghans, the Berbers, and the Ibos of Nigeria, believe themselves to be descended from the Lost Ten Tribes of Israel. Various writers, historians, and scholars have suggested that the following peoples are truly the Lost Ten Tribes: the American Indians, the Delaware Indians, the Mexican Indians, the Yucatán Indians, the Abyssinians, the Masai, the Ganges Indians, the Kareen tribe of Burma, and the Shindai of Japan.

The State of Israel has not been the only Zion that the non-Jewish world (and even some Jews) sought as a homeland for Jewry. In 1654 the British government wanted Surinam in South America as a haven for the Jews of Europe. In 1659 the French West India Company supported plans for a Jewish colony in Cayenne, French Guyana, in South America. Baron de Hirsch in 1892 established the Jewish Colonization Association for 3 million Russian Jews in Argentina. (About 45,000 came by 1914.) In the United States, Mordecai Noah in 1825 sought to establish the Jewish State of Ararat on Grand Island near Niagara Falls, New York. The London Mansion House Committee in 1884 established a colony of Russian Jews in Saskatchewan, Canada. The island of Cyprus in the Mediterranean was proposed for a Jewish homeland in 1880. In 1839 the British government sought a Jewish homeland in Syria. In 1903 the British offered both an area of Kenya and El Arish in the Sinai. Mesopotamia was investigated in 1908 by the Jewish Territorial Association. In 1928 Russia established Birobidjan. And in 1946 Ho Chi Minh of Vietnam offered David Ben-Gurion a Jewish home in exile. In 1940 the German government envisaged the settlement of 4 million European Jews on the island of Madagascar in the Indian Ocean, but Adolf Eichmann abandoned the idea!

One of the most interesting of surviving Jewish cultures is that of the Marranos and/or *conversos* of Spain and Portugal. Since the Spanish and Portuguese Inquisitions of the end of the fifteenth century, thousands have lived as "secret Jews" in remote areas of northern and central Portugal and on the islands of Majorca and Minorca in Spain. Those who were forcefully converted (the *conversos*) did not fare as well religiously as the Marranos, who secretly practiced their faith but remained externally Catholic like the *conversos*. Marranos over the centuries have migrated to the Netherlands, Mexico, South America, and throughout the world.

Visiting Jewish communities can be an exhilarating experience—there are limitless opportunities to meet and greet Jewish brethren. The Jewish traveler who visits Jewish communities will find there a "Jewish spirit"—if not always a religious community of people practicing Judaism.

This is not a regular travel guidebook, for such general tourist information is beyond our scope. We offer our knowledge and experience to guide you to places of Jewish interest. This book is *not* meant as a bible of Jewish travel; rather, it is a joyous companion to help the hurried traveler appreciate more fully the pleasures of Jewish sightseeing in today's jet age.

Our focus is on people *and* places, because the author believes that the scenery of a country cannot be fully enjoyed without a familiarity with the people who live and work there. The names and addresses of Jewish residents are occasionally listed (with their permission). Cementing relationships between the American Jew and his Jewish brother or sister abroad is one goal the author especially relishes.

Although the names, addresses, and telephone numbers listed in this guide have been checked very carefully, they are subject to change without notice. In addition, sensitive political situations in some countries have made verification very difficult. If you come across any changes that you would like to have noted for the next edition, or any other information of interest, please write to WARREN FREEDMAN, c/o E. P. Dutton, Inc., 2 Park Avenue, New York, NY 10016.

ACKNOWLEDGMENTS

This guide is the product of my travels over the past twenty-plus years. But it is also a testimonial to those wonderful friends and acquaintances all over the world who have regularly kept me informed of developments in Jewish community life. These resourceful friends reside in Stockholm, Saõ Paulo, Tel Aviv, London, Bangkok, Copenhagen, Rio de Janeiro, Oslo, Cairo, Jerusalem, Mexico City, Vancouver, Cape Town, Rome, Auckland, Wellington, Sydney, Melbourne, Johannesburg, the Fiji Islands, Paris, Hong Kong, Athens, and Montreal. Their letters, brochures, and newspaper clippings have been invaluable in making this book current, accurate, and informative. My wife, Esther, who is my constant companion, contributed her ideas and impressions as well as her personal guidance.

To all my *chaverim* (friends) a hearty appreciation and *yasher koach* (go with strength).

INTRODUCTION: THE JEW AS A WORLD TRAVELER

Since the beginning of the Diaspora, Jews have been particularly fascinated by reports of travel to remote Jewish communities by their coreligionists. In the Middle Ages, in particular, perennial conflicts with Christian and Moslem authorities made Jews rejoice whenever they heard or read that in some distant area of the world there existed Jews who were not subject to foreign domination. (Unfortunately, there was, and still is, a dearth of areas where Jews possess equally with the general population the cherished freedoms of worship and of citizenship.) Few accurate historical records of Jewish world travelers exist, and therefore the extent of the travels and of the writings of early Jewish world travelers will never be known.

In A.D. 965 an Arabic-speaking Jew, Ibrahim Ibn Ya'Qub, is supposed to have served as an envoy of the Spanish-Moslem ruler to the German court of Otto the Great; he recorded in some detail his travels through France and western Germany, into Prague and even the Baltic areas. Sulaiman, an Andalusian Jew, supposedly visited China during the second quarter of the ninth century, and was hospitably received there by Hebrew-speaking Jews. In the next century Dunash Ben Labrat traveled from Iraq (Babylonia) to Spain, and Joseph Ibn Abitur journeyed from Spain to Iraq; both travelers recorded their memorable visits. One Ibn Hawqal spent thirty years on journeys for the Fatimid intelligence service and recorded some of his adventures. Eldad Ha-Dani, an itinerant Jewish storyteller of the ninth century, has described in venturesome detail his worldwide trips (he went as far as China). Jacob Ben Nathaniel Ha-Kohen wrote of his long pilgrimage through the Holy Land. But the most prolific Jewish travel writer was Benjamin of Tudela, an affluent and learned Spanish Jew, who traveled throughout the civilized world on his precedent-setting eight-year trek between 1165 and 1173.

Leaving Saragossa in his native Spain, Benjamin of Tudela reached Rome in 1166 during the reign of Alexander III. He found that the 200 Jewish families in Rome, unlike their Spanish coreligionists, "paid no tribute to any man." He was duly impressed with the relative freedom of Italian Jewry. Arriving in Baghdad in 1168, Benjamin of Tudela reported that there were 40,000 Indian Jews maintaining twenty-eight synagogues and ten academies of learning. He recorded the presence of ten full-time Jewish officials, *batlanim,* or men of leisure, who did not engage in work except for Jewish communal administration. In Fustat (Cairo) he observed 7,000 Jewish families of Egyptian descent prospering in a city which then outranked Baghdad as the largest city in the Islamic world. Here commercial and intellectual relations were maintained with Spain and even remote India. Maimonides was then Cairo's most illustrious son, and the Genizah, or documentary depository, was a cherished Jewish mecca. In Alexandria, Benjamin of Tudela visited with many of the 3,000 Jewish families. This ubiquitous traveler even journeyed southward from Egypt to meet the Falashim of Ethiopia.

On his journey to Turkey and its capital, Constantinople, Benjamin of Tudela stopped off at the Greek islands of Corfu and Chios. In the latter he found a Jewish population of 400 persons, somewhat burdened by a hereditary tax imposed by the Turkish ruler, Constantine IX, to support a local monastery; however, Chios Jews were then exempt from all other imperial taxes. Benjamin was truly impressed by the power and glory of Constantinople: in the Jewish quarter in Pera he observed 2,500 Jewish families, "rich and good men, charitable and religious; they cheerfully bear the burden of exile." In Iraq he visited synagogues and tombs in the ancient centers of Sura, Pumbedita, and Shaf Ve-Yatib.

In 1170, Benjamin of Tudela arrived in the Holy Land. He found Jerusalem to be "a small city," fortified by three walls and inhabited by a polyglot population which included only four Jewish families. He described a "dyeing house for which the Jews paid a small rent annually to the king, upon the condition that besides the Jews, no other dyers be allowed in Jerusalem."

Benjamin of Tudela also visited Syria. In Damascus he found 3,000 Jews, and in Tyre about 500 Jewish glassblowers. In ancient Palmyra, northeast of Damascus, he observed 2,000 "warlike" Jews who took an active part in the city's battles against the Turks and the Crusaders.

Returning to Europe, he visited nearly every Jewish community in Germany, all of which, he noted, were located in centers of ecclesiastical power. He described his visit to Czechoslovakia: "The Jews who dwell there call it Canaan because the men of that land (the Slavs) sell their sons and daughters to other nations." About Paris, he said: "Scholars are there unequaled in the whole world—[they] study the law day and night. They are charitable and hospitable to all travelers and are as brothers and friends unto all their brethren the Jews."

In 1180, a German-born travel writer, Petahiah Ben Jacob of Ratisbon, traveled almost the same route as Benjamin of Tudela, except that Petahiah journeyed into Poland, the Ukraine, and the eastern lands then under Tatar domination. His enormous wealth enabled him to cover in his travels most of the civilized world. Like Benjamin of Tudela he was impressed by the Jewish communities in Turkey: "There are so many congregations that the land of Israel could not contain them, were they settled therein." He spent considerable time in the kingdom of Khazars where he found coreligionists who had been converted to Judaism in the eighth century. Petahiah returned to Germany in 1187, confirming most of the observations as to Jewish population, communal structure, medical practices, and folkways that were first recorded by Benjamin of Tudela.

The Spanish historian Salvador de Madariaga in his book *Christopher Columbus* (Macmillan, 1940) argues that Columbus was a Jew, born in Italy of Spanish Jewish ancestry. The Spanish historian Blasco-Ibáñez also claimed that Columbus was Jewish. There are indeed many facets of the life of Columbus which would lead to the conclusion that Columbus may have been a *secret* Spanish Jew— *converso* or Marrano: (1) Columbus addressed several personal notes to his son Diego in Hebrew (in one letter are the Hebrew letters *beth* and *hay,* indicating the Hebrew benediction *baruch hashem*); (2) Columbus left another diary written entirely in Hebrew; (3) Jewish financiers like Diego de Deza, Abraham Zacuto, Isaac Abravnel, and Juan Cabrero (the king's chamberlain) contributed *personal* monies to make his trips possible; (4) of the 120 men on Columbus's three ships that sailed to America there were a large number of Marrano Jews; (5) Columbus wrote long letters to two noted Marrano Jews, Luis de Santangel (chancellor of the royal household) and Gabriel Sanchez (chief treasurer of Aragon); (6) his cartographer and the manufacturer of his nautical instruments was Judah Cresques, the Jewish director of the military academy in Palma, and a personal and close friend of Columbus; (7) the first man ashore in the New World was a Jew, Luis de Torres, who landed on October 12, 1492, which day was Hoshana Raba, a Jewish holiday of rejoicing; the voyage had begun on the ninth day of Ab, a solemn Jewish holiday; (8) his family name Colom (also known as Colombo, Colón, and Colomo) was the same as that of Aaron Colom, a noted Jew from Saragossa, and Andre Colom, a Catalonian Jew who was burned as a heretic in 1479. When Columbus appeared years later before King Ferdinand, he was known as "Don Cristobal Colón," and the King was aware that the family name was associated with Jews of his realm; (9) the ship's surgeon Marco and the ship's doctor

Maestre Bernal were Jews (in 1490 Bernal was forced to do public penance for his Jewish beliefs); and (10) in his writings Columbus frequently quoted Isaiah and Jeremiah in Hebrew.

Columbus's family is believed to have fled Spain, possibly from Catalonia, after the pogroms and persecutions in the year 1391, and settled in Genoa, Italy, where Columbus was born. The Colombo family was engaged in wool-weaving like many *converso* Jews, but young Columbus soon turned his interests to navigation and the art of cosmography.

In 1844, Israel Joseph, a twenty-six-year-old Romanian Jew calling himself "Benjamin II," left his home in search of the Lost Ten Tribes of Israel. In his book *Eight Years in Asia and Africa,* he depicts his many experiences, including a visit to Shiraz in Persia (now Iran), where he found 2,500 Jews forcibly converted to Islam.

In 1857–1859, Joseph Mordecai Netter set off around the world, and in 1860 published in Vienna *The Gulls of the Sea,* a brief volume tracing his journey from somewhere in the Austro-Hungarian Empire to Istanbul (Constantinople), Jerusalem, Bombay, Hong Kong, San Francisco, Utica, New York, and back across the Atlantic Ocean to Vienna. His first Asiatic stop was Istanbul, where he spent a considerable period of time. In Bombay, India, in 1857 he dedicated a poem to the illustrious Jew David Sassoon. Netter arrived in Hong Kong on the third day of Tammuz in 1858, and together with two other "merchant princes" opened a mercantile establishment. Months later he boarded a Sassoon-owned ship out of Macao for Canton, China, and then journeyed for seventy-four days across the Pacific Ocean to San Francisco. Here Netter met with the congregations of Shearith Israel and Emanu-el, for whom he wrote two poems. After leaving California, he arrived in late September 1859 in Utica, New York. Following a voyage of forty days across the Atlantic Ocean, Netter returned to his home city of Vienna, and apparently settled down to record his epoch-making three-year journey "around the world."

The
WORLD GUIDE
for the
JEWISH TRAVELER

ADEN

Aden or South Yemen has been a home for Jewry since biblical times. In 1838, under the British there were about 8,000 Jews in the Aden Protectorate; 100 years later the population was about the same. Aden Jewry differed from their Moslem counterparts in that each Jewish family kept its own still and wine cellar. Aden Jews were the official suppliers of alcoholic beverages to the British and the wealthiest inhabitants of Aden. Anti-Jewish attacks were historical, but not until after 1933 did these attacks result in a mass exodus of Jews. As recently as December 1947, 100 Jews in Aden were killed, their houses and stores looted, and their synagogues and school set on fire. In June 1967, after the British abandoned Aden, more Jews were murdered, and the three synagogues totally destroyed. Today no Jews remain in Aden; 70 percent of them settled in Israel.

AFGHANISTAN

One of the oldest Jewish communities, allegedly descended from King Saul of ancient Israel, is found in Kabul (population 450,000), the capital city of this remote Asiatic country. As of 1983, the total Jewish population was less than 100; during the 1870s there were 40,000 Afghan Jews. Unfortunately, the several ancient but small Jewish communities of Kandahar, Ghazni, and Balkh have virtually disappeared.

There appears to be religious tolerance and respect for the Jews; most Afghans believe that they are descended from the Lost Ten Tribes of Israel. Specifically, the Pathan tribes are believed to be the remnants of the Lost Ten Tribes driven into exile some 2,700 years ago; many still bear names reminiscent of the lost tribes: Ephridi (Ephraim), Reavani (Reuven), and Shnavari (Shimon). A Jew from Afghanistan, Michael Gul, some years ago described his presence as a young child at a meeting between the king of Afghanistan, a Pathan, and a representative of the Jewish community. The king asked the Jew from which tribe of Israel he was descended, and the latter explained that following the exile, with all the tragedies and wanderings, the tribal origins had been forgotten. "In that case," said the king, "it appears that I am the real Jew because I can tell you my exact origins." Whereupon the king proceeded to outline his entire genealogy: "I am from the tribe of Benjamin, the son of Jacob," he said, and he went down the line all the way back to Pithon, the son of Micah, the son of Jonathan, the son of Saul, the first King of Israel (1 Chronicles 9:41).

Despite the small number of Jews, there is a daily *minyan* in Kabul on the second floor of a building on Charshi Torabazein Street. Kabul Jews also practice their ancient Sephardic rituals, replete with homemade bread and green wine following Friday evening services. Many Jewish shopkeepers are found in Kabul's Royal Marketplace, the Serai Shazedeh. Locally, call upon Harry Sharbat (tel. 24707) and Amnon Aqa Shlomo (tel. 25487).

In Herat, Naftali Basal is the recognized leader of the Jewish community. The mosque of Moses is just off the marketplace along a mud street but with a bright blue *Magen David* on its door. The synagogue is a square brick building with a high arched ceiling; the

2

walls are painted blue, green, and white. Colorful carpeting covers the floor, particularly since all worshipers must remove their shoes upon entering (a Moslem custom). The *aron kodesh* in the western wall of the Herat synagogue is large enough for a man to walk into.

Since 1948, over 4,000 Afghan Jews have settled in Israel. The future of Afghan Jewry is indeed bleak, especially following the Soviet invasion of 1980.

USEFUL ADDRESSES

Kabul: U.S. Embassy, Wazir Akbar Khan Mina (tel. 24230).

ALASKA*

Alaskan Jewry, numbering perhaps 900 persons (including 150 in the U.S. military), are centered in the cities of Anchorage, Fairbanks, and Juneau, but the only organized Alaskan Jewish community is the Conservative Congregation Beth Sholom at 1000 West 20th Avenue in Anchorage. (There is a Jewish family operating a lodge in Circle, a hamlet above the Arctic Circle.) Founded in 1958, this Anchorage congregation meets in the only synagogue building in all of Alaska, and in 1980 Rabbi Lester Polonsky doubled the synagogue membership. U.S. Air Force Chaplain Fred Lewin, endorsed to the military by the National Jewish Welfare Board, has traveled extensively from Elmendorf Air Force Base in Anchorage to reach Alaskan Jewry all over the state. A number of Jewish families in the Anchorage area purchase kosher meat from Seattle, 1,800 miles away. The first *mikvah* in the state was constructed at Elmendorf by Rabbi Shalom Gershon Grossbaum of St. Paul, Minnesota, assisted by the Civil Engineer Squadron of Elmendorf AFB. A *tfillin club* was organized, and classes in adult Jewish education are held weekly. There is a Jewish library and chapel at Chapel Center in Building 9-824 on 8th Street at Elmendorf (tel. (907) 752-4300).

Among the national Jewish organizations in Anchorage are Hadassah (Mrs. Enid Green, 1223 Annapolis Drive); National Council of Synagogue Youth (Debbie Green, 3742 Terrace Drive), and Hapoel Hamizrachi Women's Organization.

There is a small Jewish community in Fairbanks serviced also by the U.S. Air Force chaplain. The first Alaskan congregation was founded here in 1904, and the first Jewish cemetery was established here in 1905. The Jewish Community Council of Fairbanks is headed by Bea Kennedy (1242 Log Cabin Court). Religious services are conducted monthly at Fort Wainwright in Fairbanks.

---

*NOTE: The forty-ninth state is included in this book because (1) it is culturally remote from the metropolitan centers of American Jewish life; (2) it is geographically distant from other American Jewish communities; and (3) until twenty years ago, Alaska did not have even an organized Jewish community.

Approximately 900 miles south of Fairbanks is the city of Juneau, where seventy-five Jews reside. Some have married local Eskimos, and most have lost all semblance of Jewish life. Perhaps 85 percent of the marriages are mixed, and children are reared without contact with Judaism. However, the current struggle of the State of Israel for survival has touched their hearts; under the leadership of Sam Corwin (P.O. Box 4326), and his good neighbor Jim Butler, a Jewish community is being formed.

Early Jewish history of Alaska began with Lewis Gerstle, a German Jewish immigrant from Bavaria, who traveled to Alaska via Kentucky and California. In the 1860s, Gerstle and his brother-in-law, Louis Sloss, founded the Alaska Commercial Company and secured from the U.S. government a twenty-year exclusive contract for seal-hunting rights on the islands off Alaska. The firm prospered, organizing a line of steamers plying the waters between San Francisco and Alaska and later developing the large salmon canneries which are still a dominant industry in the Pacific Northwest.

ALBANIA

The *London Jewish Chronicle* recently reported: "Just 1,250 miles from London, less than 3 hours' flying time, a tiny and isolated Jewish community faces total disintegration." Indeed, the People's Republic of Albania has had its doors closed since 1946, and the 300 or more Albanian Jews (called *Cifuts*) apparently are lost to Judaism. In 1976 the government required that all ethnic minorities take Albanian surnames, so that even Jewish names are no longer identifiable.

Jews have lived in Albania since the twelfth century. Spanish Jews arrived in the sixteenth century at the invitation of Albania's Turkish rulers, and during the centuries that followed, other Jews found a home in this mountainous country bordering the Adriatic Sea. A few Jews of Spanish descent still reside in Valona; this naval port was a major Jewish center in the sixteenth and seventeenth centuries. The town of Berat was the refuge of the seventeenth-century false Messiah, Sabbatai Zevi, who spent his last days here.

The town of Durrës once had more than a thousand Jews, but hard times forced them to depart in the early 1800s for Greece.

Just before the outbreak of World War II, Albania under King Zog permitted political asylum for Jews escaping Nazi tyranny. But King Zog soon abdicated, and the German invasion of the country in mid-1943 brought disaster.

Today in Albania religious worship is forbidden, and possession of prayer books is a crime. Jewish observances are held only in the secrecy of homes. Albania's isolation policy foretells the end of Albanian Jewry, although current reports estimate the Jewish population at 200 to 300 people.

ALGERIA

Probably fewer than 300 Jews continue to live in Algeria, including a number in the city of Oran where the Great Synagogue, destroyed in 1960, has been rebuilt as a mosque. This brutal act was just another instance of expropriation of Jewish property by Algerian authorities. Reportedly 600 Jews are in forced labor camps, living in inhuman conditions.

There are still small Jewish communities in Algiers, Blida, Oran, Sidi Bel Abbès, Mostaganem, Tlemcen, Bougie, Constantine, and Colomb Béchar. Many elderly Jews still live in Algeria, most of whom seek shelter in the Maimonides School in the city of Algiers. The Jewish community headquarters is located at 9 rue Hassena Ahmed (tel. 628572); the Algiers synagogue is at 11 rue de Dijon. In the city of Oran the Jewish center is at 27 Boulevard Maata Mohammed El Habib (tel. 23577); and in Blida the Jewish center is at 49 rue des Martyrs (tel. 492657).

Algeria is less than an hour's flight from metropolitan France, yet little is known of the activities of Algerian Jewish communities. Over 140,000 Jews lived in Algeria just twenty-odd years ago, but large-scale emigration began in 1962 when Algeria gained full independence under the Evian agreements. (Algerian Jews were accorded French citizenship by the Crémieux decree in 1870.) Since then about 120,000 have gone to France, about 10,000 to Israel, and 10,000 or more to Spain, Argentina, and Canada.

USEFUL ADDRESSES

Algiers: U.S. Embassy, 4 Chemin Cheikh Bachir Brahimi (tel. 60-14-25).

Oran: U.S. Consulate, 14 Square de Bamako (tel. 390972).

ANDORRA

Isolated in the Pyrenees Mountains between France and Spain is the scenic principality of Andorra, well known as a shopper's paradise. And there are perhaps as many as twenty Jewish businessmen of Spanish origin making their living here. In the village of Les Escaldes there are several Jewish tradesmen, but no Andorran Jewish community per se exists.

ARGENTINA

Among the 22 million people of Argentina, 350,000 to 400,000 Jews and 1 million Arabs live side by side. (The Arabs have mainly come to Argentina since World War II as refugees from Egypt and other Arab countries.) Argentina was an early haven for persecuted Jewry, and Jewish origins date from 1862. Today Argentine Jewry constitutes the largest Jewish community in Latin and South America. Jewish community life is organized into 100 Argentine Jewish communities, only 18 percent of which are Sephardic.

Some 20,000 pupils are educated in seventy Hebrew schools in Buenos Aires where 250,000 Jews reside; another 5,000 or more pupils are enrolled in twenty-seven Jewish schools outside the capital. In Buenos Aires is the famed Jewish Museum (Libertad 773; tel. 45-2474) which depicts the role played by Spanish Jewry in the rise and spread of Spanish culture and civilization.

A few years ago a new synagogue, Comunidad Bet El, was dedicated in Buenos Aires (Sucre 3338; Rabbi M. T. Meyer and Rabbi Mordecai Edery); it is unique because it was built in memory of the late American theologian and scholar Dr. Abraham Joshua Heschel. Numbers alone do not delineate the great importance of the Argentine Jewish community. In Buenos Aires there are more than fifty synagogues and more than twenty-five rabbis, most of whom are Orthodox. The synagogues range from Ashkenazi to Sephardic to Conservative to German Reform. Every conceivable Jewish organization has its counterpart in Argentina.

A representative listing of Buenos Aires synagogues includes the following:

ASHKENAZI

Templo de la Congregacion Israelita de la Republica Argentina, Libertad 773 (Rabbi Dr. Mario Ablin)

Templo de la Asociacion Israelita de Beneficencia y Culto, Paso 423

Templo Ashkenazi Lituano, Uriburu 348

Sinagoga Adat Israel, Asamblea 73

SEPHARDI

Templo La Paz, Olleros 2876

Shaarei Tefila, Paso 773 (Rabbi S.B. Anidjar)

Asociacion Sefardi de Flores (Agudat Dodim), Avellaneda 2874

Congregacion Latina, Piedras 1164

CONSERVATIVE

Or El Congregacion (connected with David Wolfsohn Schools) (Rabbi Daniel A. Kripper)

GERMAN REFORM

Culto Israelita de Belgrano (Benei Tikva), Vidal 2049 (Rabbi Dr. A. Skorka)

Asociacion Religiosa Lamroth Hakol, Caseros 1450 (Rabbi Rev. S. Dresner)

Nueva Comunidad Israelita del Belgrano, Arcos 2319 (Rabbi Dr. H. Harf and Rabbi Dr. B. Plavnik)

Buenos Aires has many Jewish hospitals and health institutions, and at least thirty-eight kosher butcher shops supervised by the Central Rabbinate.

There are important Jewish communities in the cities and provinces of Rosario (15,000), Córdoba (10,000), Santa Fe (6,000), Tucumán (5,000), La Plata (4,000), Bahía Blanca (4,000), Mendoza (4,000), Paraná (3,000), Mar del Plata (3,500), Resistencia (2,000), Corrientes (1,500), and Salta (1,500).

In November 1984 the town of Mosesville in Santa Fe Province will celebrate the ninety-third anniversary of the arrival of the first emigrants sponsored by Baron Maurice de Hirsch's Jewish Colonization Association (JCA). These colonists have prospered; about 1,500 of the town's 4,000 residents are Jewish, and a few years ago all five members of the Municipal Council were Jewish. In 1891 Mosesville received the first 820 Jews arriving in Argentina under JCA auspices after they had escaped from Russian pogroms. There are similar Jewish colonies in Rivera (where 50 percent of the 2,000 population is Jewish) and in General Roca with 1,000 Jews. Jewish farmers cultivate about 1 million acres of Argentine land, raise livestock, and grow grain.

KOSHER RESTAURANTS

Buenos Aires: Sucat Davit at Paso 640 (tel. 88-4645).
Vidalinda at Vidal 2364 (tel. 781-1339).
Shalom (at Bar Ilan School), Rua Pompeu Loureiro 48, Copacabana (tel. 257-1571).

USEFUL ADDRESSES

Buenos Aires: U.S. Embassy, 4300 Colombia, 1425 (tel. 774-7611).
Canadian Embassy, Brunetta Building, Suipacha and Sante Fe (tel. 32-9081/8).
Israeli Embassy, Arroyo 910 (tel. 392-4481).

ARUBA

This delightful tropical island has a population of 61,000 and twenty-two Jewish families. Unlike Curaçao (forty miles to the east) which is predominantly Sephardic, the Aruba Jewish community is predominantly Ashkenazi. Nearly all of Aruba's Jewish citizens were refugees from Nazi tyranny and Eastern European pogroms.

In the capital city of Oranjestad is Beth Israel Synagogue, a distinctively simple but tastefully decorated one-story edifice on Nassau-straat near Pasteurstraat (tel. 3272). The building features a large *Magen David* on its facade, and its front door opens directly into the synagogue proper. To the left of the *aron kodesh* is a door leading into a large social hall where *oneg shabbat* services are held on Friday nights. Frequently, a *minyan* is difficult to find, but American tourists always appear just in time. Unfortunately, there is no rabbi nor cantor, and the services, in recent years, have been led by an eighty-four-year-old Polish refugee. (Contact Hugo Lampl of the New Amsterdam Store; tel. 1152.) Built in 1962, the synagogue was designed by Morris Lapidus, architect of the Aruba Caribbean Hotel.

The Old Jewish Cemetery on Aruba contains gravestones dating back to 1563, almost a century before the first Jewish settlement on the neighboring island of Curaçao. But regular use of the cemetery did not begin until 1837; moreover, most Aruban Jews were buried in Curaçao where they initially had stopped in their migrations.

The first known Aruban Jew was Moses De Salmo Levy Maduro, a member of a large and still prominent Curaçao family, who arrived in 1754 with his wife and six children. He leased land from the Dutch West India Company, and settled down. In the 1850s small quantities of gold were discovered on Aruba, and Jewish investors arrived, as they did in 1879 when the Aruba Phosphate Mining Co. was organized.

Aruba is a shopper's paradise, and it is understandable why Aruba's Jews are all businessmen. One of the most successful is Ike Cohen (and his genial wife, Grete), who not only owns Aruba's famous restaurant Talk of the Town, but also two other restaurants and two hotels. Leo Berlinski and his wife own and operate Aruba's fine jewelry store in San Nicolas. Other leaders of the Jewish community in Oranjestad are Benjamin Pick (La Moda Store, tel. 1432); Jose Isaac, Kalman Hochman, Adolf Groger, S. Elpstein, and young Issak Gottfried (Casa Haime, tel. 1235).

AUSTRALIA

The story of Australian Jewry truly began in the year 1788 when the first fleet of British convicts arrived in Australia. Among their numbers were ten Jews—just enough for a *minyan*. Within a decade there were 850 Jews, all of whom had been convicted by British justice. But no Jewish community was established until 1817 when the first Jewish burial society was organized by twenty Jews. In the 1820s Joseph Marcus, a German-born convict with a good religious background, gathered together some thirty of his fellow Jews for religious services. Organized Jewish worship commenced in May 1828 with the arrival in Sydney of a young London Jew, Phillip Joseph Cohen, who had the authority of the British Chief Rabbi to solemnize Jewish marriages.

In 1830, Chief Rabbi Solomon Hirschel of London dispatched Rabbi Aaron Levy of the London *Beth Din* to Sydney to finalize a Jewish divorce; while there, Rabbi Levy provided Australian Jewry with its first *sifrai torat*. Two years later a formal congregation of 300 Jews was established with Joseph Barrow Montefiore, a pioneer of the sheep industry, as its president. In 1841 there were 856 Jews in Sydney, and so Beit Israel Synagogue was built in 1844 on York Street near the site of the town hall. In 1859 a second synagogue, the Great Synagogue, was built in Macquarie Street, close to the present site of St. Stephen's Presbyterian Church. In 1878 the two Jewish congregations merged and established the Great Synagogue (166 Castlereagh Street; tel. 613950). Thus was organized the great Jewish community of Sydney, then numbering 1,100 persons. Today more than 30,000 Jews live in Sydney.

There were also Jews among the early settlers in other Australian cities such as Melbourne, Adelaide, and Brisbane, but immigration there on a larger scale did not begin until the gold rush of the mid-nineteenth century. When gold was discovered in 1851, Jews, like other people, came to Australia from all over the world. But most Jews came as peddlers and shopkeepers and did not gain enormous wealth immediately. The shortage of Jewish women caused these early Jewish arrivals to marry out of their faith in large numbers. Between 1870 and 1900, as the result of Russian pogroms, Jewish refugees from Eastern Europe swelled the Jewish population in Australia to 15,000. Thousands more arrived before and during World War II.

Among the distinguished Australian Jews was Sir Isaac Isaacs, Chief Justice and Governor-General, and most recently Governor-General Sir Zelman Cowen, who had been Vice-Chancellor of Queensland University. Another noted Australian Jew was Lt. General Sir John Monash who commanded Australian forces in World War I. Monash University in Melbourne is named after this great Australian soldier. Here Yiddish has been recognized as a qualifying language; proficiency in Yiddish exempts the student from study of another foreign language. Another Jew, Vabian Solomon, served as Premier of South Australia. Indeed, in nearly every field of endeavor, Jewish contributions to Australian life are far out of proportion to the Jewish population.

The Jewish population of Australia has reached 100,000, of whom 40,000 live in Victoria (capital city, Melbourne) and 35,000 in New South Wales (capital city, Sydney). There are Jewish communities also in Canberra (Capital Territory)—500; Newcastle (New South Wales)—100; Brisbane and Gold Coast (Queensland)—2,000; Adelaide (South Australia)—1,800; Hobart and Launceston (Tasmania)—150; Ballarat and Geelong (Victoria)—100; and Perth (Western Australia)—3,500.

Australian Jewry is like any other Jewish community in the world, in that it is highly organized: there are about 200 Jewish communal organizations in Sydney and Melbourne alone. Current president of the Executive Council of Australian Jewry is I. J. Leibler.

ADELAIDE (South Australia)

The Jewish community in Adelaide began in 1848 with the dedication of Beit Yisrael Synagogue on Synagogue Place (tel. 2231388). This South Australia community of 1,800 Jews was the early home of the Montefiore family, cousins of the famed Sir Moses Montefiore of England.

BALLARAT (Victoria)

Seventy-five miles northwest of Melbourne is the gold rush town of Ballarat. Within two years of the 1851 gold rush the Ballarat Hebrew Congregation was formed, and in 1861 Shearit Yisrael Synagogue was erected on Barkly Street. Despite a turbulent history, Ballarat became an Orthodox center and even had its own *matzoh* plant. But after 1890 the Jewish populace declined and today there are only fifty Jews in Ballarat.

CANBERRA (Capital Territory)

Canberra was created from a plan which was declared the winning entry in an international design competition in 1912. Walter Burley Griffin's 1912 plan was for a city of 25,000 people, but today Canberra has a population of over 200,000. The 500 Canberra Jews are proud of the Jewish community center (tel. Forrest 733038), a modern building housing a chapel and located in the center of the city. The National Jewish Memorial Center is at the corner of Canberra Avenue and National Circuit (tel. Forrest 951052).

GEELONG (Victoria)

Geelong, forty-five miles southwest of Melbourne, is a manufacturing center. In 1854 a synagogue was consecrated, but the community never grew beyond its need for the 100 seats in the synagogue on Yarra Street.

LAUNCESTON (Tasmania)

In the city of Launceston on St. John Street is located Australia's second oldest synagogue, built in 1846 but closed since 1960. (See S. Crawcour, 100 Elphin Road, tel. 2-3986.)

MELBOURNE (Victoria)

Founded in 1835 by convicts, the Melbourne Jewish community's first free Jewish settler was Michael Cashmore, who arrived from London in 1840 and opened a drapery shop. By the year 1841 there were fifty-six Jews, and in the same year the Melbourne Hebrew Congregation was founded with Michael Cashmore as president for a two-year term. In 1848 Shearit Israel Synagogue was founded; the gold rush increased Melbourne's population, so that by 1857 a third congregation was formed, the East Melbourne Hebrew Congregation of non-British Jews (Albert Street, tel: 6621372). In 1861 there were 1,796 Jews in Melbourne, and by 1940 there were more than 9,000. Today Melbourne's Jewish population exceeds 35,000. There are eighteen Orthodox synagogues and three Liberal temples in Melbourne, including the following:

> Melbourne Hebrew Congregation, Toorak Road, South Yarra. The most beautiful stained-glass windows in Australia (tel. BM262255).

> Temple Beth Israel, 76-82 Alma Road, St. Kilda (tel. 511488). Also services held at 549 Centre Road, Bentleigh, and at 33 Harp Road, East Kew (Liberal congregation).

> Moorabbin, 960 Nepean Highway, Moorabbin.

Elwood, 39 Dickens Street, Elwood (tel. 911547).

St. Kilda Synagogue, Charnwood Grove, St. Kilda.

Adas Israel, 24 Glen Eira Avenue, Ripponlea, St. Kilda (tel. 537116) [Hungarian].

Beth Yaacov, 15 Elizabeth Street, East Coburg (tel. 352980).

The B'nai B'rith office in Melbourne is at 99 Hotham Street, East St. Kilda (tel. 524491).

Among the important sights of Jewish interest in Melbourne are the Memorial to the Six Million in the local cemetery; the Bialystoker Center; Monash University; Mount Scopus College (245 Burwood Highway; tel. 288-5722); the Lubavitcher Yeshiva; and Bialik College. Jewish-owned businesses include Sydney Music Bowl, a popular retreat, and Myer Department Store, the biggest in the Southern Hemisphere.

SHEPPARTON (Victoria)

In Shepparton, a farming community 113 miles north of Melbourne, there are Jewish orchards and Jewish farming, as well as the Toolomba Training Farm for would-be *kibbutzniks* in Israel.

SYDNEY (New South Wales)

Sydney is Austrailia's second largest Jewish city and has many synagogues in its metropolitan area, including:

Adath Yisroel, 243 Old South Head Road, Bondi.

Bankstown, 41 Meredith Street, Bankstown.

Central, 13–15 Bon Accord Avenue, Bondi Junction (Rabbi Michael A. Alony is Irish-born).

Coogee-Randwick-Clovelly, 121 Brook Street, Coogee.

Cremorne, 10 Yeo Street, Neutral Bay.

Great Synagogue, 166 Castlereagh Street, (tel. 613950). "The Great," as it is fondly known to Sydney Jewry, is today Sydney's best-known Jewish landmark with its imposing main entrance in Elizabeth Street, facing Hyde Park. The synagogue interior presents an impressive picture which combines solemnity and beauty in a mellow historical setting. Beneath the Synagogue is the War Memorial Centre, constructed in the 1950s. The Rabbi A. L. Falk Memorial Library in the center houses a priceless collection of Judaica; and there is also a Jewish museum named for the late A. M. Rosenblum.

The B'nai B'rith building, located in East Sydney at 22–38 Yurong Street (tel. 319035), has three main halls, a kosher restaurant, a library, committee rooms, and boardrooms; an estimated 2,000 men and women in the Sydney area belong to the organization.

TASMANIA

Tasmania is an island off the southeast coast of Australia, and in its chief city, Hobart, is the oldest standing synagogue in all of Australia. A convict, Judah Solomon, arrived in 1833 and was well accepted by the few Jewish families already there; after receiving a royal pardon, he offered part of his garden to the Jews of Hobart in order to build a synagogue. In 1845 the Hobart Hebrew Congregation on Argyle Street opened its doors. When the nearby penal colony was closed in 1877, the Jewish population declined. Today it has fallen to 150 persons; the president of the community is Clyde Epstein.

Other representative Australian synagogues are found in the following cities:

Brisbane (Queensland): Hebrew Congregation, Margaret Street, (tel. 27389).

Gold Coast (Queensland): Hebrew Congregation, Hamilton Ave, Surfer's Paradise.

Perth (Western Australia): Hebrew Congregation, Freedman Road, Menora (tel. 2710539).
Temple David, 34 Clifton Crescent (tel. 2711485).

Newcastle (New South Wales): Hebrew Congregation, 124 Tyrrell Street (tel. 23338).

KOSHER RESTAURANTS

Melbourne: Kinnereth Restaurant, 48 Chapel Street, St. Kilda (tel. 942510).
YMHA Restaurant, 178 Collins Street (tel. 633934).
Zion Restaurant, 10 Glen Eira Avenue, Ripponlea (tel. 539637).
B'nai B'rith, 99 Hotham Street, East St. Kilda (tel. 524491).

Sydney: B'nai B'rith, 22–38 Yurong Street (tel. 336533).
Dizengoff Kosher, 15 O'Brien Street, Bondi (tel. 307393).

USEFUL ADDRESSES

Canberra: U.S. Embassy, Moonah Place, Yarralumla (tel. 733711). Office of the High Commissioner for Canada, Commonwealth Avenue (tel. 732541).
Israeli Embassy, 6 Turrana Street (tel. 731309).

Melbourne: U.S. Consulate General, 24 Albert Road South (tel. 699-2244).

Perth: U.S. Consulate, 246 St. George's Terrace (tel. 322-4466).

Sydney: U.S. Consulate General, T&G Tower, 36th floor, Hyde Park Square (tel. 264-7044).
Israeli Consulate, 100 William Street (tel. 358-5077).

AUSTRIA

The first Jewish settlers in Austria probably came with the Romans, and by A.D. 900 there were Jewish merchants throughout the country. In 1238 Emperor Frederick II granted a charter to the Jews of Vienna, thereby taking them under his protection. This medieval community soon became a center for Jewish scholarship, but in 1406 the Jewish quarter was burned to the ground, after the Jews had been charged with performing ritual murder. The period between the thirteenth and the fifteenth centuries was marked by a series of persecutions culminating in a massacre in the year 1420, followed by the expulsion of Jews from Austria in 1421. In 1670 there was another general expulsion of Jews from Austria, but Jews reappeared in the following century and finally, in 1867, Jews received full rights as Austrian citizens.

The Jews of Vienna found root in this city only after the issue of a decree of tolerance by Emperor Franz II in 1782. But even then, Jews were still proscribed from setting up a community, conducting public synagogue services, and employing a rabbi. A tolerance tax was imposed on licenses for permanent residence in Vienna, and the pursuit of professions was limited. Jews were permitted to attend secondary schools, to be wholesale merchants, and to set up manufacturing plants. But permission to reside in Vienna was only granted to those who could prove a regular profession or ownership of 10,000 gulden. This limitation prevented poorer people from settling in Vienna, a state of affairs that lasted until the revolution in 1848. In 1938 an unprecedented persecution resulting in the death of 250,000 Austrian Jews took place under the aegis of the Nazi conquest. Today only 13,000 Jews live in Austria.

BAD GASTEIN

This Austrian resort has a fine kosher hotel and restaurant, Erzherzog Johann, Gasteiner Bundestrasse (tel 2690).

EDLACH

Here in the garden of the local sanatorium is a memorial to Dr. Theodor Herzl who died in Edlach in 1904.

EDT BEI LAMBACH

At a forest here in Upper Austria, a mass grave of about 9,000 Jews killed by the Nazis was found in 1979. Documents were found indicating that the victims were Hungarian Jews who were forcibly marched here in 1944. The Vienna Jewish community has reinterred the remains in a special grave at the Mauthausen cemetery.

EISENSTADT (30 miles from Vienna)

Records of local land being held by Jewish tenants go as far back as 1515; the first mention of a Jewish ghetto dates back to 1572. After 1732 the Eisenstadt ghetto was an independent community known as Unterberg-Eisenstadt, and remained so until 1938. During this long period, the Jewish community accounted for a considerable part of the population of Eisenstadt and played an important role in the city's economic and cultural development. After the occupation of Austria in 1938 by Nazi Germany, the ghetto area, completely intact up to this point, was forcibly evacuated. The synagogue was subsequently set on fire by a mob stirred into action by Nazi racist propaganda. Today a simple plaque draws attention to what once stood there: "This was the site of the Eisenstadt synagogue, burned down on November 11, 1938, as a result of blind racial prejudice and nationalist arrogance."

S. Wertheimer's Synagogue, built in 1720, is located on Unterberggasse (second floor). The Austrian museum at Museumgasse, adjoining Unterberggasse, details the history of the local Jewish community in an interesting permanent exhibit.

GRAZ

Graz was known in Crusader days as the site of a massacre of its entire Jewish population by Richard the Lion-Hearted of England. The Jewish community center is at Grieskai 58 (tel. 86327) and has a small chapel. The local museum has collected silver *torah* shields and old Sabbath lamps.

INNSBRUCK

The Jewish community center in this mountain resort is located at Zollerstrasse 1 (tel. 6892).

JUDENBURG

A figure of a bearded Jew's head is carved in stone on the facade of the Post Hotel, and it is believed that the building at one time was a synagogue. One of the gates of the city is called *Judenthurl* because a Jew in 1469 strangled himself on it in his haste to flee the city.

LINZ

In upper Austria is the provincial capital city of Linz. The small Jewish community is centered about its community center at Bethlehemstrasse 26 (tel. 22835).

MAUTHAUSEN

Here, not far from Linz, is the former Nazi concentration camp where 250,000 people perished. The torture chambers, execution rooms, furnaces, and other horrors have all been preserved as a perennial reminder of Nazi bestiality.

SALZBURG

The local synagogue is at Lasserstrasse 8, and the Jewish community center is at Mertensstrasse 7 (tel. 72228).

VIENNA

For the Austrian Jew, Vienna has always been the center of Judaism; in 1938 there were 200,000 Jews in Vienna, but today there are only 9,000. Among the many places of Jewish interest is the home of Sigmund Freud at 19 Berggasse. Vienna's famous Jewish son, founder of psychoanalysis, was long ignored by the city fathers who exhibited a strong anti-intellectual bias and pervasive anti-Semitism. On Freud's seventieth birthday in 1926, official Vienna maintained an indecent silence as world tributes poured in. In 1971, however, the Austrian government bought Freud's home and turned it into the Sigmund Freud Museum. The flat has been furnished to look as much as possible as it did when Freud lived there (1891–1938). Freud went to London as a Jewish refugee in 1938 and died there a year later. Only the intervention of President Franklin D. Roosevelt (who paid a large ransom) enabled the Freud family to escape from Austria.

The building at Bauernfeldgasse 4, Vienna XIX, houses the offices of the Jewish community of Vienna, including the rabbinate, the rabbinical court, the matrimonial office, and the library, as well as the offices of Jewish publications. One of Vienna's true scholars on Jewish life is Dr. Leon Zelman, who operates his own travel agency at 10 Stephenplatz and who heads the Jewish Welcome Service in Vienna.

The first synagogue in Vienna, at Seitenstettengasse 4, was founded in 1826, destroyed by the Nazis in 1938, rebuilt in 1946, and reconsecrated in 1963 under the leadership of Professor Otto Niedermoser. (The Nazis destroyed Vienna's twenty-two synagogues and forty small prayerhouses.) The completely restored synagogue is located within the business center of Vienna, and has an unusual elliptical interior. It is the center of Jewish life in Vienna. There are also prayer rooms at Grunagergasse 1 (Agudas Israel); Seitenstetten-gasse 2 (Machzike Haddas); Judenplatz 8 (Misrachi); Riemergasse 9 (Misrachi); and at Grosse Schiffgasse 8 (Schiff-Schul).

Of the Viennese places of Jewish interest, the Reinhardt Theater in the famed Schonbrunn Castle must not be overlooked; nor the many Jewish busts and statues in the Hall of the Famous at the University of Vienna. St. Stephen's Cathedral has several stained-glass windows unfavorably depicting medieval Jews. The Austrian National Library, 1 Josefsplatz, has a large collection of Judaica reflecting the history of Jewish communities under the Hapsburg monarchy, a fine Hebrew book collection, and 227 Hebrew manu-scripts. Central Friedhof, Vienna's central cemetery, is in the Sim-mering district: here three generations of Vienna's Jews are buried (Gates 1 and 4). There is a well-known Jewish memorial chapel at 11 Simmeringer Hauptstrasse, which was restored after having been burned by the Nazis in 1938. The Gestapo Victims Monument on Martinplatz honors the hundreds of Austrians, including many Jews, who died on this site of Gestapo headquarters during World War II. (The Gestapo enclave was in the Metropol Hotel, destroyed by Allied bombing.)

Theodor Herzl-Hof, a city housing development between 13–15 Leopoldgasse and 7 Malzgasse, is named for the founder of political Zionism. The apartments, constructed on the site of a reception cen-ter for elderly Jews before they were sent to the death camps, is in the heart of the Leopoldstadt area, which for two centuries was the ghetto. The Jewish cemetery at 9 Seegasse dates from the fifteenth century, and is the oldest surviving Jewish burial ground in Austria; adjoining the cemetery is the Jewish Old Age Home and Hospital. Also of interest are the Jewish School at 16 Malzgasse; the Jewish Youth Home at 8 Krummbaumgasse; and the Jewish Museum, Bauernfeldgasse 4, which has an exhibit of religious and cultural articles. The Museum of Ethnology, 19 Laudongasse, has a fine collection of objects reflecting Jewish life in Austria. Also of interest is Judenplatz, or Jews' Square, which dates back to the thirteenth-century Jewish community; here are plaques commemorating the site of the synagogue and hospital.

In 1976 the city of Vienna published a short illustrated guide in English for Jewish visitors. It is distributed free by the city tourist office.

KOSHER RESTAURANTS

Bad Gastein: Erzherzog Johann, Gasteiner Bundestrasse (tel. 2690). Kurhaus Bader, Rosenzweig (tel. 2031).

Semmering: The Alexander (tel. 336).

Vienna: The Weihburg, Seilerstatte 14 (tel. 52-81-55). (Also a small room for use as an Orthodox prayerhouse.)

USEFUL ADDRESSES

Vienna: U.S. Embassy, Boltzmanngasse 16A-1091 (tel. 315511).
Canadian Embassy, Dr. Karl Lueger-Ring 10 (tel. 63 66 26).
Israeli Embassy, Anton Frankgasse 20 (tel. 31 15 06).
Israeli Information Center, Stephensplatz 10 (tel. 63 43 24).

BAHAMAS

San Salvador, one of the 700 islands comprising the Bahamas, was the very first piece of land sighted by Columbus in 1492. His Jewish interpreter, Luis de Torres, went ashore to bargain with the natives in the mistaken belief that Columbus had landed on the Spice Islands in the East Indies. It was not until 1620 that the British settled in the Bahamas. A century later Nathan Simson of New York built a trading station here, and just before the American Revolution, two London Jews, Jacob and Moses Franks, arrived in Nassau. Relatively few Jews settled here until World War II; after the war (particularly following the advent of gambling casinos in the 1950s) more than 150 Jewish families found their way to the Bahamas.

The Nassau Jewish community of almost 100 persons is made up chiefly of businessmen and professionals from the United States, England, Canada, Ireland, and South Africa. Until the 1960s occasional worship services were held in private homes or hotels, and Jewish residents often went to Florida to observe Passover and the High Holy Days. In 1965 the Nassau Hebrew Congregation (Conservative) was organized. (The nephew of the founder, Rubin Bott, today owns Rubin's Department Store, tel. 23853). The synagogue, seating fifty persons, was opened in the Hoffer Building on Market Street, off Bay Street (the founder was Hal Hoffer at 372 Bay Street, tel. 23170). The congregation has no rabbi; but a cantor and student rabbi from Florida are brought in for the major holidays, and Marcel Urbach acts as religious leader the rest of the year.

In the second largest city, Freeport, on Grand Bahama Island, stands a magnificent new edifice, the Luisde Torres Synagogue (Reform), consecrated in 1974. Located on East Sunrise Highway, with seats for 120 worshipers, it has a new library, a study, a social hall, and a kitchen.

KOSHER RESTAURANTS

(None, except for Jewish-style food at Manny's Place in the Prince George Hotel, Bay Street.)

USEFUL ADDRESSES

Nassau: U.S. Embassy, Mosmar Building, Queen Street (tel. 322-4753).

BARBADOS

The Jewish community of the island of Barbados was founded in 1655 by refugees from Brazil after its conquest by the Portuguese. Among the earliest arrivals from Brazil were members of the De Mercado family as well as Luis Dias, who became the principal organizer of Nidhe Israel Congregation of 1656. In 1678 Dias brought in a Marrano-born Spanish rabbi, Eliahu Lopez, who served the local Barbados congregation for fifteen years.

Jewish traders may have stopped in Barbados as early as 1627; by 1680 more than 300 Jews lived on the island. More Jews arrived from Cayenne in 1664 after the cession of this French colony to the Dutch. In the eighteenth century Jewish congregations existed in Bridgetown and Speightstown. The Bridgetown Sephardic synagogue Nidhe Israel ("dispersal of Israel") was erected in 1679 on Magazine Lane on a land grant by the Earl of Carlyle; the synagogue was reconsecrated on March 29, 1833, after the devastating hurricane of 1831. The community felt a special kinship with the Jewish community of London; for almost 100 years, Barbados rabbis came directly from the Bevis Marks Synagogue in London.

By 1900, the Jewish community of Barbados had fewer than twenty persons, due to the fall in sugar prices and the emancipation of slaves. The old synagogue and cemetery property were about to be sold when a young Gentile solicitor stepped in to purchase the property: Eustace Maxwell Shilstone, who had visited the synagogue as a boy, agreed to purchase the property in order to preserve it. His offer was passed over, but upon the deaths of the purchasers in 1934, the properties passed to a Mr. Hutchinson, who converted the synagogue into office space, then set about destroying the cemetery in order to erect garages for the property. Shilstone confronted Hutchinson, warning him that no good would come of his actions; and, as though a West Indian curse lay on the graveyard, Hutchinson had a stroke and soon died. With the support of newly arrived European refugees, Shilstone arranged to have the cemetery put in perpetual trust in the deeds of the island. Meanwhile, Shilstone had taught himself Hebrew, Spanish, and Portuguese. On his hands and knees, he copied 374 epitaphs which were later published by the Jewish Historical Society of England. The cemetery is located in the heart of Bridgetown near Synagogue Lane.

The synagogue building near Synagogue Lane is today used for offices by the Barbados government. The upper floor, which houses a law library, still exhibits its famed carved ceiling, once painted blue and white; this story is still entered from a covered staircase that curves around the side and rear of the building.

Today the Ashkenazi Orthodox congregation of Bridgetown, Shaare Tsedek, meets in a rented house, "True Blue," Rockley New Road, Christ Church, for social and cultural activities; inquiries can be directed to J. H. Altman, "Sea Shell," Gibbes Beach, St. Peter (tel. 22664). The leader of the small Jewish community is elderly O. Pillersdorf (Rendezvous Hill; tel. 77109). Recently a congregation of Black Jews has been formed under the leadership of Miss M. D. Beckels. This small congregation has its own synagogue, the Zion House of Israel, and services are held every Friday evening.

Twelve miles north of Bridgetown in Speightstown was a branch synagogue called Semach David ("Offshoot of David"). According to a contemporary account, this synagogue was destroyed in 1739 under the following odd circumstances: Among the guests at a Lopez family wedding was a young Gentile named Burnet, who passed himself off as a son of the island governor. Burnet complained of a headache during the festivities and was sent to the nearby home of the bride's father to lie down. Shortly thereafter, the bride's father learned of the guest's fraudulent identity, gathered a group of persons and assaulted Burnet, accusing him of theft. The young impostor raised such an outcry that a mob of townspeople forced the Jewish community to flee and tore down the Speightstown synagogue.

During the seventeenth century, Jews were in control of the island's sugar industry. Swan Street in Bridgetown was then known as Jews' Street because of the large number of Jewish businessmen. Even today there are still many Jewish businesses in Swan Street with such trade names as Altman, Karp, Kriendler, and Speisman. But anti-Semitism brought oppression, and although Barbados Jewry suffered quietly, they continued to live on Barbados. Jews were not allowed to testify in court because they refused to take the oath on the Christian Bible. It was not until a royal order of Parliament in 1674 that Jews were permitted to take the oath on the Five Books of Moses. In 1802 full political emancipation was finally granted to all minorities.

In the second half of the nineteenth century the economic decline of Barbados led to the disappearance of the Jewish community. Since 1934 the Jewish population has not exceeded 100 persons. In more recent years a new Ashkenazi community has emerged; there are sixteen families from Poland, Germany, and Romania.

Opposite the public library in Bridgetown is the splendid

Montefiore Fountain (Lucas Street), presented to the city in 1864 by John Montefiore, a wealthy member of the Jewish community. In the Barbados Museum, a former military prison one mile from the airport, there is a marble basin for washing hands (apparently belonging to the old synagogue), a pew bench from the old synagogue, a brass menorah, a London-made 1817 clock, and a charity box dating back to 1834.

A former Premier of Barbados, Hon. Errol Barrow, is the descendant of an old Jewish family (Shimon Baruch or, anglicized, Simon Barrow). In the old Jewish cemetery in Bridgetown can be found the bilingual tombstone of his eighteenth-century ancestor.

USEFUL ADDRESSES

Bridgetown: U.S. Embassy, Canadian Imperial Bank of Commerce Building, Broad Street, P.O. Box 302 (tel. 63574).

BELGIUM

Since the days of the Roman Empire, Jews have lived in the area known today as Belgium. A few Jews resided in Belgium in the thirteenth century, but most were exterminated during the Black Death of 1348. Later Duke Hendrik III of Brabant and Count of Antwerp ordered that Jews originating from southern France and Lombardy, except for a "few honest merchants," must be evicted. This order was fortunately not carried out. Again in 1549 the City Council of Antwerp objected to the expulsion decree of the Emperor Charles V against Marranos (forcibly baptized Jews who secretly remained faithful to Judaism) who had come from Portugal. The Marranos, the council fathers declared, brought profit to the city of Antwerp by their "commerce with fruits, pearls, and precious stones." In 1566, the Jewish printer Plantin produced a Hebrew Bible. Beginning in the sixteenth century, Marranos from Spain and Portugal settled in Antwerp and soon prospered as bankers and traders. Throughout this chaotic period the Marranos quietly went ahead trying to rebuild their sugar-trading businesses and to develop a diamond-cutting trade in Antwerp, while secretly worshiping as Jews. It was not until the eighteenth century when Ashkenazi Jews from Eastern Europe began to settle in Antwerp that the synagogue was legally recognized.

Formal organization of the Belgian Jewish community began under the French (1794–1814) and the Dutch (1814–1816). Under Dutch sovereignty, two synagogues were built after 1816 in Brussels and in Maastricht, Holland. When the Kingdom of Belgium was constituted in 1830–1831, religious equality became part of the fundamental Belgian law. In the 1830s there were some 80,000 Jews in Belgium, and 24,000 Belgian Jews died in Nazi concentration camps in the 1940s. Today there are 41,000 Belgian Jews who reside principally in the cities of Antwerp, Brussels, Liège, and Charleroi.

ANTWERP

There are approximately 13,000 Jews in Antwerp with forty-seven Jewish organizations and about twenty-five places of worship, including synagogues located at Terlistrasse 35; Jacob Jacobstrasse 31; Oostenstrasse 29; Van Spangenstrasse 6; Van Leriusstrasse 54;

and Mercatorstrasse 56. The main synagogue, the Romi Goldmuntz Synagogue, is at Oostenstrasse 43; and there is a Portuguese Sephardic synagogue at Hoveniersstrasse 31. (There is also a B'nai B'rith lodge at Nervierstrasse 4.)

Antwerp is synonymous with the diamond trade, and the diamond trade, with four diamond bourses, is synonymous with the Jewish community. On the Sabbath business in Antwerp is literally closed down. The official Jewish community *(Gemeente)* is Orthodox, although there is a strong Hasidic following. The Chief Rabbi directs the community which contains two of the largest and best Jewish day schools: the Tachkemoni School (Lange Leemstraat 313, tel. 390467), supported by the Gemeente, has about 800 pupils and is modern enough in its approach to be coeducational; the Yesodei Hatorah School (Lange Van Ruushroeckstrasse 14–16, tel. 392535), more conservative and under government control, has about 1,000 pupils, and boys and girls are segregated. These, and some smaller Jewish schools run by the Hasidim, account for about 75 percent of the children, most of whom emerge fluent in Hebrew. In 1970, the largest and most modern Jewish community center in Europe was opened in Antwerp—the Romi Goldmuntz Community Center at Nervierstrasse 12 (tel. 393911). Facilities include an art gallery, Judaica library, a nightclub, an electronics laboratory, a day-care nursery, and an underground parking lot.

In Antwerp the diamond exchanges, truly a Jewish craft, are located on Pelikaanstrasse, which is also the home of many Hasidim. The Plantin-Moretus Museum at Vrijdagmarkt features examples of early Jewish printing. Israelitenstraat is a street which acquired its name in 1563 when some Marrano Jews built twelve houses, each bearing the name of one of the twelve tribes of Israel.

Antwerp today continues to be a distinctly religious community with a very intensive Jewish life. It has become the haven for Orthodox Jewry fleeing the USSR and Eastern Europe, and Antwerp is justly proud of its *shtetl* atmosphere.

ARLON

The local synagogue is at rue de la Synagogue; it was built in 1865.

BRUSSELS

The international city of Brussels, with 25,000 Jews, remembers the 28,838 Jewish citizens murdered by the Nazis with a Resistance Memorial in the Square of the Jewish Martyrs (district of Anderlecht, at the corner of rue Emile Carpentier and rue Goujons). Brussels' synagogues include the Turkish Sephardic community synagogue at rue Joseph Du Pont 2; the Orthodox synagogues at rue de la Clinique 67a, rue de la Querelle 1, rue de Thy 73, rue de Merode 198 in St. Gillis; rue Rogier 126 in Schaarbeek; and rue Houzeau de Lehaye 33 in Molenbeek. The community synagogue of Brussels is at rue de là Regence 32; consecrated in 1878, its structure was not severely damaged in World War II.

There are small Jewish communities in Charleroi (community center at rue Pique-au-Croly 56); Ghent (community center at Savaenstrasse 14); Heide (synagogue at Leopoldstrasse 38); Knokke (synagogue at Van Burrenlaan 38); Liège (synagogue at rue L. Frederica 19); and Mons (community center at Grand Rue 49). On the Belgian coast is the village of Knokke where kosher hotels and restaurants predominate. And Ostend (synagogue at Maastrichtplein 10) also has a large Jewish population and attracts Jewish tourists from all over Europe and Great Britain.

KOSHER RESTAURANTS

Antwerp: A. Fruchter, Simonstrasse 10 (tel. 33-26-55).
Gelkop, Pelikaanstrasse 86 (tel. 32-91-63).
M. Herer, Pelikaanstrasse 78 (tel. 33-92-89).
Pension Fogel, Steenbokstrasse 9 (tel. 39-16-87).
Blutner, Simonstrasse 10 (tel. 33-42-72).
Jakob, Lange Kievitstrasse 49 (tel. 33-27-36).

Brussels: Jewish Youth Center, Chausse de Vleurgat 89 (tel. 648-18-59).
Sara Pauker Restaurant, avenue Clemenceau 34.
Bornstein, rue de Suede 62 (tel. 5371679).

Knokke: Chez Bernard, rue Antoine Breart 11.
Le Grand Hotel Motke, Digue de Mer 96 (tel. 60-12-62).
Dorchester Grand Hotel, Kustlaan 6 (tel. 60-27-27).

USEFUL ADDRESSES

Antwerp: U.S. Consulate General, Rubens Center, Nationalestraat 5 (tel. 2321800).

Brussels: U.S. Embassy, boulevard du Regent 27 (tel. 5133830).
Canadian Embassy, rue de la Science (tel. 5137940).
Israeli Embassy, avenue de l'Observatoire 40 (tel. 3749080).

BERMUDA

Bermuda is perhaps the only West Indies community where no Jewish settlement occured. There never was a synagogue building or cemetery, although in the early eighteenth century Jewish traders lived here, and American Jews have vacationed here for many years.

History reveals that Jews who traded here from 1694 to 1761 were subject to heavy discriminatory taxes. A syndicate headed by Moses and Jacob Franks was the largest purveyor of supplies to Bermuda's British forces during the two decades before the American Revolution. Until World War I no more than ten Jews ever resided here; Jewish guests were excluded from Bermudan hotels until after World War II. After the United States leased air and naval bases on Bermuda in 1940, Jewish civilian employees and military personnel organized the first Jewish community. Visiting Jewish chaplains from the mainland today conduct services several times a year at the U.S. Air Force Chapel.

As of 1946, Bermuda had four Jewish residents and today perhaps ten to fifteen Jews live here permanently, excluding the personnel at the American military bases. (Kosher food is available at the Princess Hotel in Hamilton.) U.S. Navy Commander Bernard Schattner (tel. 3-8111, ext. 2111) leads religious services also in private homes.

USEFUL ADDRESSES

Hamilton: U.S. Consulate General, Vallis Building, Front Street (tel. 295-1342).

BOLIVIA

After 1920, Polish Jews migrated into this landlocked South American nation. German refugees began arriving in 1935, and by 1942 there were more than 7,000 Bolivian Jews. Marranos worked in the silver mines of Potosí more than 400 years ago, and they were among the pioneers who founded the city of Santa Cruz in 1557. To this day, the possible Jewish ancestry of the old families in that region is suggested by their custom of lighting candles on Friday nights and sitting on the ground when mourning. The Marrano community went into decline with the establishment of the Inquisition in neighboring Peru in 1570.

In the early 1950s there were as many as 10,000 Bolivian Jews living in the capital city of La Paz and in the towns of Cochabamba, Oruro, Sucre, and Potosí. Many Jews came as agriculturists to develop the fertile tropical lowlands. Various Jewish agricultural settlements were attempted on the free homelands offered by the Bolivian government. The Sociedad Colonizadora de Bolivia (SOCOBO), founded in 1940 with the help of $1 million from the Jewish tin magnate Mauricio Hochschild, sponsored these settlements. For a variety of reasons, one being the inaccessibility of markets, these Jewish agricultural colonies failed.

Bolivia provided a haven for European Jewry after the Holocaust, despite the fact that Bolivia also achieved notoriety as a haven for former Nazis. For many years Bolivia refused French extradition demands for Klaus Altmann, the alias used by Klaus Barbie, the "Butcher of Lyon." (Bolivia has never been pro-Nazi, but the government does not concern itself with the past history of its immigrants. The Bolivians did not incarcerate Altmann. Once Altmann was struck by a Jewish storeowner while walking down a shopping street. He decided to press charges and went to court. The shopkeeper rolled up his shirtsleeve in order to show the judge his concentration camp number. The Jewish merchant explained that he could not help his rage when he saw Altmann walk in front of his store. The charges were dismissed.)

Bolivia is today one of Israel's staunchest friends. Israelis have built a vegetable oil factory, and a series of scholarships has enabled many Bolivians to study in Israel.

The Circulo Israelita de Bolivia, located at Calle Landaeta 84 (tel. 24938), was organized in 1955 and occupies a four-story building in La Paz. Here also are a B'nai B'rith lodge, a women's Zionist organization, a society for the protection of immigrants, two synagogues, a Maccabee organization for young people, and an all-day school for 100 children.

In recent years, economic conditions in Bolivia have prompted thousands of Bolivian Jews to depart for the United States, Brazil, and Argentina; hundreds have migrated to Israel. Today fewer than 600 Jews live in La Paz and about 200 in Cochabamba and Santa Cruz. The Bolivian press frequently reprints anti-Semitic articles from releases by the Federation of Bolivian Arab Organizations in La Paz.

Other than the small Circulo Israelita synagogues in La Paz, the only synagogue is in the tourist town of Cochabamba at Calle Junin y Calle Columbia.

USEFUL ADDRESSES

La Paz: U.S. Embassy, Banco Popular del Peru Building, corner of Calles Mercado and Colon (tel. 350251).
Israeli Embassy, Avenida Mariscal Santa Cruz, Edificio Esperanza, Casilla #1309, #1320 (tel. 358 676).

BRAZIL

Brazilian Jewry, numbering nearly 175,000 (120,000 are Ashkenazim) centers about the great metropolitan areas of Rio de Janeiro and São Paulo, where 80 percent of Brazilian Jewry reside. All Brazilian Jewish life is linked together in an effective organization, the Confederacio Israelita do Brasil. In many ways, the Jewish lifestyle is comparable to that of any Western country. But the history of the Jews here is a strange and turbulent one, going back to the founding of Brazil itself in the late fifteenth century. Almost 500 years ago the first colonizers came to Brazil from Portugal, and among their company was at least one Jew, Gaspar da Gama. He was followed by a number of New Christians, who were of Jewish birth and still secretly practiced Jewish rites. When the Dutch colonized northern Brazil at the end of the sixteenth century, Jewish community life truly began, for the Dutch proclaimed freedom of religious observance for all colonizers and natives. Shortly thereafter formal Jewish communities in the towns of Recife, Maranhão, Ceará, Pernambuco, and Bahia ("The Rock of Israel") were established. In 1641 the Jewish colony of Recife had a rabbi from Amsterdam ministering to its two congregations. But a few years later in 1649, the Portuguese successfully waged war on the Dutch, and the victorious Portuguese ordered the Jews out of Brazil in 1655. A large number found their way to New York City, while others drifted to the West Indies.

The next stage of Brazilian Jewish life came with the liberation of Brazil from Portuguese domination in 1822. Jews began to filter back into Brazil from as far away as Morocco. In 1824 Brazilian Jews built a synagogue in Belém, the capital of the State of Pará. The beginnings of Brazil's modern Jewish community came in 1903 when the southern communities, initially agricultural settlements of Russian refugees, were formally organized. The stream of refugees continued, and by World War I Brazil had a Jewish population of about 6,000. The years following brought increases in immigration—between 1920 and 1930, 28,820 Jews entered Brazil. However, after 1930, government authorities tightened up on immigration and maintained that policy until the end of World War II when the barriers were again relaxed.

Adolfo Bloch owns *Manchetti,* South America's top newsweekly, and thirty other major Brazilian periodicals. In his skyscraper building in São Paulo there is a museum of modern Brazilian art and a 700-seat theater used for public performances of classic plays. In sharp contrast is David Markus (Rua Julio Conceicao 449) who publishes virtually singlehandedly the only Yiddish newspaper in Brazil.

BRASÍLIA

In Brasília, the new federal capital 600 miles northeast of Rio de Janeiro, there are seventy Jewish families, mostly civil servants who arrived in 1960 when the capital city was carved out of the jungle. In 1977, the Jewish community built a synagogue at a cost of $350,000; the site was donated to the community by the city council of Brasília (ACIB, Entrequadros Norte 305–306 Lote A).

RIO DE JANEIRO

In 1979 Dr. Israel Klabin, a leading Brazilian industrialist, took office as mayor of Rio de Janeiro, the first Jew to hold that post in the 400-year history of the city. In Rio de Janeiro, where 60,000 Jews dwell, there are synagogues of every persuasion; a representative list includes the following:

Uniao Israelita Shei Guemilut Hassadim (Orthodox Sephardic), Rua Rodrigo de Brito 37 (tel. 2264885)

Associacao Religiosa Israelita (Liberal), Rua General Severiano 170 (tel. 2269666)

Bethel, Rua Barata Ribeiro 489 (tel. 2379688)

Grande Templo Israelita, Rua Tenente Possolo 8 (tel. 2323656)

Kehilat Moriah (Orthodox), Rua Pompeu Loureiro 48 (tel. 2574299)

Kehilat Yakov, Rua Capelao, Alvares da Silva 15 (tel. 2361601)

Monte Sinai (Orthodox), Rua Sao Francisco Xavier 100 (tel. 2488448)

B'nai B'rith offices in Rio de Janeiro are located at Avenida Rio Branco 128, Sala 1207.

SALVADOR

In this capital city of Bahia in northern Brazil, there are about 120 Jewish families, two Hebrew teachers for sixty Jewish youngsters, but no rabbi. The small synagogue at Rua Alvaro Tiberio 60, Campa da Folvera, is painted blue and white with blue Stars of David on the walls flanking the entrance. Here are also the offices of the Sociedad Israelita da Bahia. There is a Jewish social club on Avenida Otavio Mangabiera, Boao do Rio.

SÃO PAULO

Recently the Federacao Israelita Do Estado De São Paulo, the representative body for São Paulo's 75,000 Jews, was accorded special status, which made it exempt from Brazilian federal taxes. At the same time São Paulo's Carlos Chagas Foundation (which coordinates scheduling for many Brazilian universities) stated publicly that it would not schedule examinations on Jewish holidays. These developments were warmly welcomed by São Paulo Jewry. Of São Paulo's many synagogues, the following may be noted:

Israelita Paulista (Hungarian), Rua Augusta 259 (tel. 256-5970)

Templo Beth-El (Ashkenazi), Rua Martinho Prado 128 (tel. 256-8671)

Israelita Bras (Sephardic), Rua Odorico Mendes 174

Centro Israelita (Orthodox), Rua Newton Prado 76 (tel. 220-0185)

Congregacao Israelita (Liberal), Rua Antonio Carlos 653 (tel. 256-7811)

Congregacao Mekor Haim (Sephardic), Rua Sao Vincente de Paula 254 (tel. 67-2029)

Machzikei (Orthodox), Rua Padre Joao Manoel 727 (tel. 282-6762)

The Hebraica or Jewish community center of São Paulo occupies six square blocks of prime residential property in the downtown area. For its 25,000 members there are three Olympic-size swimming pools, two restaurants, a gymnasium seating 5,000, a theater with 1,000 seats, two synagogues, and beautiful surrounding gardens.

There are Jewish communities in Belo Horizonte (synagogues at Rua Rio Grande do Norte 477 and at Rua Pernambuco 326); Belém (synagogues at Rua Alcipreste Manoel Teodoro 842 and at Travessa Campos Sales 733); Manaus (synagogues at Rua 7 de Setembro and at Rua Leonardo Malcher 630); Curitiba (synagogue at Rua Cruz Muchado 126); Santos (synagogue at Rua Campos Sales 137); and Petrópolis (synagogue at Rua Aurelio Coutinho 48). In Recife, which has probably the oldest Jewish community in South America, there are 250 Jewish families; the synagogue is at Rua Martins Junior 29.

Other Jewish communities may be found in Rio de Janeiro State at Campos (synagogue at Rua 13 de Maio 52) and at Niterói (synagogue at Rua Viscondedo Uruguai 255); in Rio Grande do Sul State at Erechim (synagogue at Avenida Pedro Pinto de Souza 131); Passo Fundo (synagogue at Rua General Osorio 1049); Pelotas (synagogue at Rua Santos Dumont 303); and Santa Maria (synagogue on Trav Augustura). In the city of Pôrto Alegre, where 15,000 Brazilian Jews reside, there are Orthodox synagogues at Rua Henrique Dias 73, Rua Bento Figueredo 56, Rua Joao Telles 329, and at Rua Barros Cassal 750. In São Paulo State there are Jewish communities at Campinas (synagogue at Rua Barreto Leme 1203) and São Caetano do Sul (synagogue at Rua Para 61).

KOSHER RESTAURANTS

Rio de Janeiro: Shalom, Rua Pompeu Loureiro 48 (tel. 2574299).

São Paulo: Buffet Wegh, Rua Correa de Mello 172 (tel. 227-7304). Carlitos Lanches, Rua Tres Rios 488 (tel. 220-4908).

USEFUL ADDRESSES

Brasília: U.S. Embassy, Avenida das Nocoes, Lote 3 (tel. 223 0120). Israeli Embassy, Avenida das Nocoes, Lote 38 (tel. 244 5886).

Rio de Janeiro: Canadian Embassy, Edificio Metropole, Avenida Presidente Wilson 65 (tel. 242-4140).

BULGARIA

The earliest Jewish settlement in Bulgaria was a colony of Greek Jews from Salonika who arrived in Sofia in the second century. Hebrew tombstone inscriptions found near Oescus (now Gigen) attest to these ancient communities. From the thirteenth to the fifteenth centuries perhaps 30,000 Jews came from Spain and Greece to settle in Bulgaria, including Joseph Karo, the codifier of the *shuchan aruch*. Years later Ashkenazi Jews from Bavaria established a synagogue in Sofia; their Rabbi Benjamin ben Meir Halevi authored the famed prayer book bearing his name.

Ladino, a language derived from Spanish, Portuguese, Hebrew, and Arabic, is still spoken among present-day Bulgarian Jews. The Central Jewish Cultural Organization in Sofia, at Al Stamboliyski 50 (representing 7,000 Bulgarian Jews), is proud of the fact that the Nazi Holocaust did not touch Bulgaria's 45,000 Jews. They remember "the protective concern and heroic intervention" of the Bulgarian government for its Jewish citizens in the 1940s. However, from 1948 to 1949, some 38,000 Bulgarian Jews left for Israel, principally for political, economic, and religious reasons.

Unfortunately, present-day Jewish leadership seems little concerned about the survival of the Bulgarian Jewish community. In 1957, the government dissolved the Jewish national religious organization, and today there are no Jewish schools, no rabbis, and no meaningful Jewish cultural existence, except for the few synagogues that are open to visitors as national cultural attractions.

In Sofia the synagogue at Exarch Iosif Street 16 (tel. 87-49-95) still shows the effects of World War II bombings. Under its 100-foot dome is an immense chandelier; and the outer iron gate is topped by a large Star of David. The meanderings of the foreign tourist are apt to be watched by the government; upon visiting the Sofia synagogue, one may be surprised by the unannounced appearance of a Bulgarian official who may announce that he is a government student of "Jewish culture."

SOFIA

In the building of the Central Jewish Cultural Organization at Al Stamboliyski 50 there is housed a permanent exhibition entitled

"The Rescue of the Bulgarian Jews, 1941–1944"; the offices of the Jewish newspaper, *Evreiski Vesti* (tel. 87-0354); and the offices of the *Annual,* published by the Social, Cultural, and Educational Association of the Jews of the People's Republic of Bulgaria. President of Sofia's only synagogue is Isaac Moscona, a collector of prayer books and a world-famous authority on the Ladino language.

In Plovdiv is another synagogue, making a total of two open synagogues among the fifty-two synagogue buildings in Bulgaria. Plovdiv has an interesting Sholom Aleichem Cultural Center offering lectures and music recitals; there are four closed synagogues in Plovdiv.

Sofia has a Jewish population of 4,000; Plovdiv about 400; Varna 250; and 1,000 Jews are scattered among nine other Bulgarian communities. In Samokov and in Vidin there are old defunct synagogues restored as monuments and cultural museums of the government.

USEFUL ADDRESSES

Sofia: U.S. Embassy, Alexander Stamboliski Boulevard (tel. 88-48-01).
Israeli Legation, Luben Karavelov Street 34 (tel. 85-19-70).

BURMA

Jews first settled in Burma in the mid-nineteenth century, shortly after the British occupation in 1824. They came from Baghdad, Calcutta, Tehran, and Cochin. In 1850 two Ashkenazi Jews arrived in Rangoon, one from Romania and the other from Poland; within a few years they became wealthy, deriving profits from teakwood and supplying the occupying British army. In 1857 the first congregation was formed in Rangoon by Iraqi Jews from Baghdad—Motzmeach Yeshuah at 85 26th Street. In 1907 a second Burmese synagogue was built in Mandalay but after a few years it fell into disuse as Mandalay Jewry moved away. But the Motzmeach Yeshuah Synagogue in Rangoon continues to function for the few Jews remaining there. It is a simple stucco structure, lovingly cared for by a young Jewish businessman, Jacob Samuels (Rangoon tel. 75062), whose philanthropy has kept the synagogue open. There are two *sifrai torat* remaining from the 126 *Torah* scrolls which were in Burma in 1942.

The old Jewish cemetery recalls the fact that Rangoon was once a thriving Jewish community. In 1939 there were 2,200 Jews, but in 1942, when the Japanese invaded, almost 2,000 Jews escaped to India, England, and Israel. In 1945 about 400 Jews returned to Burma, but after Burmese independence in 1948 and the Moslem violence of 1956, hundreds of Jews left the country. No more than seventy still live in Burma. Yehuda Ezekiel Street in Rangoon honors the memory of an illustrious Jew who was mayor of Rangoon.

USEFUL ADDRESSES
Rangoon: U.S. Embassy, 581 Merchant Street (tel. 82055).
Israeli Embassy, 49 Prome Road (tel. 84188).

CANADA

Of 20 million Canadians, approximately 310,000 are Jewish, and they reside principally in Montreal (100,000), Toronto (125,000), Winnipeg (18,000), Ottawa (8,000), Vancouver (14,000), and in another 150 cities and towns throughout Canada. There are more than 200 Canadian synagogues, 75 percent Orthodox.

From a humble beginning in 1759 when only ten Jews lived in Canada, Canadian Jewry benefited greatly from the large-scale migrations from Eastern Europe at the end of the nineteenth century. One of the earliest Canadian Jews was David Gradis, a wealthy French shipowner from Bordeaux, who with his son helped commercial development of the French colony of Quebec. The first Canadian synagogue, built in 1768, was Shearith Israel Synagogue in Montreal. It was not until 1849 that a second synagogue was built, in Toronto.

Atlantic Maritime Provinces

More than 2,000 Canadian Jews reside in the four Atlantic provinces of Nova Scotia, New Brunswick, Prince Edward Island, and Newfoundland. In Nova Scotia, Jews have played important roles in commerce and industry; an Associate Justice of the Nova Scotia Supreme Court is the Honorable J. L. Lubinsky (P.O. box 2314, Halifax, Nova Scotia). In the city of Yarmouth there are eighteen Jewish families who have, despite many hardships, maintained a semblance of Jewish life. The Yarmouth synagogue is the Agudath Achim Synagogue at 8 Park Street.

HALIFAX

Halifax, home to 500 Jewish families, has a particularly flourishing synagogue, the Orthodox Beth Israel at 1480 Oxford Street; Rabbi M. Pritzker, 6674 Quinpool Road, heads the congregation. Halifax Jewry supports five Hadassah chapters, two B'nai B'rith lodges and chapters, ORT, Mizrachi, Z.O.A., two cemeteries, and Camp Kadima, a summer camp for Jewish children. Halifax's other synagogue, Shaar Sholom, is at 1981 Oxford Street, and the Z.O.A. office is at 5675 Spring Garden Road.

In New Brunswick Province, there are three Jewish population centers. Moncton, Saint John, and Fredericton. In Moncton, the synagogue, Tiferes Israel, is at 50 Steadman Street. In the capital city of Saint John the Shaarei Tzedek Synagogue is at 76 Carleton Street. (Neil Franklin, P.O. Box 1174, tel. 693-3302, is a local B'nai B'rith leader.) And in Fredericton, Sgoolai Israel Synagogue is at 170 Westmoreland Street. Rabbi David Spiro, 317 Wright Street, heads the Fredericton Jewish community.

In the Province of Newfoundland, the local congregation is headed by Lawrence Nathanson, 105 Rannies Mill Road, St. John's.

The Province of Prince Edward Island does not appear to have any organized Jewish community.

SYDNEY

Sydney, home to 120 Jewish families, has two synagogues, and is actively involved in Jewish organizational life; there is a B'nai B'rith Lodge, Hadassah, and Sisterhood. The Temple Sons of Israel Congregation has a fine library of Judaica, an auditorium, and classrooms for fifty-five students; Rabbi S. Simon, 120 Hospital Street, heads the congregation. Adath Israel Synagogue at 84 Mt. Pleasant Street (Whitney Pier) is the older synagogue, and Sabbath morning services here are well attended by local businessmen. The city of Glace Bay, near Sydney, with forty Jewish families, has a synagogue on Prince Street and a full-time rabbi. In nearby New Waterford there are twelve Jewish families; the Sons of Israel Congregation at 48 Hudson Street is headed by Rabbi M. Tabachnik.

Ontario

In the heavily populated province of Ontario, a listing of representative synagogues includes:

Belleville: Sons of Jacob, 211 Victoria Avenue

Brantford: Congregation Beth David, 50 Waterloo Street

Chatham: Children of Jacob Congregation, 29 Water Street

Cornwall: Beth El, 321 Amelia Street

Hamilton: Beth Jacob, 375 Aberdeen Avenue
Ohav Zedek, 77 Hess Street N.
Adas Israel, 125 Cline Avenue S.
Anshe Sholom, King Street at Cline Street

Kingston: Beth Israel, 124 Centre Street

Kirkland Lake: House of Israel, Station Road

Kitchener: Beth Jacob, 161 Sterling Avenue

London: Congregation Or Sholom, 532 Huron Street
Beth Tefilah, 1210 Adelaide Street W.

Niagara Falls: B'nai Jacob, 1328 Ferry Street

North Bay: Sons of Jacob, 302 McIntyre Street W.

Oshawa: Beth Zion, 144 King Street E.

Ottawa: Beth Shalom, 151 Chapel Street
Agudath Israel, 1400 Coldrey Avenue
Machzikei Adas, 2310 Virginia Drive
Young Israel, 627 Kirkwood Avenue

Peterborough: Beth Israel, Weller Street at Hopkins

Port Arthur: Shaarei Shomayim, Main Street

St. Catherine's: B'nai Israel, Church Street at Calvin Street

Sarnia: Ahavath Israel, 202 Cobden Street

Sault Ste. Marie: Beth Jacob, Bruce Street (145 Pim Street)

Stratford: B'nai Israel, 122 Downie Street

Sudbury: Shaar Hashomayim, 158 John Street

Thunder Bay: Shaare Shomayim, 5 Cumberland Street

Timmins: House of Israel, 23 Cedar Street N.

Toronto: Adath Israel, 37 Southbourne Avenue, Downsview (Conservative)
Agudath Israel, McGillivray Avenue
Ahavas Achim, 33 Wilmington Avenue, Downsview
Anshei Minsk, 12–14 St. Andrew's Street (just off Spadine in colorful Kensington Market)
Anshei Stashov, Sultana and Bathurst Streets
Beth Meyer, 272 Codsell Avenue, Downsview (Conservative)
B'Nai Torah, 5949 Bathurst Street, Willowdale
Chevre Shas, 3545 Bathurst Street, Willowdale
Clanton Park Congregation, Clanton at Lowesmoore, Downsview
Holy Blossom Temple, 1950 Bathurst Street, Downsview (Canada's largest Reform synagogue, built in 1938)
Kielce Congregation, 2941 Bathurst Street

Kiever Congregation, 25 Bellevue Avenue (around the corner from Anshei Minsk)
Knesseth Israel, 52 Maria Street
Machzikei B'Nai Israel, 279 Dovercourt Road
Mizrachi-Hapoel Hamizrachi, 86 Vaughan Road at Wilson Street
Petah Tikva Anshe Castilla, Donby and Bathurst Streets
Shaarei Emunah, Wilmington at Overbrook, Downsview
Shaarei Shomayim, 470 Glencairn Avenue (east of Bathurst)
Shaarei Tefilah, 3600 Bathurst Street
Shlome Amunei Yisroel, 567 Lawrence Avenue W.
Shomrei Shabbos, 585 Glengrove Avenue
Temple Emanu El, 100 Old Colony Road, Willowdale (Reform)
Temple Sinai, 210 Wilson Avenue (Reform)
Tifereth Joseph, 44 Edinboro at Bathurst Street, Downsview (Lubavitcher)
Torath Emes, 1 Viewmont Avenue and 1344 Bathurst Street
Yavne Zion, 788 Marlee Avenue
Yeshiva Torath Chaim, 475 Lawrence Avenue W.

Welland: Anshe Yosher, 144 Summit Avenue

Windsor: Shaar Hashomayim, 115 Giles Boulevard E.
Shaarei Zedek, Giles Boulevard at Lillian Street
Temple Beth El, 2525 Mark Avenue (Reform)

Toronto has laid claim to having the largest Jewish day school in the world. Associated Hebrew Schools of Toronto occupies a five-acre site, has 1,200 pupils from kindergarten to high school, thirty-six classrooms, a chapel, library, gymnasium, and swimming pool. Another 1,600 pupils attend four branches of the school. Holy Blossom Temple in Toronto with a membership of 2,500 families is the second largest Reform congregation in North America; its name is derived from the Hebrew *pirchei kodesh*—flowers of holiness. The synagogue was founded in 1849 and was Orthodox in tradition until 1920 when Rabbi Maurice Eisendrath, a graduate of Hebrew Union College in Cincinnati, Ohio, assumed the rabbinical chair.

Quebec

Montreal's Jewish history began in 1768 with the arrival of British Jews of Sephardic origin. Their synagogue, Shearith Israel (today at 4894 St. Kevin Road) was not only the first synagogue, but the first non-Catholic house of worship. It was not until 1858 that Ashkenazi Jews founded Shaar Hashomayim (450 Kensington Avenue in Westmount). Today Montreal has more than forty synagogues for its 100,000 Jews. (A Reform synagogue is Temple Emanu-El, 4100

Sherbrooke West, Westmount (tel. 937-3575), built in 1927 as the fourth home of the 1,650-family congregation; the synagogue seats 1,800 congregants.) In the Province of Quebec a representative listing of synagogues would include:

Montreal: Shaare Zion, 5575 Cote St. Luc Road (Conservative)
Adath Israel, 1500 Ducharme Avenue, Outremont
Chevra Kadisha, B'Nai Jacob, 5237 Clanranald Avenue
Young Israel, 6235 Hillsdale Road

Quebec City: Beth Israel Ohev Shalom, 939 de Salabery

St. Agathe-des-Monts: House of Israel, 31 Albert Street

Sherbrooke: House of Israel, 531 Montreal Street

Saskatchewan, Manitoba, and Alberta

In the western provinces of Saskatchewan, Manitoba, and Alberta are the following representative synagogues:

SASKATCHEWAN

Moose Jaw: House of Israel, Caribou Avenue at Third Avenue

Prince Albert: House of Jacob, 10th Street E. and 1st Avenue

Regina: House of Jacob, 1640 Victoria Street at Olsler Street

Saskatoon: Agudath Israel, 715 McKinnon Avenue (250 families)

Yorkton: Shaarei Shomayim, Betts Avenue (exceptionally majestic interior)

ALBERTA

Calgary: Shaare Tzedek, 103 17th Avenue, S.E. and Center Street S. (large building)
House of Jacob*, 1212 12th Street, S.W.

Edmonton: Beth Israel, 10219 119th Street and 102nd Avenue
Beth Sholom, 11916 Jasper Avenue

Lethbridge: Beth Israel, 914 15th Street S.

---

*Rabbi Ginsberg is known throughout Canada as the Orthodox rabbi who dresses up as Santa Claus at Christmas to collect money for the Salvation Army.

Medicine Hat: Sons of Abraham, 540 5th Street S.E.

MANITOBA

Portage La Prairie: House of David, Main Street South

Winnipeg: Shaarei Zedek, N.E. Academy Road at Wellington Crescent (largest congregation)
Independent B'Nai Abraham, 235 Enniskillen Avenue
Ashkenazi, 297 Burrows Avenue
Rosh Pina, 123 Matheson Avenue (beautiful stained-glass windows)
Herzlia Adas Yeshurun, Brock Street at Fleet Street
Lubavicher, 551 Magnus Avenue
Chevra Mishnayes, 700 Jefferson Avenue

Pacific Northwest

The Jews of the Pacific Northwest constitute perhaps Canada's most interesting community. According to British Columbian historian Bruce A. McKelvie, in the sixteenth century itinerant Jews from Asia settled on the coast of what is now the Canadian Province of British Columbia and the American State of Washington. These seafaring Jewish traders are believed to have crossed the Pacific Ocean in junks from the Chinese mainland. The absence of ethnological traces of these early Jewish settlements in the Pacific Northwest is attributed to the fact that there were no intermarriages with the Indians. But Jewish presence in the Pacific Northwest is attested to by (1) the many Hebrew words in the forty-seven native Indian dialects; (2) the absence of pork from the Indian diet (the Siwash tribe still abstains from pork); and (3) the similarity of the mitered helmet, necklace, and apron of the Indian medicine man to the ceremonial costume of the high priest of ancient Israel.

It was not until the 1850s that recorded Jewish settlement began in the Pacific Northwest. The first synagogue, Congregation Emanu-el, was founded in Victoria in 1863, although Jewish traders had visited the area earlier. In the 1870s, Jewish community life in the Pacific Northwest centered around Victoria, British Columbia. Samuel S. Hyams, one of the founders of the Victoria Jewish community, regularly visited the Jews of Seattle, Washington, during 1859–1861, to help them maintain their Jewish identities. Today in Victoria there is but one small synagogue (originally built in 1863) for the fifty Jewish families, Temple Emanuel at 1461 Blanshard Street (tel. EV2-0615). When built in 1863, it was the first synagogue in western Canada. A Victoria architect, John Wright, designed the structure in the Romanesque style. Original brick detailing remains on the rear and south facade, while the other facades have been unsympathetically plastered. An interesting feature about the congregation is a clause in the deed of property, which states that should at any time the Jewish

population of Victoria be unable to raise a *minyan,* the building is to
become the property of the city of Victoria, to be used as a public
institution. The local Jewish cemetery in Victoria, which opened in
1859, is located at Cedar Hill Road and Hillside.

Vancouver is today the hub of Jewry for the Canadian Pacific
Northwest. Some 14,000 Jews attend the various synagogues,
mostly located on Oak Street (locally known as Jerusalem Street):

> Congregation Schara Tzedeck (Orthodox), 3476 Oak Street (tel. 736-
> 7607), housed in a magnificent white stone edifice and possessing the
> only *mikvah* in town
>
> Beth Israel Congregation (Conservative), 4350 Oak Street (tel. 731-
> 4161), under the leadership of Rabbi Wilfred Solomon
> Temple Sholom (Reform), 4426 West 10th Street (tel. 224-9221)
> Sephardic Congregation, 3231 Heather Street (tel. 266-8276)
> Jewish Community Center Chapel, 940 West 41st Avenue

In neighboring Richmond (a young Conservative congregation
under Rabbi Daniel Segal), North Vancouver, West Vancouver,
Burnaby, New Westminster, Port Coquitlam, and Surrey there are
local Jewish community associations holding services for the High
Holy Days and serving as the local centers of Jewish life. (Burquest
Jewish Association, tel. 299-9466, serves Burnaby, New Westminster, Port Coquitlam, and Surrey; Louis Brier Home and Hospital
Chapel, 1055 West 41st Street, tel. 261-9376, has religious services
for its residents and the general community; and the North Shore
Jewish Community Association, tel. 277-2731 or 274-4873, also
serves.) There is an impressive Talmud Torah in Vancouver at 998
West 26th Avenue (off Oak Street), tel. 736-7307; a truly attractive
senior citizens' home and hospital at 950 West 41st Street, tel. 261-
9376; kosher restaurants and butchers, four summer camps, a country club, Jewish educational services from preschool to university,
and more than 100 active Jewish organizations. Widely heralded is
the local Jewish newspaper, the *Western Jewish Bulletin,* edited and
published by Sam and Mona Kaplan.

At Prince George, British Columbia, a remote town of 35,000
people some 400 miles from Vancouver, there are half a dozen
Jewish families. Jack and Lil Horlick own and operate a fine fur store
at 1277 Third Avenue; Sid Bereskin is the court recorder; Myron
Sandbad, Sam Arbour, and Dave Segal all give local color to the
small Jewish community.

Northwest Territories

The first successful Jewish farm settlement in Canada was developed between 1886 and 1907 when fifty Jewish families from
southern Russia and Bessarabia took up homestead lands offered to

them by the Canadian Government; this area later became a part of the Province of Saskatchewan, twenty miles from the Manitoba border. The history and social life of the Wapella Settlement from pioneer days to modern times is delightfully described in "Wapella Farm Settlement," by Cyril E. Leonoff, published in 1975 by the Historical and Scientific Society of Manitoba and the Jewish Historical Society of Western Canada. One Wapella homesteader was Ezekiel Bronfman, founder of Canada's famed Bronfman family.

KOSHER RESTAURANTS

Kingston, Ontario: Hillel House, 26 Barrie St. (tel. 542-1120).

Montreal: YM & YWHA, 5500 Westbury Avenue (tel. RE 7-6551).
Gan Eden, 5810 Decarrie Boulevard (tel. 731-1744).
El Morocco II, 3450 Drummond Street (tel. 844-6888).
Chabad House, 3429 Peel Street.

Toronto: Kol-Tov Delicatessen, 3023 Bathhurst Street (tel. 787-5231).
Matti's Felafel House, 836 Sheppard Avenue W., Downsview (tel. 633-9591).
Marky's Kosher Pizza, 3799 Bathurst Street (tel. 638-1081).
Hamefgesh (the Meeting Place), 361 Wilson Avenue.

Vancouver: Bagel Barrel Bakery, 3885 Oak Street (tel. 733-6815) (kashrut certified).
Leon's Kosher Korner, 3710 Oak Street (tel. 736-6348) (kashrut certified).
Max's Delicatessan and Bakery, 3150 Oak Street (tel. 733-4838) (kashrut certified).
Vancouver Kosher Meat, 3832 Oak St., (tel. 733-9210) (kashrut certified).
Wander Inn Coffee Shop, 950 West 41st Street (tel. 266-9111).
(Kashrut Committee, c/o 3476 Oak Street, tel. 688-2756 or 736-7607, is responsible for assuring the observance of the Jewish dietary laws in British Columbia institutions and food stores.)

Victoria: Sheiling Shalom, 1010 Langley Street.

Winnipeg: Elite Kosher Snack Shop, 686 McGregory Street (tel. 586-3734).
The Town Pump, 1415 Main Street (tel. 582-9218).
YMHA, 370 Hargrave Street (tel. 943-7624).

USEFUL ADDRESSES

Ottawa: Israeli Embassy, Apt. 601, 410 Laurier Avenue W. (tel. 237-6450).
U.S. Embassy, 100 Wellington Street (tel. 238-5335).

CHILE

In Chile there is a closely knit Jewish community of more than 30,000 persons, of Russian, Turkish, and Yugoslav origin. About 28,000 Jews live in Santiago, and fewer than 2,000 in Valparaíso; there are also small communities in Arica, Concepción, La Serena, Temuco, Valdivia, and the resort of Viña del Mar.

In the capital city of Santiago are the following representative synagogues:

Bicur Joilim (Orthodox), Avenida Matte 624 (tel. 561257)

Circulo Israelita, Serrano 214 (tel. 393872)

Comunidad Israelita Ashkenazi (Orthodox), Cura Marchant 1015 (tel. 465927).

Circulo Israelita is probably the best-known synagogue in all of Chile. Some 1,200 Jewish pupils, about a quarter of the total number of children, attend the secondary Jewish Integral School in Santiago. There are two Jewish weekly newspapers: the Spanish-language *Mundo Judío* (Jewish World), and *La Palabra Israelita* (Jewish Word) published in Spanish and Yiddish. Santiago also has two homes for elderly Hebrews, several Jewish sports clubs, plus the entire array of typical Jewish institutions and organizations, including seven B'nai B'rith lodges. Santiago has a very large and impressive Jewish community center, Estadio Israelita, with 2,500 family memberships.

Valparaíso has a synagogue and community center located at Alvarez 490, Viña del Mar (tel. 80373). The day school is attended by 200 pupils.

When the Allende government came to power in recent years, many Jews left Chile. When this Marxist government was ousted in September 1973, the Chilean military junta had many prominent Jews among its leaders, all active in Jewish communal affairs. In contrast, Jewish members of the Allende government maintained few links with Jewish life.

The local synagogue in Arica is at 21 de Mayo 669; in Concepción at Rengo 111; in La Serena at Cienfuegos 650; in Temuco at General Cruz 355; and in Valdivia at the local community center in town.

Communal headquarters for Chilean Jewry is at Avenida Miguel Claro 196, Providencia, Santiago (tel. 465927).

KOSHER RESTAURANTS

Santiago: B'nai Jisroel Kosher, Portugal 810 (tel. 221993).

USEFUL ADDRESSES

Santiago: U.S. Embassy, Codina Building, 1343 Agustinas (tel. 710133).
Canadian Embassy, Ahumada 11 (tel. 62256).
Israeli Embassy, San Sebastian 2812, Avenida El Bosque Las Condes (tel. 246-1880).

CHINA

(People's Republic of China)

The Jewish presence in China goes back more than 3,000 years. The prophet Isaiah sang of the return of Jews from the land of the *Sinnim* (Chinese), but there is little scientific evidence that the ancient Hebrews could have known about their existence. Small, scattered bands of Jews may have entered China around 200 B.C. (early Han Dynasty). However, there is written evidence of the presence of Jews in the Chinese Empire during the T'ang Dynasty (A.D. 619–907). Jews came as traders of silk, furs, beaver skins, swords, slave girls, and eunuchs in exchange for cinnamon, spices, musk, and camphor.

The first settlement of Jewish immigrants was probably during the Sung Dynasty (A.D. 960–1279) when Chinese merchants turned to maritime trade with India and the Arab countries. Arab records attest to the fact that Jewish merchants from Baghdad were actively engaged in trade with China, trading silk for the dyed clothes and glassware of Europe. Eventually these Jews established trading posts in China, and intermarriage made them indistinguishable from other Chinese. They participated fully in Chinese politics and culture; some became governors of provinces and ministers of state. Chinese Jews worshiped in synagogues and had a distinctive religious environment.

K'AIFENG

K'aifeng, capital city of the Sung Dynasty on the banks of the Yellow River in the province of Honan in north China, was the most important Jewish settlement in China. K'aifeng was founded during the early twelfth century by a group of Jewish families from Persia. The Jews occupied a small street in the eastern section of the city, alongside a larger settlement of Moslems and a few Nestorian Christians. The K'aifeng Jews were led by two *Ustad* (rabbis) named Leih-Wei (Levi) and Yen-tu-la (Abdullah). Besides religious leaders and teachers, their population of about 350 included merchants, tradesmen, and physicians. They observed the Sephardic rite of rabbinic Judaism, and had brought Torah scrolls and prayer books with them from Persia. The Chinese, who saw little difference between the Jews and their neighbors, referred to them collectively as *hue-hue* (Moslems). Later, the Jews came to be known as *chu-hu* (from the Persian *djuhud*), *yi-tzu-lo-yeh* (Israelites), and *t'iao-chin-chiao* ("Sect that Extracts Sinews")—a reference to Jewish ritual slaughter.

In the official dynastic history of the Mongol Empire (1279–1368) there are several references to Jewish communities in China. Christian missionaries and travelers also described these Jewish communities. Marco Polo (who departed from the Crusader city of Acre, Israel, in 1273) wrote about Jews residing in the Mongol capital at Cambalue (near present-day Peking). In 1280, when Kublai, Genghis Khan's grandson, ruled China, Chinese Jewry occupied positions of honor and power. The Mongols were tolerant of other religions, and Jewish enclaves existed in Khanbalik (Peking), Hanchow, Yangchow, Ningpo, Nanking, and Zayton (Ch'uanchou). When the K'aifeng synagogue was damaged by local fighting, Kublai had it rebuilt so magnificently on two acres of land at the foot of Earth Market Street that the synagogue withstood the elements for 600 years. After the death of Kublai in 1294 the Mongol Dynasty fell victim to factionalism; secret societies openly revolted and attacked foreign minorities. But the Ming Dynasty soon granted foreigners all the rights of Chinese citizenship, including the right to own property and enjoy freedom of religion—provided that all males had Chinese wives. Assimilation of the Chinese Jews took a major step in 1421, when a Jewish physician, An San Hassan, exposed local corruption; in recognition of this service to the throne, he became Chao Ch'eng, an assistant commissioner in the Embroidered Uniform Guard. In 1436 a Jew named Kao Nien passed the government's civil service examination and received a judicial post. Another Jew, Al Chun, became household administrator to the Imperial Prince. Within a short time, Chinese Jews had all adopted Chinese surnames and spoke and dressed like their Chinese neighbors. The K'aifeng synagogue continued to receive financial support from the government, including salaries for the community's rabbis, Li Liang and Li Jung.

A stone tablet dating from 1489 found in the courtyard of the K'aifeng synagogue is an invaluable source of information about Chinese Judaism in the fifteenth century. It recounts the fact that the Torah scrolls had been brought to K'aifeng from Jewish communities in Ningpo and Ningsia; that prayers were offered "morning, noon, and night"; that the congregation observed the Sabbath every seventh day, and fasted four times a year; and on the Day of Atonement, "men abstain from all food and drink for a full day, while respectfully addressing Heaven, filled with contrition for their trespasses." Other traditional observances delineated on the tablet were Sukkot, Simchat Torah, Chanukah, Tisha B'av, and Shavuot.

K'aifeng Jews celebrated Passover, called the "Feast of Dry Wheat"; the New Year, the first day of Tishri, was called the "Festival of the Greater Patriarchs." A great annual fast was the day after Tisha B'av, called the "Fast of the Judge's Gate," commemorating the destruction of the Holy Temple in Jerusalem. Two festivals unknown to Western Jewry were the "Festival of Escape from the Sword" and the "Festival of the Minor Patriarchs." Circumcision was rigorously practiced; the eating of pork was forbidden; and *mezzuzoth* were attached to the doors of homes. The community maintained dietary laws, and circumcised male children on the eighth day after birth. The Chief Rabbi bore the Chinese title *chang-chiao* (custodian of the Teaching); his assistants were called *man-la* (mullah), an Arabic term commonly used among Chinese Moslems. The synagogue had about twelve *man-la*, who were responsible for assisting at prayer and at community observances, for performing ritual slaughter, and for educating children. The stone tablet also reveals the extent to which Chinese Judaism assimilated Chinese values: "The Confucian Teaching and this Teaching agree on essential points and differ on secondary ones only. Thus, their common principles of making the mind resolute and making conduct appropriate are nothing more than acknowledging the Way of Heaven. By venerating our ancestors, observing the proprieties between ruler and subject, revering our parents, living harmoniously with our wives and children, preserving the distinction between superior and inferior, and living peacefully with our friends, we accord with the Five Confucian Relationships."

K'aifeng thrived as more than 400 Jewish families participated in Chinese life and civic affairs. But many factors soon contributed to the decline of K'aifeng Jewry: (1) there was no proselytism to increase their numbers; (2) there was an absence of other synagogues, i.e., visible symbols of Jewish identity; and (3) most important, for some unknown reason, these Jews never translated their Torah or Hebrew prayer books into Chinese. When contact with Persia was cut off around 1450, it was no longer possible to import trained rabbis. Knowledge of Hebrew declined, as well as access to Mosaic Law; the Torah scrolls became little more than incomprehensible cult objects. By 1512, the synagogue had more than a dozen Torah scrolls from former Chinese Jewish communities that had failed.

In 1605, a K'aifeng Jew named Ai T'ien traveled 700 miles to Peking and visited the Italian Jesuit missionary Matteo Ricci, who questioned him at great length. The Jewish community then numbered about 1,000 persons; the Grand Rabbi had died several years earlier and had been succeeded by his son, whose knowledge of the Law was incomplete. There was friction between Jews and Moslems, and the community had begun to ignore traditional dietary restrictions and the practice of circumcision. This community leader, casting about desperately for a solution, offered to make Matteo Ricci the Grand Rabbi if he would give up eating pork.

In 1642, rebel armies left K'aifeng in ruins after six months' siege; the city was defended by Li Kuang-Tien, a Jew, who cut the dikes and forced the Tartars to withdraw, although 1 million persons perished in the flood. A contemporary account of the fighting, *Diary of the Defense of Pien,* records the heroism of a Jewish company commander named Li Yao who, with a small detachment of Jewish and Moslem troops, perished while defending the city's walls. The battle ended when the waters of the Pien River inundated the city, and most of K'aifeng was destroyed, including the synagogue, its Torah scrolls, prayer books, and the single copy of a Chinese guide to Hebrew pronunciation, without which prayers could not even be recited.

Jews did not return to K'aifeng until 1653, and in 1663 the new Temple of the Pure and True was completed. According to Jean Domenge, a French Jesuit who visited K'aifeng in 1722, the temple grounds contained five courtyards, around which were arrayed the sanctuary, the front hall, two school buildings, the ancestral hall, a kitchen, a slaughtering ground, ritual baths, and living quarters for the Grand Rabbi and *man-la.* Roofs were of green tiles, the columns and wooden latticework of red lacquer. Above the doorways and on either side of numerous archways, congratulatory inscriptions were written in golden Chinese characters. Inside the sanctuary, which was surrounded by a white marble balustrade, were housed the Ark, an altar, the Imperial Spirit Tablets, and the Chair of Moses, upon which the Torah was placed for reading. In the Ark were thirteen Torah scrolls—one for each of the twelve tribes and one for Moses; twelve of these had been copied from the single scroll pieced together between 1653 and 1656.

In 1665, the Ch'ing Dynasty banned all missionary activity, and the Jewish community once again faded into the surrounding Chinese population. In 1850, in a letter to T. H. Layton, the British consul at Amoy, the K'aifeng Jewish community described their difficulty: "In reply to inquiries we have to state that during the past forty or fifty years our religion has been but imperfectly transmitted, and although its canonical writings are still extant, there is none who understands so much as one word of them. . . . Morning and night, with tears in our eyes and with offerings of incense, do we implore that our religion may flourish. . . . It has been our desire to repair the synagogue and again procure ministers to serve in it, but poverty has prevented us, and our desire has been in vain." At the same time, Bishop George Smith in Hong Kong was instructed to inquire into the condition of the Jews in K'aifeng. His findings: "A few Jewish families, sunk in the lowest poverty and destitution, their religion scarcely more than a name, and yet sufficient to separate them from a multitude around, exposed to trial, reproach, and the pain of a long-deferred hope, remained the unconscious depositaries of the oracles of God, and survived as the solitary witnesses of departed glory."

A Protestant missionary wrote in 1866 that barely a shadow of Jewish life remained. The synagogue, which had been rebuilt in the early seventeenth century, was dismantled and abandoned, its stones and timbers used for building the Great East Mosque. Only a few stone markers with terse Hebrew inscriptions remained; a few copies of the Torah were being sold on the open market. In 1932 David Brown, an American Jew, visited K'aifeng and met with several assimilated Jewish families. "They know they are Jews," he wrote, "but know nothing of Judaism. They realize they are Chinese, completely assimilated, yet there is pride in the knowledge that they spring from an ancient people who are different from other Chinese in K'aifeng." In 1957 a Czech sinologist visited K'aifeng and was told that at least 200 Chinese in the city identified themselves as being of Jewish nationality, although in the same year another historian reported some 2,000 persons of Jewish ancestry in K'aifeng.

According to "Journey Into China" (National Geographic Society, 1982) K'aifeng today has a population of 500,000, "and the streets of the downtown bazaar are very crowded. There is a narrow lane known as 'South Alley of the Teaching of the Scriptures' and a 'Foreign Heaven Chapel' once stood just behind this lane. Its wall still contains the Chinese words, 'Hear, O Israel, the Lord our God, the Lord is One.' Indeed, over the centuries at least three synagogues stood here where today is a hospital."

Recent History: In the 1830s Elias Sassoon arrived in Shanghai from Baghdad and established a trading company which was to prosper until the Communist takeover in 1949. Soon other Western Jews opened up trade with the mainland Chinese, and by 1900 colonies were established in Shanghai and Tientsin. Russian Jews arrived in Harbin in 1899; by 1910 there were 10,000 Jews there with an organized community of Hebrew schools and synagogues. The Bolshevik Revolution brought the Jewish population over 12,000. Shanghai and Hong Kong then had Jewish populations in the several thousands; Jews also resided in Tientsin, Mukden, Dairen, and Peking. Each Chinese community had its own synagogue and communal facilities, including newspapers. During World War II the surviving Chinese Jews suffered badly at the hands of the Japanese—but as Chinese, not as Jews. At the end of the war, Chinese Jews departed for other countries, including the USSR—at the express invitation of the Soviet government. After 1949, the Jewish population in China dwindled to a few families in Shanghai and Harbin—in 1964, according to newspaper reports, six Jews were still residing in Harbin and an equal number in Shanghai. Yet in 1983 a Singapore rabbi reported a village in South China with 115 Jews.

While there are few if any Jewish landmarks extant in China today, there are many Jews living and working in China. Teaching English in Shanghai is Tom Gold, a Harvard exchange scholar; and Margo Landman of New York is at a university near Tientsin. A civil servant in the Chinese government is Israel "Eppi" Epstein, a native of China, who migrated to Canada and later returned to China. Epstein now works for the Foreign Language Press in Peking. Solomon Adler, who worked as a U.S. Treasury representative in Chungking during World War II, and David Kruk are employed by the Foreign Language Institute in China. Sidney Rittenberg, a Reform Jew from Charleston, South Carolina, has spent more than thirty-eight years in China. He was the first American adviser to the Academy of Social Sciences in Peking. In 1945 Rittenberg was sent to China by the U.S. Army and remained there as an employee of the United Nations Relief Agency. He spent sixteen years in prisons on espionage charges. In the January 1981 issue of *Reform Judaism,* Rittenberg is quoted: "The Jews, like the Chinese, are an ancient people with an ancient religion that has survived since the beginning of recorded time. . . . We share many traditions and outlooks, including the importance of the family, the supremacy of scholarship, and an emphasis on a life of righteous actions rather than words. If this were more widely known among the Chinese, it would bring about better Israel–China relations as well as improve U.S.–China ties."

USEFUL ADDRESSES

Guangzhou: U.S. Consulate General, Doug Fang Hotel (tel. 69900, ext. 1000).

Peking (Beijing): U.S. Embassy, Guang Hua Lu 17 (tel. 522033). Canadian Embassy, San Li Tun #16 (tel. 521475; 521571; 521648).

Shanghai: U.S. Consulate General, 1469 Huai Hai Middle Road (tel. 379-880).

COLOMBIA

The 12,000 Jews residing in Colombia are scattered throughout the country, including Bogotá, Popayán, Barranquilla, Cali, and Medellín. It is believed that in the Antioquia region there are also descendants of Marranos who have maintained a number of Jewish customs. Jews began to arrive in the 1850s from the Caribbean, and settled principally in the port cities. However, many converted and were assimilated. The present Jewish community is made up of Sephardic Jews from the Mediterranean and of Jews from Eastern Europe (mainly Poland). The last group to arrive in Colombia were German Jews who arrived between the world wars. The Colombia immigration law of 1939 closed the door to Jewish immigration.

In Bogotá (about 7,000 Jews) are the following representative synagogues:

Centro Israelita, Calle 23 #12–37 (tel. 416-662)

Magen Ovadia, Calle 79 #9–66

Montefiore, Carrera 20, #37–54 (tel. 455-264)

Bogotá Jewry are organized under the umbrella organization Confederación de Asociaciones Judias de Colombia at Carrera 16A, #28–33, affiliated with the World Jewish Congress. It is made up of three congregations, the Sephardic, Ashkenazi, and German Reform, each with its own communal organizations. There is one Jewish school, the Colombo Hebrew School in Bogotá, with 1,000 students, including non-Jews.

Cali has a prosperous community of about 3,000 Jews, nearly all of whom arrived in the 1930s. Sinagoga Maguen Eliahu is located at Calle 44A Nort 5–00 (tel. 686918).

In Barranquilla (1,000 Jews) Centro Israelita Filantropico is located at Carrera 43 #85–95 (tel. 51197), and the local community center is at Apartado Aereo 142. In Medellín (about 1,000 Jews) Max Wagner (tel. 17538) presided over Union Israelita de Beneficencia, Calle 56, #52–73 (tel. 417538).

The remote Andean mountain city of Popayán is known as a Catholic mecca; but on Calle de Reloj there is a modest synagogue.

Here a handful of mostly Syrian Jews *eke* out a bare existence—yet all ten families provide a *minyan* regularly.

USEFUL ADDRESSES

Bogotá: U.S. Embassy, Calle 37, 8–40 (tel. 285-1300).
Israeli Embassy, Calle 35, 7–25 (tel. 245-6603).

CORSICA

This French island is the third largest of the Mediterranean islands and has a distinctive Jewish history apart from France. Corsica has a population of about 300,000, only 250 of whom are Jews. Jews have, however, lived in Corsica since the Middle Ages. Turkish Jews first arrived in 1916, settling in the port city of Bastia, which was the only Corsican place to give them hospitality and permanent residence.

A small synagogue at 3 rue Castagno in Bastia (tel. 310196) was built in 1925; but without a rabbi and with few links to mainland France, the synagogue did not prosper. In the 1950s North African Jews arrived, and in 1974 the French Consistoire put Corsica under the jurisdiction of Rabbi Jean King, former Chief Rabbi of Lyons. Recently the Jewish community in Bastia elected David Sabbagh (18 rue Napoleon) as president; Joseph Nino (13 Boulevard Paoli) as secretary general; and appointed Tangier-born Moses Cubby as their rabbi (Maison Toledano, Route de Ville, tel. 324919).

In the capital city of Ajaccio there are fewer than twenty Jewish families. (Contact Victor Bohbot, tel. 224200.) There are scattered Jewish families in Corte, Ile Rousse, Pietranera and Porto Vecchio. Corsican independence leaders recently destroyed the million-dollar wine cellars of Joseph Cohen-Scali, a prominent member of the Marseilles Jewish community. The attack was not upon Jewish property, but upon absentee ownership of Corsican wine cellars.

COSTA RICA

Almost 2 million people inhabit the Central American republic of Costa Rica. These citizens, including 2,500 Jews, enjoy the social and political benefits of the most democratic country in Central America. Costa Rica is also one of the world's friendliest countries, especially in its continued relationship with the government of Israel.

Between 1929 and the 1940s Ashkenazi Jews fleeing from Eastern Europe settled in Costa Rica; about 250 more arrived after World War II. While most Jews live in the capital city of San Jose, a few families live in Cartago and Alajuela, not far from San Jose. The central representative body for Costa Rican Jewry is the Central Israelita de Costa Rica in San Jose (Apartado Postal 1473: tel. 225449).

On the Paseo Colon in San Jose stands the Jewish community center and synagogue. Its leader is Isaac Ligator, born in Poland, past resident of Cuba and New York. Another leader is Arthur Green, who works for the United States Information Service and the U.S. Embassy in San Jose. Unfortunately, Costa Rica has no rabbi, but there is a kosher delicatessen, a Jewish sports club, and a Weizmann Institute where Jewish children are enrolled. There is a central Zionist organization and youth movement (Hanoar Hazioni), a WIZO branch, a B'nai B'rith lodge, and a women's welfare organization (Sociedad de Damas Israelitas de Beneficencia). A monthly Jewish periodical in Spanish, *Baderej,* established in 1964 with the help of the Federation of Central American Jewish Communities, is circulated throughout Central America.

USEFUL ADDRESSES

San Jose: U.S. Embassy, Avenida 3 and Calle I (tel. 331155). Israeli Embassy, Calle 2, Avenidas 2 y 4, Apartado 5147 (tel. 216011).

CUBA

The first European to set foot on the soil of Cuba was Luis de Torres, a Marrano Jew and the official interpreter for Christopher Columbus. He remained in Cuba, worked the land as a tobacco planter, and eventually died there. Other Marranos seeking refuge from the Spanish Inquisition followed Torres' lead. Hernando Alonso came with the Spanish fleet that conquered Cuba in 1511, and later helped Hernando Cortez build in Cuba the ships used to conquer Mexico. Unfortunately the Inquisition also came to Cuba, and it was not until 1783 that religious persecution ended; Inquisition laws were not formally abrogated until 1823, and public worship for non-Catholics was forbidden until the island's liberation from Spain in 1898. Nevertheless, Jewish merchants from Newport, Philadelphia, New York, Curaçao, Jamaica, and the Virgin Islands traded extensively with Cuba throughout the eighteenth and early nineteenth centuries.

Cuban Marranos have disappeared as a group, although some aristocratic old Cuban families boast of Marrano ancestry. One of the earliest Cuban freedom fighters was Juan Ellis, a Jew who helped organize an underground movement in Santiago in the 1820s and later served with Simón Bolívar. Jose Martí, the nineteenth-century Cuban patriot, imbibed some of his libertarian ideas from Jewish labor leaders while working in New York as a journalist; and in his struggle for Cuban independence he enlisted the support of a number of Florida Jews.

Jews have played an important role in Cuban history. In 1898 a Jewish lawyer from Brooklyn, New York, Horatio Rubens, became a colonel in the Cuban Liberation Army. Colonel Rubens raised funds for the movement among wealthy Florida Jews, many of whom later settled in Havana. After the 1905 pogroms in Eastern Europe, the Havana Jewish community was augmented by hundreds of refugees.

American Jews served in Cuba during the Spanish-American War and were the first Jews to establish themselves permanently as planters, industrialists, and corporate representatives. Among them was Sgt. Frank Steinhardt, who built Havana's first streetcar line. The trickle of Sephardic Jews from the Near East and Morocco that began after 1900 turned into a steady stream during the Balkan Wars of 1910–1913. After 1940, Jewish refugees exceeded 10,000. On the eve of the Castro revolution in 1959, Cuba had 15,000 Jews.

Many Cuban Jews came to the forefront during the Castro revolution. Among those who marched with Castro were many Jewish men and women wearing both *mezzuzoth* and revolutionary emblems. Castro's first minister of communications was twenty-nine-year old Enrique Oltuski, son of a Jewish immigrant who owned a Santa Clara shoe factory. Manuel Novygrod, whose parents had come from Poland, was only twenty-two when Castro appointed him chargé d'affaires in Canada. Maximo Bergman, also the son of an immigrant, led the pre-Castro revolutionary youth movement at the University of Havana. Jewish leaders contributed heavily to Castro's funds, and Castro himself, in return, treated the Jewish community well.

Castro, being a great devotee of modern agricultural techniques, was especially intrigued by Israeli experts. He was so fascinated by a scholarly paper by Professor Dan Goldberg on "drip irrigation" that he invited Professor Goldberg from Israel to lecture in Havana.

Havana's four synagogues, including one of Sephardic origin, have been the pride of the Cuban Jewish community: Adath Israel (Ashkenazi Orthodox) at Jesus Maria 103; Union Hebrea Shevat Ajim (Sephardic Orthodox) at Prado 557; United Hebrew Congregation (Reform) at Avenida de Los Presidentes 502; and Patronado Synagogue (Orthodox Ashkenazi) at Calle 13 el Vedado, with 150 members. Cuban Jews worship without governmental interference, although there are no rabbis. The Albert Einstein Jewish School, built for 2,000 students, has only thirty, because so few young Jews wish to attend. Two kosher butcher shops in Cuba still operate, and *matzoh* for Passover has been imported with government permission from the Canadian branch of the World Jewish Congress. These anomalies are consonant with Cuban communism which permits ethnic foods for minority groups; on Passover and Rosh Hashanah every Jewish family is given a chicken by the government. Provision has also been made for Jewish "soul food," such as herring and borscht. Jewish students in the national educational system are given time off to study Hebrew, Yiddish, and Jewish religion and culture. The imposing Patronado Jewish Club in Havana provides communal facilities, including the best Russian food outside the USSR. Its auditorium is leased to the government for use as a national drama institute.

In recent years much of Cuban "anti-Semitism" has been the by-product of certain Jews who were members of the Communist Party long before Castro and who now publish a weekly Yiddish paper containing vicious attacks on the State of Israel. (One member is also employed as secretary of a small ultra-Orthodox synagogue in Havana.) Cuba today is influenced also by an influx of Arab terrorist organizations, although Cuban communism has nothing to do politically with spurious Arab socialism, which is strictly anti-Israel. According to the latest reports, Cuban Jews still practice their religion openly: Moises Baldes is the seventy-five-year-old leader of the Patronado Synagogue, Cuba's largest. But the Jewish community has dwindled since the exodus began in 1959; today more than 10,000 Cuban Jews make their homes in Miami, Florida.

USEFUL ADDRESSES

Havana: U.S. Interests Section, Swiss Embassy, Calcado entre L and M, Vedado Seccion (tel. 320551).
Canadian Embassy, Calle 30 #518, Esquina a7a, Miramar, Marano (tel. 224924).

CURAÇAO

(Netherlands Antilles)

Jewish settlement on the island of Curaçao began in 1652 when a Dutch charter was granted to one David Nassy to encourage it. But there is evidence that at least one Jewish settler, Samuel Coheno, arrived earlier, in 1634. He was the interpreter for a Dutch expeditionary fleet that captured Curaçao from the Spanish. Coheno had lived in Brazil in the 1620s and was fluent in Dutch, Portuguese, Spanish, and Indian dialects. He searched unsuccessfully for gold on Curaçao, then returned to his wife and child in Amsterdam. In 1657 an agricultural settlement, founded by a Portuguese Jew, Joao Ilhao, prospered, and within three years refugees from Brazil arrived. The first congregation was organized in 1659, and by 1674 the local community had grown strong enough to bring from Amsterdam as *haham* (rabbi) Josiau Pardo, whose father and grandfather had served as Amsterdam rabbis. There was great prosperity on Curaçao in the eighteenth century, and the early Jewish businessmen (almost 2,000) shared this wealth. When Congregation Shearith Israel in New York City was building its synagogue in 1729, the Jewish community of Curaçao sent a generous donation. Curaçao Jewry also helped pay the cost of building Touro Synagogue in Newport, Rhode Island, in 1763. For the history, see *History of the Jews of the Netherlands Antilles* by Isaac and Suzanne A. Emmanuel (KTAV Publishing Company, London).

Curaçao served as a center of Jewish learning and Jewish practice for the world Jewish community until the last quarter of the nineteenth century; and then, unfortunately, as a center for further migration of Jews to every corner of the world.

The Sephardic Mikve Israel-Emanuel Synagogue (today called the United Netherlands Portuguese Congregation) is the oldest in the Western Hemisphere. The original building dates from 1732 and was dedicated in 1763. It is located on a square block at the corner of Columbustrasse and Kerkstrasse in the center of the city of Willemstad. Its pastel yellow walls dominate the adjacent commercial buildings. The synagogue's outer doorways open onto a tiled courtyard, and its outer rear stairway leads to the women's gallery. The picturesque curve of its gable betrays the influence of the Spanish colonial baroque; tall columns support the vault, while shorter columns carry the women's gallery, as in the Portuguese Synagogue in Amsterdam. White sand covers the floor like a thick carpet (symbolic of the sands of the desert where the Israelites camped during their long journey from slavery to freedom). The Holy Ark is seventeen feet high and fifteen feet wide, fashioned of heavy, richly carved mahogany with solid silver ornamentation. Inside are fifteen Torah scrolls, wound on silver rollers. In the balcony directly over the entrance is a nineteenth-century pipe organ from Amsterdam. And there are magnificent brass chandeliers everywhere, all suspended from the high arched ceiling, each carrying twenty-four sconced candlesticks.

In the early days, imitating their mother-congregation in Amsterdam, the leaders of Mikve Israel enacted regulations that governed the life of every Curaçaoan Jew for the next two centuries. Infractions were often punished by excommunication. Today Mikve Israel-Emanuel, though Orthodox-Sephardic in origin, has become Reconstructionist, following its merger in 1964 with the Reform Emanuel Synagogue. (The Emanuel Synagogue, built in 1867, is on Hendrikplein, about two blocks away.) Today Rabbi Aaron L. Peller (Kerstraatza, tel. 11067), and Cantor Pavel Slavinsky lead the worshipers.

Adjacent to the synagogue in two buildings dating from 1728 is the Jewish Cultural Historical Museum. It possesses striking mementos of the Jewish past, including Torahs dating to 1492; a unique mahogany "Chair of Elijah" for circumcisions; a 200-year-old battered silver tray, used for smashing wineglasses during wedding ceremonies; a silver Chanukah lamp of 1716; a Havdalah spice box of 1704; and silver-gilt Torah crowns of 1711. But the prize exhibit may be a centuries-old ritual bath, or *mikvah,* recently unearthed in the courtyard during restoration work; it is now located on Hanchi de Banio (Street of the Bath). The museum's curator is a charming young lady, Miss Mae Capriles, whose family arrived in Curaçao in 1759.

There is also an Orthodox-Conservative synagogue, Shaarei Tsedek (Ashkenazi), at Scharlooweg 39 (tel. 12515). Here Rabbi A. Bokow and Cantor A. Truzman lead the congregation of 120 members. This synagogue was incorporated in 1958; most of its members are recent refugees from Eastern Europe. In December 1978 it was reported that the congregation purchased $20,000 worth of kosher meat from New York City since there is no longer any kosher butcher on Curaçao. Recently a Sephardic Reconstructionist congregation was formed.

Near Emmastad is a seventeenth-century Jewish cemetery, Bet Hayim, containing venerable graves of prominent Curaçaoan Jewish families. The cemetery was consecrated in 1659 and offers hundreds of fascinating examples of Jewish sepulchral art in Portuguese, Spanish, Hebrew, and other languages. Although Bet Hayim Cemetery was originally laid out in open country, it has been surrounded since 1915 by the huge Shell Oil refinery, whose pollution has unfortunately eaten away the markings on most of the gravestones. A newer Jewish cemetery is located on Berg Altena.

The Jewish residential section of Curaçao is the fashionable Mahaai area. Damacor and Vanengelen are other prominent Jewish residential areas, as is the old Scharlooweg area with its ornate mansions where old Curaçaoan Jewish families lived many generations ago. There is an active B'nai B'rith leadership here; Schura Vorona, owner of Vorona's Department Store, P.O. Box 532 (tel. 13969), served as president of Curaçao Lodge No. 2389.

Also of interest is the monument to Elias S. L. Maduro, a nineteenth-century philanthropist; it was erected in 1911 at Julianaplein. Five streets are named after prominent Curaçaoan Jews:

Madurostraat: The Maduro family, in Curaçao since 1672, played a leading role in island commerce and industry, developing land, creating the deep inland harbor and shipping piers, providing water and electricity, and serving as bankers, brokers, and agents for Shell Oil and KLM.

Dario Salas Straat: Named for the poet and writer.

A. M. Chumaceirokade: Named for Abraham Mendes Chumaceiro, a prominent lawyer.

Dr. Caprilesweg: Named for David Ricardo Capriles (1837–1902), a pioneer in local public health.

George Maduroweg: Named for a young scion of the Maduro family, a Dutch war hero who died in 1943 at Dachau.

Curaçaoan Jews are credited with a number of island food specialties: *pastechi,* a fried meat *kreplach;* and *funchi*, a cornmeal mush, plus the now frequent addition of raisins, prunes, olives, and capers to meat and fish dishes. Kosher frozen meals are available at the Curaçao Plaza Hotel and at the Avila Beach Hotel.

USEFUL ADDRESSES

Willemstad: U.S. Consulate General, St. Anna Boulevard 19 (tel. 613066).
Israeli Consulate, Santarosaweg 60 (tel. 35039).

CYPRUS

Of all the islands in the Mediterranean, Cyprus has been perhaps the most frequently occupied by foreign forces. Jews first settled on Cyprus in the middle of the second century B.C. Hasmonean coins have been found here, and history records that formal links between the Jews of Palestine and the Jews of Cyprus were forged by the marriage of a granddaughter of King Herod to a wealthy Cypriot Jew. In A.D. 115, the 40,000 Jews of Cyprus were expelled after rebelling against Roman rule. During the Middle Ages, Cypriot Jews suffered severe persecution at Christian hands, including the requirement introduced by Archbishop Giovanni Del Conte that Jews must always display a yellow badge of identification. With the conquest of the island by the Turks in the sixteenth century, there were attempts to settle more Jews on Cyprus to negate the Christian influence. A small number of Jews from Eastern Europe settled here at the end of the nineteenth century.

Today, more than twenty years after Cypriot independence, political tensions between its Greek and Turkish citizens still persist. Cyprus in pre-1948 days was a large transient center for more than 50,000 Jewish "illegals" on their way to Palestine. Cyprus was also the locale for the motion picture *Exodus*.

About thirty Cypriot Jews reside in Nicosia and in Famagusta. The only organized Jewish religious facility is the cemetery in Margo; the cemetery at Larnaca is no longer used. Cyprus is less than one hour's flying time from Israel, and is a favorite resort for Israelis.

USEFUL ADDRESSES

Nicosia: U.S. Embassy, Therissos Street at Dositheos Street (tel. 65151).
Israeli Embassy, 44 Archbishop Makarios III Avenue (tel. 45195).

CZECHOSLOVAKIA

Jews have lived in what is now Czechoslovakia for more than 1,000 years. This fact is attested to by customs documents issued more than 1,000 years ago; Jewish merchants crossing from Bohemia were subject to fines. Even the coat of arms of the city of Prague bears an identification of its Jewish populace, the Star of David. Although Prague's Jews had been herded into a ghetto since the Middle Ages, the area was given autonomy, and by the seventeenth century was a focal point for Judaic culture. The old Jewish town hall, with its famed wooden tower and its clock of Hebrew letters as numbers on the dial, still stands on Maislova Street 18 (next to the Staronova Synagogue) and houses the Council of Jewish Communities.

In 1848 Czech segregation laws against Jews were abrogated, and by the end of the nineteenth century the ghetto became the Josefov district.

Some 300,000 Jews lived in Czechoslovakia before World War II, and despite the Nazi destruction, thirteen synagogues remain standing, only two of which are in active use; the remaining eleven are museums maintained by the government. The Great Synagogue at Jerusalemska 7 at one time accommodated 1,800 worshipers on the High Holidays, according to official government statistics. (It is the only synagogue in Prague open daily for worship.) Prague is the home of almost 2,000 Jews; another 10,000 are scattered throughout Czechoslovakia in dozens of communities including Brno (the residence of Chief Rabbi of Bohemia and Moravia Dr. Richard Feder, Leitnerova 6; the synagogue is at Skorepka 12, and the Jewish community center is at Hybesova 14). Karlovy Vary has a synagogue at Vridelni 59. One thousand Orthodox Jews live in Bratislava; the synagogue is at Heydukova Street 15. There are also synagogues in the following Czech cities and towns: Dolni Kounice, Komarno, Kosice (Puskinova 3), Galanta (Partizanska 907), Liberec, Marianske Lazne, Mikulov, Nove Zamky, Olomouc (Komenskho 7), Ostrava (Revolucni 17), Piestany (Hviezdoslavova 59); Plzen (Leninova Street); Podebrady, Presov, Pribor (the birthplace of Sigmund Freud), and Trnava (Kaitulska Street 7).

The Judaic heritage has been carefully preserved by the government in Prague's many synagogues, museums, and cemeteries, though the atmosphere surrounding them is sterile. The oldest existing synagogue in Europe is the Staronova, or Altneuschul (Old-New), Synagogue, dating back to 1268–1270. It is constructed in early Gothic style, has a five-ribbed vaulted ceiling with fluted pillars dividing the nave into two aisles, and its interior still retains richly decorated artistic works. Legend has it that the synagogue was built by exiles from Jerusalem after the destruction of the Temple in the year 70; these exiles brought with them Temple stones for the synagogue's foundation. Outside on the lawn is a statue of Moses. Nearby is the equally old Pinkas Synagogue on Josefska Street, once the main street of the ghetto; here also is a stark stone memorial to the 77,297 known Czech victims of Nazi brutality, along with a list of twenty-eight concentration camps from Terezin to Trostinec. The Spanish Synagogue (named for its architecture, not for its worshipers) on Dusni Street houses a collection of almost 1,000 Ark curtains stolen by the Nazis from synagogues all over Europe for inclusion in an "anti-Jew" museum which the Nazis expected to build in Prague.

The Prague State Jewish Museum (Statni Zidovske, Stare Mesto, Jachymova 3), located in the old Klaus Synagogue and open daily except Saturdays, is probably the largest Jewish museum in the world, a result of Hitler's plunderings. It is endowed with a unique collection of 200,000 ritual objects from silver to textiles. The collections tell the tragic tale of the extinction of most of the 300,000 Jews who lived in Czechoslovakia before 1939. There are Ark curtains from former synagogues in Boskovice and Mikulov, double chairs used for circumcision, Chanukah menorahs, ritual garments, mantles, jewelry, silver "hands" for pointing to one's place in the Torah, knives and axes of kosher butchers, prayer books, and countless other items of Judaic significance. Of all the museums in Czechoslovakia, the State Jewish Museum is the most frequented (1 million visitors annually).

The Old Jewish Cemetery nearby dates back to the first half of the fifteenth century. Although it was extended several times, it was never large enough to accommodate the needs of Prague Jewry, so new graves were piled upon the old although the cemetery was closed in 1737. The oldest preserved tombstone is that of the scholar and poet Avigdor Karo, who died on April 25, 1439. Other identifiable tombstones include Rabbi Loew (Yehuda Levi Ben Bezalel, also known as the Maharal, identified in legend as the inventor of the *Golem,* a miracle worker whom even Death was reputed to be afraid of); David Gans, a Renaissance astronomer (1613); and Mordechai Maisel, mayor of the Prague Jewish community from 1528 to

1601. The thousands of tombstones, thrusting from the ground in clusters, resemble the leaves of an artichoke; most are elegantly carved and lettered. Prague is still proud of its many distinguished Jewish sons, including Sigmund Freud, Gustav Mahler, Max Brod, Franz Werfel, and Franz Kafka (buried in the New Jewish Cemetery at Strasnice). President of the Jewish community is Dr. Desider Galsky.

In Prague the Rabbi Loew statue at the entrance of the Prague town hall is especially impressive; on the ceiling are three heavy chains once used to close the gates of the ghetto. St. Sigismund Cathedral has a seven-branch menorah which it is believed once stood in the Temple in Jerusalem. Other points of Jewish interest include the following:

Charles Bridge, the historic crossing of the Vltava River linking the Old Town with the newer city, has a monument to Jewish degradation in the shape of a large crucifix encircled by gilded Hebrew letters spelling the traditional sanctification, "*Kadosh, Kadosh, Kadosh, Adonai Tzvuoth* (Holy, Holy, Holy is the Lord of Hosts)." A plaque underneath explains that in 1609 a Jew was accused of desecrating this crucifix and, as punishment, the ghetto community was forced to pay for affixing the Hebrew letters. The original gold was stolen during the Nazi occupation.

Klaus Synagogue, next to the Pinkas Synagogue on Josefovska Street, is the largest surviving ghetto synagogue. It was founded by the famed Rabbi Judah Loew in the late sixteenth century. The baroque structure houses an exhibit called *Crimes Not Forgotten* which depicts Nazi crimes in Czechoslovakia.

Meisel Synagogue, Maislova Street, another sixteenth-century structure, rebuilt in the nineteenth century, now houses one of the world's largest collections of spice boxes, menorahs, Torah pointers and crowns, and other treasures of the old Jewish community and the destroyed synagogues.

Other places of great Jewish interest in Czechoslovakia include Mauthausen (in nearby Austria), site of a Nazi concentration camp where tens of thousands of Czech Jews were tortured to death, and Terezin, which was built before 1780 as a military fortress and served as a Nazi concentration camp during the 1940s for more than 150,000 Jews from all over Europe. Over one-fourth of all these people died from maltreatment and disease, and 20,000 died from exhaustion and starvation; yet Terezin was but a transit station for the Nazi gas chambers farther east.

The city of Holesov has a sixteenth-century synagogue (later re-modeled in baroque style) and a cemetery with the gravestone of the legendary Rabbi Sabbatai Meir Kohen (Schach); and the city of Mlada Boleslav is proud of its old cemetery which contains the tomb of Jacob Bashevi. In Bratislava, near the Danube, there is an underground Jewish cemetery containing tombs of famed talmudic scholars from the seventeenth century.

KOSHER RESTAURANTS

There are kosher restaurants in Bratislava (Zamocka 49a); Piestany Spa, and Kosice (Zvonarska ul 5). The dying Jewish community in Prague confirms the fact that there are no kosher facilities, except for the food brought from Bratislava for the Old Jewish Town Hall kosher restaurant at Maislova 18 (tel. 62541 or 62543), open only for lunch.

USEFUL ADDRESSES

Prague: U.S. Embassy, Trziste 15-12548 (tel. 536641).
Canadian Embassy, Mickiewiczova 6 (tel. 327124).

DENMARK

In 1622 the first Jews invited to come and live in Denmark settled in the City of Gluckstadt in the Danish province of Schleswig-Holstein. These early arrivals from Amsterdam and Hamburg were invited by King Christian IV at the prompting of his Jewish mint-master, Albertus Denis, and his physician and friend, Dr. Jonah Charizi. They were granted full religious freedom and commercial privileges. Other Sephardic Jews followed in 1657, serving as financiers and jewelers to the royal family and to Danish nobility. The talmudic scholar Benjamin Musafia was named the king's personal physician in 1646, and his son-in-law, Gabriel Milan, was appointed governor of the Danish West Indies (now the Virgin Islands) in 1684.

Also in 1684, synagogues were opened in Fredericia, East Jutland; Nakskov; and Copenhagen. Nine years later the first Jewish cemetery was established in Copenhagen. In 1814 the Jews of Denmark were accorded the civic rights and duties of Danish citizens.

But the date October 1, 1943, is one of unusual significance in modern Danish-Jewish history. By the heroic action of all the people of Nazi-occupied Denmark virtually every Jewish citizen was spirited out of the country on the very eve of their scheduled shipment to Nazi concentration camps and were provided with sanctuary in neutral Sweden for the balance of World War II.

The Nazis had planned to round up the country's 8,000 Jews on the first day of Rosh Hashanah that year—when everyone would be conveniently assembled in the synagogue or at home, easy prey for the special Kommando units of the Gestapo, handpicked by Adolf Eichmann himself for their mission. German troopships were anchored in Copenhagen harbor, ready to transport the intended victims to the death camps of Central Europe. But when the stormtroopers, in a series of carefully executed, simultaneous raids, descended upon the synagogue and on Jewish homes, they found that their prey had vanished. Every Jewish man, woman, and child in the country had been hidden away in Danish homes, in basements and attics, in churches and hospitals. During the ten days that followed, between Rosh Hashanah and Yom Kippur, Danish Jews were smuggled out of the country and taken by an improvised fleet of fishing vessels and rowboats to safe haven in Sweden, separated from Denmark by the narrow waters of the Oresund.

This wartime escape began when G. F. Cuckwitz, a German consular official in Copenhagen, leaked to Danish leaders details of the plan to deport all the Jews. The underground informed Rabbi Marcus Melchior who sounded the alarm from his pulpit on the first night of Rosh Hashanah. Most of the Jews fled north to the area around Helsingor, where they were hidden in seaside inns, churches, and woods along the beach until the Danish resistance forces and fishermen could carry them to safety in Sweden. (Only 472 Jews were captured by the Nazis and shipped to the Theresienstadt concentration camp in Czechoslovakia.)

During Nazi occupation Danish Jews had a special reason to feel proud: their king, Christian X, wore in public the same yellow armband which the Nazis had ordered all Danish Jews to wear. Even Jews who fell into Nazi hands and were sent to Theresienstadt were kept alive by Danish food packages smuggled into the camp. A New York lawyer, Richard Netter (remotely related to the world traveler Jacob Mordecai Netter), got the idea in the 1950s to thank the Danes for their decency by raising money for scholarships to be held by Danish students in both American and Danish universities. Subsequently Netter broadened the base into Thanks to Scandinavia Scholarships, which grants ten scholarships annually.

Today there are approximately 8,000 Danish Jews among 5 million Danes; most Danish Jews reside in Copenhagen, where the Great Synagogue, built in 1833, is located (Krystalgade 12). Its plain exterior contrasts with the white-and-gold elegance of its interior. King Christian X attended its centennial in 1933. When the Nazis invaded Copenhagen the king helped to hide the Torahs in a neighboring church. Ministering to the needs of Denmark's Jews is Chief Rabbi Bent Melchior, 27 Frederiksborggade in Copenhagen (tel. 01-138282). Machsike Hadass Synagogue is located at 12 Ole Suhrsgade in Copenhagen also.

COPENHAGEN

In front of the Copenhagen cathedral in Norregade is a life-size sculpture of Moses holding the Ten Commandments. Denmark's most important center of Judaism is the famous Bibliotheca Judaica Simonseniania, housed in the Royal Library at Christians Brygge 8. Here are 50,000 volumes of Judaica, including more than 400 manuscripts printed before 1500, and some 900 Hebrew prints from the sixteenth century.

The Museum of the Resistance on the Esplanaden features an exhibit of maps and photographs depicting the rescue of the Danish

Jews from Hitler, their escape route, their reception in Sweden, and the welcome accorded them upon their return to Denmark in 1945.

The Administration Office of the Jewish community in Copenhagen (Ny Kongensgade 6; tel. 01-128868) houses the offices of a council of twenty delegates, who are elected by approximately 1,800 Jewish taxpayers, the board of directors, and a board of trustees in charge of the synagogue. The building also contains a small museum, a library, and a *mikvah*. Adjoining is one of the three government-supported Jewish old people's homes. The building also houses a number of adult and youth organizations, including a choir. The unified Jewish community centers about the Great Synagogue where Orthodox services are conducted.

The old Jewish cemetery on the Moellegade (tel. 01-371342) dates back to 1693; Vestre Kirkegard Cemetery is at Kirkegarde Alle (tel. 01-211158). Israelsplads (Israel Square) in the center of Copenhagen was so named in 1968 on the twenty-fifth anniversary of the rescue of Danish Jewry; its Jerusalem counterpart is called Denmark Square—a token of Israel's "Thanks to Scandinavia." Bohr Alle is a street named in honor of Niels Bohr, Denmark's greatest scientist. It was at Bohr's Institute for Theoretical Physics at the University of Copenhagen (on Amelienborg Square) that atomic physics had its great synthesis in the 1920s. Bohr, under the cover name of "Mr. Baker," directed a secret laboratory at Los Alamos, New Mexico, where the first atomic bomb was assembled and tested. Bendixgade is a street name for Victor Bendix, a noted Jewish composer. Melchior's Plads is named for Moritz Gerson Melchior, nineteenth-century merchant and friend of Hans Christian Andersen. Brandes Alley is named for Dr. Ludwig Israel Brandes, one of Denmark's greatest physicians.

The Museum of Danish Resistance Movement offers somber reminders of Nazi bestiality, including the section called "The Persecution of the Jews." Round Tower, adjoining Trinity Church, on Kobmagergade—within sight of the Great Synagogue—is one of several seventeenth-century Copenhagen buildings on which the name of God is inscribed in Hebrew; the sacred Torahs of the community were hidden here during the years of Nazi occupation. Holmen's Church, on the Holmen's Canal, also has God's name inscribed in Hebrew over its gateway; many Jews were first hidden here, in the church belfry, in 1943 during their escape to Sweden. Caroline's School, 18 Bomhusvej (tel. 299500), was founded in 1805 by Mendel Levin Nathansen. A kindergarten and elementary school, it provides secular and religious education for 200 boys and girls.

FREDERICIA

This town of 30,000 people was built as a fort with straight streets intersecting at right angles and encircled by ramparts. Its harbor services the largest ships of any Danish port. In town is an old Jewish cemetery erected more than 250 years ago. (The oldest Danish Jewish cemetery is in Nakskov.)

HELSINGOR

In the local ferry station is a sculptured Jewish refugee memorial by Harald Isenstein, recalling the heroism of the Danish underground of 1943. The monument represents a fishing boat with Jewish refugees.

HORNBAEK

During the summer months the local synagogue at Granvej 7 is open for daily services (tel. 200731).

ODENSE

In this town, where Hans Christian Andersen lived and wrote his world-famous stories, is an old Jewish cemetery dating back to 1825. (The two oldest Danish Jewish cemeteries, over 250 years old, are located in Nakskov and Fredericia.) In the Andersen Museum are Hebrew and Yiddish translations of his writings. As a child, Andersen attended a Jewish school in Copenhagen and his writings paint sympathetic pictures of Jews and Jewish life.

KOSHER RESTAURANTS

Copenhagen: Arne Cohn, Rorholmgade 2 (tel. 133012 or 138867).
Bielefeld, Ole Suhrsgade 8.
Hotel Aviv, Colbjornsensgade 13.
Apelts Kosher Food A/S, Vendersgade 16 (tel. 117063) (caterers for SAS Airlines).
"Copenhagen Kosher," Classensgade 5 (tel. 420981).
Hakoah is a Jewish sports club at Bremensgade 9.

USEFUL ADDRESSES

Copenhagen: U.S. Embassy, Dag Hammarskjolds Alle 24 (tel. 01-423144).
Canadian Embassy, Prinsesse Maries Alle 2 (tel. 01-122299).
Israeli Embassy, Trondhjemsplads 4, 3rd floor (tel. 01-260088).
Israel Government Tourist Office, 6C Vesterbrogade (tel. 01-119679).

DOMINICAN REPUBLIC

Jews first settled in the Dominican Republic in the eighteenth century, although Luis de Torres, a Marrano, had in 1492 been ashore here as a member of Columbus's expedition. (In fact, the tree trunk to which de Torres moored his boat, along with the "ashes" of Columbus, are preserved in Santo Domingo's cathedral.) From 1509 to 1520, the island of Hispaniola (of which the Dominican Republic occupies the eastern half) was governed by Columbus's son Diego who, like his father, is believed to have been a Marrano.

The eighteenth-century Jewish settlers were Sephardim from the Netherlands and the Netherlands Antilles and they soon became assimilated with the local population. The 1794 slaves' revolt forced thousands of landowners and merchants to flee; the few Santo Domingo Jews also left for the United States, and settled in the South where they figured prominently in later Confederate history.

The oldest existing Jewish community is in the capital city of Santo Domingo where Jews from Curaçao settled early in the nineteenth century, to be joined around 1890 by Russian Jews. In 1917 several Jewish families from the Virgin Islands arrived, and in 1933 others arrived from Cuba after the overthrow of the Machado government.

The Jewish community grew rapidly in the late 1930s and during World War II by the arrival of refugees from Nazi persecution. Indeed, the Dominican Republic was the only nation that offered unlimited asylum for Jewish refugees. But after the war many of the refugees moved to other countries. Today there are only about 150 Jews in Sosua, 150 in Santo Domingo, and 12 in Santiago.

In terms of Jewish history, the city of Sosua on the northern coast has a special significance, for in April 1940, Jewish refugees from Hitler were promised asylum there. Only 705 Jews were able to come. Dictator Trujillo had offered to accept 100,000 Jewish and non-Jewish refugees, but the shortage of sea transportation prevented Sosua from becoming a real haven. Of the young Jewish refugees who arrived in 1940, fewer than 400 stayed on, and these intermarried with Dominican women. Each settler was given seventy acres of land and ten cows plus a small cash allowance that came from Jewish sources. Overseas Jewish organizations expended $3 million on transportation, land improvement, roads, and housing. A cooperative dairy, truck farming, and cattle breeding were begun, and soon Sosua Jews had their own hospital, school, synagogue, and even a radio station. Shortly thereafter, many Sosua Jews were attracted to Puerto Rico, the United States, and Israel. Today, the 150 who remain own cooperatively two prosperous factories for making cheese and sausages. The local synagogue, built in 1941, is open. Jewish businesses include a boutique (Amber Collection), Koch Guest Houses, and La Roca Restaurant.

In the capital city of Santo Domingo, there is an attractive synagogue (Centro Israelita, Avenida Ciudad da Sarasota 5; tel. 533-1675). A fine jewelry store is owned by Rudi Frankenburg, and a furniture store is owned by Misza Mainster, both prominent leaders of the Jewish community. There are two pro-Israel organizations: the Instituto Cultural Dominico-Israeli, which promotes cultural ties between the Dominican Republic and the Jewish State; and Shalom, an association of Dominican students trained in Israel.

USEFUL ADDRESSES

Santo Domingo: U.S. Embassy, corner of Calle Cesar Nicolas Pensen and Calle Leopoldo Navarro (tel. 682-2171).
Israeli Embassy, Avenida Ciudad de Sarasota 38 (tel. 533-2359).

ECUADOR

In Ecuador's capital city of Quito there are about 200 Jewish families, all of whom are justly proud of their three-man choir, billed as the "oldest choirboys" of any synagogue in the world. This unique ensemble has sung in many South American countries. Most of Ecuador's 1,100 Jews came in the 1930s from Germany, Czechoslovakia, and Poland, although there are a few Sephardic families who have lived here for many years. Ecuador's Jewish population peaked in the year 1950 with 4,000 Jews, 80 percent of whom lived in Quito. The liberal Ecuadorian constitution of 1936 had guaranteed freedom of religion. But in 1938 and in 1952 government orders detrimental to Jews were introduced; aliens had to provide evidence that they were working in the occupations listed on their immigration papers, and Jews not engaged in agriculture or industry were asked to leave the country. Fortunately, with the aid of the World Jewish Congress, these laws were rescinded.

The Asociación de Beneficencia Israelita, founded in 1938, represents the Jewish community. There are a number of Jewish organizations such as B'nai B'rith, WIZO, and Maccabi. There is an elementary school, Albert Einstein, for approximately 220 children, although only half of them are Jewish. It is considered prestigious for upper-class Ecuadorians to send their children to a Jewish school with better-paid teachers than government schools. The Jewish Community Center is located at 18 de Septiembre 954, Casilla 2873 (tel. 233765).

Jews also live in the large coastal city of Guayaquil (ten families) and in Cuenca (six families). In Guayaquil, the port city of Ecuador, the Jewish Community Center is at Luque 127, 5 piso.

Jews in Ecuador work mostly in industry; very few are in the professions. Some Jews attempted agriculture but were unsuccessful. Many own factories of furniture, textiles, clothing, underwear, and shoes; others have attained some prominence in pharmaceuticals. However, compared to the Jews in other Latin American countries, those in Ecuador are not affluent.

The government of Ecuador has become friendly with Israel, and there is a network of technical cooperation between the two countries.

USEFUL ADDRESSES

Guayaquil: U.S. Consulate General, 9 de Octubre y Garcia Moreno (tel. 511570).

Quito: U.S. Embassy, 120 Avenida Patria (tel. 548000).
Israeli Embassy, Avenida 12 de Octubre 532, Casilla 2463 (tel. 528100).

EGYPT

The Patriarch Abraham, progenitor of both the Jews and the Arabs, visited Egypt almost 4,000 years ago, as did the other two Patriarchs, Abraham's son Isaac and his son Jacob. Jacob actually settled in Goshen in eastern Egypt, after being reunited with his eleventh son, Joseph, who had been sold into slavery by his jealous brothers. Joseph was later promoted by Pharaoh to be his chief minister. After Joseph's death at the age of 110, "there arose a new king over Egypt who knew not Joseph," and the bondage of the Jews began. The "Pharaoh of the Oppression" is generally considered to have been Rameses II, who not only set taskmasters over the Israelites (Jewish forced labor built the cities of Pithom and Raamses), but also was the first man in history to devise a systematic plan to destroy them. Rameses II is thought by some scholars to have lived between 1300 and 1234 B.C. Scholars disagree over whether Rameses II was the Pharaoh of the Exodus as well as the Pharaoh of the Oppression. However, the circumstances of Egyptian history indicate that the Pharaoh of the Exodus was Rameses' son, Meneptah, or Mernepta, and that the Exodus took place between 1225 and 1215 B.C.

In the year 586 B.C. Nebuchadnezzar, King of Babylonia, conquered Judah and destroyed Solomon's Temple in Jerusalem, appointing Gedalia as Governor of Judah. When, shortly afterward, Gedalia was assassinated, his supporters fled to Egypt, taking with them the Prophet Jeremiah. The last recorded prophecy of Jeremiah is a condemnation of the Jews of Egypt for worshiping idols. But, idol-worshipers or not, the Jews of Egypt did not lose their identity or forsake their Judaism. In the fifth century B.C., 100 years after the Persian conquest of Egypt, a flourishing Jewish settlement with its own synagogue existed on the Nile island of Elephantine, opposite Aswan in Upper Egypt. (The ruins of an ancient Jewish temple can be seen here today.)

In 332 B.C., Alexander the Great conquered Egypt, founded Alexandria, and designated it the capital city. Alexander the Great organized a new government and then, a year later, withdrew to Phoenicia. Jews streamed into Egypt in the wake of Alexander's conquest, most of them settling in Alexandria. The great port city became the focus of Jewish life in Egypt, the seat of that great Hellenistic-Jewish culture which brought Judaism to the pagan world and the achievements of the Greeks to the Jews. Its best-known exponent was the philosopher Philo. Jewish settlement in Egypt was at its zenith; the community was the largest it has ever been, about 1 million Jews! It was in Alexandria that seventy Jewish scholars, all working independently, translated the Bible into Greek—the Septuagint—on the order of Ptolemy II (285–246 B.C.).

Egypt came under Roman rule in 30 B.C., remaining within the Roman Empire until the Moslem conquest of A.D. 640. The Jews of Egypt rebelled against Roman rule in A.D. 115. It took the armies of the Emperor Trajan two years to subdue them, virtually wiping out the Jews of Alexandria in the process. The Christianization of the Roman Empire led to a deterioration in the condition of Egyptian Jewry, and the invading Arabs in A.D. 640 found a community which had dwindled into insignificance. The Arabs enforced the traditional Moslem anti-Jewish code, but despite this, the situation of the Jews was fairly favorable, with the exception of the period under Caliph Hakim (A.D. 996–1021), when there was savage persecution of the Jews.

ALEXANDRIA

Alexandria has perhaps 150 Jews under the leadership of Clement R. Setton. (In 1948 Alexandria had 26,000 Jews.) In 1979 Mr. Setton was included in the official Egyptian welcoming party for Prime Minister Begin at the Alexandria airport. He stood next to the Vice President of Egypt as the Egyptian band played "Hatikva," and many of the Jews of Alexandria cried unashamedly. A minha service for Begin was scheduled at the magnificent Eliahu HaNavi Synagogue at 69 Nebi Daniel Street. When the Egyptian security people came to arrange the seating of the official party and the press, Setton mentioned that he had invited all 150 members of the community but that there was obviously room for many hundreds more. An Egyptian security officer corrected him: "There are 300 Jews in Alexandria and they will be here." (The size of the community had doubled overnight.) Funds for the maintenance of the Alexandrian synagogue came from the sale or rental of the community's once-extensive properties and the sale of cemetery plots. Unlike the Jewish cemetery in Cairo, which had been invaded by homeless squatters desperate for a place to live in a city bursting at the seams, the Jewish cemetery in Alexandria is well fenced and guarded. It is well worth a visit—not only for the elaborate mausoleums of the wealthy Jewish families, but also as a reminder of one of the most colorful episodes in modern Jewish history. Here in Alexandria were organized the men of the Zion Mule Corps and the Jewish Legion of

World War I, who fought as units of the British army, with the dream of winning an independent Israel in Palestine; and here are buried many of the men who died in that struggle. Gravestones mark their names and the place where many of them fell—Gallipoli, the peninsula off the Turkish coast which Winston Churchill, in one of the worst blunders of his career, had targeted as the landing place for a British expeditionary force. In a terrible slaughter, the English army, including the 562 Jews who had signed up in Alexandria, were driven back into the sea by the defending Turks.

CAIRO

The Jew of Cairo in the eleventh century was, above all, a successful businessman, according to Dr. Stefan Reif, of Cambridge University. Dr. Reif has uncovered written records of early Jewish life: "Do not leave a single penny idle—buy when God gives you the chance, and export on the first ship to set sail." Jewish businessmen continually complained of fluctuations in prices: "Prices are in God's hands; they follow no principle."

These and other records of Jewish life in Cairo have been found in Ben Ezra Synagogue in Old Cairo (6 Harett-il-Sitt-Barbara). For about a thousand years this synagogue has served as a repository or *genizah* for every conceivable written record of Jewish life. It is a unique archive of Jewish life in the Middle Ages, and scholars have spent years reconstructing the everyday life of the Cairene Jew. The Ben Ezra documents also spelled out the problems and harassment faced by Jewish businessmen from government tax and customs collectors. Every boat on the Nile was scrutinized for evaders. Jews also had to pay a special Jewish tax, and payment of the tax for the Jewish poor was a great *mitzvah*. The synagogue is now closed for repairs. The only functioning synagogue is at 17 Adli Pasha Street in the business district, near the Nile Hilton Hotel.

During the centuries of Arab rule, Cairo became the greatest Jewish center of Egypt. There were Jews in Fustat (Old Cairo) when the new city of Cairo was founded in the tenth century; Jews were among its first citizens. Cairo became the seat of the local *Nagidim,* or heads of the community, in the eleventh century. When the great Moses Maimonides (the Rambam) arrived in Egypt in the second half of the twelfth century, he became the spiritual head of the Cairo community, and his descendants held the office of Nagid in succession for a considerable period of time.

The Turks captured Cairo in 1517 and incorporated Egypt into the Ottoman Empire. Although the position of Egyptian Jewry improved to some extent, their record until the nineteenth century was undistinguished. During the first half of the nineteenth century, the star of

Egypt's Jews began to rise again, following the reforms of Mohammed Ali and after the opening of the Suez Canal. European Jews began settling in the country, and Alexandria became a commercial center. Soon Alexandria's Jewish population again exceeded that of Cairo. In 1897 there were 9,800 Jews in Alexandria and 8,800 in Cairo. More Jews immigrated after the outbreak of World War I in 1914. By 1917, the Egyptian census showed 59,580 Jews. Between 1937 and 1947, Egypt's Jewish population grew to 65,600.

This was not to last. In 1945, the Cairo Jewish quarter was attacked. A synagogue, a hospital, and a home for the aged were burned down and many Jews were injured or killed. This was the first anti-Semitic disturbance of its kind in modern Egypt. Two years later the Companies Law came into force, decreeing that at least 75 percent of employees in any undertaking must be Egyptian citizens. This hit the Jews particularly hard, since only about one-fifth of them had Egyptian citizenship; the remainder, although in many cases born in Egypt where their families had lived for generations, were either aliens or stateless. Then came May 15, 1948, the establishment of the State of Israel, and King Farouk's declaration of war. Hundreds of Jews were arrested and the property of many was confiscated. The second exodus from Egypt began. Between 1948 and 1950, 25,000 Jews left, 14,000 going to Israel. Nasser's seizure of power in 1954 was followed by more arrests of Jews. The 1956 Sinai campaign was the signal for the internment of 3,000 Jews and the deportation of thousands of Jews with little more than the clothes on their backs. By 1957, there were only 8,560 Jews left in Egypt, 5,560 in Cairo, 2,740 in Alexandria, and the remainder scattered in a number of smaller localities. Ten years later, the Egyptian community numbered a mere 3,000; in 1970, fewer than 1,000. Today fewer than 250 Jews are left in Egypt. The Jewish community center in Cairo is at 13 Sebil-el-Khazender Street (tel. 824613 or 824885).

USEFUL ADDRESSES

Alexandria: U.S. Consulate General, 111 Avenue Horreya (tel. 801911).

Cairo: U.S. Embassy, 5 Sharia Latin American 9, Garden City (tel. 28219).
Canadian Embassy, 6 Sharia Mohammed Fahmi el Sayed, Garden City (tel. 23110).
Israeli Embassy, 6 Shariah Ibn-El Maleck, Giza (tel. 982000).
Israeli Consulate, Tarik Al-Hurrya 453 (Rushdi), Alexandria (tel. 846040).

EL SALVADOR

Fewer than 300 Jews reside in El Salvador. Jews first arrived in the 1800s and settled in the small city of Chalchuapa. French Jews came later to the capital city of San Salvador; Eastern European Jews arrived in the 1920s, and German Jews during World War II.

The Comunidad Israelita de El Salvador is located in San Salvador (Apartado Postal [06] 63) under the leadership of Enrique Guttfreund. The Conservative synagogue under Rabbi Alexandre Granat is at 23 Avenida Norte (tel. 215466).

In 1979 the honorary Israeli consul Ernesto Leabes was kidnapped and murdered. Two years later civil war broke out and many Jews emigrated.

USEFUL ADDRESSES

San Salvador: U.S. Embassy, 25 Avenida Norte 1230 (tel. 267100).

ENGLAND, WALES, and NORTHERN IRELAND*

[United Kingdom]

A small number of Jewish financiers from Rouen, France, followed William the Conqueror into England in 1066, and during the course of the next generation, Jewish communities were established in London, York, Bristol, and Canterbury. Protected by the Crown, Jews flourished as traders and moneylenders. But 1144, in the city of Norwich, brought the first recorded ritual-murder accusation against English Jews, and for the next century there was much bloodshed. In 1190 escapees from an English riot in the city of York burned themselves alive rather than submit. One hundred years later, almost 5,000 Jews were expelled from England.

In 1655, Manasseh Ben Israel of the Netherlands negotiated with Cromwell for the readmission of Jews, and within ten years official recognition was given to a new Marrano group from the Netherlands. By 1690 Ashkenazi immigrants from Germany and Central Europe had built their first synagogue in London. In the nineteenth century the rise of Sir Moses Montefiore brought Judaism into its greatest prominence; in 1858 Lionel de Rothschild was admitted to Parliament. After 1881, refugees from Russian persecution added to the growing Jewish population in England. Today approximately 410,000 Jews have found Great Britain a wonderful place in which to live.

AYLESBURY

Mentmore Towers in Buckinghamshire, England, was the first of six great mansions built or reconstructed within an eight-mile radius of Aylesbury by the English Rothschild family after 1840. Some 30,000 acres encompassed Mentmore Towers; it was designed by Sir Joseph Paxton, architect of London's Crystal Palace, as a

---

*Scotland is covered separately because of its independent Jewish character.

Rothschild family residence. The only one of the six great houses still occupied by a Rothschild as a residence is neighboring Ascott, a National Trust property. The Rothschild family represented Aylesbury in the House of Commons for almost sixty years.

BASILDON

This small community in Essex has a "Whiteway" synagogue on Basildon Road, Laindon.

BIRMINGHAM

Jews have resided here since 1730; the first synagogue was in The Froggery in 1780. Today there are more than five synagogues, the oldest known as "Singers Hill" at Ellis Street (tel. 021-6430884).

BLACKPOOL

The Orthodox synagogue is on Leamington Road (tel. 025-328614), and the Reform synagogue is at 40 Raikes Parade (tel. 025-323687).

BOURNEMOUTH

The Bournemouth Hebrew Congregation was established in 1905; since then this resort community has grown to more than 3,000 Jews. The Orthodox synagogue is at Wooton Gardens (tel. 020-227433) and there is a Reform congregation at 53 Christchurch Road (tel. 020-227736).

BRADFORD

In this West Yorkshire community German Jews developed the export trade of wool yarns and fabrics. The Orthodox synagogue is at Springhurst Road, Shipley, and the Reform congregation meets at Bowland Street, Manningham Lane.

BRIGHTON

Brighton is a seaside resort just an hour from London. The fountains, illuminated gardens, promenade, and "lanes" for antique and curio shops make Brighton a premier holiday city with a large Jewish population. Jews have lived in Brighton since 1767. There are synagogues at Landsdowne Road 6 (Progressive); Middle Street, Holland Road 22 (Orthodox); and Palmeira Avenue (Reform), all in the suburb of Hove.

BRISTOL

Bristol was the center of medieval England; the rich Jew whose teeth were extracted one by one until he surrendered his fortune to King John is a historical figure here. The synagogue at 9 Park Row (tel. 027-223538) dates back to 1870, although its predecessor was erected in 1786. There is a Progressive synagogue at 48 Bannerman Road.

BURY ST. EDMUNDS

Here in Yorkshire is the famed "Jews House" in Lincoln and Moyses Hall, one of England's oldest houses. Its northeast wall has a recess which once held a Torah.

CAMBRIDGE

There is a small synagogue at Ellis Court, Thompson's Lane, built in 1938 for Jewish students at Cambridge University; it houses a kosher restaurant. Mary Frere Hebrew Library at Girton College has an important collection of manuscripts in Hebrew. The Cambridge University Library with its twenty miles of shelves has the finest collection of Judaica in England, including the Schecter-Taylor Geniza writings of the ninth to the eleventh century. The Herbert Loewe Memorial Library is housed in the small synagogue.

CANTERBURY

There is no synagogue today in Canterbury, but Jewry Lane and the old cemetery near St. Dunstan's Street are reminders of the past when Jews resided here.

COVENTRY

In September 1970 the Jewish community here celebrated the bicentenary of its synagogue on Barras Lane. The first synagogue in Coventry was founded in 1770 on Butcher Row by Isaac Cohen who lived to the ripe old age of ninety-seven. Coventry's proximity to Birmingham enabled the latter Jewish community to help save the Coventry Jews from time to time.

EXETER

A German Jew named Lemel who resided in Exeter over 300 years ago was responsible for the introduction of rum into the British navy. Lemel changed his name to Lemon Hart, and gave his name to one of the best-known trade names for English rum.

Jews first came to Exeter in the year 1181 when it was one of the cities set aside by the Normans for the registration of Jewish debts to the Crown although, in truth, it was usually the Crown that owed money to the Jews. After the Resettlement of the Jews in the seventeenth century, Exeter became one of the places used extensively by Jewish peddlers and other traders. They established the local synagogue, which still stands in Synagogue Place, Mary Arches Street, and (after the Plymouth synagogue) is the second oldest outside of London still standing on its original site. In Exeter's early days local Jewish traders offered Jews from the larger cities the "bribe" of unrestricted credit on the understanding that they would make their home in Exeter and so help to make up a *minyan*. The present Jewish population is fewer than fifty persons.

Exeter's Jewish cemetery at Magdalen Street has inscriptions dating back to 1728.

GATESHEAD

Here on the River Tyne is the famed Jewish Teachers Training College for Women organized in 1944, as well as a yeshiva for training young men. One hundred fifty Jewish families also reside in Gateshead; the local synagogue is at 180 Bewick Road (tel. 063-2781472).

HARROGATE

The pleasant city of Harrogate has an ultramodern "oblong" synagogue located on St. Mary's Walk.

HULL

This seaport has been the home of Jewry since 1780. More than 500 Jewish families reside here. The Old Hebrew Synagogue, destroyed in World War II, was rebuilt in 1955 on Osborne Street.

LEEDS

The Jewish community of Leeds exceeds 15,000 and dates back only to 1804; the first synagogue was built in 1860. The New Central Vilna Synagogue is at 245 Harrogate Road; Shomrei Hadass Synagogue is at 368 Harrogate Road; Sinai Reform at Roman Avenue, Street Lane; and the United Hebrew Congregation is on Belgrave Street (tel. 053-245516).

LEICESTER

Jews have been in Leicester since the Middle Ages, but the earliest synagogue was built in 1861. Its present-day structure is on Highfield Street; there is a Progressive Jewish congregation in town.

LIVERPOOL

The organized Jewish community began in 1750. The Old Hebrew Congregation on Princes Road (tel. 051-7093431) was first built in 1807 (on Seal Street). The Progressive synagogue is at 28 Church Road N.; the Sephardic congregation meets at 2 Dovedale Road; and the Greenbank Drive Hebrew Congregation meets on Greenbank Drive.

LONDON

The city of London, where almost 300,000 Jews (mostly Orthodox) reside, is the exciting hub of Anglo-Jewish life. The City, the East End, Golders Green, Edgware, and Stamford Hill are Jewish suburbs of London; there are perhaps 100 Orthodox, Conservative, Sephardic, Reform, and Liberal synagogues, as well as countless Jewish communal organizations. (Consult the London telephone directory.) Jewish travelers should visit Bevis Marks Synagogue (St. Mary Axe) which is England's oldest Jewish edifice; for an opulent synagogue, visit Marble Arch Synagogue, Great Cumberland Place.

In London's galleries and museums there are Jewish memorabilia of every description: in the Victoria and Albert Museum, there is a collection of Jewish wedding rings; at the British Museum, a fine Judaica collection; and at the Tate Gallery, Jacob Epstein's magnificent sculptures (also in Parliament Square).

Visit Woburn House (Upper Woburn Place; tel. 01-3875937), administrative headquarters for Anglo-Saxon Jewry, which has an outstanding collection of Jewish antiquities. In the House of Commons there is a special Bible in Hebrew used for swearing in Jewish Members of Parliament. In the academic world, Jews' College (11 Montagu Place; tel. 01-7232041) is of international renown. Founded in 1856 it is the oldest rabbinical seminary in England; this school trains Orthodox rabbis, cantors, and educators for traditional services. Leo Baeck College (33 Seymour Place; tel. 01-2627586), established in 1956, prepares rabbis and educators for Liberal-Progressive congregations. Westminister Synagogue (Rutland Gardens, Knightsbridge) is the site of hundreds of Torah scrolls rescued from the Nazis. These Holocaust Torahs are being repaired and restored and are sent to synagogues all over the world.

The nine-floor B'nai B'rith London Hillel House, 1/2 Endsleigh Street, Tavistock Square (tel. 01-3875278) was opened in the fall of 1971; it has a synagogue, dormitories, kitchens, dining hall, lounges, library, and meeting rooms. The edifice not only accommodates 3,000 Jewish students in London, but also the District B'nai B'rith offices.

In Brick Lane, East London, stood a synagogue building with a history dating back to 1743—the Spitalfields Great Synagogue. Originally built for French Huguenots, the building subsequently underwent surprising changes in ownership: in 1819 the Wesleyans leased the church and school; shortly thereafter the Jewish Evangelical Society took over the church and tried to convert local Jews to Christianity; later the East End Mission occupied the premises with a similar effort; and finally in 1894 the Yiddish Talmud Torah rented the school premises. Two years later, in 1896, the Talmud Torah leased both the church and school for a term of eighty years. The consecration of the synagogue in 1898 was an exciting event with a solemn street procession in which twenty-six scrolls of the Law were carried under two marriage canopies, led by a band of musicians. In 1922 the freehold of the synagogue and Talmud Torah was purchased by Machzike Hadas and soon became the "citadel of the Orthodox." Both the Talmud Torah and the Spitalfields Great Synagogue flourished, until the former was finally closed in 1968 due to a scarcity of pupils. Recently the synagogue building was demolished to enable a Pakistani mosque to be built there.

Few Jewish visitors to Windsor Castle are aware that the Queen's Presence Chamber and the Queen's Audience Chamber have seven tapestries depicting the eventful life story of an ancient queen, Esther, the wife of Ahasuerus. Woven at the French royal factory at Gobelins in the 1780s, from paintings by Jean François de Troy (1679–1752), they show: Esther's Swoon, Esther's Coronation, The Banquet, Triumph of Mordechai, Esther's Toilette, Mordechai's Disdain for Haman, and the Condemnation of Haman.

MANCHESTER

More than 35,000 Jews dwell in Manchester, whose Jewish cemetery dates to 1794 and whose Great Synagogue (Stenecourt, Holden Road; tel. 061-7403019) also dates back to the days of the earliest community. There are synagogues at Cheltenham Crescent, Salford; Upper Park Road, Salford; Leicester Road, Salford; Altrincham Road; 190 Cheetham Hill Road; Park Lane, Whitfield; Jackson's Row; and 62 Singleton Road. Every conceivable Jewish organization has an office and membership in Manchester.

NEWCASTLE-UPON-TYNE

This community was established about 1831, although Jews had lived here since 1775. About 700 Jewish families reside here now and attend synagogues at Great North Road, Gosforth; 37 Eskdale Terrace; and at Graham Park Road, Gosforth.

NORWICH

There is today only a small Jewish community in this isolated coastal town. The synagogue is located at 3 Earlham Road (tel. 060-323948). Evidence of Jewish life survives in the Music House at Norwich, the oldest remaining Jewish residence in England.

OXFORD

When Jews started to arrive in England in the wake of William the Conqueror, they chose Oxford as one of the first places in which to settle. In 1177 Jews were allowed to purchase land outside London, and the first purchase in Oxford was land for a cemetery known as "The Jews' Garden." In 1308, after the expulsion of the Jews from England, the local synagogue became a tavern. Oxford University was the first to admit Jews as teachers; Cambridge had the first Jewish students, but they were unable to proceed to a degree. Another lesser-known, though still notable, "first" for Oxford was the 1650 opening of England's earliest coffeehouse by "one Jacob, a Jew." Both Jews and Oxford have come a long way since then, and nowadays a thriving residential community coexists with a well-established university Jewish Society, coming together at the bright, modern synagogue and communal center at 21 Richmond Road, a modest little street on the west side of the town, not too far from the railroad station.

The university library has a fine Judaica collection. At least three of the oldest buildings, Jacob's, Moyse's, and Lombard Halls, were Jewish homes in the twelfth century. Oxford's Bodleian Library houses a great collection of priceless Judaica. (Sir Thomas Bodley, for whom the great library was named, was a student of Hebrew.) Isaac Wolfson College is named after the Jewish philanthropist who contributed heavily to this postgraduate institution. The Jewish cemetery in use from 1231 to 1290 is now part of the Botanical Gardens and the very ground on which the Hospital of St. John stands.

Probably the most colorful of all Oxford Jewish personalities in recent memory was the great Jewish historian Cecil Roth, who held the readership in postbiblical Hebrew studies for many years after establishing the post in the 1930s. Another distinguished Oxfordian is Sir Isaiah Berlin, Fellow of All Souls' College and one of the most distinguished living philosophy scholars.

Five miles beyond Oxford lies the imposing seventeenth-century manor house of Yarnton. Today this is the home of the Oxford Center for Post-Graduate Hebrew Studies under the direction of Dr. David Patterson. With access to an outstanding collection of Hebrew and Yiddish books and manuscripts, the Center makes an important contribution to contemporary Jewish scholarship. Many under-graduates take advantage of the modern Hebrew and Yiddish classes offered at the Post-Graduate Center.

PLYMOUTH

This Devonshire Jewish community was founded in 1752, and in 1762 the Ashkenazi synagogue was built on Catherine Street; it is the oldest Ashkenazi synagogue building in England still used for its original purpose.

SHEFFIELD

The Jewish community dates back to 1837 and is proud of its stately synagogue on Wilson Road, its community center at 127 Psalter Lane (tel. 07-4252296), Talmud Torah School, and an at-tractive residence for the Hebrew aged. There is also a Hillel House for Jewish students attending Sheffield University.

YORK

English Jewry regard York as the city of dishonor because of the tragic events of 1190 when Richard the Lion-Hearted, after his coro-nation, was believed to have issued an order to attack the Jews. This ugly and false rumor ignited a riot, and mobs looted Jewish homes, beating and killing in a wild frenzy. After the king learned of this brutal attack, he insisted that three of the leaders of the mobs be put to death and instructed his people not to harm the Jews in any way. Nevertheless, when King Richard left England shortly thereafter to lead a Crusade, new riots broke out against the Jews. Crusaders, bent on robbing the Jews, were joined by noblemen who owed them money and fanatical priests who sought to convert them. Together, they mounted an all-out attack on the Jews of York. About 500 Jews managed to take refuge in the royal castle in York, where they fought off their attackers. After a few days, their meager food supplies were gone and they faced a bitter choice—baptism or death at the hands of those besieging the castle. They chose neither. Instead, they de-cided to take their own lives. Following the example of the defenders of Masada (who were hopelessly outnumbered by the Roman legions in A.D. 73), the Jews of York committed mass suicide on Friday, March 16, 1190, the evening of the Great Sabbath before Passover. The few Jews who were ready to accept baptism in order to survive were killed by the leaders of the mob when they entered the castle. The marauders then moved to the cathedral where they burned the records of all the debts owed to the Jews.

A widely held tradition among English Jews is that a *cherem,* or ban, was placed on the city of York, forbidding Jews to live there.

The story of the massacre was told by Sir Walter Scott in his novel *Ivanhoe*. York Cathedral has five stained-glass windows, traditionally known as the "five sisters" or "Jewish windows" because they were paid for by money extorted from the Jews of York.

There is a mound of earth close by the River Ouse called Baile Hill, upon which stands Clifford's Tower, built in the thirteenth century to replace a wooden Norman tower burned during the "Jewish riots" of 1190. It is a memorial to Jewish suffering and Jewish heroism. Nearby are several small cemeteries where ancestors of the leading Jewish families of England were buried. The local synagogue (established in 1892) is on Aldwark Street. (At nearby King's Lynn there was once a medieval Jewish community.)

Wales

The first documented Jewish presence in Wales was in 1749 when one David Michael came from Germany. His son Levi was the first Welsh-born Jew (1754), and he settled in Swansea. Other Jews followed and a Jewish burial ground was established there in 1768. The next Welsh Jewish settlement was in Cardiff in 1840. The advent of the steamship and the demand for coal and steel after 1870 brought Jewish settlers to Tredegar, Neath, and Merthyr Tydfil.

The old synagogue on Church Street in Merthyr Tydfil (no longer in use) is a three-story stone building, approachable from steps above the level of the street. The facade resembles twin towers; toward the back is a higher facade culminating in a triangular peak.

Today there are synagogues in only six Welsh communities: Aberdare (19A Seymour Street); Cardiff (Cathedral Road, Moira Terrace, and Bandreth Road); Llandudno (Church Walks); Pontypridd (Wood Road); Rhyl (Queen Street); and Swansea (Ffynone). Today there are fewer than 3,000 Jews in all of Wales.

Northern Ireland (Belfast)

One of the earliest references to Jews in the city of Belfast appears in the second volume of Benn's *History of Belfast* (1880): "About sixty years ago a Jewish rabbi proposed to give some lectures in Belfast on the Hebrew Scriptures, in a large room in Commercial Court. He was countenanced by the intelligent inhabitants, but a rabble gathered at the place and with drums and riots prevented the lecturer proceeding." Unfortunately, the description is all too familiar. Forty years later organized Jewish life began in Belfast, though the first Jews had been living there since 1652. In 1871 Daniel Jaffe founded the synagogue on Great Victoria Street, which later became Orange Hall.

In Belfast's early days Russian refugees joined the community, and today their descendants make up most of Northern Ireland's 1,500 Jews. At the beginning of the century Belfast had a Jewish mayor, Sir Otto Jaffe, who in 1907 built the Jaffe School as a free school for students of all religious denominations.

Jewish social life centers around the Jewish Institute at 33 Ashfield Gardens. There is a new synagogue at 49 Somerton Road (tel. 0232-77974) in the Fortwilliam section. Belfast also has a new communal center, Northleigh, built in 1966. About 350 Jews call Belfast their home. Close ties with Dublin Jewry are maintained.

KOSHER RESTAURANTS

The vast number of Kosher restaurants (and hotels) in London and other English communities permits only a listing of a few:

BELFAST: Belfast Jewish Institute (tel. 0232-77149).

BIRMINGHAM: Social Club, 91 Church Road, Mosely (tel. 021-449-1573).

BLACKPOOL: Guest House, 26 Longton Road (tel. 0253-27964).

BOURNEMOUTH: Cumberland Hotel, East Cliff (tel. 0202-20722). Grosvenor Hotel (tel. 0202-28858). Green Park Hotel (tel. 0202-34345). New Ambassador Hotel, East Cliff (tel. 0202-25453).

BRIGHTON: King's Hotel, 139 Kings Road (tel. 0273-29133).

GANTS HILL (Greater London): Sharon Restaurant, 376 Cranbrook Road (tel. 01-554-2471).

LIVERPOOL: Hillel House, 25 Arundel Avenue (tel. 051-722-5671).

LONDON: Aviva and Avna Hotels, 1 Platts Lane, Finchley Road, N.W. 3 (tel. 794-6756).
Bloom's, 90 Whitechapel High Street, E. 1 (tel. 247-6835).
Carmel Restaurant, 143 Clapton Common, E. 5 (tel. 800-4033).
Gershon's Fish Restaurant, 1017 Finchley Road, N.W. 11 (tel. 455-6141).
Kohn's Snack Bar, 14 Stamford Hill, N. 16 (tel. 806-3978).

MANCHESTER: Filson Catering Ltd., 70 Bury Old Road (tel. 061-773-7625).
J. S. Kosher Salt Beef Bar, 7 Kings Road (tel. 061-773-2909).

NOTTINGHAM: Supernosh, 182 Highbury Road, Balwell (tel. 060-227-8102).

USEFUL ADDRESSES

LONDON: U.S. Embassy, 24/31 Grosvenor Square, W.1 (tel. 499-9000).

Office of the High Commissioner for Canada, Canada House, Trafalgar Square, S.W.1 (tel. 01-930-9741).

Israeli Embassy, 2 Palace Green, Kensington (tel. 01-937-8050).

BELFAST: U.S. Consulate General, Queen's House, 14 Queen Street (tel. 228239).

ETHIOPIA

The prophet Jeremiah (13:23) once asked, "Can the Ethiopian change his skin, or the leopard his spots?" This ancient Hebrew was raising the question of man's ability to change, but the prophet Amos (9:7) reminded us of our racial intolerance: "Are ye not as the children of the Ethiopians unto Me, O Children of Israel? saith the Lord." Nowhere is this reminder more pertinent than in the northwest provinces of Ethiopia (near the town of Gonder) where there are almost 20,000 remnants of Falashim, or Black Jews, who call themselves "Beta Israel." Only in recent years has world Jewry opened its heart to these ancient Hebrews who, since the destruction of the Second Temple in Jerusalem, have practiced Judaism despite great poverty, persecution, and isolation. In the early 1600s, the Falashim population exceeded 500,000; the last Jewish kingdom was overthrown by the Copts.

The Jewish traveler to Ethiopia is immediately made aware of Jewish influence. Not only does the Ethiopian calendar follow the Hebrew calendar, but the biblical names of Solomon, Samson, and Isaac are heard everywhere. Orthodox Ethiopians do not eat pork, and even their ritual killing of animals is similar to the Jewish method. Three Ethiopian cities important to the Jewish traveler are: Lalibela, with its mighty twelfth-century rock churches, is called New Jerusalem; Aksum has priests still guarding what is allegedly the original Ark of the Covenant; and Gonder (former capital of Abyssinia) is the home of most Falashim. On the island of Tanka Cherkos in Lake Tana, legend has it that King Menelik I and the Levites fled from Jerusalem with the Ark of the Covenant and built a temple to house it. (The Ark is now at Aksum.) Three large stones with hollows for catching blood are believed to be the sacrificial stones carried from Jerusalem. The emperors of Ethiopia have been crowned in Addis Ababa (8,200 feet above sea level) upon the Throne of David with the eternal proclamation: "Verily, verily, thou art the King of Zion, son of David and Solomon." Haile Selassie, who was emperor from 1930 to his death in 1975, was called "The Lion of Judah of the Tribe of Judah, elected by God, Emperor of Ethiopia."

The Falasha synagogue at Wallaka is built of poles and tree branches, covered by a thatched roof, and crowned by a *Magen*

David. The interior of the synagogue is bare, except for the Ark containing the Torah written in Ge'ez, the ancient Semitic language of Ethiopia. The Falashim have their largest settlement at Ambo Ber, about twenty miles from Gonder, where they have a synagogue, a sectarian school, and several rabbis. In Addis Ababa, the local "white" synagogue belongs to the members of the Aden community who settled there as refugees from Arab hostility (tel. 211725).

These Black Jews, long unrecognized by the Jewish world due to their geographical remoteness as well as the indifference of white Jews, claim descendance from the marriage of the Queen of Sheba and King Solomon. It was the son of that marriage, King Menelik I, who brought the Ark of the Covenant to Ethiopia.

The Falashim observe the Judaic precepts governing *kashrut,* the Sabbath, circumcision on the eighth day, and marriage. The Falashim still burn offerings as a sacrifice to God and, according to the ancient ritual rules of the Bible, slaughter only male animals. The sacrificial animal is slaughtered by a rabbi with a two-edged knife specifically kept for this purpose in the synagogue. In most cases the male firstborn of each family is ordained for the priesthood but if a member of his family has committed a serious violation of the biblical laws (for example, adultery), he is not entitled to become a priest. Every community with a *mesjid* (synagogue) has a *kahen* (rabbi; the word is a derivative of the Hebraic *kohen*). Every Falasha household contributes *asrat* (one-tenth) of its income in cash or in kind to the synagogue. Besides sacrifices, the Falashim bring *meswaet,* offerings to the priests. On the Sabbath morning or at any lunar or yearly festival the women bring bread and *tella* (beer) to the synagogue as offerings. The deacon accepts them and the priest, turning toward Jerusalem, recites the benediction over them; then either he or the deacon cuts the bread down the middle for all to partake. The Falashim's feasts and fasting days are the same as those observed by Orthodox Jews everywhere, but their observance of the Sabbath is exceptionally strict. They regard the Sabbath as a goddess who can bless and destroy at will; on this day, a Falasha would rather pay someone else to work for him than do a stroke of work himself. They adhere to the Jewish calendar and have lunar months and solar years. So rigorously do they follow the Mosaic laws and other biblical injunctions that an infringement of any one of them may entail severe penalties. A Falasha who changes his religion or marries a non-Falasha is automatically thrown out of the community. A girl who loses her chastity before marriage is made an outcast for life.

The Bible of the Falashim consists of the Five Books of Moses, together with the books of Joshua, Judges, and Ruth. Unfortunately, these people have no knowledge of Hebrew, and their priests make great use of the canonical and apocryphal books (Enoch and

Jubilees) of the Old Testament in Ge'ez, their native language. Two of their religious books, *Te'ezaza Sanbat,* or "Ordinance of the Sabbath," and *Abba Elijah,* or "Father Elijah," are given Hebrew titles. Falashim observe all the Jewish holidays except Purim and Chanukah, which are postbiblical.

For the most part, the Falashim are an agricultural people, living in small villages and hamlets in the mountains around Gonder, a city of 80,000. The men are ironsmiths, weavers, and carpenters, crafts their fellow Ethiopians despise as being beneath their dignity; the women are experts in pottery-making.

While little is truly known about the history of the Falashim, it has been established that they were victims of continuous persecution not only by rapacious landowners but by missionaries who sought to convert them to Christianity. The renowned Jewish "missionaries" Joseph Halevy and Jacques Faitlovich made trips to Ethiopia at the beginning of the twentieth century to bring the Falashim into contact with European Jewry and introduce them to a more modern form of Judaism.

Probably the first meaningful recognition of the Falasha community of Ethiopia occurred in 1921, when Rav Kook, Chief Rabbi of Palestine, addressed an appeal to world Jewry to "save our Falasha brethren from extinction and contamination . . . and to rescue 50,000 holy souls of the House of Israel from oblivion." In more recent years there have been attempts to raise their standard and to bring them back into contact with world Jewry. In 1954 the Jewish Agency opened a seminary in Asmara for Falasha students from the Gonder area. But funds ran dry, and the school was not reopened until 1967. A settlement project was launched in the lowland areas (20,000 acres of heavily wooded land with fertile soil, sufficient to accommodate all the Falashim) through efforts of the Ethiopian government with the assistance of the United Nations. Cotton, sesame, and sorghum are being grown under the guidance of technical experts from Israel.

In 1972, Rabbi Shlomo Goren, the Ashkenazi Chief Rabbi of Israel, publicly stated that the Falashim are part of "the community of Israel." Rabbi Ovadia Yosef, the Sephardic Chief Rabbi of Israel, had earlier received the Falashas into the Jewish community. In 1975 the Israeli Interministerial Commission ruled that the Falashim were true Jews entitled under the Law of the Return to a home in Israel. The door to Israel was open for those Ethiopian Jews fortunate enough to be permitted to emigrate. For detailed information on the lot of the Falashim, call on the American Association for Ethiopian Jews, 340 Corlies Avenue, Pelham, NY 10803 (Graenum Berger). In Great Britain the Falasha Welfare Association in London (H. Gershon Levy) is also very active. Over the years many distinguished leaders have concerned themselves with the plight of the Falashas: Professor Norman Bentwich established the Falasha Welfare Association in England; Dr. Aryeh Tarakower headed the pro-Falasha committee in Israel; and Dr. Wolf Leslau lived among the Falashim and studied their history and customs. (Dr. Leslau's book, *Falasha Anthology,* published by Yale University in 1951, is an important contribution to our knowledge of the Falashim.)

In Eritrea lives a small community of Jews who migrated from the Arabian state of Aden. About fifty families, non-Falashim, earn their living in commerce in the capital city of Asmara. The community has a small synagogue in Asmara at via Hailemariam Mammo 34 (see Kenzen T. Cohen, Avenue Empress Menen 152; tel. 11682) and another in Addis Ababa (tel. 211725).

USEFUL ADDRESSES

Addis Ababa: U.S. Embassy, Entoto Street (tel. 110666).
Canadian Embassy, African Solidarity Insurance Building (tel. 48335).

FIJI ISLANDS

In Suva, capital of the Fiji Islands, one might encounter Mark Israel, who is a member of the Suva City Council. His granduncle Sir Henry Marks emigrated from Australia and established a large commercial organization in Fiji; he was a member of the Fiji legislature for many years. In Suva today Herbert Thaw, a German Jew, owns a jewelry and watch shop along Victoria Parade where once many Jewish businessmen had their stores. Rodney Ackreman is another prominent Fijian Jew, as are Jacob Prowellor, a Polish Jew who owns a banana-drying business in Fiji, and Chief Justice Clifford Grant, who was knighted by Queen Elizabeth in 1977.

Suva's once prosperous Jewish community included Abraham and Alfred Hort who operated a fleet of sailing vessels; retail stores, owned by Brodziaks, Lazurus, Joske, Benjamin, and Samuel, all Jews who had come to Fiji from New Zealand or Australia in the early 1920s; and Philip Samuel Solomon, editor of the newspaper *Fiji Times* who also served as Acting Attorney General. Overlooking Suva harbor is an old Jewish cemetery where these prominent Fijian Jews are buried.

Visas have not been required for Israeli citizens ever since Fiji became an independent sovereign state on October 10, 1970. With independence, however, Fijian Jewry apparently has declined.

USEFUL ADDRESSES
Suva: U.S. Embassy, 31 Loftus Street (tel. 23031).

FINLAND

The Finnish Jewish community of 1,000 persons is one of the youngest in Scandinavia and certainly among the sturdiest. Until 1809, Finland was part of the kingdom of Sweden where Jews had been prohibited from settling. In 1809, Finland became a grand duchy in the Russian Empire; Czar Alexander I did not change any existing Swedish laws, so Jews were still barred. Indeed, the first Jews to settle in Finland came in 1830 as Russian soldiers, and then as Russian refugees in 1860. Having served in the Russian army garrison, they were permitted by the Czar to stay in Finland. But these Russian Jewish settlers, called "Cantonists" or "Nicolaievskis," were all young Jewish males who had been drafted into the Russian army for a period of twenty-five years and had been assigned to garrison duty in remote outposts of the czarist empire—places such as Siberia and Finland. The harsh conscription law had been designed to alienate the youthful recruits from their own people and their religion, thus forcing their conversion to the Russian Orthodox Church. Each Jewish community within the Pale of Settlement was assigned its quota of young draftees, and there were special Jewish officers, known in Yiddish as *khapers* (kidnappers), who had the task of impressing the conscripts into the army. There was a reluctance to draft the older youth, who might already be married and supporting families; often boys as young as eight or nine years old would be chosen instead—with witnesses on hand to swear that the eight- or nine-year-olds had actually reached the statutory age of twelve.

These early Russian Jews settled in the cities of Helsinki and Viipuri, and every residence permit issued to them was bitterly opposed by the local authorities. After failing to have revoked the Jewish permit granted by the Russians, the Finnish authorities endeavored to undermine the Jews' position by a series of severe restrictions. Jews were subject to constant control by the Finnish police, who required them to renew their residence permits every three months. They were permitted to deal only in secondhand clothes, and forbidden to leave their city of residence or to attend trade fairs. The slightest violation of any of these rules served as a ground for expulsion from Finland.

The first Jewish religious services in Finland were held in the Sveaborg fortress at Helsinki. In 1865 Jews won permission to build a synagogue which took forty years to build because they could not afford the price of a building, even on land donated by the city. The struggle for equal rights for Jews began in 1872 and continued for many decades. A law authorizing Jews to reside in the cities of Helsinki, Turku, and Viipuri was enacted in 1889; at that time there were 1,000 Jewish residents in Finland. Jews did not receive full civil rights until 1918, when Finland became independent.

During World War II, there was an unyielding determination in Finland to protect its Jewish citizens—even though Finland ended the war in alliance with Germany against the Soviet Union. All able-bodied Jews fought in the Finnish army during the Russo-Finnish War of 1939–1940, and continued to serve in the Finnish forces when they later fought beside the Germans against the Russians. When the town of Viipuri was annexed by the Soviets, about 300 Finnish Jews evacuated along with the Finns, and returned to Finland. Field Marshall Mannerheim, who commanded the Finnish army during both wars, refused to enforce anti-Jewish legislation, despite strong pressure. The 1945 peace treaty between Finland and the Allies, banning racial discrimination and reestablishing full civil rights for Jews, confirmed the status of equality the Finnish Jews had enjoyed before the war and which they have enjoyed ever since.

Helsinki is the home of 850 Jews who maintain a synagogue at Malminkatu 26 (tel. 6941297), founded in 1906 by former Russian soldiers. A wreath preserved under glass memorializes the Finnish Jews who lost their lives in the Russo-Finnish War. The community center adjoining the synagogue is a modern complex, housing a Jewish preparatory and day school, a small hospital and old people's home, the Maccabi Sports Club, a choir, a theater, and numerous recreational facilities. Helsinki University Library, Rikhardinkatu 3, possesses many original documents on Jewish history in Finland; it also has a rare collection of Hebrew and Yiddish books printed in Russia between 1825 and 1917. Tuomiokirko, the Lutheran cathedral located in the heart of the city between the university and the House of Parliament, has the Hebrew word *Adonai* chiseled over the western main entrance and also on the eastern wall.

There is a Jewish community center in Turku (Brahenkatu 17; tel. 12557); it was erected in 1956. Next door is a small synagogue built in 1912 for Turku's 250 Jews; Feibel Hasan is president. And in Tampere a communal center (Nasilinnankatu 38; tel. 27397) serves Tampere's twenty Jews; Solomon Steinbach is president. The Ahvenanmaa Islands in the Gulf of Bothnia contain the ruins of Bomarsund, a Russian fortress built partly by Jewish military conscripts and destroyed by British and French naval forces during the

Crimean War in 1854. Nearby are the graves of a number of Russian-Jewish soldiers. And in Hameenlinna, the Old Cemetery has graves of the Cantonists, the earliest tombstones dating from 1835.

Jews in Finland are fully integrated citizens. Max Jacobson, member of a prominent Jewish family, headed Finland's delegation to the U.N. and was president of the U.N. Security Council in 1969. His mother, Mrs. Jonas Jacobson, was head of Finland's Women's International Zionist Organization for many years. In modern Finland, Jews are engineers, industrialists, and intellectuals, as well as merchants and traders.

KOSHER RESTAURANTS

Kosher food will be served by previous arrangement by Mrs. Sarah Smolar, Kalevankatu 40, Helsinki (tel. 642094).

USEFUL ADDRESSES

Helsinki: U.S. Embassy, Itainen Puistotie 14A (tel. 171931).
Israeli Embassy, Vironkatu 5a (tel. 175177).
Canadian Embassy, Pohjois Esplanadikatu 25B (tel. 171141).

FRANCE

Where Roman armies pitched their camps in Gaul, the first cities in that part of the world sprang up. Jewish settlers arrived in the region of Marseilles about 500 B.C. Close behind the Roman armies came migrant Jewish peddlers trying to escape from the limited economic opportunities of overcrowded Rome. Thus Jews helped lay the foundations of early French commerce, particularly in Paris, Orléans, and Lyon. Centuries later, as conditions became unsettled because of constant warfare, Jews moved from commerce into farming. Under the Frankish rulers Jews prospered, but the Christian clergy, disturbed by the favorable positions held by Jews, prevailed upon the populace to compel Jews to convert. In A.D. 629, Jews were expelled from the kingdom of Dagobert in central France; some settled around the city of Narbonne in the territory later called Provence, where Jewish cultural activity blossomed. After the Crusades turned Christian against Jew, French pogroms became more frequent. In 1171, in Blois, in the Loire Valley, Jews were accused of killing a Christian in order to use his blood for religious purposes; in 1321, 160 Jews were buried alive in a pit in Chinon in the Loire Valley; and in 1388 no Jew was allowed to live in the city of Strasbourg. Jews were banished from much of France in 1394. Starting in 800, Jews settled in Verdun, Metz, Nancy, Rouen, Paris (1182), Bray, Sens, Troyes, Lyon (where Jews were expelled in 1420), Limoges, Bordeaux, Bayonne, and Toulouse (where the Jewish community was annihilated in 1420). The greatest concentration of French Jewish life before 1500 was in the general area of the Côte d'Azur.

Jews returned to France in the seventeenth century, and at the time of the French Revolution, organized Paris Jewry was founded; in 1791 the full emancipation of French Jewry was celebrated. There were still, however, bursts of anti-Semitism such as the Dreyfus Affair. During World War II, the Nazis executed or sent to concentration camps more than 175,000 French Jews. Today, after the influx of Jews from Algeria, Tunisia, Morocco, and Eastern Europe, France has 650,000 Jews, constituting the fourth largest Jewish community in the world; more than half dwell in Paris. Indeed, more Jewish refugees have found a haven in France since the end of World War II than in any other country except Israel.

Three Jews have served as Prime Minister of France: Léon Blum served twice, first in 1936 and then in 1946; René Mayer in 1953; and Pierre Mendes-France in 1954. The distinguished French scholar Regis Michaud (1880–1939), in his book *Modern Thought and Literature in France* (1934), pointed out that the leading French philosopher (Bergson), the foremost French novelist (Proust), the chief French controversialist (Benda), and the favorite French essayist (Maurois) "are Jews or half-Jews." Indeed, the history of France is intertwined with the history of its Jewish citizens, in both the positive aspects indicated above, as well as less pleasant episodes of continuing anti-Semitism.

AIX-LES-BAINS

One of France's premier resorts has its local synagogue on rue du Roosevelt, and the local *yeshiva* on Route de Tresserve. There is also a JDC home for the aged and a girls' school.

AVIGNON

The synagogue for the small Jewish community is at Place de Jerusalem 2, a modern edifice with many memorial plaques.

The ancient Jewish ghetto here was called *carrière*. Several years ago an underground garage was built under the Place du Palais; the entrance was constructed through the rue de Vieille-Juiverie. This street has disappeared, along with its century-old buildings. Rue Pente-Rapide and rue Petit-Reille, both very small streets, remain as vestiges of the ancient Jewish section, where Jews lived from the fifth to the thirteenth century. In 1211, the *carrière* was transferred to the area of rue Jacob and Place de Jerusalem, where the synagogue is located today. The ancient synagogue on this site was destroyed by fire in 1845 and replaced by the present synagogue, built in the Romanesque style.

BAYONNE

This southern Jewish community serves a wide area in which 200 Jewish families reside. Rabbi Amar M. Mirene presides over the synagogue at 35 rue Maubec (tel. 59-550395).

BIARRITZ

The local synagogue at rue de Russie has been closed in recent years.

CANNES

The local synagogue (tel. 381654) is at Boulevard d'Alsace 20; it was built in 1955 through the generosity of an Egyptian Jew. The community center is at 3 rue de Bone (tel. 381654).

CARPENTRAS

The ancient synagogue in Place de la Mairie, built in 1367 and rebuilt in 1741, is a French national monument; it is the oldest French synagogue still in use. The community today is composed principally of Algerian Jews who arrived in 1962.

CAVAILLON

The fourteenth-century synagogue here is a historical landmark, maintained by the community as a tourist attraction. Located on rue Hebraique, it is the oldest surviving synagogue building in France, a national monument, and an outstanding example of medieval craftsmanship.

CLERMONT-FERRAND

There is a small synagogue at rue des Quartre-Passeports 20 and a community center at rue Blatin 6. The B'nai B'rith lodge, Auvergne Emile Kahn, had as its president Dr. Elie Wurm (rue Blatin 58); and as its secretary R. Slama (rue Rameau 6).

DEAUVILLE

A house of worship was established in 1978 at 41 rue Robert Fossorier in the center of town. This is a newly organized Jewish community.

DIJON

The local synagogue is located appropriately at rue de la Synagogue 5. Dedicated in 1879, the edifice has been restored since its use by the Nazis as a warehouse in the 1940s (tel. 305791).

GRASSE

Grasse has a synagogue at rue Mougins-Roquefort 6, just across from the town hall (tel. 879132). It adjoins the remains of the thirteenth-century ghetto at Place aux Herbes.

GRENOBLE

Grenoble has a small community of 7,000 French and North African Jews. The local synagogue is the Consistoire Israelite at rue Maginot 14 (tel. 870280).

L'ISLE-SUR-LA-SORGUE

This ancient Jewish community disappeared shortly after the French Revolution. The Place de la Juiverie occupies the site of the ancient *carrière,* or ghetto. The balustrade in front of the high altar of the Church of St. Laurent was taken from the remains of the synagogue when it was demolished in the 1850s. There is also an ancient cemetery, densely covered by trees and bushes, which the municipality has begun restoring. The Jewish cemetery at nearby St. Rémy-de-Provence has already been restored.

LYON

France's third largest city has a Jewish population of over 35,000, worshiping at the Grande Synagogue, 13 quai Tilsitt (tel. 873-1343); Neveh Chalom, 317 rue Duquesclin (tel. 858-1874); Chaare Tsedek, 18 rue St. Mathieu (tel. 872-0161); La Fraternite, 4 rue Malherbe (tel. 884-0432); Ecole Juive, 40 rue Alexandre Boutin (tel. 824-3891); Oratoire Loubavitch, 3 Impasse Cazenove (tel. 860-5433); and Oratoire Etz Hayim, 60 rue Crillon. The new Jewish community center at 3 rue de Turrenne is a five-story building with all facilities.

Jews first settled in Lyon in Roman times—rue Juiverie dates back to that era. Today 70 percent of Lyon Jewry are Sephardim from North Africa, Turkey, and other Mediterranean areas. (In 1979 Lyon Jewry welcomed Iranian Jews.)

MARSEILLES

Marseilles has the second largest Jewish community in France; more than 80,000 Jews, chiefly from Algeria, Egypt, Morocco, and Tunisia, reside here. Marseilles is the main port of entry for North African Jews coming to France, and is also the main transit point for Jews en route to Israel.

The Temple Consistorial Synagogue (tel. 377184) is at 119, rue Breteuil, presided over by Grand Rabbi Joseph Sitruk; recently the congregation celebrated its 100th anniversary. The synagogue's stained-glass windows are especially interesting, particularly the 1846 Montpelier windows.

Marseilles has other synagogues and fourteen "houses of prayer," plus twelve kosher butcher shops. There are Jewish community centers at 112, Avenue Paul-Claudel and at 4, Impasse Dragon.

The Jewish visitor should also stop at the office of the Fonds Social Juif Unifié (United Jewish Social Fund) at rue Breteuil 67; Casim (Jewish social welfare agency) which handles reception and aid for thousands of Jewish families including refugees at 61 rue de la Palud;

and the ORT vocational and training school for refugee children at 3 rue des Forges. The Edmond Fleg Student Center (dedicated in 1968) is a haven for young people.

NICE

Some 90 percent of Nice's 30,000 Jews are originally from North Africa; most of them were part of that grand exodus of close to 2 million French citizens—Christians, Jews, and 200,000 Moslems— who fled after France's North African empire turned into the independent states of Tunisia, Morocco, and Algeria.

The synagogue at rue Gustave de Loye 7 (tel. 854435) is Sephardic, and the one at rue Blacas 1 is Ashkenazi. The temple is located at 8 rue Marceau (tel. 853484). Jews have resided in Nice since the fourth century. The ancient ghetto ruins on rue Benoit-Bunico are a reminder of the past. There is a community center at rue de Voltaire 1. The B'nai B'rith lodge, Loge Côte d'Azur No. 1625, had as its president Victor Aouizerat ("Les Cigales," Boulevard Pasteur 35); and as its secretary Raphel Avidgor ("Palais Arimda," Avenue Mariana).

The National Museum of the Bible Message Marc Chagall (tel. 81-7575) is truly of consuming interest to the Jewish traveler. Located at Avenue du Docteur-Menard in Olivetti Park in Cimiez, this museum was built in 1970 by the French government from Chagall's own plans, and houses seventeen major Chagall oil paintings, delineating the Bible in all its splendor. Picasso once remarked of Chagall: "He must have an angel in his head somewhere." And that angel, multiplied many times, seems to have descended from his head to his palette to his brush and onto the enormous canvases hanging on the stark-white museum walls. Soft-focus angels swirl about the humans portrayed in each of the twelve canvases in the Great Hall, the largest of the several galleries in the building; sensuous blues and greens are dominant in these illustrations of scenes from Genesis and Exodus— "The Creation of Man"; "Paradise"; "Adam and Eve Driven from Paradise"; "Noah's Ark"; "Noah and the Rainbow"; "Abraham and the Three Angels"; "The Sacrifice of Isaac"; "Jacob's Dream"; "The Combat of Jacob and the Angel"; "Moses Before the Burning Bush"; "The Smiting of the Rock"; "Moses Receiving the Tablets of the Law"; "The Song of Songs I"; "The Song of Songs II"; "The Song of Songs III"; "The Song of Songs IV"; and "The Song of Songs V." The first ten of these magnificent paintings are devoted to Genesis and Exodus, and the dominant colors are blue and green. These ten canvases were painted between 1954 and 1967. In another room are the sculptures of David, of Moses, and of Christ, as well as two bas-reliefs in honor of the four biblical women, Sarah, Rebecca, Rachel, and Leah. The inner courtyard of the building features the mosaics of the pool, and shows the prophet Elijah in his chariot of fire surrounded by the signs of the zodiac. The concert and lecture hall within the building contains three magnificent stained-glass windows by Chagall. Another fascinating section of this building displays over 200 of Chagall's preliminary studies leading to the large canvases of the "Bible Message." These preliminary sketches are moving in their simplicity. In addition, Chagall has assembled forty-odd engravings showing Joshua and the Children of Israel, David, Solomon, the Prophets Elijah, Isaiah, Jeremiah, and Ezekiel.

PARIS

Paris has many places of Jewish interest, but, above all, is the Tomb of the Unknown Jewish Martyr, a ponderous memorial to the 6 million Jews who died at the hands of the Nazis (17, rue Geoffroy-l'Asnier). The building surrounding the tomb has four floors of mementos of ghetto existence from all over Europe. In the basement is the Hall of Remembrance where six chests, built into the walls, contain books in which are inscribed the names of thousands of Jewish martyrs. The memorial, dedicated in 1956, centers around a black marble tomb, is shaped like a Star of David with a flame flickering in its center, and holds the ashes of Jews who perished in concentration camps.

Nearer to the center of Paris, in a garden behind Notre Dame, is the *Memorial de la Déportation,* the French government's crypt-memorial to the 200,000 Frenchman killed by the Nazis (130,000 were Jewish). Inscribed in stone are the poignant words: "Forgive... Do not forget." The walls are studded by 200,000 glass-headed nails. Here is a place of reverent pilgrimage for all mankind.

The Jewish traveler must visit the Pletzl area of the Marais district and the rue des Rosiers, where the scenes are reminiscent of New York's East Side many years ago. (Place Saint Paul was once called "Jews' Place.") The old synagogues range from the largest building at 10, rue Pavée (its interior is decorated in red velvet), the most beautiful at 21, rue de Tournelles (its ornate facade is architecturally unusual), to the many storefront and parlor synagogues accommodating fewer than twenty worshipers. Thousands of North African Jews live here today.

The Alliance Universelle, which operates a remarkable network of schools all over the Jewish world, has its headquarters in Paris at 45, rue de la Bruyère. Its library has volumes of Judaica and rare manuscripts. On the facade of the Hotel de Castille at 37, rue Cambon (on the right bank, in the heart of Paris) is the Theodor Herzl Memorial Plaque, erected in 1961 to commemorate the site where he wrote *The Jewish State* in 1894. The famed Jewish actress Sarah Bernhardt is remembered by a lovely statue on the Place Malesherbes.

On the left bank the facade of the Medical School on rue des Saints Pères bears a medallion showing Moses Maimonides treating a patient.

French Jewry is governed by the Grand Consistoire, established by Napoleon in 1809 and headquartered at 17, rue St. George (fourth floor).) There are ninety subdivisions throughout France, and their activities are centralized in the main body. Paris today has nineteen synagogues and another thirty-seven in its suburbs. Visit the Ashkenazi synagogue at 15, rue Notre Dame de Nazareth, the oldest synagogue in Paris. Originally built as an Anglican church, its construction was stopped in June 1819 due to architectural problems, and the building was then sold to the Jewish community.

There are Jewish community centers at 42, rue de Saules (which also has a museum), and at 19, Boulevard Poissonière; in the Mercaz de Montmartre is a community center patronized by Tunisian Jewry. The magnificent "Rothschild" Synagogue at 44, rue de la Victoire is the main Paris synagogue, built in 1874, and rebuilt after a 1941 bombing. When the synagogue was built a century ago under Napoleon III, the empress allowed the Jews to have only a very modest entrance on the main street of rue de la Victoire. Other must visits in Paris include the Cluny Museum with its Jewish monuments and tombstones and the rabbinical seminary at rue Vauquelin. At Notre Dame Cathedral, on both sides of the central portal, are feminine figures representing the Church triumphant over the defeated Synagogue, the former beautiful and resplendent, the latter shattered with her eyes covered by a snake and with a tablet of the Law slipping from her fingers. A visit to the tombs of Emile Zola and Heinrich Heine at the Montmartre cemetery is worthwhile. Wealthy Parisian Jews reside in the 16th Arrondissement, particularly the stately Avenue Foch. One familiar story (pre-1975) asked the difference between Avenue Foch and the Suez Canal; the answer: "As to the latter, Jews occupy only one side."

PERPIGNAN

The local synagogue is at 54 rue Arago. In the nearby cemeteries at Haut Vernet and Rivesaltes there are monuments to the thousands of Jews deported from these areas to Auschwitz.

RHEIMS

In 1979, leading French civic and military representatives joined the Jewish community in celebrating the centenary of the Rheims synagogue at 49 rue Clovis (tel. 476847).

ROUEN

Recent excavations unearthed the remains of a medieval Jewish academy of learning—complete with Jewish graffiti on its walls! The building is Romanesque and the Palace of Justice courtyard in Rouen had apparently been built on top of it. The building fronts on the ancient rue aux Juifs, built as an institution of higher learning by early Norman Jews. Unfortunately the French government has not yet opened the site for public viewing. The local synagogue and community center is at 55 rue des Bons Enfants (tel. 710144).

ST. CIRQ-LAPOPIE (near Cahors)

Fifteen hundred prosperous Jewish artisans, mostly goldsmiths and dyers, lived here in the Middle Ages. Today there are fewer than 100 artisans, and they carve stoppers for wine casks. The Jewish quarter is still visible; the lintels of the stone houses are carved in Hebrew with the owners' names and dates.

SARCELLES

Twenty minutes from Paris live 8,000 Sephardic Jews in this bedroom community of high-rise apartment houses and modern shopping centers. Here is an outstanding day school, Torah Emeth with several hundred students; a nursery for Jewish children; a Talmud Torah; six kosher butcher shops; a *mikvah;* a large synagogue (74 Avenue Paul Valery); and a Jewish community center at 11 rue Louis Lebrun.

STRASBOURG

Strasbourg, after World War II, was probably the first site where the European Jewish community rebuilt some of its past. Strasbourg became known as the place where Jewish orphans from all over Europe were welcomed with open arms. Today the Jewish community numbers 14,000, and is justly proud of its new Synagogue de la Paix and community center at 16, Avenue de la Paix (tel. 356135). Unfortunately, the Notre Dame Museum in Strasbourg and the Strasbourg Cathedral still exhibit the famed thirteenth-century statues representing the "Synagogue Defeated."

The University of Strasbourg has a chair in Modern Hebrew (established in 1955); at 14 rue Sellenick, in an old building, is the ORT Trade School. Chief Rabbi Max Warschawski (tel. 324337) presides over the lower Rhine region of which Strasbourg is the center and largest city.

TOULON

The Jewish community center and synagogue is at rue de la Visitation 6 (tel. 926105).

VICHY

The synagogue is at rue de Maréchal Foch 2b; Helene Kosher Restaurant at Avenue Thermale 47 is frequented by Jewish tourists. This city, which served as the capital during the infamous Nazi occupation, is one of the world's most famous watering places.

There are synagogues in the following French communities:

Agen: 52, rue de Montesquieu.
Aix-En-Provence: 3, rue Montperrin.
Amiens: 38, rue du Pont-d'Amont.
Angers: 12, rue Valdemaine.
Annecy: 18, rue de Narvick.
Antibes—Juan-Les-Pins: Villa "La Monada," Chemin des Sables.
Arcachon: Avenue Gambetta.
Belfort: 6, rue de l'As-de-Carreau.
Besançon: 2, rue Mayence.
Béziers: 19, Place Pierre-Semard.
Bordeaux: 213, rue Sainte-Catherine, and 8, rue Labirat; the community center is at 15, Place Charles Gruet.
Caen: 46, Avenue de la Liberation (tel. 934632).
Chalon-Sur-Saône: 10, rue Germigny.
Colmar: 1, rue de la Cigogne; the community center is next door.
Douai: Place Barlin.
Dunkerque: 18, rue Jean-Bart.
Epernay: 2, rue Placet.
Epinal: 9, rue Charlet.
Haguenau: 3, rue du Grand-Rabbin-Joseph-Bloch.
Le Havre: 38, rue Victor Hugo.
Le Mans: 4 et 6, Boulevard Paixhans.
Lens: 87, rue Casimir Beugnet.
Lille: 5, rue Auguste Angelier.
Limoges: 27, rue Pierre Leroux.
Lunéville: 5, rue Castara.
Menton: 1 bis rue Albert 1er.
Metz: 39, rue du Rabbin-Elie-Bloch.
Montauban: 12, rue Sainte-Claire.
Montpellier: 5, rue des Augustins.
Mulhouse: 19, rue de la Synagogue.
Nancy: 13, Boulevard Joffre.
Nantes: 5, Impasse Copernic.
Nîmes: 40, rue Roussy.
Obernai: 5, rue du Selestat.

Orléans: 16, rue Robert de Courtenay.
Pau: 8, rue Trois Freres Bernadac.
Perigueux: 13, rue Paul-Louis-Courrier.
Roanne: 9, rue de Beaulieu.
Saint-Etienne: 34, rue d'Arcole.
Saint Fons: Avenue Albert Thomas.
Saint-Quentin: 11, Boulevard Henri Martin.
St. Tropez: Frejus-St. Raphael, rue du Progres.
Sarrebourg: 12, rue du Sauvage.
Sarreguemines: rue George V.
Saverne: rue du 19-Novembre.
Sélestat: Place Vanolles.
Toulouse: 2, rue Palaprat; 14, rue du Rempart-Saint-Etienne; 36 rue du Pech; 3 rue Jules Chalande.
Tours: 37, rue Parmentier.
Troyes: 5, rue Brunneval.
Valence: 1, Place du Colombier.
Valenciennes: 36, rue de l'Intendance.
Verdun: Impasse des Jacobins.
Versailles: 10, rue Albert Joly.
Villeurbanne: 4, rue Malherbe.
Vittel: rue Crois-Pierrot.

KOSHER RESTAURANTS

Of the myriads of kosher restaurants, note the following in addition to those mentioned earlier:

Caen: Lasry, 26 rue de l'Engannerie

Grenoble: Community Center, 11 rue Maginot.

Marseilles: Community Center, 4 Impasse Dragon (tel. 37-33-44); Fleurette, rue Vincent Scotto (tel. 20-73-91).

Nice: Guez, 26 Avenue Pertinax (tel. 856142) and Av Roi David, 9 rue Clement Roassal.

Paris: Centre Communautaire, Boulevard Poissonière 19 (tel. 2338021).
Restaurant Universitaire, 5, rue de Medicis (6e): Jo Goldenberg's, 7 rue des Rosiers (tel. 887-2016).
Restaurant Gan Eden, 2 rue Ambroise Thomas (tel. 5231918)
Restaurant A la Bonne Bouchée, 1, rue des Hospitalières, St. Gervais (2e) (tel. 5088602).
Le Relais, Boulevard de Belleville, 69 (11e) (tel. 3578391).
Centre Rachi, Boulevard Port Royal, 30 (5e) (tel. 3319820).
Restaurant Gagou, rue de la Grange Batelière, 8 (9e) (tel. 7700502).

Strasbourg: Shalom, 1, rue du Grand Rabbin René Hirschler; and Universitaire, 11 rue Sellenick (tel. 351568).

USEFUL ADDRESSES

Paris: U.S. Embassy, Avenue Gabriel 2 (tel. 2961202).
Canadian Embassy, 35 Avenue Montaigne (tel. 2259955).
Israeli Embassy, 3 rue Rabelais (tel. 2669149).

GERMANY: WEST AND EAST*

Jews are naturally and understandably reluctant to visit Germany. The evils of Nazism and the death of 6 million Jews make the case against travel to Germany insurmountable. But the fact remains that there are 38,000 Jews in West Germany and perhaps 1,000 Jews in East Germany, longing for contact with Jews from other parts of the world. For more than twenty-five years, the Jews of West Germany and East Germany have been isolated from the mainstream of Jewish life. These German Jews have returned to the "scene of the crime" because they wanted to live as German Jews. They remember the scientist Albert Einstein, the theologian Martin Buber, the diplomat Walter Rathenau, the producer Max Reinhardt, and the medical scientist Paul Ehrlich, among many others. There are growing Jewish communities in Dusseldorf, Hamburg, Munich, and West Berlin and many other West German cities.

Jews have lived in Germany since the earliest Roman times. By A.D. 300 there were Jewish settlements along the Rhine. Between A.D. 500 and 1000, Jewish settlements were founded in Cologne, Frankfurt, Mainz, Worms, Speyer, Wurzburg, Magdeburg, Merseburg, Augsburg, and Ratisbon on the Danube River. In the next 500 years Jewish communities began in many other towns.

BERLIN—West

The present 7,000-odd member Jewish community of West Berlin is indicative of a remarkable growth since 1945, and its youthful membership has increased beyond all expectations. A Jewish youth center and organizations like the Maccabees, Zionist Youth, and several youth commissions are active. Though many young German Jews today study in Israel, a number attend the religious school in the Jewish Community Center in West Berlin.

The new and spacious Jewish Community Center was erected in 1959 on the site of the famed Fasanenstrasse Synagogue which was gutted during Hitler's *Kristallnacht* rampage of November 9 and 10, 1938. The building's outer facade encompasses a small stone col-

---

*West Germany is known formally as the Federal Republic of Germany; East Germany is the German Democratic Republic.

umn (bearing in tragic irony the Mosaic legend "Love thy neighbor as thyself"); and at the main entrance there is an archway from the ruins of the old synagogue which had been built in 1912 and had more than 1,000 seats. The first rabbi of the Fasanenstrasse Synagogue was the respected Dr. Julius Galliner; years later Dr. Leo Baeck preached here, although Rabbi Baeck regularly officiated in the later years of the Nazi regime at the Lutzowstrasse Synagogue (at that time the newest and architecturally most imposing synagogue in Germany). As an aged rabbi, Dr. Leo Baeck was perhaps the last to preside during the liquidation of the Berlin Jewish community. (In the winter of 1943 this seventy-year old man was taken by the Nazis to Terezin, or Theresienstadt, in Czechoslovakia, the antechamber to the crematoria at Auschwitz. But twenty-seven months later he was miraculously rescued, and went to live in England with his daughter. His subsequent teachings and lectures in the United States were an inspiration to future teachers of Judaism. He died on November 2, 1956, at the age of eighty-three.) Another distinguished Berlin rabbi was Dr. Joachim Prinz who began preaching in 1933 at the age of twenty-three and continued until 1937, when he was officially expelled by the Nazis. Rabbi Prinz (whose pulpit has been in Newark, New Jersey, ever since) has pointed out that the majority of German Jews were totally unprepared for the Hitler regime. They considered themselves either Germans of the Jewish faith or simply Jewish Germans. Indeed, four months after the last free elections to the Reichstag the renowned Martin Buber in June 1933 concluded an article in *Unser Bildungsziel* with these words: "Let none ask for which country we want to educate [our children]. For Palestine if it may be so, for any foreign country if it must be so, for Germany if it can be so."

West Berlin Jewry attend the Liberal synagogue at Pestalozzi Strasse 14 (its interior walls were recently restored with the aid of public funds), the Conservative synagogue at Fraenkelufer Strasse 10–16; and the Orthodox synagogue at Jachimstalle Strasse 13. In addition, religious services are held at the Hebrew Old Aged Home on Iranische Strasse 3. There are hundreds of Jewish cemeteries in Germany, but the largest and oldest, containing more than 100,000 graves, is found in East Berlin. In West Berlin other places of Jewish interest include the Leo Baeck House at Baselerstrasse 11; the Anne Frank Youth Center at Brabenterstrasse 5; the International Center for Documentation and Research into Nazism and Its Consequence, on Limonenstrasse; and the Kafka Memorial House at Grunewaldstrasse 1e.

A survey of West German communities reveals the presence of Jewish community life.

AACHEN
The local community dating back to the ninth century attends the synagogue at Oppenhoffallee 50 (tel. 501690). There are about 300 Jews in Aachen.

AMBERG
Synagogue at Salzgasse 5 (tel. 13140).

AUGSBURG
Synagogue at Halderstrasse 8 (tel. 517985).

BADEN-BADEN
Synagogue at Werderstrasse 2 (tel. 22142).

BAD NAUHEIM
Community center and synagogue at Karlstrasse 34 (tel. 5605).

BAYREUTH
Community center at Maxstrasse 74 (tel. 64994).

BONN
Synagogue and community center at Tempelstrasse 2 (corner of Adenauer Allee).

BREMEN
Synagogue and community center at Schwachthauser Heerstrasse 117 (tel. 495104).

COLOGNE
Synagogue and community center at Roonstrasse 50 (tel. 235527).

DUSSELDORF
Synagogue and community center at Zietenstrasse 50 (tel. 480314).

ESSEN
Community center at Sedanstrasse 46 (tel. 273413).

FRANKFURT

Rabbi Joseph Schlesinger, former Israeli army rabbi, heads the local synagogue at Schefelstrasse 32 (tel. 590117). The Jewish community numbers 4,800.

FURTH

There is a beautifully restored synagogue at Julienstrasse 2; the community center is at Blumenstrasse 31 (tel. 770879).

HAMBURG

The Reform movement, which has exerted such profound influence on American Jewish life, had its origins in Germany following the civil emancipation of the Jews in the early nineteenth century. While the first Reform worship services were instituted in 1801, the earliest formal congregation was organized in Hamburg in 1817. A year later, the new group dedicated the world's first Reform synagogue, the Hamburg Temple. The Temple became the "Mother Synagogue" of the liberal movement in Germany, and influenced Progressive Judaism throughout the world. The pioneer Reform congregations in the United States turned to the Hamburg Temple for support and guidance in religious matters and used the Hamburg Prayer Book and Hymnal in their early days. The Hamburg Temple remained the center of the classic German liberal tradition in Judaism, and eventually became one of the leading congregations in Europe. In November 1938, one month after the celebration of the 120th anniversary of the dedication of the first Hamburg Temple, and shortly after the erection of a new building, the sanctuary of the congregation was desecrated and looted, and its members deported to Nazi concentration camps. Rebuilt in 1961, the Hamburg Synagogue is located at An Der Hohe Weide 34 (tel. 492904). Hamburg has about 1,500 Jews today.

Hamburg is only fifty miles from Belsen Belsen, notorious Nazi concentration camp.

MUNICH

The German Jewish community of Munich has 4,700 members. There is a great deal of community activity centered about four synagogues (Possartstrasse 15, Reichenbachstrasse 27, Schulstrasse 30, and Georgenstrasse 71); the Hebrew home for the aged (Kaulbachstrasse 65); the very active Jewish Women's League (Schneckenburgerstrasse 34); the Union of Jewish Students in Bavaria (Prince Regentstrasse 91); the community-minded, seventy-member B'nai B'rith lodge (Lillenstrasse 70); and the lively Jewish newspaper,

Muncher Judische Nachrichten (Dachaustrasse 123). In addition, there are three Talmud Torahs with 120 students, and an elementary day school (Mohlstrasse 14) with fifty students.

Today the Jewish community of Munich is probably 90 percent Hassidic, which may explain its emotional involvement in total Jewish community life. The new Jewish community center building at Possartstrasse 15 (an unexplained fire destroyed the old building) has a synagogue seating 250 persons, several large meeting rooms, community offices, a kosher restaurant, and what Munich Jewry regard as Europe's finest *mikvah*. The Munich City Counsel, the Bavarian state government, and the federal government of West Germany contributed $1 million toward its building costs.

The Chief Rabbi of Munich is Rabbi H. I. Grunewald, who lived in Israel for twenty-five years before he returned to Munich in 1970 to accept his present position. Rabbi Grunewald is one of only nine ordained rabbis still officiating in West Germany today.

Twenty miles north of Munich is Dachau, and the only Jews living in Dachau, site of the notorious concentration camp, are the Nikolai Lehner family. Lehner was himself a prisoner of the camp, and when released after World War II, he settled down here. He owns and operates a carpentry and building material business.

WORMS

The oldest Jewish cemetery in Europe and the oldest synagogue in Europe are found here amid 75,000 residents among whom not a single person is Jewish. Recently the city has built the Rashi House Museum for Jewish Survival.

In West Germany there are synagogues in the following cities and towns:

Bad Homburg Holderlinweg 28.
Bad Kreuznach Gymnasialstrasse 11.
Bamberg Willy-Lessingstrasse 7.
Bielefeld Stapenhorstrasse 35.
Brunswick Steinstrasse 4.
Darmstadt Osannstrasse 11.
Dortmund Prinz Friedrick Karlstrasse 9.
Emden Petkumrstrasse 48.
Frankfurt-am-Main The synagogue at Freiherr Vom Steim 30 is a magnificent stone and stucco building occupying almost one square block; there are also synagogues at Roederberg Weg 29, Baumweg 5, and Altkonigstrasse 22 and the Central Welfare Organization of Jews is at Hebelstrasse 17.

Freiburg Holbeinstrasse 25.
Fulda Rangstrasse 23.
Furth Blumenstrasse 31.
Gelsenkirchen Reckerstrasse 9, built in 1958.
Hagen Pottshofstrasse 16, built in 1960.
Hanover Haeckelstrasse 10, built in 1961.
Heidelberg Hausserstrasse 10–12.
Herford Goltzstrasse 11.
Hildeshein Mellingerstrasse 32.
Hof Karolineanstrasse 13.
Karlsruhe Kriegsstrasse 154, opened in 1970.
Kassel Bremerstrasse 3.
Krefeld Rheinstrasse 2.
Mannheim Maximilianstrasse 6.
Minden Kampstrasse 6.
Munster Klosterstrasse 6, built in 1957.
Neustadt Weinerstrasse.
Offenbach Kaiserstrasse 109, built in 1956.
Saarbrucken Lortzingstrasse 8.
Stuttgart Hospitalstrasse 36, built in 1952.
Wiesbaden Friedrichstrasse 33, dedicated in 1966.
Worms Judengasse, rebuilt in 1961.
Wuppertal Freidrich Eberstrasse 73.

Many West German communities hold special significance for Jewry. In the city of Worms, the original Rashi Synagogue built in the eleventh century is the oldest synagogue in Europe. The Worms synagogue was destroyed by the Nazis in 1938, but reconstructed in 1961. In Friedberg/Hessen the *mikvah* at Judengasse 20 was built in 1260. Near the border with Belgium is the delightful West German town of Wittlich where in 1977 the old synagogue was restored and reopened as a municipal cultural center since there are presently no Jews in Wittlich.

East Germany

In East Germany today there are perhaps 750 Jews officially belonging to the eight *Gemeinden,* or Jewish religious communities recognized by the East German government. There are an additional 7,000 unaffiliated Jews living in East Germany. There are probably also thousands of East German Jews who left Judaism in 1933 and who still feel ill at ease in revoking their renunciation of Judaism. A number of these uncommitted Jews (and even Jewish atheists) do participate in Jewish social and cultural events. The eight *Gemeinden* centers are found in East Berlin, Leipzig, Dresden, Magdeburg, Halle, Chemnitz, Erfurt, and Mecklenburg. The Jewish community of East Berlin has 430 registered members, presided over by a forty-three-year-old neurologist, Dr. Peter Kirschner.

In East Berlin there is a Jewish Community Center at Oranien-burgerstrasse 28 (tel. 2823327). The Rykestrasse Synagogue at Ry-kestrasse 53 is open, and is currently being equipped, at a cost to the government of $120,000. There has been no rabbi here since Rabbi Singer left for Budapest many years ago. In Dresden the community center is at Bautznerstrasse 20, and the synagogue at Fiedler-strasse 3. In Erfurt the local community center is at Juri-Gagarin-Ring 16. In Leipzig it is at Lohrastrasse 10; and in Magdeburg at Groper-strasse 1a. There are community centers in Chemnitz (now called Karl Marx Stadt) at Stolbergerstrasse 28; in Mecklenburg at Schlach-terstrasse 3; and in Halle at Gross Markerstrasse 13.

East Berlin is a dying Jewish community of the aged and infirm. The crumbling walls and the empty rows of seats in the Rykestrasse Synagogue are most depressing. Built in the 1920s as a model syna-gogue (with seating for over 2,000 people), it was the proud center of the thriving Berlin community. During World War II the building was used as a vegetable warehouse. In 1952 the East Germans rebuilt the synagogue and renamed it "the Temple of Peace." The burned-out skeleton of the old Oranienburgerstrasse synagogue stands as a pitiful monument to those killed by Hitler's Germany. East Berlin has four cemeteries, one being Weissensee, the largest Jewish cemetery in Europe, with a total of 114,500 graves. There are about 200 Jewish cemeteries in East Germany. The Hebrew Home for the Aged in Niederschoenhaugen is still serving thirty-eight Jew-ish pensioners.

KOSHER RESTAURANTS

West Berlin: Restaurant der Judischen Gemeinde, Fasanenstrasse 79/80 (tel. 8813031); Fleischmann's, Dahlmannstrasse.

Cologne: Gemeindehaus Restaurant, Roonstrasse 50 (tel. 235527).

Frankfurt-am-Main: Gemeinde Restaurant Jawne, Friedrichstrasse 27 (tel. 728618).

Furth/Bayern: Familie Rosenfeld, Julienstrasse 2 (tel. 776422).

Munich: Gemeindehaus Restaurant, Reichenbachstrasse 27 (tel. 241577).

Stuttgart: Restaurant der Israelitischen, Hospitalstrasse 36 (tel. 295629).

USEFUL ADDRESSES

Bonn (West Germany): U.S. Embassy, Deichmannsaue (tel. 3393390)

Canadian Embassy, Friedrich-Wilhelm Strasse 18 (tel. 231061).
Israeli Embassy, Simrockallee 2 (in Bad Godesburg, a suburb of Bonn) (tel. 228-8231).

East Berlin (East Germany): U.S. Embassy, Neustaedtische Kirch-strasse 4–5 (tel. 2202741).

GIBRALTAR

Beginning with the British occupation of "The Rock" in 1704, Sephardic Jews from Spain, Portugal, and North Africa poured into the area. (Five hundred years previously, thousands of Jews who had escaped from Spain and Portugal to come to Gibraltar were mistaken by the local inhabitants for Moors and were massacred.) By 1776, Jews numbered one-third of Gibraltar's 3,000 inhabitants, but fled to England in large numbers during the siege of 1779–1783. Many Jews returned in the years that followed; in the 1850s there were about 2,000 Jews on Gibraltar, but by World War II the figure had dropped to 1,000. The Jewish community today numbers about 500 among the Rock's 20,000 inhabitants.

The oldest of the four synagogues, Shaar Hashamayim, at Engineer Lane 47–49 (founded in 1724), was built during the middle of the eighteenth century. It became known as the "Cathedral Synagogue" because of its size and prominence, although today it is hidden from the main thoroughfare. As preserved, it is a typical Sephardic synagogue (tel. 4069—Rev. J. M. Benzecry). Other synagogues are Ez Hayim, opened in 1759, located at Irish Town 91 (tel. 5563—Rev. Samuel Benaim); Nefusot Yehuda, of Moorish architecture, founded in 1790 and renamed the Flamenco Synagogue, at Line Wall Road 65 (tel. 3213—Rev. Haim A. Sananes); and Abudarham at Parliament Lane 20 [tel. 3165—Rev. Raphael D. I. Garson). The Chief Rabbi is Rabbi S. Haliwa, 7 Bomb House Lane (tel. 4764), but he is on an extended leave.

There are many retail stores on Gibraltar owned by Jewish merchants. The extensive Jewish commercial influence is illustrated by the names of its streets: Ben Zimrah Avenue, Benoliel Passage, and Serraya Ramp. The local library contains many important Jewish archives. In the 1840s Jewish influence was so tangible that theaters shut down on Friday evenings and all day Saturdays. The present Prime Minister, Sir Joshua Abraham Hassan, is Jewish and native-born. (Sir Joshua, a politician for over thirty years, is extremely popular among the populace; prior to taking up his present appointment, he had been elected mayor twenty-one times. The current mayor, Abraham Serfaty, is also Jewish.

There is a Hebrew School at Bomb House Lane 10; in the same building is the Jewish Social and Cultural Club, which serves kosher meals (tel. 3158). There is an ancient Jewish cemetery at Upper Rock. The old Jewish cemetery in the neighboring Spanish city of La Línea is especially worthwhile visiting, as is the Mackintosh Jewish Old Age Home at 34a Line Wall Road, Gibraltar.

KOSHER RESAURANTS

The Kosher Shop, 5, Governor's Parade, Gibraltar (near the Holiday Inn) (tel. 5965)

Kosher food is available at the Jewish Social and Cultural Club, Bomb House Lane 10.

USEFUL ADDRESSES

Israeli Consulate, City Mill Lane 3 (tel. 5955 or 5966).

GREECE

Since biblical times Jews have lived in Greece; stone inscriptions identify Jewish settlements during the second century B.C. (The oldest city in Europe with continuous Jewish existence is Chalkis, which was founded in 200 B.C.) In fact, the Greek alphabet was derived from that of the ancient Hebrews. The Apostle Paul founded many synagogues in Greece and organized Jewish communities in all of the principal cities; he addressed epistles to the major synagogues of Corinth and Thessaly. Most Greek Jews were traders; many were engaged in silk-weaving and a few in agriculture.

Large numbers of Spanish Jews arrived at the end of the fifteenth century after their expulsion from Spain. The local Jewish communities soon lost their Grecian character and became entirely Sephardic in culture. In 1912 the city of Salonika or Thessalonika was one of the largest Jewish communities in all of the Mediterranean—90 percent of its population was Jewish.

Before World War I there were 125,000 Jews in Greece, but World War II and the Nazi occupation of Greece brought death to vast numbers of Jews. Today there are fewer than 6,000 Jews in all of Greece: approximately 3,000 are in Athens; 1,100 in Salonika; and the remainder in such small communities as Larissa (650 Jews), Chalkis, Patras, Cavalla, Kardista, Florina, Volos, Trikkala, Ioannina, and on the islands of Rhodes, Corfu (130 Jews), and Kos.

Few are aware that since 1948 the Greek government has provided compensation for Jewish property losses caused by the Nazi invaders. This property fund, known as *Opaie,* has restored ancient synagogues and built Jewish schools and communal centers throughout Greece; it is supervised by the Central Board of the Jewish Communities of Greece.

ATHENS

Athens has a colorful Sephardic synagogue, Beth Shalom, at Odos Melidoni 5 (Rabbi Yaacov Arrar, tel. 5221225). Begun before World War II, it was completed after hostilities ceased. There is a B'nai B'rith office at Paparigopoulou 15 for some 400 members. The B'nai B'rith lodge, Loge Philon No. 993, had as its president Dr. Asher Moissis (Rue Parnassou 2), and as vice-president, attorney Daniel

Alhanatis (Nikis Street 2; tel. 227598). The Central Board of Jewish Communities of Greece is located at Sourmeli 2 (tel. 8839951), and the Jewish Youth Center at Vissarionis 9 (tel. 3637092). In the Jewish cemetery at Kolinia there is a Martyrs Memorial and in the center is a pyramid listing the Jews killed by the Nazis in every Greek city. Two large menorahs grace the marble pedestals. Other places of Jewish interest in Athens include the Athens Jewish School at Kameleon and Antheon Streets, in the fashionable suburb of Psychico, operating since 1960 and serving 250 children; the new Jewish Communal Center, Georgion Karitsi Place 6, has a library, chapel, lecture hall, and kosher restaurant.

CHALKIS

Of all the cities, towns, and villages in Europe, Chalkis is famed for having the oldest continuous Jewish community. Jews have lived here since 200 B.C. Until the last century the community was called "Koutsouk Safet" because of its strict religious devotion like that of the medieval Safed in Israel. Only fifty-four miles northeast of Athens, Chalkis (population 25,000) is the chief town and port of the large island of Euboea. (The island is joined to the mainland by a bridge; curiously the straits here have alternating currents which change direction at least ten times every twenty-four hours. Legend has it that Aristotle threw himself into the strait in despair of ever being able to understand it.) A short distance from the bridge is the former ghetto on Kotsou Street where there is a modern synagogue. Inside, the white walls and marble floors have a peaceful, cool aura. The youthful Rabbi Menasseh Zacharias Cohen (never ordained), who resides at Mavromichali Street 6, owns a general store and ministers to the needs of the thirty Jewish families.

Greek Jews have fought in all the wars of Greece; the first senior Greek officer who died in battle during World War II was a Jewish colonel, Mordecai Frizis of Chalkis. During the Nazi occupation, Jewish suffering was alleviated by the friendly Greek people of Chalkis and, in particular, Monsignor Gregorios who protected the synagogue from the Nazis.

In the Chalkis synagogue there are many old books of Hebrew poems written in Greek or Turkish characters; on the enclosure wall are several slabs with Hebrew inscriptions. Indeed, the synagogue wall itself consists of tombstones removed from the ancient Jewish cemetery; the only slab not a tombstone is that above the entrance to the synagogue, and that stone commemorates the inauguration of the present synagogue in 1849 on its original foundation.

The ancient Jewish cemetery here containing 1,200-year-old graves has been desecrated by vandals throughout the ages. In 1897 Ferdinand Rothschild visited Chalkis and donated a sum of money to build a protective wall around the cemetery.

CORFU

This beautiful Greek island has an ancient synagogue at Rue Palaiologu 4, serving only forty Jews. The synagogue is in an old quarter of town, up a narrow cobbled street; it proudly displays large white metal *Magen Davids* on each side of its outer doors. Inside, the large rectangular hall has bare boards scrubbed scrupulously clean and whitewashed walls. Two enormous crystal chandeliers hang from the ceiling. There are four Torah scrolls, each enclosed in carved olivewood holders, dressed in red, green, or blue velvet. The caretaker is a survivor of Nazi concentration camps. President of the community is Armando Aaron (tel. 23802). The local agent for Olympic Airways is Jewish—Moishe Soussis, c/o King Alkinos Hotel. Corfu Jewry includes one tinsmith, several taxi drivers, and many hardworking businessmen.

Not far from the waterfront are the remains of a hideous ghetto where the Jews of Corfu were confined for centuries under Venetian rule. Yet these very Venetians tolerated a Jewish monopoly of trade and banking because the Jews were so skilled at these professions. Centuries later the Nazis carted off the Greek Jews of Corfu to death camps.

CORINTH

In the local historical museum is preserved the door of an ancient synagogue of the third century.

CRETE

In the former capitol, Canea, there is a Jewish quarter, Evraiki, which was mostly destroyed by World War II bombing; the old Beth Haim Synagogue has been closed for centuries, but Hebrew inscriptions are still visible (Parodos Kondulki 20). It dates from the fourteenth century, and the Athens Jewish Museum is reconstructing it.

In Heraklion the old synagogue building area serves as an office and partly as a soccer field.

DELOS

This small island possesses the "seat of Moses," a fragmented chair from an ancient synagogue. Also found amid the ruins of this island (legendary birthplace of Apollo) are pieces of marble columns with Hebrew inscriptions.

IOANNINA

Ioannina has a small group of native Greek-speaking Jews who constitute the only remnants of Romaniot Jews except for their brethren on Corfu and in Chalkis. They are descendants of Greek

Jews of the Byzantine Empire of the fourth century. As Diaspora
Jews, they adjusted first to pagan Greece, then to Byzantine Christianity, and to Venetian, Serbian, Bulgarian, Norman, and Italian inva-
sions before the Turkish conquest. Their basic prayers are Sephardic
but their language and culture are Greek. When Constantine the
Great ruled the Roman Empire (288–337) these Greeks became
subjects of Rome and so Romaniot Jews were identified.

The Ioannina Jewish community has always been the center of
commerce here. As late as 1910 the commerce of Ioannina was
totally in the hands of Ioannina Jewry. During the sixteenth and
seventeenth centuries Ioannina had a Jewish population of 7,000. In
1940, just before the Nazi occupation of Ioannina, there were 1,950
Jews living there, and Ioannina emigrés, observing the Roman tradition, have settled all over the world. (The local synagogue is in
Volmoundo Street; call Moise Eliasaf, tel. 29429.) In New York City
they built one synagogue at 280 Broome Street and another, the
Mapleton Synagogue, in Bensonhurst, Brooklyn. Jerusalem has two
Romaniot synagogues, Beth Avraham and Ohel Sara.

PATRAS

Thousands of Greek Jews embarked from Patras in the early
1900s for New York City. The Patras Jewish community has only
two families today, but many lived here in ancient times. (Note Hebrew inscriptions in the local Church of St. Anastasias.) Benjamin of
Tudela visited Patras in the second half of the twelfth century and
found fifty Jews living here. In the sixteenth century, Sephardim and
even Ashkenazim founded congregations in Patras, but during the
Turko-Venetian war, they fled the town and did not return until
1715, when Turkish rule was reestablished. During the Greek War of
Independence (1821–1829), the Jewish community of Patras
ceased to exist and was not restored until 1905. In 1940, just before
the Germans occupied Greece, there were 337 Jews living in Patras.
In 1947, 152 survivors returned to their native city. The local synagogue is at Pantanassa 34.

RHODES (Dodecanese Islands)

Jews have lived on Rhodes since biblical times. There were 400
Jews on Rhodes in the twelfth century and perhaps 2,000 before
World War II, but only forty live there today, mostly Egyptian refugees. Points of interest on Rhodes include the **Jewish Cemetery** on
the outskirts of the island's main city. There is a triple-arched entrance gate beyond which are row after row of neat white crypts with
inscriptions dating back many centuries; a marble monument

identifies the 2,000 Jews of Rhodes and Kos killed by the Nazis. The **Shalom Synagogue** (1 Symmion Street) was built in the seventeenth century, restored in 1731, and rebuilt after World War II; it is the only remaining synagogue of the four which once stood in the walled Jewish quarter. It is open to tourists daily from 10 A.M. to 11 A.M. and from 5 P.M. to 6 P.M. The two yellow stars on the synagogue were probably painted by the Nazis, who destroyed Rhodes' other three synagogues. Another place of Jewish interest is the **Square of the Martyrs,** the name given to a large open area encircled by debris which was once the Jewish quarter. The central fountain, dominated by a seahorse and topped by the Star of David, was erected by the Rhodes government as a memorial to the murdered Jews. The Jewish Community Office is located at Polydorou Street 5 (tel. 22364).

SALONIKA

The 1,100 Jews here were involved in trades unlike those practiced by Jews elsewhere. Salonika Jews worked in the maritime trades as shipbuilders and chandlers, as dock and harbor workers, and as sailors and ship pilots. Hence the ancient ghetto of Salonika lies along the quays of the harbor.

In 1909 the Alatinis were the most prominent Jewish family of all the Spanish Jews who founded the settlement here. The baroque splendor of the Villa Alatini is today dwarfed by tall apartment buildings and mazes of winding lanes. (Kemal Ataturk, the great Turkish reformer, was born here.) After Sultan Murad II's conquest of the city in 1430, Salonika was left devastated for hundreds of years. In the late seventeenth century the influence of Sabbatai Zevi, the false messiah, led to the founding of the Donmeh sect of Jews, who followed Islam but preserved Jewish customs. In the early twentieth century Jewish merchants made Salonika the commercial center of Turkey in Europe; an international fair was held there in 1926. Salonika's 50,000 Jews were almost all exterminated by the Nazis in World War II. Today the Aristotelian University stands on the grounds of the Jewish cemetery.

Salonika's synagogues are to be found at Syngrou Street 35 and at Odos Vassiliou Irakliou 24; the latter is Ashkenazi and also houses a Jewish community office. Kosher meals are available at the Jewish Center at Odos Megalou Alexandrou (tel. 75701). In the local cemetery at Stavroupolis is a striking memorial to the 50,000 Greek Jews whom the Nazis murdered in Auschwitz. (The old cemetery was destroyed in 1943 by the Nazis.)

In Larissa (population 60,000), Trikkala (population 30,000), Veroia (population 30,000), and Volos (population 50,000) there are small Jewish communities with ancient synagogues that are worthwhile visiting. The Larissa synagogue is located at Odos des Six. Trikkala's synagogue is on Odos Diacou, and in Veroia's sixteenth-century Jewish quarter, the synagogue is being restored. The Volos synagogue is on Moisseos Street; call Raphael Frezis (tel. 25640).

The small Greek island of Chios has a long history of Jewish settlement from the time of Herod during the Hellenistic period, through Byzantine, Genoese, and Turkish domination. There are Jewish tombstones on Chios dating back to 1543; however, the first Jewish school was built in 1892 through the financial support of the Rothschilds. The island of Zante (near Corfu) was occupied by the Nazis during World War II, but the local town council prevailed upon the Nazis to spare the lives of all Jews. There is a mosaic pavement containing inscriptions of a fourth-century synagogue in the harbor area of Aegina; this synagogue is being restored by the Athens Jewish Museum.

KOSHER RESTAURANTS

Hotel La Cite in Porto Heli (Athens) is a unique kosher hotel comprising eight buildings with 147 rooms. It opened in April 1977 for the spring, summer, and fall seasons. Its large swimming pool is 12 meters by 25 meters, and the hotel features water-skiing, mini golf, two tennis courts, a volleyball court, and a basketball court.

USEFUL ADDRESSES

ATHENS: U.S. Embassy, Vassilissis Sofias Avenue 91 (tel. 7212951).
Canadian Embassy, 4 Ioannou Ghennadiou Street and on Ypsilantou (tel. 739510).
Israeli Diplomatic Representation, Marathonodromon 1, Palaion Psychichon (tel. 6719530).

SALONIKA: U.S. Consulate General, 59 King Konstantine Street (tel. 266 121).

GUADELOUPE/MARTINIQUE

The French islands of Guadeloupe and Martinique had seventeenth-century Jewish communities. Jewish refugees from Recife, Brazil, landed in Guadeloupe in 1654. In 1671, the French minister Colbert established religious freedom and liberty for all citizens, and by 1676 a synagogue was erected on Martinique. But in 1685, the Black Code of the Jesuits banned Jewish settlement on French islands, and Jews had to leave. The 1902 eruption of Mt. Pelée on Martinique destroyed all vestiges of early Jewish life.

Today, about 120 Jews reside in the Martinique capital city of Fort-de-France. (The Association Culturelle Israelite is at 25 rue Emil Zola.) Joe Koubi, a refugee from North Africa, left mainland France several years ago to seek his fortune. He prospered and could even afford to fly in a rabbi from France for the High Holy days which the Jews on the island tried to observe in the traditional fashion. Pointe-a-Pietre, Guadeloupe's commercial center, is named after a Dutch Jew, who fled from Brazil in 1654 and pioneered the island's sugar-cane industry as did his coreligionists in other parts of the Caribbean. (See Aron Braesch, 106 rue St. Louis, Pointe-a-Pietre.) Religious services are held at the Hilton Hotel here.

USEFUL ADDRESSES

Fort-de-France: U.S. Consulate General, 14 rue Blenac (tel. 719301).

GUATEMALA

There are about 1,500 Jews in this Central American republic, and virtually all live in Guatemala City. In 1848 Guatemala had only two Jewish families; between 1872 and 1880 a number of German Jews arrived, and the first Jewish cemetery was established. In the 1920s Jews from Eastern Europe and the Middle East arrived, and in 1923 the Sephardim established the Sociedad Maguen David; in 1928–1932 Polish Jews founded the Centro Hebreo, and later German Jews founded the Sociedad Israelita de Guatemala. All three organizations constitute the Consejo Central. The Sephardic synagogue is at 7a Avenida 3–80, Zone 2—about five blocks from the National Palace and the National Cathedral. The Ashkenazi synagogue is at 7a Avenida 13–51, Zone 9, in the northern section of the city. A new German Reform congregation, Bet El, has recently been established at 15 Calle 7–59, Zona 11.

Guatemala has not always favored Jewish migration. In 1932 the government sought to deport all "peddlers," so Jews came off the roads and established stores.

Perhaps 15 percent of Guatemalan Jews are millionaires today. One of these Sephardic Jews is Dr. M. Behar, who invented a milk substitute. The most prominent members of the Jewish community were the Stahl family who built cotton mills and were also active in finance and banking. However, Guatemala's turbulent history discouraged the community's growth. Eduardo Gerstenhaber is a Jewish communal leader; during the devastating earthquake of February 1976 he was instrumental in getting the State of Israel to send to Guatemala several consignments of emergency relief supplies. The Jewish community in Guatemala City did not suffer casualties or any serious damage.

Guatemala City has a Jewish elementary school, Colegio Guatemaleco Israelita, with 110 pupils, 80 of whom are Jewish, but with slightly fewer than half from mixed marriages.

Max Trachtenberg is president of the local B'nai B'rith in Guatemala City; he is also director of volunteer firemen. B'nai B'rith International Council correspondent in Guatemala City is Marcel Rugg. Roberto Stein is the head of the Jewish community, and Mordecai Allon is the honorary Guatemalan consul in Israel.

A Jewish community of about twelve families lives in the mountain city of Quetzeltenango. Of Turkish origin, they appear to have abandoned the practice of religion.

USEFUL ADDRESSES

Guatemala City: U.S. Embassy, 7–01 Avenida de la Reforma (tel. 311541).
Israeli Embassy, 13 Avenida 14–07, Zona 1 (tel. 325334).

HAITI

The first Jew to set foot upon this island of exotic natural beauty was Luis de Torres, the Marrano interpreter to Christopher Columbus. In 1697 Spain ceded the western third of the island of Hispaniola to the French; a century later the native population revolted and established the only independent French-speaking nation in the Western Hemisphere.

The earliest Jews in Haiti were Marranos who settled near Cap Haitien; soon Jewish traders entered other Haitian ports. These included the Gradis family of Bordeaux and their rivals, the Mendes family, who have had trade depots in Haiti since 1750. The Pass family owned several Haitian plantations. Abraham Sarzedas from Bordeaux was Haitian agent for the important Newport Jewish merchants, Aaron Lopez and Jacob Rodriguez Riviera, from 1764 to 1774. A 1765 tax list shows twenty-nine Jewish family heads in Cap Haitien, plus eight more in other areas of Haiti. A synagogue existed in the town of Jérémie (the birthplace of Alexandre Dumas); another synagogue may have existed in Cap Haitien. One early Jewish planter was Jacob Toussaint—there has been speculation as to his relationship to Haiti's great black liberator, Pierre Dominique Toussaint L'Ouverture. The black revolt of the 1790s scattered the Jewish community, but some Jews remained in the town of Jérémie and their black descendants live there today. The town of Jacmel may have a similar Jewish background.

It was not until after World War I that Jewish immigrants from Syria and the Balkans arrived in Haiti. After World War II a few families from Poland and Germany settled here. But no Jewish community was organized; today there are about forty-five Jewish families and a large Israeli Embassy staff. (Israeli Ambassador Zvi Loker, born in Yugoslavia, serves as the rabbi.)

Haiti has been a strong supporter of Israel since 1948. Israeli citizens are involved in an agricultural mission at Croix de Bouquets in Haiti's Cul de Sac Valley, outside Port-au-Prince.

In the capital city of Port-au-Prince Jewish businessmen and merchants make their living. (Visit Shalom art gallery.) There are many mixed marriages including that of the owner of a Pétionville hotel whose father was a Syrian Jew and whose mother was a black

Haitian (his infant son was circumcised by a visiting *mohel*). In 1969, American novelist Herbert Gold found many black Haitians of Jewish descent. He met an anti-Semite named Cohen who imported kosher wine from the United States; he discovered a French Jew named Calmann who had fled the Nazis, a Russian Jew named Lazareff living in a mountaintop home with his Haitian wife and a fine library, and an aged Jewish tailor named Schneider. Gold later attended Schneider's funeral, a voodoo ceremony conducted by his black children. A voodoo cup proved to be a kiddush cup with a Hebrew inscription—made in Dublin in 1788.

USEFUL ADDRESSES

Port-au-Prince: U.S. Embassy, Harry Truman Boulevard (tel. 20200).

Canadian Consulate, Camille-Leon Street, intersection of Des Marguerites Street (tel. 2-2358).

Israeli Embassy, 8 rue Berthe Street, Pétionville (tel. 70001).

HAWAII*

While there were Jewish settlers in Hawaii before World War II, it would appear that Jewish community life in Hawaii did not begin until after the war. There is a story that the first Jew in Hawaii was a cook in the entourage of King Kamehameha the Great in 1798. He came aboard the whaling ship *Neptune* and then was "bought" by the Hawaiian king. After Hawaii was annexed by the United States in 1898, Jewish businessmen began to arrive. The Hawaiian royal family is said to have had a Torah and a *yad* or hand-pointer in its possession since 1888, and the Jewish community customarily borrowed the scroll and the pointer on holidays before 1930, when the scroll suddenly disappeared. But the *yad* may be seen today in the state's principal Reform synagogue, Temple Emanu-el (2550 Pali Highway, Honolulu), established in 1951. A Conservative congregation, Sof Ma'arav, has recently been established at 2500 Pali Highway, Honolulu.

There was no organized Jewish community in Hawaii until the founding of the Hebrew Benevolent Society in 1901, and in the same year a Jewish cemetery was consecrated at Pearl City. In 1923 the National Jewish Welfare Board established the Aloha Center in Honolulu; and under the direction of Mr. and Mrs. Alexander Linczer, the center served the needs of transient Jewish military personnel at many installations in the islands.

The present Jewish community of 250 families (estimates of the transient Jewish population, including military, run as high as 5,000 persons) traces its beginning to 1938 when the Honolulu Jewish Community was incorporated. It held services at a church building on Young Street from about 1946 to 1949, and at the JWB Center on Beretania Street under the leadership of Rabbi Emanuel Kumin. The first president of the synagogue, now known as Temple Emanuel in Honolulu, was Barnett Sapiro. The growing Jewish community was fortunate to have among its members a young attorney, Bernard H. Levinson, who arrived from Cincinnati in 1945, and pro-

---

*The fiftieth state of Hawaii, like Alaska, is included in this book because it is culturally and religiously remote from the metropolitan American centers of Jewish life; and it is a relatively recent American Jewish community.

ceeded to reorganize the community. In 1949 he drafted the amended charter and by-laws for the Congregation of the Honolulu Jewish Community, and in May 1950 he became president. The following year a house at 2207 Oahu Avenue was purchased and converted into a synagogue. In 1959 the premises on Oahu Avenue were sold, and a building fund campaign was conducted under the leadership of the late James Zukerkorn. In 1971 Rabbi Julius J. Nadel, who served many years in St. Louis, Missouri, and Portland, Oregon, accepted the pulpit. Attorney Levinson, who had presided over the Honolulu Jewish community for a ten-year period, also served as a Circuit Court judge in 1966 and 1967 and as Associate Justice of the Hawaii Supreme Court from 1967 to 1974. He retired in September 1974 to practice law in Honolulu. In its early days, Temple Emanu-el was not identified with the Reform movement, but in 1952 the congregation voted to become a Reform congregation and affiliate with the Union of American Hebrew Congregations. The current president is Dr. Ira J. Lichton.

The first navy chapel—the Aloha Jewish Chapel—to be built for use specifically as a synagogue was dedicated and consecrated in December 1975 at Pearl Harbor. Its features include a sanctuary, a *mikvah,* a kosher kitchen, a library, a lounge, four classrooms for the Sunday school and midweek Hebrew school, and a Judaica shop. The chapel serves as a center for the Jewish families on the base and has a men's club, a women's guild, and a young adults' program. One of its Torah scrolls was brought to the United States by Jews who left China after World War II. Rabbi Fred Natkin presides.

Local chapters of Hadassah in Hawaii are very active as are the sisterhoods of both synagogues. The Hawaii Jewish Community Council has been organized. Hawaiian Jewry today includes an unusual number of prominent and leading citizens, but unfortunately, few of these people have identified themselves with Jewish community life.

On the outer islands there are small bands of Jewish residents: at Lihue, Kauai, Arthur Ross and Harold F. Birnbaum; at Hilo, Hawaii, Andrew Levin and Mrs. Molly Zimring; and on Maui, Philip H. Lowenthal, among others.

KOSHER RESTAURANTS

Kosher meals are available at the Kuillima Hyatt Hotel on the north shore of the island of Oahu.

HONDURAS

In this Central American nation beset by internal and external political conflict, about 200 Jews have made their home. In the 1920s, Ashkenazim from Russia, Poland, and Romania found their way here. In the capital city of Tegucigalpa (with 25 Jewish families) the Hotel Prado is Jewish-owned (Helmut Seidel, owner); the Honduras Maya Hotel is Jewish-managed. Tegucigalpa's Jewish community was not organized until 1963. In Tegucigalpa the Israeli consulate in the Midence-Soto Building works closely with the local Jewish community. In 1983 Israel and Honduras signed a cultural agreement and laid plans for closer economic cooperation.

In the city of San Pedro Sula is the only synagogue in Honduras. Built in 1952 it serves sixty Jewish families (call Mauricio Weizenblut).

A few Jewish families also reside in Tela, Comayagua, and Choluteca.

USEFUL ADDRESSES

Tegucigalpa: U.S. Embassy, Avenido la Paz (tel. 32 3120).
Israeli Consulate, Midence-Soto Building 411 (tel. 22-2529).

HONG KONG

It has been said that the quest for righteousness is Oriental and the quest for knowledge is Occidental. Israel Zangwill in his *Dreamers of the Ghetto* (1898) wrote, "His soul was of the Orient, but his brain was of the Occident. His intellect had been nourished at the breast of Science, that classified everything and explained nothing. . . . Oh, it was a cruel tragedy." Jewish migration to the Far East never reached the proportions of Jewish entry into the Western or Occidental world for geographical reasons, but the Jewish mentality has always been based upon righteousness combined with the intellectual quest for knowledge. The Jew is at home in the West and in the Orient.

Today approximately 500 or more Jews reside on Hong Kong Island, Kowloon, and in the New Territories. It is difficult to ascertain the number of Hong Kong residents since many Jews come temporarily for business purposes. Israelis comprise a substantial proportion of local Jewry. Some residents originate from Shanghai which had a thriving Jewish community of 25,000 before World War II.

Jews first made their appearance in Hong Kong (twenty-nine square miles) shortly after the Opium War waged by Great Britain against China in 1842. With the opening of Hong Kong to Western trade in that year, the Sassoon family, "the Rothschilds of the East," which had amassed great wealth in Baghdad and Bombay, opened a branch in Hong Kong. The Sephardic family of Kadoorie followed, and by 1857 there was an organized Jewish community in Hong Kong. (In 1855, the Sassoon family purchased a large tract of land as a Jewish burial ground.)

Hong Kong has served as a city of refuge for Eastern European Jews since the beginning of the twentieth century, and especially during World War II for escapees from Nazi tyranny. The several Jewish families still residing in Hong Kong are extremely wealthy (the Kadoorie and Sassoon families, for example). The community is nominally Sephardic but Ashkenazi in practice, and consists mostly of transient Jews in business, education, and the consular corps. Although the Jewish community was established in 1857, it did not build its synagogue until 1901. (It was built by Sir Jacob Sassoon in memory of his mother, Leah.) The Ohel Leah Synagogue (70 Robinson Road; tel. 229872) is situated on prime commercial land and includes an adjacent Jewish Recreation Club with lovely tropical gardens from which one can view the magnificent Hong Kong harbor. Built in the Sephardic style, it is resplendent with white wooden pillars painted golden. The *bima* is raised and centered, and women are relegated to the balcony overlooking the main floor. The adjoining Jewish Recreation Club was erected by Sir Elly Kadoorie in 1909. Rabbi David Hirshberg greets the Jewish visitor, along with the Chinese *shammas* of the past twenty-five years, Chan Loin. Rabbi Hirshberg is an Israeli who previously held a pulpit in Trondheim, Norway, for seven years. President of the synagogue is Richard L. Elman (tel. 225-611).

In addition, there is a Jewish Benevolent Society, Jewish cemetery, a Hebrew Sunday school, and a *mikvah*. The history of the Jewish community of Hong Kong is dramatically portrayed in the Jewish cemetery at 13 Shan Kwong Road, dedicated in 1855. Engraved in marble in Hebrew letters, the inscription states that the cemetery was purchased by the Sassoon family from Her Majesty Queen Victoria *b'kesef molay*—full price—the same term used in Genesis to describe the purchase of the *m'aarat hamachpela* by Abraham. Many of the monuments were constructed from pure imported marble, and the fascinating inscriptions in both Hebrew and English dating back to the 1850s give one a bird's-eye view of the local Jewish settlement.

In early March 1974 in the "thieves' market" on Cat Street in Hong Kong, four ancient and invaluable sacred Hebrew scrolls were discovered by Father Herbert Vogt, a German Salesian friar living in Hong Kong. Father Vogt immediately contacted Sir Lawrence Kadoorie, past president of Ohel Leah Synagogue in Hong Kong, because it saddened him to see these scrolls among the Mongolian machinery and good-luck amulets. Sir Lawrence purchased the Torahs for about $5,000. The Torahs were identified as belonging to the Hankow, China, Jewish community which had prospered fifty years earlier. These Torahs were housed in wooden chests marked "Shanghai"; inside of the housing were found a German prayer book dated 1907, and two photo albums of a Chinese Jewish family. The Ohel Leah Synagogue is the storehouse for these Chinese Torah scrolls.

The Kadoorie family is still active in the Jewish community. Lawrence Kadoorie, president of the Jewish Club, and his brother, Horace, contribute large sums of money for philanthropic purposes.

The future of Hong Kong Jewry is dim, because today there are better opportunities elsewhere to earn a living. (The nearness of Communist China is like a Sword of Damocles, which can cut off

Hong Kong from the free world in a matter of hours.) The Talmud (Gittin, 70a) says that three things sap one's strength: worry, travel, and sin. Curiously, within the bounds of travel, Hong Kong can transform these debilitating signs of worry and sin into a satisfying experience. May the Jewish community of Hong Kong find a new life in the years to come.

KOSHER RESTAURANTS

Prepackaged kosher food is available upon request at the Hong Kong Hilton Hotel (religious services are held on the fifth floor) and at the Imperial Hotel on Kowloon.

USEFUL ADDRESSES

Hong Kong Island: U.S. Consulate, 26 Garden Road (tel. 239-011).

Israeli Consulate, 1122 Prince's Building, Chater Road (tel. 220177).

HUNGARY

Despite the bestial murder by the Nazis of 600,000 of the 825,000 Hungarian Jews, the Hungarian Jewish community today remains one of the largest in Europe. There are perhaps 80,000 Jews, including more than 60,000 in Budapest alone, and 100 synagogues, although many are not open for worship. Soviet forces "liberated" the country in January 1945, and helped to stabilize postwar dislocation and to normalize living conditions, but did not encourage Jewish life. The Hungarian constitution expressly provides for the separation of church and state to enable all minorities to live in freedom, and this legal affirmation of Jewish rights was conducive to continued Jewish survival in Hungary. Hungary is probably the only Communist country where Jews are still members of the Politburo, the supreme body of the Communist Party.

Jews have lived in what is now Hungary since the third century A.D., as evidenced by Hebrew tombstone inscriptions found at Gran. In fact, Judaism is very much alive in Hungary; there are more Hungarian rabbis and more functioning synagogues in Hungary than in all of the other Eastern Europe countries combined. There are *yeshivoth, talmud torahs,* kosher slaughtering facilities (according to the *Jerusalem Post* there are "twelve kosher butcher shops which export 25 wagon loads of kosher meat to Israel each month"), a one-hundred-year-old rabbinical seminary, and three kosher restaurants. There are also twelve old-age homes, a Jewish orphanage, and even a state-owned matzoh factory. Budapest's Kozma Street Jewish Cemetery, dating to 1700, is the resting place for 600,000 Hungarian Jews. But Israel is almost an unknown country to Hungarian Jewry, for no information about Israel is available in Jewish schools; there are no lectures about Israel, nor visits to Israel by Hungarian Jews—all in keeping with the official policy of the government which equates Judaism with Zionism and the State of Israel.

Jewish communal facilities in Budapest include a Jewish hospital and a twenty-five-year-old Jewish newspaper, *Uj Elet,* an effective unifying force and information source within the community. One of its stories described a Budapest Jewess, Dr. Margit Koricsoner, who had been a heart specialist at the Budapest Jewish Hospital from 1942 to 1944 while serving as the leader of the Iron Network Resistance Organization. Operating under the code name "Magog," Dr. Koricsoner regularly reported to Allied intelligence agencies on the military movements of the Nazis, and at the same time helped countless prisoners of war escape. Dr. Koricsoner's work was enhanced by a two-way radio hidden in her portable electrocardiograph. In 1969 she was posthumously awarded the highest honor of the Association of Former French Resistance Fighters and Deportees.

The Jewish community of Budapest before World War II was large and relatively prosperous. The Nazis took over the Manfred Weiss Works, Hungary's largest munitions enterprise, but allowed its Jewish owners (forty-eight members of the family) to migrate to Portugal. Today the Hungarian government owns the renamed Csepel Iron and Steel Works. Dr. Imri Haber, a lawyer, has served as president of the Central Board of Jewish Communities of Hungary as well as the head of the Budapest Jewish community (VII Sip Utca 12; tel. 226-478). Conservative Chief Rabbi is Dr. Laslo Salgo (tel. 421180) who is also a member of Parliament. The Orthodox Chief Rabbi is Dr. Marton Weisz (tel. 221-172).

Budapest's Dohany Street Synagogue, built in 1854, is a stately and dignified structure, and is the second largest synagogue in the world, seating 3,300 persons and accommodating up to 5,000 worshipers on the High Holy Days. This huge edifice has four balconies and a giant organ with over 5,000 pipes, once played by Liszt and Saint-Saens. (Several years ago an American television network was disappointed to learn that the government had at the last moment canceled its scheduled telecast of the Kol Nidre services from this synagogue.) The synagogue, the largest in Europe, is one of the glories of a once-proud community of Jews. One hundred and thirty years old, it occupies prime real estate in the heart of Budapest, and is surrounded by the offices of the Jewish community, a dormitory for the Jewish aged, and the Jewish Museum. The Hungarian government maintains the synagogue as an official monument and cultural attraction.

Theodor Herzl was born on the very site of the Jewish Museum; its collection of mementos of Herzl's life is unequaled anywhere. However, few tourists are aware that Budapest was his birthplace because Zionism, which he founded, is not acceptable within Hungary. In the courtyard of the Dohany Street Synagogue there is a memorial plaque to Hanna Szenes (or Senesh), a twenty-two-year-old Hungarian Jew who lived in Palestine and in 1943 volunteered to organize Jewish resistance in Hungary. She was captured and shot as a spy by the Nazis. During World War II, the synagogue here was enclosed by a wooden fence, creating a concentration camp for the city's Jews. The indelible sorrow of the Hungarian Jewish experience is recorded by various memorials. A memorial "To the Unnamed

Martyrs, 1942–45" is in the cemetery behind the Jewish Museum. Here 2,000 Jews who died in the ghetto are buried in a mass grave.

Other places of Jewish interest in Budapest include Ghetto Memorial, a simple tablet in the side wall of a former Jewish school at Wesselenyi Utca 44, marking the site of Budapest's World War II ghetto; the Hungarian Academy of Sciences, Roosevelt Terrasz 2, which in its Oriental section has the famous Kaufmann Collection of illuminated Hebrew manuscripts and printed Judaica, including a magnificent fourteenth-century hand-illustrated Haggadah; and the Jewish Theological Seminary of Hungary, Jozsef-Korut 27, which has been a renowned center for Jewish scholarship for over eighty years. In 1944, the seminary was used as a detention center through which 20,000 Hungarian Jews passed en route to concentration camps; a plaque honors those who died. The building also houses a 150,000-volume Jewish library, including 500 volumes that are more than one thousand years old. Other places of interest are Martyrs' Memorial, in the Jewish Cemetery at Kozma Utca 6, which contains the names of more than 10,000 Budapest Jews who perished in the Nazi occupation; the Monument to the Unknown Jewish Forced Laborer, which is in the Rakoskeresztur Jewish Cemetery; and Temple of Heroes, at the entrance of Wesselenyi Utca 5, an imposing domed structure at the end of the arcade leading from the new wing of the Dohany Street Synagogue, erected as a memorial to the more than 10,000 Jews who died fighting for Hungary in World War II.

Dr. Pal Schwartzmann, seventy-five years old, widely known for his work in geriatrics, heads the new 200-bed Jewish Hospital in Budapest. (Dr. Schwartzmann escaped from a slave labor camp in 1944, returned to Budapest, and in exchange for medical services, he was hidden in basements until the German defeat.) At 41 Kazinsky Street is the kosher salami factory; owned by Dezso Kovari the factory also turns out fine kosher liverwurst. Nearby is the Orthodox bathhouse, a three-story building. On Kazinsky Street there is a basement wine shop where kosher wines from the Eger region of Hungary are sold. There is also a communal kitchen serving 1,200 free hot meals each noon to old Jewish pensioners. The matzoh factory works year-round, shipping 450 tons of matzohs each year to Jewish communities in East Germany, Czechoslovakia, and Poland.

At 26 Tancsics Street in the Castle Hill district of Budapest the remains of an ancient synagogue were discovered in 1965 during the renovation of a house. On the basis of the Turkish character of the Hebrew lettering on the interior walls it was determined that the synagogue was in operation during the Turkish occupation of the city in the seventeenth century, although tombstones were found nearby from as early as 1268. Also unearthed was a candelabra, several pieces of enamelware for liturgical use, a copy of the charter of emancipation issued by King Bela IV in 1251, and even fragments of shells which demolished the synagogue during the Turkish siege of Budapest in 1686. The restored synagogue is open to the public.

SOPRON

In 1950, in the little Hungarian border city of Sopron, three Gothic windows were discovered in a two-floor dwelling at 11 Uj Street (formerly known as Jewish Street). Further excavation revealed the presence of an ancient synagogue, consisting of a spacious two-story hall with a single nave and without columns. Later excavators found a niche in the east wall for the Ark of the Covenant with Hebrew inscriptions reading: "Find out whom you are facing." According to documents dated 1440, the synagogue had been built around 1350. Across the street from the synagogue was a one-story ritual bath, which has also been restored. Nearby tombstones revealed that Jews had settled here circa A.D. 650. When Jews were driven out of Sopron in 1526, the synagogue was converted into a dwelling house by "building in" the east and south sides of the synagogue and adding another story to the building. Today the restored Sopron Synagogue is a Jewish Museum operated by the government.

The tangible signs of Jewish life—synagogues, the Jewish press, Hebrew schools, rabbinical seminaries, *matzoh* bakeries—are shadowed by relentless pressure to assimilate. Where religious institutions do exist, the government controls and manipulates them for its own political aims. More insidious is the denial of Jewish identity and the exploitation of Jewish experience. Although history books treat the fate of Jews in wartime Hungary sympathetically, they do not mention the Jewish identities of the many who were prominent in Hungarian political, economic, and cultural life. The murdered deportees are referred to as "martyrs to fascism." Anti-Semitic acts, which are subject to punishment, are considered solely as expressions of fascism, the enemy of the Communist society. In this climate, then, something which is generally considered a good thing—the fact that the designation "Jew" does not appear on identity cards—reinforces the pressure on Jews to assimilate.

There are synagogues in the following Hungarian towns and cities, but whether they are still open for prayer is not known: Debrecen (Bacji Zsilinaty Utca 26); Eger (Hibay Karol Utca); Miskolc (Kazincsky Utca 7); and Pécs (Furdo Utca). In Szeged (about two hours from Budapest) is a magnificent synagogue of Moorish design and cathedrallike proportions. Its stained-glass windows depict the symbols of the Jewish holiday cycle. Built in 1903, the 1,100-seat synagogue (with only 400 members today) has a distinctive memorial plaque listing its 4,000 members who died in the Holocaust.

KOSHER RESTAURANTS

Budapest: Central Kitchen, XIII Katona Jozsef Utca 9–11 (tel. 121372).
Die Soziale Kuche Hannah, VII, Dob Utca 35 (tel. 226-620 or 421-072).
Mio Udulo, VII, Sip-utca (tel. 226-478).
Balatonfured Hotel, Liszt Rerenc-utca 6; Supervision: Orthodox Rabbinate (Chief Rabbi Martin Weisz), VII Dob Utca 35 (tel. 421-072).

Miskolc: Restaurant of the Orthodox Worship Community, Kazinczy Ferenc Utca 7 (tel. 15-276).

Szeged: Izr Hitkozseg, Gutenberg Janos Utca 20 (tel. 14-283).

USEFUL ADDRESSES

Budapest: U.S. Embassy, V. Szabadsag Terrace 12 (tel. 329375).

INDIA

The Jewish community of India is over twenty centuries old. Jews probably reached India in 175 B.C. by traveling through Persia or through the Persian Gulf, both as traders and refugees. The port city of Daybul (not far from Karachi) was a famous trading post in A.D. 800 for Radanite Jewish merchants traveling from Europe to China. When Jews first arrived on the west coast of Bombay the Hindus welcomed them with open arms and have ever since permitted the practice of Judaism without hindrance or fear. Earliest Jewish settlements were in Bombay, Goa, Cranganore, Cochin, Madras, and Quilon. (In 1170 Benjamin of Tudela found 3,000 Jews on the island of Ceylon or Sri Lanka, off the southeastern coast of India.)

Unfortunately, Indian Jewry have not prospered in recent years, and there are fewer than 8,000 Jews living in India today. But in the mid-1940s about 26,000 Jews were living in the territory which in 1947 became the Republic of India, including some 5,000 wartime Jewish refugees from Asia and Europe. Since the establishment of the State of Israel in 1948, more than 30,000 Indian Jews (at the rate of almost 1,000 per year) have migrated there. Thousands of other Indian Jews have gone to Canada, England, and Australia. These great migrations have left Indian Jewry in fear of disintegration after more than 2,000 years of history. Congregational leaders in Bombay observed the centenary celebration of the Thane Synagogue in 1979; Thane is twenty-one miles northeast of Bombay, and only 250 Jews of B'nai Israel descent attended the ceremonies presided over by Judah David Garsulkar, president of the United Synagogues of India and vice-president of the (Conservative) World Council of Synagogues. Today about 6,000 Jews live in Bombay and about 250 in Calcutta. In the cities of Poona and Ahmedabad there are about 500 Jews, but only 200 Cochin Jews live on the Malabar coast in the far southwest of India.

Indian Jews have held high positions in government, in the army, and in the professions of medicine, law, and teaching. The people of India (as opposed perhaps to the government of India) are sympathetic to the State of Israel. The Israeli Consulate and the Jewish Agency function freely in Bombay. But 100 million Indian Muslims plus the considerable trade between India and Arab countries make impossible any overt public display of favor toward Israel.

BOMBAY

Bombay (population 5 million) was first settled by Baghdadi Jews, although the "Bene Israel" community here had been native to the city for centuries. (Their women dress in saris and their men wear Hindu shirts and white trousers and caps; they are believed to be descended from the Lost Ten Tribes of Israel, although records show their possible departure from Palestine in 175 B.C.) Despite their isolation from world Jewry the Bene Israel respect the Sabbath, kashrut, circumcision, and the prayer Shema. Maghain David Synagogue at Byculla (Victoria Gardens Road) was named for David Sassoon, an Iraqi Jew who settled here in 1832 and prospered as an importer and exporter of textiles and yarn. (Another Iraqi synagogue is Knesset Eliyahoo at Forbes St. 1.) By 1864 there were 3,000 Jews in Bombay, and the Sassoon enterprises were extended to banking, insurance, industry, and dock facilities. Sha'ar Ha-Rahamin or Gate of Mercy Synagogue (254 Samuel Street, Mandavi), erected in 1796, is of Bene Israel origin as are Sha'ar Rashon or New Synagogue (at Don-Tad, Khadok 9), Tifereth Israel (at 92 Clerk Road, Jacob Circle), Etz Hayim Prayer Hall (19 Umerkhadi), and the Magen Hassidim Synagogue (8 Moreland Road) which is Bombay's largest synagogue and the most modern and has more than 600 members who celebrated their golden jubilee in 1983. The Bene Israel Reform Congregation, Rodef Shalom, is at 23 Sussex Street. Relations between the white Iraqi-descended Jews and the brown-skinned Bene Israel have not been happy because skin color in India marks differences in social status. But their common love for the State of Israel has brought the two communities a little closer together.

Today worship in Bombay is still carried on in at least ten synagogues, seven Bene Israel, two Baghdadi, and one Progressive.

Among the places of Jewish interest in Bombay are the following: the Sir Elly Kadoorie School, on Mazagaon Road; the Sir Jacob Sassoon School at 340 Victoria Gardens Road in Byculla; the Flora Fountain; the David Sassoon Reading Room and Library at Kala Ghoda, Fort Bombay; the Bene Israel cemeteries on Mazagaon Road, Grant Road, and Haines Road; the Iraqi cemetery at Deslile Road; the David Sassoon Reformatory School at Matunga; the Sassoon Docks at Colaba; and the Royal Institute of Science. Visitors to Bombay should call upon Shellim Samuel, a distinguished lawyer, able judge, and author of a treatise on the history of the Bene Israel (Supreme Court of India, Colaba Court, 3rd floor, Colaba Causeway; tel. 255942).

Visitors may also contact the Central Jewish Board (tel. 24-1858) or the Council of Indian Jewry, 137 Mahatma Gandhi Road.

CALCUTTA

In Calcutta (population 7 million), most Jews trace their ancestry to Baghdad or Syria; both the Ezra and Sassoon families of great wealth hailed from Baghdad. In 1825 Neve Shalom Synagogue (9 Jackson Lane) was built, followed twenty-five years later by Beth El Synagogue at 26/1 Pollack Street, then the center of Calcutta Jewry. The largest synagogue in Calcutta is the Maghain David, a brick structure with a high steeple at 109a Beplabi Rash Bihari Bose Road, erected by the Ezra family in 1884. Other synagogues include Maghain Avoth, 25 Blackburn Lane, and Shaare Rasone, 16 Sudder Street. The Jewish Association of Calcutta is at 1 Old Court House Corner (tel. 22-4861).

From 4,000 Jews in 1945 Calcutta Jewry has rapidly declined in numbers, due to emigration, and community life for the 250 remaining Jews in Calcutta is depressing. Worship is still carried on in five synagogues, but only by means of a paid *minyan*. The suggestion to congregate together in one synagogue for High Holy Day services was coldly rejected by the community's leaders. The Jewish Girls' School at 63 Park Street (tel. 445741) is practically bereft of Jewish girls, and the Jewish Club possessed only six regularly attending Jewish members before it closed.

NEW DELHI

India's capital city was settled by Persian Jews in the sixteenth century. The present city has a small Jewish population (six families or thirty-five persons), but the heart of New Delhi Jewry is the small and pleasant Judah Hyam Hall (2 Humayun Road), a simple structure built in 1956 and trimmed with two rows of Stars of David and a menorah on orange-colored glass. The Jewish Welfare Association at 74 Babar Road (tel. 384252) is constructing an annex to the Judah Hyam Hall, to be known as the Institute of Jewish Studies. Adjoining the synagogue is a cemetery in which all tombstones face west toward Jerusalem. (Call Ezra Kolet, 74 Babar Road; tel. 384252.)

POONA

In the city of Poona the Ohel David Synagogue at 9 Rastas Peth and the Succath Sholomo Synagogue at 93 Rastas Peth are open. (E. J. Mazgaonkar at 12 Todiwala Road is a leading Jewish citizen of Poona.)

COCHIN

Cochin is at India's southwestern tip in the State of Kerala. In the Mattancherry district is Jew Town—a community of black and white

Jews of fewer than seventy persons. Over 400 years ago Paradesi Synagogue was founded by Sephardic Jews who fled the Spanish Inquisition. On December 12, 1968, the fourth centenary of Paradesi Synagogue was nationally celebrated: it was marked by the Indian government's issuance of a special stamp showing the synagogue's interior and by the attendance of the Prime Minister of India. Paradesi Synagogue (whose famed clock tower has dials in English, in Hebrew, and in native Malayalam) is separated from the former Rajah's palace grounds by a fence and is just thirty yards away from a Hindu temple. It has crystal chandeliers and hanging silver lamps of unique proportions; the floor of the synagogue is made of Chinese tiles (installed in 1762) in a willow pattern. These blue and white tiles give an immediate impression of brightness. Like all synagogues in the State of Kerala, there is a *bima* in the gallery and another in the center of the synagogue; the top one is used for the reading of the Law and for services during the Sabbath and festivals, while the bottom one is used for the ordinary daily prayers and for *Musaf* (additional prayer) on Sabbaths and festivals. The synagogue is ringed by a gallery for women.

Of great community pride are the "copper tablets" attesting to the existence in the eleventh century of a free Jewish state on India's southwestern coast near Cranganore—perhaps the first free Jewish state in the Diaspora. These heavy copper plates are inscribed in Sanskrit and in an ancient form of the Tamil language of south India. Cochin Jews date the copper plates from A.D. 379, although other historians place them as late as the eleventh century. The plates record the grant by the Maharajah of Cranganore, of the State of Anjuvannam to a Jew, Joseph Rabban, and his descendants. Other privileges given to Rabban included the right to bear arms, otherwise granted only to the aristocracy, and the privilege to fire a gun salute on the marriage of his daughter, a privilege shared only with the Maharajah himself. Anjuvannam was the only independent Jewish sovereignty ever to exist outside ancient Israel. It lasted until 1524 when its population, enlarged by refugees from the Inquisition, was wiped out by a combined force of Portuguese and Moors.

Some scholars believe that the first settlement of Jews in Cochin followed the Assyrian and Babylonian captivities of the First Temple era. Legend also has it that Jews who first settled here at the time of King Solomon were visited by St. Thomas in A.D. 50 to make them converts. The thirteenth-century explorer Marco Polo, at any rate, mentioned that Jews were settled in various places along the Malabar coast, and that by the year 1000 the Jews of Cochin were well established and enjoying the favor of their rulers. Cochin Jewry, comprising white, black (somewhat brown-skinned), and the emancipated brown-skinned, have been repeatedly torn asunder by their "color" problem. After the introduction of the caste system in India, about 400 years ago, the Jews of Cochin became divided into White Jews and Black Jews, the former immigrants (hence the name Paradesi or "strangers") from Spain and Portugal, via the Ottoman Empire, and the latter Bene Israel, the mysterious Jews of India, who to the foreigner are indistinguishable from the native Indian. Later, a third caste arose, the Brown Jews, made up of slaves of the White Jews who were freed by them in accordance with Jewish law, but not without a great deal of pressure from rabbis and Jewish communal leaders everywhere. The White Jews, who were in the minority, refused to mix with their Black or Brown brethren, religiously as well as socially. The White Jews lived at the upper end of Jew Town, close to the Rajah's palace, "for immediate protection" from the wrath of their fellow Jews, the Black and Brown Jews at the lower end of Jew Town. They refused to intermarry, although rabbis in Palestine and elsewhere to whom the Black Jews appealed, pronounced this segregation to be contrary to the letter and spirit of Judaism and called upon the White Jews to mend their ways on pain of *cherem* (excommunication). White Jews also worshiped exclusively in their own synagogue; Black and Brown Jews were not allowed to enter the White synagogue and had to pray in the forecourt. The only time they were allowed to be "called up" to the Reading of the Law was on Simchat Torah, which was celebrated in Cochin with special fervor.

By 1768 there were forty White Cochin Jewish families, but four times that number of Black Jews practicing in their own synagogues. Efforts at integration finally succeeded in 1932 in the Paradesi Synagogue (where the two copper plates are housed), and at the birth of the State of Israel in 1948 the problem became moot, for most of the Black and emancipated brown-skinned Jews of Cochin migrated to Israel, and today are on Israeli agricultural settlements. Few of the White Jews have left Cochin because Indian government regulations bar the transfer of monies out of India. Today only the Paradesi Synagogue in Jew Town, Mattancherry, and the "Black" Kadavumbhagam Synagogue are still in use.

Cochin Jews have succeeded remarkably in Israel. A moshav in the Upper Galilee, Kefar Yuval, had failed with Iraqi farmers before young Cochinese immigrants produced fruit trees whose produce is known throughout Israel and in foreign markets. Many Cochin Jews live at Nevatim, near Beersheva, and have attained success in engineering, medicine, and the civil service.

USEFUL ADDRESSES

Bombay: Israeli Consulate, 50 Kailash, G. Deshmukh Marg 26, Cumbala Hill (tel. 362793).

New Delhi: U.S. Embassy, Shanti Path, Chanakyapuri 21 (tel. 690351).
Office of the High Commissioner for Canada, 4 Aurangzeb Road (tel. 618191).

INDONESIA

Jews have lived in this elongated Asiatic nation of over 150 million people on 13,000 islands since the seventeenth century when Jews arrived from Holland. By 1850 there were twenty Jewish families from Germany and Holland living in Batavia, now Jakarta. Soon Jews from Baghdad and Aden arrived and established Jewish settlements in Surabaja and Semarang. (Many worked as clerks with the Dutch East India Company.) By 1921 there were 2,000 Jews in Indonesia, but many became assimilated with the Dutch citizens. After 1921 Russian Jews arrived, German Jews in the 1930s, and in 1939 another 2,000 Dutch Jews. After World War II there was even a Jewish newspaper, *Contactblad.*

When Indonesia achieved independence in 1949 there were anti-Semitic outbreaks among its Moslem citizens, and Jews left to find homes elsewhere. The fact that the Indonesian government did not recognize the State of Israel contributed to the emigration. In 1951 there were 1,500 Jews, but six years later, only 450 remained. Today only 100 Jews live in Indonesia in Jakarta, Bandung, and Surabaja in eastern Java.

In fall 1972 the leader of the Jewish community in Surabaja died at the age of fifty-two—David Mussry (married to a convert to Judaism) who had built the local wooden synagogue in 1946. Another recently deceased Indonesian Jewish leader was the son of the Chief Rabbi of Sweden. Today the remaining 100 Jews suffer from illiteracy in Hebrew and are unable to read their few prayer books. The local Jewish cemetery with seventy graves has been frequently vandalized, and the marble tablets on many Jewish monuments are illegible. (Local custom requires Jews to stop off at non-Jewish premises before returning to their homes from the Jewish cemetery.)

In Jakarta there are a few Jews, mainly Western businessmen and intergovernmental exchange persons. See Mr. and Mrs. Daniel Goldsmith (P.O. Box 3154); Dan is general manager of Diamond Cold Storage, and Vivi teaches physical education at the Joint Embassy School; she is also an interior designer.

USEFUL ADDRESSES

Jakarta: U.S. Embassy, Medan Merdeka Selatan 5 (tel. 340001-9).

Medan: U.S. Consulate, Djalan Iman Bonjol 13 (tel. 322290).

Surabaja: U.S. Consulate, Djalan Raya Dr. Sutomo 33 (tel. 69287).

IRAN

"Thus saith Cyrus King of Persia. The Lord God of Heaven hath given me all the kingdoms of the earth; and He hath charged me to build him a house in Jerusalem, which is in Judah."

The above quotation from Isaiah firmly established the Persian King Cyrus in Jewish history. He had freed the Jewish exiles after conquering Babylonia, and showed justice and mercy toward the Jewish people in permitting them to return to Palestine.

Perhaps no country in the world, outside of Israel, Egypt, and Iraq, has such a continuous history of Jewish settlements as Iran (or Persia). Beginning with the conquest of northern Israel in 722 B.C., the northern tribes of Israel were banished by the conquering Assyrians to the cities of Persia and Media. In 586 B.C., the Assyrian King Nebuchadnezzar deported a large part of the Jewish population to Babylon. When Babylon itself was conquered fifty-two years later by the Persian King Cyrus, these Jewish exiles settled in Persia. Esther and Mordecai and Haman and King Ahasuerus and the city of Shushan are all part of Persian Jewish history. Benjamin of Tudela, the famed world traveler (see Preface) found 15,000 Jews in Hamadan in the twelfth century. Persia was then a renowned seat of Hebrew scholarship and learning, but 300 years later Jewish life in Persia encountered much hardship, including conversion by coercion. But converted Jews in Persia did not have to pay a head tax nor wear the badge of shame, as did their European counterparts. In the city of Meshed there are still converted Jews practicing a mixture of Islam and Judaism.

Today there may be as many as 70,000 Jews in Iran, two-thirds of whom reside in the capital city of Tehran. Jews live in Isfahan (4,000), Shiraz (8,000), Ahwaz, Hamadan, Abadan, and in Kashan where there are two synagogues dating back to the fifteenth century. There is no centralized Jewish organization, and each community elects its own rabbi and pays for maintenance of its own synagogue. Perhaps 50 percent of Iranian Jewry still live in the grim and wretched poverty conditions of ghetto slums. Before the Khomeini revolution in 1979 Iranian Jews were mostly engaged in commerce, wholesale and retail, although a sizable number worked in banking, heavy industry, food processing, the plastic and synthetic fiber industries, and textiles. Several large hotels in Tehran were Jewish-owned. But the majority of Iranian Jews are living below or close to the poverty level. Jewish children over twelve years of age sit at the ubiquitous carpet looms weaving the intricate and magnificent Persian rugs. Jewish women work too, and are virtually indistinguishable from their Moslem counterparts, wearing the same dress and shawl masking the face.

HAMADAN

Hamadan—ancient Ecbatana—was the ancient royal city that was the locale for the Purim holiday. Here Queen Esther made her mark in Jewish history as the beautiful Jewess who married King Ahasuerus. French excavations in Hamadan during the past hundred years attest to the splendor of the royal Achaemenian palaces, as described in the Bible: coaches of silver and gold set upon colored marble floors; marble pillars from which hung white, green, and blue curtains fastened with royal purple cords and silver rings; gold and silver beds on floors of red, blue, white, and black marble.

In Hamadan the so-called tomb of Esther and Mordecai is probably the tomb of a much later Jewish queen, Shushan-Dukt, of the fifth century A.D. Esther and her uncle are more likely to have been buried at Susa.

In Hamadan, Darius the Great, searching through his predecessor's archives, discovered Cyrus the Great's decree which contained instructions for the Jews to be given funds from the royal treasury and assistance to return to their homeland and rebuild the temple at Jerusalem. Today Hamadan has a Jewish population of less than a hundred families.

ISFAHAN

South of Tehran is Isfahan, the ancient capital of Persia, home of some 4,000 Jews, most of whom are poverty-stricken and live within the *mahalleh* (Jahanbareh area). Just thirty years ago, there were 15,000 Jews in Isfahan, but migration to Tehran and to Israel greatly reduced the population. Hundreds of years ago, Isfahan was known as a Jewish city; in Arabic its name *Dar Ol Yahud* meant "House of Jews." Indeed, the Jews of Isfahan claim to be the direct descendants of the exiles sent from Palestine by King Nebuchadnezzar in 586 B.C. Even the Talmud ascribes the founding of the city to those exiled Jews. Graves dating back 2,000 years attest to Isfahan's early Jewish settlement.

Tradition links at least three Hebrew prophets with Isfahan. In the cemetery of Takht-e Foulad, close to the airport, a brick mausoleum contains a large stone tomb blackened with smoke from candles burned by pilgrims; it is known as the tomb of Joshua. The better-known Harun-i Vilayat with its famous tiled facade, near the Masjid-i Jumeh, is revered by Moslems, Jews, and Christians. Moslems believe this shrine contains the body of a descendant of the Imam Ali, Harun ibn Ali. For many years the shrine was under the guardianship of a Jewish caretaker and the Jews believe that the son or brother of Moses was buried here. In the courtyard of the Imamzadeh Ismail, also close to Masjid-i Jumeh, is the little Masjid-i Shaia, standing on the site of a very early Abbasid mosque. Many people believe that this mosque stands over a crypt containing the remains of the Prophet Isaiah, and the tomb itself is enclosed in a carved wooden *zari*, covered with a green cloth. The false messiah, Ishak Ben Yakub Obadiah Isa-Al-Isfahani, was born in Isfahan; he fought against the rulers of Persia before meeting his death in a violent battle.

Today there are seventeen synagogues (few are open daily) in this ancient city of Isfahan. In the Dardasht area there are two synagogues under the leadership of a Mr. Saghian for twenty Jews; in the Golbahar area there is one synagogue for fifteen Jews led by a Mr. Shemooelian; and on Shah Abas Street the only synagogue is led by a Mr. Sedighpoor. The famed Ramban Synagogue in the ghetto has unfortunately been closed.

Places of Jewish interest in Isfahan include the cemetery, still in use, and alleged to be 2,000 years old; there is an ancient Persian Jewish custom which requires Persian Jewry to sleep in the cemetery during the High Holy Days. Nearby are three Jewish villages with a population that speaks in a Judeo-Persian dialect.

Just eighteen miles from Isfahan is the little village of Linjan, within sight of the early fourteenth-century shrine of Pir Bagran, an ancient Jewish cemetery with tombs that date by inscription from the second century A.D., including the legendary tomb of Sarah, the daughter of the patriarch Asher (son of Jacob). While there are few Jewish residents in Linjan, the large shrine of sixty rooms and two synagogues is well protected, and elderly Jews visit the area during the month of Ab preceding Yom Kippur.

MESHED

Here was the center of Iran's Marranos or forcibly converted Jews who were called *Jedid Al-Islan* or New Moslems. In 1839 a fanatical mob overran the Jewish quarter and burned the synagogue. But later the Jews of Meshed secretly resumed their Jewish practices. However, because of local pressure and suspicion, many *Jedidim* left their homes and settled in Afghanistan, Turkestan, and Bukhara;

others found their way to Bombay, London, and Jerusalem, where they established synagogues.

SHIRAZ

Shiraz is some 800 miles south from Tehran. Here perhaps 6,000 Jewish citizens reside and attend ten synagogues. The Jews of Shiraz are indistinguishable in physical appearance from their Moslem neighbors, but they are a closely knit, observant Jewish community living in the ghetto in the style of their forefathers. These Persian Jews are mainly artisans, eking out a modest existence making gold jewelry, some with semiprecious stones; some are small grocery store owners, and others sell draperies.

Near Kirman in southeastern Iran, tradition says that the great desert of the Dasht-e-Lut was once an inland sea in which the present city of Yazd was an island, and that the now-extinct volcanoes of Basman and Tuftan in Baluchistan rose by its shores. Here, according to legends, Jonah was swallowed by the whale and cast up at a place now known as Yunsi, a small village.

There are perhaps 8,000 Iranian Jews still living in Meshed, Tabriz, Sanandaj, Yazd, and Kirman. At Persepolis and Pasargadae, near Shiraz, are the ruins of the great palaces of the ancient Persian kings, similar to those of Shushan near the Iraqi border.

SUSA

In Susa (called Shushan in the Bible), excavations have located the royal palace mentioned in the Book of Esther. Here also is the Tomb of the Prophet Daniel, a beautiful shrine with a white conical dome which has become a place of pilgrimage for all Iranians. The Book of Daniel relates how one night the King of Babylon feasted with his guests; and, while the revelers were drinking out of the holy goblets of the Temple of Jerusalem, there suddenly appeared writing on the wall in burning letters, warning of the downfall of Babylon and her king, an event that occurred some hours later. The Book of Daniel also relates the story of Daniel in the lion's den. Daniel held a high place in the Kingdom of Darius the Mede, who ruled Babylonia, and also in the kingdom of Cyrus. (No one can be certain that Daniel's bones are really interred here.) Arab invaders first discovered the tomb in the seventh century A.D.—a triangular pool of water in a beautiful Persian garden.

TEHRAN

Prior to 1979 the 50,000 Jews living in Tehran resided in various parts of this city of 3 million. Off Cyrus Street, in downtown Tehran, are the remnants of the ghetto or *mahalleh* where once the dark, twisting alleys were knee-deep in mud; today the streets have been paved, food stalls cleaned, and running water piped into the courtyards. The low mud-brick buildings are still bare and poor, and house an entire family's meager possessions. Here about thirteen small synagogues (of the fifty in Tehran) may be found, attended by approximately 3,000 Jews who live side by side with the city's poorest Moslems. The largest synagogue is the Iraqi Synagogue on Avenue Anatole France; the compound includes a school, kindergarten, and community social hall. The rabbinate here descends from father to son without formal ordination (a rabbi is called *haham,* or learned man). Orthodoxy is practiced widely and *kashrut* observed. In addition, there is the Haim Synagogue in Gavamossaltaneh Street and the Meshedi Synagogue in Kakh Shomali Avenue—both apparently open and available for prayer.

Prior to 1979, at the University of Tehran there were approximately 22,000 students, of whom 800 were Jewish; the faculty included three full professors, twenty-five associates, and 55 assistants of the Jewish faith. The Khomeini revolution has apparently closed much of the university.

KOSHER RESTAURANTS

Kosher food may be available in Tehran at the Commodore Hotel, 10 Takhte Jamshid Avenue (tel. 613154)—owned by Mayer and Jacob Nazarian, an old Jewish family. Other Jewish-owned hotels include the Sinai, King's, and the Victoria, all in Tehran.

USEFUL ADDRESSES

Tehran: Canadian Embassy, Bezrouke House, corner of Takhte Jamshid Avenue and Forsat Street (tel. 48306).

IRAQ

There are fewer than 450 Jews in Iraq, the remnants of a once-flourishing community which was the greatest and most prosperous of all Jewish communities in the Middle East. In 1948, over 125,000 Jews began their exodus. For 2,500 years, since the First Temple, Jews had lived here. Earliest Jewish migrations (about 2,000 B.C.) began in such towns as Ur, Babylon, and Mari. (Abraham and his father, Terah, left Ur in Chaldea.) Centuries later, 722 to 586 B.C., Jews returned and settled in such cities as Ava, Sippara, Mahoza, Cutha, Sura, Nippur, Pumbedita, and Ellasar. Recent history begins in A.D. 637 when the area was conquered by the Arabs, and the large and ancient Jewish community assisted the Arab advance in hope of being delivered from Sassanid persecution. Soon Jews from all over the Arab world settled in Kufa and other villages, and Iraq became the center of world Jewish life. In A.D. 700, there were 800,000 Jews living in Mesopotamia. The authority of its Exilarch and of the Gaon was recognized throughout the Diaspora. Jews from all over the world submitted their questions on religion to the Gaon, and the Exilarch enforced these verdicts by bans and imposition of fines. Beginning in A.D. 850, Iraqi Jews were subjected to heavy taxation, restrictions were placed upon their residence, and they were forced to wear a yellow badge on their clothing. In A.D. 1000, Jews were subjected to punitive taxation, and by the year 1040 Iraq lost her central position in the Jewish world when the Exilarch was suspended.

Jews continued to live in the cities of Baghdad, Basra, and Mosul as tradesmen and craftsmen. Discrimination against Jews ran rampant until the Mongol invasion in the second half of the thirteenth century. When Islam took over centuries later, persecution of Jews continued. The Turkish conquest of Iraq in 1534 brought better times for the Jews. By 1900 Iraqi Jewry numbered 125,000. In 1917, under British rule, Jews prospered and even held high government posts. Iraqi independence in 1932 was accompanied by persecution of Jews. In 1941, hundreds of Baghdad Jews were killed in a pogrom, and in 1948 Jews left by the thousands.

Even before the Six Days' War, in 1956 synagogues and schools were closed; a 200-year-old cemetery was destroyed and its tombs desecrated; yellow identity cards were issued to the Jews, and the sale of Jewish property was forbidden. After 1956, even harsher measures against the Jews were instituted: all Jews were dismissed from jobs in public institutions; Jewish property was expropriated and Jewish bank accounts frozen; businesses were shut down and trading permits canceled; telephones were disconnected; Jews were placed under house arrest for long periods or restricted in movement; departure from the country was totally prohibited; and applications for passports were summarily rejected. All this was openly and plainly expressed in official statutes and regulations. Official persecution was at its worst in late 1968 and early 1969. Scores of Jews were jailed on the strength of the alleged discovery of a local spy ring. Nineteen of them were sentenced to death in staged trials and then barbarously hanged in the public squares of Baghdad; others died in prison under torture. Since 1971, many Jews have been either jailed or murdered in cold blood. Those Jews who have been able to escape from Iraq have done so, and only the old remain. There is no future for Iraqi Jewry.

Ancient Babylon (*Babil* in Arabic, which means "gate of the gods") was located fifty-five miles south of Baghdad. Led by Hammurabi (1792–1750 B.C.) the Babylonian Empire extended as far as the Mediterranean. Around 689 B.C., the city of Babylon was destroyed by the Assyrians, but was rebuilt on a grandiose scale during the reign of King Nebuchadnezzar between 605 and 562 B.C. At that time, Babylon was surrounded by a moat, an outer wall ten miles long and an inner wall four miles long. Within the walls were palaces, temples, residential buildings, and the grand processional way. Today, virtually nothing is left of the ancient Hanging Gardens of Babylon or the biblical Tower of Babel.

IRELAND

Jews have lived in Ireland since the Middle Ages, but it was not until the end of World War I that the office of the Chief Rabbi of Ireland was established. Of course, Jewish community life had long been viable, but rapid growth necessitated a more formal organization. The first Chief Rabbi in 1918, incidentally, was Isaac Herzog, who later became the Chief Rabbi of Israel. During his nineteen years in Dublin, Herzog won enormous respect and was a close friend of Eamon de Valera, father of modern Ireland. De Valera drew up the 1937 Irish constitution, bestowing full minority rights on the Jewish community, and recognizing the Chief Rabbi as appointed by its Representative Council, to which all communal organizations belong.

Almost 2,000 Jews reside in the Irish Republic. Marranos, fleeing the Spanish Inquisition, settled in Ireland in the early seventeenth century. However, it was not until 1660 that the Jewish community was permanently established with the organization of a congregation in Dublin. Since that time the small Jewish segment of Ireland's population has flourished and, despite a protracted struggle for full civil rights in the nineteenth century, has been happy and secure among its neighbors.

The Irish Jew is perhaps a rare breed, though he is as loquacious an Irishman as any other citizen of the Shamrock Isle. Michael Carr (born Michael Cohen), a Dublin-born Jew, wrote many popular Irish songs including "Did Your Mother Come From Ireland?" On the other hand, the great Irish novelist James Joyce (1882–1941) once wrote: "Ireland has the honor of being the only country which never persecuted the Jews . . . because she never let them in." The truth is that Jews are accepted in Ireland, and the role of the Irish Jew is not insignificant; he is unequivocably both a concerned Jew and a politically concerned Irish citizen. Politics in Ireland is a natural avocation, and James Joyce was simply wrong.

DUBLIN

In Dublin there is an Orthodox synagogue, the Dublin Hebrew Congregation (tel. 766745), on Adelaide Road (not far from the

Royal Victoria Hospital); this Victorian synagogue is a direct descendant of Ireland's first synagogue which was built in Crane Lane in 1660. Another synagogue, Terenure, is on Rathfarnham Road (tel. 906383). There are synagogues in the Dolphin's Barn area on South Circular Road (United Hebrew Congregation [tel. 753182]); on Lennox Street; at 77 Terenure Road North; and on Walworth Road. A relatively new Progressive or Reform synagogue is located at 7 Leicester Road (tel. 973955). Virtually all Jewish children here have some Jewish education. Half attend the two Jewish day schools—Zion Primary School and Stratford College, the secondary school (destroyed by arson in 1980 and rededicated in April 1983)—which provide daily Hebrew and Judaism lessons. Of the other 50 percent, two-thirds attend afternoon Hebrew classes, while the remainder have private tutors. There are also active youth movements, the most popular being the religiously-inclined Bnei Akiva, with 100 members aged ten to seventeen.

Clansbrassil Street, which runs perpendicular to Adelaide Road, is the street of Jewish merchants, including competitive kosher butcher shops under the same family name of Rubinstein. In the Ballybough Jewish cemetery is buried Barnaby "Pencil" Cohen, who is said to have invented the lead pencil. The cemetery is located on Fairview Strand Road 67 in back of a house. The old cemetery is at Ballybough across the river Liffey. The Old Age Home for Hebrews is located on Denmark Hill, Leinster Road West (tel. 972004).

In the library of Trinity College (part of the University of Dublin) the famed Book of Kells is kept. There is also a fine collection of ancient Hebrew texts and manuscripts. Morrison Hall, at Trinity College, was a gift of B'nai B'rith's Jack Morrison of England. One of the past presidents of the Dublin Lodge No. 1989 of B'nai B'rith is H. H. Briscoe, son of the late mayor of Dublin and himself a member of the Irish Parliament. Mansion House on Dawson Street features a portrait of Robert Briscoe, first Jewish Mayor of Dublin.

Ireland's Chief Rabbi David Rosen has his office at 9 Crannagh Park, Dublin (tel. 904383).

CORK

Ireland's second largest city is Cork, where Sephardic Jews first settled in the seventeenth and eighteenth centuries. The present synagogue at 10 South Terrace (tel. 241091) was built by Russian Jews in the late nineteenth century, but unfortunately the building is closed, except for Sabbath services. There are seventeen Cork Jews today, including former Lord Mayor Goldberg. The remains of an ancient Jewish cemetery were recently unearthed in Cork, when workmen excavating a site for a bacon factory uncovered the graveyard which is believed to corroborate the existence of a Marrano community in the seventeenth century. The Dublin Jewish community has assumed responsibility for its restoration and maintenance.

Not far from Cork is the legendary Blarney Castle with the famous Blarney Stone which bestows gifts of eloquence and persuasiveness on those who kiss it. According to tradition, this stone is part of the rock on which the biblical Patriarch Jacob rested his head during his dream at Beth-El—a "fact" which makes Ireland's Jews doubly proud.

LIMERICK

The only Jew in this city of 60,000 Irishmen is a Mr. Fine who owns a fine jewelry shop. But eighty years ago there were hundreds of prosperous Jewish merchants and moneylenders; however, one Father Creagh of the Redemptorist order of priests encouraged boycotting of Jews, and prosperity soon vanished for all the inhabitants.

KOSHER RESTAURANTS

Dublin: Mr. & Mrs. D. Hyman, 37 Hazelbrook Road (tel. 904911).
Mrs. L. Danker, 226 South Circular Road 8 (tel. 753874).
Maccabi Sports Association, Kimmage Road West (tel. 504935).

USEFUL ADDRESSES

Dublin: U.S. Embassy, 42 Elgin Road, Ballsbridge (tel. 688777).
Canadian Embassy, 10 Clyde Road, Ballsbridge (tel. 680628).

ISRAEL

How and what can one Jew tell another about Israel? Jews for centuries have prayed for their return to Israel—yet not even a majority of American Jews have visited Eretz Yisrael. Israel is a traveler's mecca for a myriad of reasons including the simple pleasure of visiting a modern, thriving democratic nation with its heart in tune with the thrust of Western civilization: life, liberty, and the pursuit of happiness.

The modern State of Israel was founded May 14, 1948. Although this small bastion of democracy has been engaged since its birth in war with its Arab neighbors, Israel has built more than 160 hospitals with 30,000 beds and 2,000 libraries containing 13 million books.

Israel covers an area of 8,000 square miles (excluding territories occupied after the Six Days' War). Israel's population of almost 4 million people includes approximately 400,000 Moslems, 100,000 Christians, 34,000 Druzes, and other sects. The approximate population of Jerusalem is 300,000; Tel Aviv/Jaffa 400,000; Haifa 215,000; Beersheva 120,000; and Natanya 60,000. The new port city of Ashdod has had more than an 800 percent increase in population since 1961, from 4,600 to over 45,000. And the industrial town of Dimona in the Negev increased over the past ten years from 5,000 to more than 25,000 persons.

It is the author's feeling that the best way to see Israel is by automobile, following a routine much like the one a baseball player might take on a baseball field, to wit:

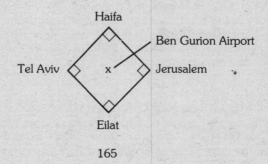

HAIFA

Upon landing at Ben Gurion International Airport (the "pitcher's mound") drive northward for two hours (approximately sixty miles) to the northern city of Haifa ("second base"). Here, built on the slopes of Mount Carmel, is a city whose port facilities accommodate ships from all over the world and whose climate is mild year-round. Almost a quarter of a million Jews, Arabs, Christians, and others live here.

For the tourist Haifa has much to offer: Technion or Israel Institute of Technology; the Bahai Shrine and Gardens; the Cave of Elijah the Prophet; Marc Chagall's Artists' House; Haifa Maritime Museum; Haifa University; Daliyat-el-Carmel, a nearby Druze village; and Rehov Yefe Nof (Panorama Street), from which there is a breathtaking view of the city and port below.

From Haifa there are three routes by automobile recommended for a full day's trip: the Northward Route, the Eastward Route, and the Southward Route, which ends at Tel Aviv.

I. Northward Route from Haifa

ACRE

At Haifa Bay intersection turn left northward toward Acre, twelve miles ahead. Acre probably has the largest native Arab population in Israel. It is a walled city throbbing with unchanged Phoenician spirit. Four thousand years ago Acre was of great importance, particularly as a glassmaking center and as the main Crusader port and fortified city. The Turks later conquered it but Richard the Lion-Hearted took it back in 1191. Of special significance is The Citadel, the British penitentiary (featured in the motion picture *Exodus*); Israel has turned it into a hospital and mental institution. Other attractions include the Mosque of Jazzar Pasha, the clocktower and marketplace, the bazaar, and the Purple Beach (its color due to an extract from snails). Napoleon lost an important battle in Acre in 1799.

About twelve miles Northeast is the settlement of **Karmiel** amid old olive groves. At **Rama,** approximately six miles farther (just past a left fork in the road), is an observation point from which one can view the entire local terrain. Approximately four miles westward, off the same road, is the village of **Peki'in,** where there is a restored third-century synagogue.

SAFED

Retracing the route past Rama, the road finally reaches Safed, one of Israel's most sacred cities, famous during the sixteenth century as a center for Kabbala. Only forty-three miles from Haifa, Safed is perched on the side of a mountain. It is today a resort and artists' colony; summer evenings are cool, although days are quite warm. There are several holy caves in this region, including one where Noah's son Shem and his grandson studied the Torah.

From Safed, driving eastward, the traveler reaches **Rosh Pina,** one of the premier settlements in Upper Galilee. At Rosh Pina there is a large kibbutz, Ayelet Hashachar, which accommodates tourists. Turning north at Rosh Pina for approximately twenty-four miles on a straight road, one reaches **Metulla,** the northernmost village in Israel, founded in 1896 by Baron Rothschild. Here the view of Lebanon is spectacular. Returning from Metulla, stop at **Tel Hai** to see the awe-inspiring monument to the Israeli hero Joseph Trumpeldor. Next is the agricultural village of **Kiryat Shemona** (approximately one-half mile before Kiryat Shemona is a road which leads into the Golan Heights); then, past the *kibbutzim* of Dan and Dafna, the road leads to the headwaters of the Jordan River at **Banias.** Mount Hermon, bordering Israel, Lebanon, and Syria, has three white-peaked summits over 3,000 feet high. Its snows feed and form the Jordan River. From here the long twenty-five mile drive into the village of **Kuneitra** is unspectacular except for the relics of the Six Days' War, such as Russian tanks and trucks, which have been left at the roadside as a permanent reminder of Israel's struggle to live in peace. From Kuneitra it is twenty-five mile miles back, past the village of **Hatzor,** one of the earliest Canaanite towns conquered by Joshua. From the main highway at Hatzor the traveler can return to Haifa via Ma'alot, Nahariya on the coast, and Acre.

II. Eastward Route from Haifa

The road to **Nesher** (cement works) climbs and offers one of the most beautiful views in northern Israel. Six miles away is **Yagur,** one of Israel's larger *kibbutzim.* At the intersection less than one-half mile before the *kibbutz,* take the northerly road into **Kefar Ata,** and then at the next intersection turn right to **Shefar'am,** which is both a Jewish and a Christian village. Approximately five miles ahead on the left is **Beit Netufa,** a man-made lake. Within four miles of **Nazareth** and just off the main road on the left is the village of **Tsippori,** once the largest city in Galilee. (Tsippori was destroyed by the Romans in the fourth century; according to Christian tradition, Mary, mother of Jesus, was born here.)

NAZARETH

Nazareth, city of Jesus, has over twenty Christian churches and convents, the most famous being the Church of the Annunciation, erected on the site of the Grotto of the Annunciation. Among other important sights in Nazareth are: Mary's Well; Maronite Church; Greek Orthodox Church of the Annunciation (over 300 years old);

St. Joseph's Workshop; Nazareth Elit (an Israeli suburb on a hill east of town); the Frank Sinatra Club and Cultural Center; and the Synagogue-Church where Jesus worshiped.

TIBERIAS

From Nazareth turn left northward on the road to Tiberias, approximately twenty miles from Nazareth. Tiberias is 700 feet below sea level and the principal city on the Sea of Galilee (or Kinneret, or Lake Tiberias). Built 2,000 years ago, the city became the most important center for Jewish learning after the destruction of Jerusalem. Bathing facilities, boating, and even water-skiing here are excellent.

The road north leads to the Tabgha Valley with its many churches, one of which tells the story in mosaics of the Multiplication of the Loaves and Fishes. Just one-half mile from Tiberias is **Capernaum** (Kfar Nahum) with its partly restored ancient synagogue with many ornamental engravings. The Mount of Beatitudes (two and one-half miles north of Tiberias) adjoins this area; a convent and church overlook the Sea of Galilee.

Returning to Tiberias the road southward along the Sea of Galilee leads first to **Beit Yerah** where there are the remains of a second-century synagogue, a fourth-century Roman bathhouse, and a sixth-century Byzantine church. Less than a mile away is **Deganya,** the oldest kibbutz in Israel. Thirty miles south is one of the most important ancient cities of the Middle East, **Beit Shean,** some 400 feet below sea level. For more than 6,000 years civilization has continued here; the Roman theater and municipal museum are worth visiting. Westward from Beit Shean the road leads to Afula in the Jezreel Valley, then southward six miles to **Megiddo.** Christian tradition places Armageddon here; on one hill the ruins of twenty cities and Canaanite temples 4,000 years old have been found. From Megiddo we retrace the direct route back to Haifa via Nesher.

III. Southward Route from Haifa

From the slopes of Mount Carmel drive southward past **Atlit,** a port town with a fort built by the Crusaders in the twelfth century. Approximately twelve miles from Haifa is **Ein Hod,** a self-governing community of artists and sculptors; it is high above the shoreline and off the road to the left. Another nine miles down the coastal road and perhaps one-half mile to the left is the mountainous village of **Zichron Ya'akov,** site of the beautiful Baron Edmund de Rothschild Gardens, old wineries, and a magnificent view of the Mediterranean coast.

CAESAREA

Returning to the main road and turning westward to the Mediterranean, about five miles south are the ruins of Caesarea, built by Herod in 20 B.C. to honor Augustus Caesar. Here the large Roman excavations include an amphitheater, Byzantine mosaics, aqueducts, a hippodrome, and an ancient synagogue. The Caesarea Hotel has the only eighteen-hole golf course in Israel. Returning to the main highway south, one passes through the village of **Hadera,** where the original malarial swamp has been replaced by large citrus groves and many of Israel's paper mills. At Hadera, return to the coastal road; twelve miles farther south is a large Mediterranean resort town with a very picturesque beach, **Natanya.** Another five miles south along the coastal road is the Wingate Physical Training Institute, named after Brigadier Wingate, a British officer who trained the Palmach before 1948. Six miles farther is **Herzliya,** another resort town with excellent beaches.

TEL AVIV

"Hill of Spring" is the English translation of Tel Aviv ("third base" on our baseball diamond), which began upon the sand dunes outside ancient Jaffa. Israel's largest metropolis, with 400,000 residents, it is the commercial, industrial, and cultural capital of modern Israel. Beaches, sidewalk cafes, treelined boulevards, large apartment houses, and skyscrapers have indeed made Tel Aviv a modern world center.

Interesting to the tourist are Carmel Market with its colorful open stalls; Mann Auditorium, home of the Israel Philharmonic Orchestra; the boutiques along Dizengoff Street; the innumerable museums and art exhibitions; and ancient Jaffa with its winding narrow streets and old port, which includes Hapisgah Park, Andromeda's Rock, the Clock Tower, the Flea Market, the Machmudiah Mosque, St. Peter's Monastery, and the Russian Cathedral. In Tel Aviv proper, see the Shalom Tower Observatory, the zoo, the Habima Theater, and the Great Synagogue. Tel Aviv University (Diaspora Museum) and other educational institutions should not be missed. The B'nai B'rith building at Rehov Kaplan 10 has a particularly fascinating mural on its ground floor. On Rehov Arlosoroff is the national headquarters of Histadrut, whose more than 1 million members constitute a distinct majority of the working population of Israel.

From Tel Aviv, four motoring routes are recommended for a full day's trip: I—Southeastward Route, II—Southcoastal Route, III—Northeastward Route, and IV—Southward Route:

I. Southeastward Route from Tel Aviv

Driving through ancient Jaffa, visit both the archaeological museum and other attractions and the new resort area along the waterfront.

From Jaffa, stop off at **Bat Yam** with its beaches and artists' colony. Past **Holon** one arrives at **Rishon Le-Zion,** "First in Zion" (established in 1882), famed for its wine cellars. Six miles farther is **Rehovot,** home of the Weizmann Institute of Science. Rehovot is a prosperous city in the center of Israel's citrus region. From Rehovot the highway turns southwestward to **Yavne,** built around an ancient city, including a mosque built upon a Crusader church. From Yavne continue westward to the sea past Palmahim Beach, and then return to Tel Aviv via the coastal road through Holon and Bat Yam.

II. Southcoastal Route from Tel Aviv

About two miles northward from Tel Aviv is the industrial center and suburb of **Ramat Gan,** noted for its chocolates and fruit-processing plants, lovely gardens, expensive residences, and sports stadium. The Ramat Gan National Park has a lake, waterfall, zoo, and amphitheater. Two miles farther is **B'nai Brak,** now a center for citrus culture, although famous in the second century as a site of Jewish learning. B'nai Brak is still one of modern Israel's leading religious centers with many *yeshivot.* Continue northeastward to **Petah Tikvah,** and then turn right and head southward past Ben Gurion Airport to **Ramla.** Ramla has a distinguished landmark in the form of a white tower built in the fourteenth century as the minaret of the Great Mosque, and is today one of the best examples of Crusader architecture. Approximately twelve miles away is **Gedera.**

ASHDOD

At the next intersection to the south, turn right (westward toward the sea), and approximately seven miles ahead is Israel's newest deepwater port, Ashdod. Built in 1957 on sand dunes, this port is an inspiring tribute to the energy of the Israeli people. The ruins of biblical Ashdod are three miles south of the main road.

ASHKELON

Return two miles to the main road and head south approximately fifteen miles and again turn off the main road toward the sea to reach the biblical town of Ashkelon, which has been converted from its ancient Philistine past to a new garden resort with a beautiful Mediterranean beach. Antiquities Park is really unique: it has Greek and Roman sculptures. Approximately nine miles south along the same main highway is **Yad Mordechai,** which is a *kibbutz* established in memory of the leader of the Warsaw Ghetto uprising in World War II. (The Gaza Strip is less than two miles farther south.) Returning to the main road, drive due east approximately fifteen miles to the development town of **Kiryat Gat,** which has long served as an immigration depot. The road out of Kiryat Gat continues east and then northward to **Beit Shemesh,** an important town in biblical days. Approximately seven miles north, turn left to return to the principal highway to Tel Aviv, less than thirty-five miles away.

III. Northeastward Route from Tel Aviv

Drive north from Tel Aviv along the coastal road, turning off toward the east at **Ramat Hasharon,** and then continue north past **Kfar Saba** and **Tira** and visit a large Arab village, **Tulkarm,** approximately thirty miles from Tel Aviv. From Tulkarm the road eastward takes one past **Sebastia,** or **Shomron** (its ruins mark the ancient capital of biblical Israel), to **Nablus,** a Canaanite town in the days of Abraham. Ancient **Shechem** is south of the city at the Arab village of **Balatah.** Archaeological expeditions are ever present here, and the ruins reveal Early Bronze Age relics. Here are Jacob's Well, Joseph's Tomb, the twin mountains of Mount Gerizim and Mount Ebal, and the Samaritan Quarter. Then go southward for thirty miles, passing through **Ramallah** where the curving road bends westward and returns past **Beth Horon,** south again onto the principal highway into Tel Aviv.

IV. Southward Route from Tel Aviv

BEERSHEVA

Leave Tel Aviv via the principal highway south (sixty-six miles) to Beersheva, a biblical town dating from the time of the Patriarchs and today the capital of Negev. Every Thursday morning there is a Bedouin camel market here. In Beersheva visit Abraham's Well, the Biological Institute and Museum, the numerous excavation sites in the area, and of course, Ben Gurion University of the Negev.

ARAD

Taking the north road toward **Hebron,** proceed seven miles to the first intersection; here take the right fork and continue to Arad, approximately twenty-seven miles, passing near **Tel Arad,** site of the excavated ruins of a Canaanite town, at the foot of the Hebron Mountains. Arad, a new town established in 1961, though in the center of the Judean Desert, has a cooler climate than is found on the shore of the Dead Sea. Israel's first atomic reactor, in the Negev at **Nahal Rubin,** began operations in July 1960.

DEAD SEA

Proceeding southeast toward the Dead Sea, pass **Rosh Zohar,** 3,000 feet above the Dead Sea. Another eighteen miles of curving roads lead to the shore of the Dead Sea, 1,500 feet below sea level. Slightly north of **Neve Zohar** on the shore are bathing facilities and numerous new hotels. One cannot sink in the Dead Sea due to the very high saline content of the water. Six miles farther north is **Ein Bokek,** where there are sulfur springs as well as a bathing beach and several new hotels.

MASADA

Approximately twelve miles north from Ein Bokek and off the westerly side of the shore road is Masada, appearing like a high island in the desert as it rises dramatically 700 feet from the shore of the Dead Sea. Here was the last stronghold of the Jewish rebels against Rome. Carefully preserved are Herod's palace, a Byzantine church, storerooms, swimming pool, synagogue, royal villa, and cisterns. After a long siege, Masada fell in A.D. 73. The climb up Masada is not easy; it takes several hours of arduous climbing to reach the peak. The best time to climb is before the sun rises between 3 and 6 A.M. (The weary may prefer the cable car!) There is also an approach to Masada from the west, although this rough road from Arad is not favored.

Finally, twenty miles farther up the shore of the Dead Sea is the spectacular oasis of **Ein Gedi,** where King David found shelter from King Saul in biblical days. Here in the desert is a natural waterfall, where a local *kibbutz* is engaged in hydroponic agriculture. A few miles farther north are the **Qumram Caves** where the Dead Sea Scrolls were found. The return route to Tel Aviv requires retracing the route to the Neve Zohar intersection, then proceeding south past the ancient city of Sodom (six miles from the intersection). At the next intersection, eight miles south, take the right turn westward to **Dimona.** (From this intersection the road south leads to **Eilat.**) Dimona is the largest new town in the Negev. From Beersheva take the return highway north directly to Tel Aviv.

EILAT

The Egged Bus Tour from Tel Aviv through the Negev to Eilat ("home plate") is recommended as an alternative to a car; the tourist not only can mingle with Israelis but can benefit from the fascinating narrative by the experienced Israeli guide accompanying the tour. (Arkia Israel Inland Airlines also operates daily flights to Eilat.) The Egged bus trip first stops at Beersheva for a morning snack. Leaving Beersheva, the bus passes the first intersection: off to the left is the partially reconstructed Byzantine town of **Shivta,** whose early ruins date back to Nabatean times. About nineteen miles south is the village of **Yeroham.** From Kefar Yeroham it is another eleven miles to the desert *kibbutz* of **Sede Boker,** where Ben Gurion lived. Also slightly off the main road and six miles farther south is **Ein Avdat,** where the desert has produced a spring and pool in a beautiful 200-foot-deep canyon. Three miles farther is the ancient Nabatean town of **Avdat,** high up on the hill overlooking the entire countryside. Avdat overlooked the caravan route of the Nabateans; in later periods the town was occupied by the Romans and the Byzantines. Today it has been partly restored. Another fifteen miles south through the desert is **Mitspe Ramon,** a lookout point above the Ramon Crater, a unique geological formation. From Mitspe Ramon to **Yotvata** is slightly more than sixty miles across some of the bleakest and driest areas in the world. Yotvata, an agricultural settlement established in 1959, is at the base of the Jordanian mountains, one or two miles away. Ten miles farther south and off the main highway is **Timna,** the site of King Solomon's ancient copper mines. In recent years the mines have been opened and a small yield of copper is being produced.

From Timna it is approximately fifteen miles to Eilat, which is Israel's resort on the Red Sea. Here is year-round swimming and skin diving, as well as rich corals and exotic fish. Eilat's many attractions include its beautiful coral beach, Cactus Park, marine museum, and Red Canyon. Not more than a mile eastward is the Jordanian city of **Aqaba.** In ancient times, halfway between Eilat and Aqaba was the ancient city of **Etzion Geber,** which was King Solomon's port and the city where the Queen of Sheba landed on her visits to ancient Israel. An overnight stay in Eilat is recommended; some of Israel's finest accommodations are available here.

From Tel Aviv to Jerusalem

Leaving Tel Aviv on the highway to Jerusalem thirty-six miles away, approximately ten miles from Tel Aviv is the ancient city of **Ramla.** From the eighth century until the time of the Crusades this was the Arab capital of Palestine; a large minaret in the center of town marks the fact. Today this dusty Arab village has been turned into a thriving business community approximately one mile away from Ben Gurion International Airport at Lod. On the main highway eastward is the **Latrun** crossroads, where one of the most important battles in the 1948 War of Liberation was fought. From this intersection the road leads through the historical Ayalon Valley, a major pass into the Judean hills. Here Joshua bid the sun to stand still; Judah the Maccabee defeated the Greeks; and Richard the Lion-Hearted fought against Saladin. Along the road is Kefar Shmuel, named after the great American Rabbi Stephen S. Wise. The road passes through the Valley of Sorek, where Samson lived; the Martyrs' Forest of six million trees can also be seen from the roadway. In the village is a Crusader church built in 1142. East from Abu Ghosh is the Roman fortress at **Kastel,** and below in the valley is **Aquabella,** site of the ruins of a twelfth-century Crusader monastery.

JERUSALEM

Jerusalem, sacred center of three world religions, and capital of Israel, has been a mecca for many centuries. Crowning the Judean hills, this eternal holy city ("first base" on our baseball tour) is one of the most attractive tourist areas in the world. About 300,000 people inhabit the city today. In Jerusalem the "must" attractions for *all* religious faiths include:

Bezalel National Museum. Founded in 1906. One of Israel's leading receptacles of ancient and modern ceremonial Jewish art.

Biblical Zoo. Every animal, bird, and reptile mentioned in the Bible is exhibited here.

Church of Gethsemane, or **Church of All Nations.** Built in 1924. Especially important to the Christian world.

Hadassah Hebrew University Medical Center. The finest hospital complex in the Middle East is located in **Ein Kerem,** just outside the city limits. Its synagogue houses the famous Chagall Windows depicting the Twelve Tribes of Israel.

Hebrew University. World-famous university. The educational complex and the campus include the unique umbrellalike Israel Goldstein Synagogue and the Williams Planetarium.

Hechal Shlomo. The seat of the Chief Rabbinate and the religious hierarchy for all Israel.

Israel Museum. A magnificent collection; the five-acre Billy Rose Sculpture Garden adjoins the modern building.

John F. Kennedy Memorial and Peace Forest. High in the Judean hills stands this edifice, shaped like the trunk of a tree cut down before its time. An awe-inspiring building, it has fifty-one pylons representing the fifty states and the District of Columbia.

Knesset. Israel's parliament. A gigantic menorah presented by Great Britain faces the entrance.

Mea She'arim. The traditional ghetto dating from 1877 is inhabited by the deeply devout Jews who retain the traditional dress of Eastern European ghetto life.

Mishkenot Sha'Ananim. Of the many miracles accomplished by human hands in Israel, few compare with the beauty and peacefulness of Mishkenot Sha'Ananim. Located just outside the ancient walls of the Old City, it is a 120-year-old retreat for artists, writers, musicians, and scholars.

Mount Herzl. A simple yet solemn memorial in black marble to Theodor Herzl, father of Zionism.

Mount of Olives. Traditional as a sacred burial place; also referred to as the site of Jesus' ascension.

Mount Scopus. Site of the original Hebrew University campus and Hadassah Hospital.

Old City. Here are ancient alleys, covered souks, and narrow streets, and thousands of shopkeepers and tourists. Within its two and one-half mile wall, the Old City is built upon several hills including Mount Moriah. Eight gates provide entrances and exits to this walled city. Inside the Old City are such world-renowned spots as:

   (a) **Church of the Holy Sepulchre:** On Calvary, or Golgotha, the site of the Crucifixion and the Tomb of Jesus; many churches have been built here over the centuries. The present church was built by the Crusaders.

   (b) **Dome of the Rock:** Sacred to Moslems, it is also the site of King Solomon's Temple. Here Abraham prepared his son Isaac for the sacrifice. Mohammed is believed to have risen to heaven from the Rock.

   (c) **Mosque of Aksa:** This silver-domed mosque dating back to the eighth century was partially destroyed by arson in 1969.

   (d) **Via Dolorosa:** The famous street where Jesus walked, followed by Christian pilgrims over the centuries.

   (e) **The Wailing Wall:** The surviving "western wall" of the Second Temple, the focal point of Jewish pilgrimages.

Outside the Old City, the city of Jerusalem includes:

Sanhedra. The tombs of the Sanhedrin, the courts and judges of Israel during the days of the Second Temple.

Shrine of the Book. Houses the Dead Sea Scrolls and other important recent findings from the past.

Synagogues. In view of Jerusalem's many synagogues of so many nationalities, including Italian, Persian, and Spanish, the Synagogue

Tour on late Friday afternoons before sundown is recommended. The tour (nominal charge) begins at the International Cultural Center for Youth in Jerusalem.

Tomb of King David. On Mount Zion; here is also the Room of the Last Supper.

YMCA. Called the most beautiful "Y" in the world, this building on Rehov David Hamelech serves people of all religious faiths.

Yad Vashem. Mount of Remembrance, dedicated to the memory of the 6 million Jews murdered by the Nazis. A stirring and solemn tribute to their memory, the shrine is built upon an immense open concrete platform.

Yemin Moshe. Just outside the ancient walls of the Old City of Jerusalem is the village of Yemin Moshe, rebuilt along the lines of an 1855 village which had attracted the very first American dollar to be invested in the Holy Land.

From Jerusalem, there are three motoring routes: I—Southward Route, II—Westward Route, and III—Eastward Route—all full-day trips.

I. Southward Route from Jerusalem

Leaving Jerusalem, proceed south to **Bethlehem** to view Rachel's Tomb, the birthplace of King David and Jesus, and the home of Ruth. Because of its holiness to Christianity this city has been spared much of the destruction that ravaged other Israeli cities over the centuries. In Bethlehem, also visit the Church of the Nativity and the Milk Grotto.

Six or seven miles south of Bethlehem on the principal road to **Hebron** is Solomon's Pools, a unique bathing resort preserved from biblical times. Back on the main road drive eighteen miles to reach Hebron, the city of Abraham, and one of the oldest villages in the Holy Land, having been inhabited for over 5,000 years. Located in a fertile valley, its winding alleys, vineyards, and bazaars are great tourist attractions. The **Cave of Machpela,** where are buried Abraham, Isaac, and Jacob, and their wives Sarah, Rebecca, and Leah, respectively, is a solemn sight; and the cave itself is resplendent with such marvelous attractions as the ancient wall stones, the Mosque, and the cenotaphs. From Hebron return northward to Jerusalem.

II. Westward Route from Jerusalem

Proceed northward from Jerusalem to reach the important city of **Ramallah,** approximately ten miles away. From Ramallah slowly wind your way west, visiting Arab villages. Ultimately the route leads to the city of **Beit Shemesh** (House of the Sun). Here Samson was born (in Tsoris, one-half mile to the north). Beit Shemesh is also the home of Israel's jet engine factories, an industrial city in a biblical pastoral setting.

Turning eastward on the way back to Jerusalem pass **Beit Gamal** (where there is a fifth-century Byzantine church) and drive through the Valley of Elah, where David killed Goliath, to **Ein Kerem,** where John the Baptist was born and where the Hadassah Medical Center is located.

Herodian is just a few miles from Bethlehem; it is a hilltop fortress where King Herod's body was carried on a bier of solid gold for burial.

III. Eastward Route from Jerusalem

Jericho: The drive from Jerusalem to Jericho is over excellent roads, but in view of the extreme heat in summer make the drive as close to sunrise or to sunset as possible. Jericho is the oldest city in the world—for more than 10,000 years people have resided here. It is situated on a fertile plain 886 feet below sea level. Oranges, bananas, dates, and vegetables are grown in the region. Jericho, during its years under Jordanian control, became a year-round resort, with posh Arab villas and hotels. There are many ancient ruins, including Hisham's Palace, dating back to A.D. 724. A winter palace, it was destroyed by a severe earthquake in 747. Except for some primitive settlements on the site, the building was never reoccupied. Of particular note is the use of human and animal forms as stone motifs. The *ancient* city of Jericho, which was built over by many civilizations, has been unearthed. A Greek Orthodox monastery built near the site of Jesus' baptism is also interesting.

The road south from Jericho toward the Dead Sea passes by the Mosque of **Nebi Musa,** where Moses is believed to be buried.

KOSHER RESTAURANTS

Every restaurant and every hotel in Israel serves kosher food unless designated otherwise.

USEFUL ADDRESSES

Jerusalem: U.S. Consulate, 18 Agron Road (tel. 234271).

Tel Aviv: U.S. Embassy, 71 Hayarkon Street (tel. 654338). Canadian Embassy, 220 Hayarkon Street (tel. 228122).

ITALY

Italy and Greece are probably the only countries in Western Europe in which the settlement of Jews has been continuous from before the Christian era to the present day. Jews first settled in Rome in the second century B.C., both as free men and as slaves. In the next few centuries there were at least forty Jewish settlements in southern Italian ports and along established trade routes. Jews also came to Italy in A.D. 70 when the Diaspora began with the sacking of Palestine by Roman legions. As slaves, they had no privileges and certainly could not practice their religion. The Christianization of the Roman Empire in the fourth century brought death to many Jews, although several popes protected Jews against the worst excesses. There was even a Jewish pope who took a Christian name and served as Pope Anacletus II. His great-grandfather was a pious Jew.

Jews settled before 1600 in such Italian communities as Turin, Milan, Soncino, Cremona (in 1597 over a thousand Jews were expelled), Mantua, Parma, Ferrara, Venice, Genoa (in 1550 all Jews were expelled), Ravenna, Lucca, Pisa, Livorno, Florence, Fano, Ancona, Foligno (where a conference of Italian Jews in 1310 discussed measures to help the persecuted German Jews), Rome, Gaeta, Capua (where in 1000 a Jew was collector of revenues and director of the mint), Naples, Trani (where in 1268 all synagogues were changed into churches), Bari, Lavello, Amalfi, Salerno, Venosa, Matera, Taranto, Oria, Brindisi, and Otranto. On Sicily, Jews lived in Palermo (in 887 the Muslim ruler Ibrahim made Jews wear "the badge of shame"), Catania, Messina, and Syracuse. When Sicily was ruled by the House of Aragon between 1391 and 1474, massacres of Jews were commonplace.

During the Middle Ages and the Renaissance, Jews from Spain and Germany arrived in Italy, and the influx resulted in a thriving Jewish community of wealthy synagogues, rabbinical schools, *yeshivoth,* and printing houses. The great center of Jewish life then was the city of Bari, a trading mecca, until supplanted by Venice. In contrast, 40,000 Jews in Sicily were largely manual laborers until expelled in 1492 by the Spanish. Jewish bankers flourished for a time in Naples, and later, in 1541, many escaped to towns in central and northern Italy. The first Jewish community in Florence dates back to 1437 when Jews were invited to establish loan banks for the poor. Under the protection of the Medici family, Jewry flourished in Florence. But in 1571, the ghetto was instituted, and not until 1860 was there emancipation. From 1899 to 1930 the Collegio Rabbinica Italiano was located in Florence.

The early Jewish settlers in Rome, known as *libertini* or liberated slaves, built their first synagogue near the present Piazzi di Santa Cecilia and the Vicolo di Santa Maria in Cappella. From the earliest days in Rome Jews built synagogues; as many as seventeen synagogues had been erected in Rome by the end of the second half of the first century. Unfortunately, no traces have been found of these ancient synagogues, except for the miraculous findings in 1961 of the remains of a synagogue built in A.D. 400 at Ostia Antica, the ancient part of Rome. In 1555 Pope Paul IV instituted the ghetto in Rome, and other Italian communities followed suit. Italian Judaism entered its decline in the middle of the nineteenth century, as Italian Jews intermarried and assimilated. Leaving small communities they migrated to the metropolitan centers or emigrated to other countries. During the early years of Italian Fascism (1922–1938) Italian Jewry managed to survive; but in 1938 Mussolini adopted an anti-Semitic policy, though less brutal than that of his Nazi allies. Before Nazi occupation came to an end more than 20,000 Italian Jews were massacred. On October 16, 1943, for example, over 2,000 Roman Jews were deported by the Germans and murdered. In September 1943 the Nazi captors demanded from Roman Jewry fifty kilograms of gold within twenty-six hours. The Jews of Rome succeeded in collecting wedding rings, gold coins, and spoons, not only from Jews but from Gentiles to whom they paid exorbitant prices. After the ransom had been paid, on a rainy Saturday the Nazis sealed off the Jewish quarter and rounded up 1,127 Jews in German trucks to be killed at the nearest concentration camp.

Today fewer than 41,000 Jews live in all of Italy—with such wonderfully Italian names as Fano, Tagliacozzo, Polacio, Luzzatto, Luciano, Navarro, Pavia, Valobra, Laras, and Ottolenghi.

ANCONA

On the Via Astagno a seventeenth-century building housed both an Ashkenazi synagogue and a Sephardic synagogue. There is also a small synagogue at Via Fanti 2 (tel. 22-905). In Ancona sixty-three Jews met their death in 1556 for refusing to be baptized; a prayer commemorating their martyrdom is still recited annually in all Italian synagogues. There is evidence of an ancient ghetto off the Via de Bagno.

Today there are 400 Jews in Ancona headed by Chief Rabbi Cesare Tagliacozzo, who resides at Via S. Marcellino 11 (tel. 55-654).

ASTI

French Jews expelled by Charles IV took refuge here in 1322, and were the progenitors of today's small Jewish community of thirty persons. The synagogue at Via Ottolenghi 4 is located on a street named after Asti's distinguished Jewish philanthropist of that name.

BARI

All that remains of the ancient Jewish community of Bari is Strada Synagoga, one of the many local streets.

BOLOGNA

Bologna's small Jewish community of 250 members under the leadership of Ancona's Rabbi Cesare Tagliacozzo has its synagogue on the Via Maria Finzi (tel. 232066); it was built with government funds in 1954 to replace the older synagogue destroyed in World War II. The president is Isaaco Cohen, and the *hazan* (cantor) is Jaacob Malki. The Civic Museum at Portici Del Pavaglione 2 contains Jewish tombstones; the municipal library has Jewish manuscripts of the seventeenth century. One elementary school is named after a young Jewish hero of World War II, Franco Cesena, who died on a commando raid at the age of thirteen. Jewish communal offices are at Via Gombruti 9 (tel. 232066).

BRINDISI

Here the ferries depart for Greece; on Via Giudea are the only remnants of the ancient Jewish community, such as a Hebrew grave marker.

CASALE MONFERRATO

Perhaps Italy's most famous synagogue (an Italian national monument) is found in this small Jewish community. At Vicolo Salomone Olper 44 stands an impressive building built in 1595 and restored in 1866. At one time it was so embellished with art treasures that its fame spread throughout Europe. Although the synagogue was plundered by the Nazis, most religious objects were saved. (Visitations are limited to civil holidays.) President of the synagogue is Dr. Giorgio Ottolenghi (tel. 71807).

FERRARA

The Jewish communal center and synagogue at Via Mazzini 95 (tel. 47004) serves the small Jewish community of fewer than 200 persons who live in Ferrara and the neighboring towns. The synagogue was originally acquired in 1481, and thoroughly rebuilt in the mid-nineteenth century with beautifully paneled walls, candelabra, and ritual objects. The Chief Rabbi is Professor Simone Sacerdoti (tel. 34240), and the president is Marcello Pesaro, Via Borgoleoni 76 (tel. 34173). Ferrara Cathedral has likenesses of Moses, Isaiah, Jeremiah, and Daniel on the columns of its portals. At Via Vignatagliata 33 is the restored residence of the famous Jewish physician and teacher Rabbi Isaac Lampronti (1679–1756).

The Ferrara Jewish cemetery is at Via delle Vigne 2.

FLORENCE

The earliest Jewish settlers in Florence arrived in the year 1430 at the express invitation of Florentine ruling families. It seems that the commercial life of the city then required the services of Jewish moneylenders. Those Jews who accepted the invitation were given full and equal rights, including the right to live in any part of the city. For 140 years Jewish commercial life prospered. Not until 1570 were Jews relegated to a ghetto—the area between Piazza Res Publica and the Piazza del l'Olio. The decree explained that the Jewish moneylenders were breaking the laws, that Jews were fraternizing too much with non-Jews, and therefore Jews must be carefully watched.

In the early eighteenth century, the Church of Santa Croce was built from the plans of a Jewish architect, Niccolo Matas D'Ancona. It was his dying wish to be buried there; this architect also achieved the satisfaction of seeing the Jewish star on the outer facade of this world-famous church; some decades later, a reigning pope decided that the Jewish star must be topped by a Christian cross.

In 1848 the entire ghetto area was demolished to make way for a rebuilding of the city. Florentine Jewry then reached the pinnacle of its fame, and its institutions were known throughout the Jewish world. One outstanding leader of the Florentine Jewish community, David Levi, requested in his will dated March 15, 1868, that his assets be utilized to build "a monumental Temple worthy of Florence." The result was the construction of the majestic synagogue at Via L. C. Farini 4 (tel. 210763). Completed in 1882, its three-tier facade is crowned by a huge dome. Its architecture is Moorish in style; the interior walls are completely covered with priceless frescoes and rich Venetian mosaics. (Rabbi Luciano Caro, tel. 270524.)

The Nazi occupation of Florence decimated the Jewish community. When Allied troops entered the city on August 11, 1944, they found that very few Jews had survived. Extensive damage to the beautiful synagogue was soon repaired. But in November 1966, the Arno River flood caused severe losses: 90 out of 120 Torah scrolls as well as 15,000 books from the ancient library were destroyed. There was water damage to the priceless frescoes, the ornate pews, the prayer books, and the taleisim. With aid from Jews all over the world, the losses are being replaced.

Among the sights of Jewish interest is the Laurenziana Library at Piazza San Lorenzo 9 which houses many Hebrew manuscripts. Jewish cemeteries are at Via di Caciolle 14 and at Via Ludovico Ariosto 14. Outside Florence on the hills of Settignano is the Villa i Tatti where Bernard Berenson, the famous art critic, lived until his death in 1960. Major sights of Jewish interest include:

Baptistery: The pair of bronze doors on the east portal by Ghiberti depict ten episodes of the Old Testament; at the north portal, the three bronze statues by Leonardo da Vinci have Hebrew inscriptions on their garments. **Pitti Palace:** Note the statue of Moses by the sculptor Corradi. **Uffizi Gallery:** A large number of paintings depict Old Testament subjects, including "Esther and Ahasueros" by Veronese. **Academia delle Belli Arti** has the original statue of David by Michelangelo. The fifteen-foot masterpiece stood at the Piazza della Signora until 1873 when it was replaced by a copy. **Martyrs' Memorial:** In the courtyard of the Florence Synagogue is a large marble tablet with the names of 248 Florentine Jews who perished during the Nazi period. On the fountain in the courtyard are the names of twenty-seven soldiers killed during World War I. **Old People's Home:** Via Carducci, dedicated in 1959, replaced the former Casa di Riposo on Via Amendola, whose Jewish residents were deported by the Germans.

GENOA

The hometown of Christopher Columbus has a Jewish community of 700 persons. The Chief Rabbi is Dr. Jehuda Zegdun; the synagogue is located at Via G. Bertora 6 (tel. 891513), and its president is Vittorio Tedeschi, Via Caffaro 12a/7 (tel. 292982). There is a fine Hebrew school at Via Maragliano 3–4 (tel. 591402).

IVREA

Here was born the founder of the Olivetti typewriter and business machines firm, Camillo Olivetti, who died in 1944 and is buried in the local Jewish cemetery at Biella. The local synagogue on Via Palma is headed by Guido Publiese, Via S. Nazario 22 (tel. 40285).

LIVORNO

This busy Tuscan city has a modern synagogue at Piazza Grande, Via del Tempio (tel. 24290); rededicated in 1962, it was first built on the same site in 1602. World War II bombing completely destroyed the synagogue and its Jewish museum. The Italian government contributed perhaps 60 percent of the reconstruction cost.

Jews first came to Livorno at the beginning of the seventeenth century upon the invitation of the Grand Duke of Tuscany. The free port's prosperity worked to the advantage of the Jewish community, and no ghetto was ever instituted. More than 15,000 Jews resided here at the beginning of the nineteenth century. Today Livorno has fewer than 1,000 Jews. Chief Rabbi is Isidoro Kahn, Corso Mazzini 15 (tel. 810265). The president of the synagogue is Luciano Cassuto, Corso Mazzini 15.

Be sure to note the memorial plaque on the wall of the Jewish community center facing the building where Sir Moses Montefiore was born (on Via Reale opposite the Great Synagogue). The Jewish community center is at Via del Lanzi 23.

MANTUA

Mantua has a small Jewish community of 150 persons (including neighboring Bergamo, Brescia, and Cremona) with its synagogue and communal center at Via G. Govi 11 (tel. 21490). The synagogue rests upon the remnants of the Great Synagogue which was demolished in the 1920s. Here are the community archives, housing the records of the Mantuan Jewish community, president of which is Italo Bassani.

MILAN

Ten thousand Jews live in Milan and neighboring Como, Pavia, Sondrio, and Varese. President of the Jewish community is Dr. Marcello Cantori, via Eupili 6 (tel. 389031 or 313354). The Great Synagogue, located at Via Guastalla 19, has the largest membership (Rabbi Professor E. Kopciowski with offices at Via Guastalla 19; tel. 791892). Though leveled to the ground by Allied bombing in 1943, this magnificent building was rebuilt with a choir loft suspended from the ceiling. In contrast to this Sephardic synagogue is the more simply designed Ashkenazi synagogue, Ohel Jacob, at Via Cellini 2 (Rabbi G. H. Garelik). Other synagogues in Milan include Beth Sholomo (Corsi di Porta Romana 63) and the Persian Sephardic Synagogue (Via Sally Mayer 4; tel. 4151660). There is also a New Synagogue (Via Eupili 8), whose *hazan* is Annibale Momigliano; this building also houses the B'nai B'rith office. The B'nai B'rith lodge, Milano No. 1992, had as its president A. Mortara (Piazza Giovine Italia 5).

Via Sabatino Lopez was named in honor of the Jewish playwright, and Via Sally Mayer is in honor of the Jewish industrialist and philanthropist. There is a medieval statue of Moses with horns standing in the Palazzo Arcivescovile. Two Jewish educational institutions are exceptional: "Angelo Donati" Beth Hamidrash at Via Sally Mayer 4—

6 (Rabbi Moshe Lazar), and the Talmud Torah at Via C. Poerio 16. In a modern building with sixty classrooms, two gymnasiums, and eating facilities is the Jewish School of Milan at Via Soderini 16. Dedicated in 1963, it has over 1,000 pupils in all grades. There is a "rest home," Casa Di Reposa, on Via Jomelli 18 (tel. 496331), and also a home for the aged at Via Leone XIII, #1.

MODENA

Angelo Donati, who was responsible for saving the lives of many of his fellow Jews during the Holocaust, resided here. He was the scion of an old Jewish family; his father was a wealthy banker who contributed heavily to the Jewish National Fund. Donati had served in World War I as a French-based liaison officer between the Italian and French air forces, and in 1919 he had settled in Paris. As a banker he amassed a considerable fortune and became the dean of the French diplomatic corps. When the Nazis took Paris, Donati took refuge in Nice and established a refugee base for Jews fleeing the Nazis. When the Vichy police came to arrest the Jewish refugees, Donati "arranged" with the local authorities for Italian soldiers to arrest the Vichy police before the latter could accomplish their mission. In 1943, after Mussolini was overthrown, Donati attempted to arrange transportation for Jewish refugees to North Africa by chartered ships, but he was unsuccessful.

The Modena Synagogue is located at Piazzi Mazzini 26 (tel. 223978); in the front is a memorial to another heroic Italian Jew, Franco Cesena. The Estence Library at Piazza San Agostina has a fine collection of Hebrew manuscripts.

There are 114 Jews in Modena and the Chief Rabbi is Dr. Raffaello Lattes, Via Coltellini 10; president of the Jewish community is Massimiliano Eckert. There is a kosher butcher, Macelleria Duomo, on Via Mercato Coperto (tel. 217269).

NAPLES

The synagogue at Via S. M. a Capella Vecchia 31 (tel. 416-286) is under Chief Rabbi Isidoro Kahn; the building is over 200 years old and is located within a courtyard. President is Dr. Gianfranco Moscati, Via Polizzi 81 (tel. 243554). The Jewish community of 500 persons was first established through the efforts of the Rothschild brothers who lived in Naples during the middle of the nineteenth century. Naples had a unique Jewish platoon, founded in 1948, within the Italian Secret Police for the detection of former Nazis; over 1,000 Nazis were convicted through their efforts. The National Museum has several ancient Jewish tombstones dating back to 14 B.C. The Grand Hotel at Rettifilo 55 observes *kashrut*.

ORIA

In this small town near Brindisi stands the *Porta degli Ebrei* (Gate of the Jews), a reminder of the prosperous Jewish community of the tenth century. Oria was also the home of Sabbatai Ben Abraham Donnolo who was a tenth-century physician and astrologer. Today the square outside the gate is called Piazza Sabbatai Donnolo.

OSTIA

In 1961 during excavations for Rome's Fiumicino Airport, Italian archaeologists unearthed the remains of an ancient and prosperous synagogue. During the fourth century B.C., Ostia was Rome's great trading port and naval base, and had 100,000 inhabitants.

The synagogue was built in the fourth century A.D. upon the remains of an earlier, first-century synagogue, and stood on the outskirts of Ostia between the sea and the Via Severiana. The entrance door faced east toward Jerusalem, and led into a large vestibule. Ahead were three large doors, behind which was the synagogue proper. In the middle of this large hall there were four marble Corinthian columns, and at the far end stood the *bima.* On the left of the four columns and facing the *bima* was the Holy Ark, made of bricks. Two small columns stood in front of the Holy Ark, and on these columns were engraved a seven-branch menorah, a *shofar,* and a *lulav* and *esrog.*

PADUA

The Jewish community center and synagogue in Padua is located at Via S. Martino e Solferino 5 (tel. 23524), and dates back to 1548. Its interior is most unusual in that the Ark rests against the long wall and the *bima* faces it from the opposite long wall. Little remains of the ancient ghetto of Padua, off Via Daniele Manin. The Jewish cemetery on Via Zodio dates to the seventeenth century. The University of Padua is noted as one of the first European universities open to Jews. Two hundred Jews live in Padua, and the Chief Rabbi is Shimon Achille Viterbo (Via B. Pellegrino 96; tel. 30476). President of the Jewish community is Vittorio Sacerdoti, Via Barzon 6.

PISA

A beautiful synagogue, built in 1595 (Via Palestro 24, near the Teatro Verdi), is maintained by the small Jewish community. There are about 200 Jews in Pisa (including neighboring Lucca and Viareggio). The Chief Rabbi is Dr. Ariel Toaff, and the president is Guido De Cori (tel. 27269).

PITIGLIANO

Sixty miles north of Rome is the village of Pitigliano where a small seventeenth-century synagogue was reopened to the public in 1964.

REGGIO EMILIA

The local synagogue at Via Monzermone 4 serves the small community. The Temple of Via dell Aquila, built about 1870, was destroyed by the Nazis during World War II; the few surviving remnants were transferred in 1948 to Temple Kyriat Shemuel near Haifa, Israel.

ROME

Rome has approximately 16,000 Jews including those in the neighboring towns of Aquila, Cagliari, Chieti, Frosinone, Nevoro, Perugia, Pescara, Rieti, Sassari, Teramo, Terni, and Viterbo. The imposing Orthodox synagogue, Tempio Israelitico, at Lungotevere Cenci 9 (tel. 655051) was built in 1900 and houses an excellent Jewish museum with a collection of memorabilia from the 2,000 years of Jewish history in Italy. Other Orthodox Ashkenazi synagogues may be found at Via Balbo 33 (tel. 479881) and at Via Agostino de Pretis 77; the Spanish Temple is at Via Catalana. There is a synagogue at the local hospital on Via della Borgata della Magiana (tel. 5232634), and also at the Polacco School at Lungotevere Sanzio 12 (tel. 5803668). The Chief Rabbi of Rome is Rabbi Elio Toaff at Via Catalana 1 (tel. 655-219). The president of the Roman Jewish community is Fernando Piperno.

The Jewish history of Rome began in the year 139 B.C., when Simon the Maccabee sent a delegation to renew the friendship pact between Judea and Rome. Thereafter the first Jewish tradesmen and money-changers settled in Rome. Their number increased considerably in 61 B.C., when Pompey sent many Jewish prisoners to Rome to be sold as slaves; and in A.D. 70, when Emperor Titus destroyed the Jewish state and dispersed its inhabitants, more Jews came to Rome. The earliest Jewish inhabitants are believed to have settled on the right bank of the Tiber (Trastevere). Later, other Jews settled along the Appian Way, on the Esquilinus and the Aventinus hills. While the Roman Empire flourished, Jews enjoyed a certain degree of civil and religious freedom. Their number reached 40,000, grouped around ten or more communities *(collegia)* spread across the town, each with its synagogue and cemetery.

Four Jewish catacombs have been discovered along the Appian, Nomentana, Labicana, and Portuense roads. The last of these contains the remains of the Jews of Trastevere, and is probably the most ancient Jewish cemetery so far discovered in Italy. A large collection of first- to sixth-century gravestones from the catacombs, with Jewish symbols and inscriptions in Greek, Latin, and Hebrew, can be seen in the Sala Judaica at the Vatican Museum. They provide precious documentation of the civil and religious life of the first Jewish settlers in Rome.

The ancient ghetto in Rome was established by Pope Paul IV in 1556 beside the left bank of the Tiber River (between the Roman Forum and the Trastevere section of ancient Rome). Its maze of narrow alleys, however, dates back to the early days of the Roman Empire. Jews were confined to this walled area under rigid curfews until 1847. Within the confines of the ghetto today still live 300 to 400 Jews. One ghetto resident was Lorenzo Da Ponte, who under his own Jewish name, Emanuele Conegliano, wrote the librettos for Mozart's *Marriage of Figaro, Don Giovanni,* and *Così Fan Tutte.*

Another distinguished Roman Jew was Ernesto Nathan, born in London but the first Jewish mayor of Rome (1907–1913); he was also a ghetto resident.

Many Roman names suggest Jewish origins and Jewish traditions: Piazza della Azzimelle, for instance, takes its name from the ovens where Passover *matzoh* were prepared. Via Catalana was so called because it was inhabited by families descended from Jewish refugees from the Spanish Inquisition. Piazza delle Cinque Scuole recalls the great building housing five synagogues, and the Hotel della Catena derives its name from the chains used to close the ghetto. Piazza Navona was once an agonizing place for Jews; during the fifteenth and sixteenth centuries it was customary at carnival time to force half-naked Jews to race around the Piazza Navona to the accompaniment of jeers and beatings by the populace. Among the ruins nearby is the Church of Sant' Angelo in Pescheria, where ghetto Jews were forced to listen to sermons for their conversion. Close by is the Church of Santa Maria delle Pianto, so called because of the lament of Christians who did not succeed in converting the Jews. Engraved on its facade in Latin and Hebrew are verses 2 and 3 of Chapter 65 of Isaiah, meant to be a perennial Christian reproach to Jewish stubbornness: "I have spread out My hands all day unto a rebellious people, that walketh in a way that is not good, after their own thoughts; a people that provoketh me to anger continually. . . ." In front of the church is Piazza Giudia, or Jewish Square.

A monument, Fosse Ardeatine, just outside the Porta San Paolo, is dedicated to the memory of the 335 Jewish and Christian citizens of Rome who were massacred by the Nazis in 1944. The Arch of Titus has a solemn meaning for Jewry: it was built to commemorate the Roman victory over Jerusalem in the year 70.

The interior of the arch depicts Jewish captives bearing the spoils of the Temple—the menorah and the silver trumpets. For centuries,

Jews were forbidden to walk under the arch, but in 1944, upon the liberation of Rome from fascism, the Jewish Brigade marched under it. The Capitoline Museum contains a number of Jewish items and the Lateran Museum has a Jewish Room. Michelangelo's "Moses" is located in the Church of San Pietro in Vincoli. (This statue was designed to be the centerpiece of an unfinished tomb which Michelangelo was ordered to make for Pope Julius II. The overwhelming figure of Moses is flanked on the left by Rachel, symbol of meditative life, and on the right by Leah, symbol of the active life. The horns on Moses stem from an incorrect translation from Exodus 34:35 in which the Hebrew word *keren* is rendered "horn" instead of "ray of light.")

On an island in the Tiber River, near the ancient ghetto, is the Jewish Hospital and Home for the Aged. Jew's Bridge, the oldest in Rome, connects the island to the city. In the Villa Borghese is a beautiful statue of David by Bernini, created when the sculptor was only sixteen years of age. One of Marc Chagall's stained-glass panels is to be found in the Vatican Audience Hall. The Sistine Chapel has frescoes representing the life of Moses, and on the ceiling are Michelangelo's framed biblical scenes. In St. Peter's is a marble column (to the right of the Pietà Chapel) believed to have come from the Temple of Solomon.

Other worthwhile sights of Jewish interest in Rome include the Mamertine Prison in the Forum, which goes back to ancient times; the prison is below street level. An inscription records the names of famous captives, including Peter and Paul and the Jewish King Aristobulus II. The last name is that of Simon Bar Giora, the general who defended Jerusalem in A.D. 70. Also of interest is the rabbinical college, housed in a building on the Lungotevere Sanzio, dedicated in 1964.

Two of the Jewish-owned hotels in Rome are the Hotel Napoleon, Piazza V. Emanuele 105 (tel. 737646); and the Hotel Delle Muse, Via Tommaso Salvini. Kosher butchers are Fratelli Terracina, Via Portico d'Ottavia 1B (tel. 6541364); Tammam, Via Filippo Turati 110 (tel. 733358); Massari, Piazza Bologna 11 (tel. 429-120); Buhnik, Via Urbana 117 (tel. 487743); and Habib, Tripolitania 105.

SANNICANDRO

Sannicandro is a small town in southern Italy where, in 1932, twenty-three peasant families adopted Judaism. The spontaneous conversion resulted from a vision of a local winegrower, Donato Manduzio, in which he was told to return to the faith of Moses. In face of opposition from the local clergy, government officials, and even the Rome rabbinate, his disciples accepted Judaism. In 1949 the group settled in Israel, and was soon dispersed throughout the country.

SARDINIA

Jews lived on the island of Sardinia for centuries until their expulsion in 1492. The Church of Santa Croce in the city of Cagliari was built on the site of a synagogue as was the Church of the Trinity in Sassari.

SICILY

Although only a few Jews now live in Messina and Palermo, there is a long and varied history of Jewish settlement here. Jews first came to Sicily in the first and second centuries. By the late Middle Ages there were 40,000 Jews. When Spain captured Sicily in 1282, Jews were massacred along with other inhabitants. The Spanish Inquisition began here in 1474 and by 1492 all Jews had been expelled.

SIENA

Jews have lived here since the beginning of the thirteenth century. Jewish loan-bankers became wealthy in Siena, and it became a center of Jewish scholarship in the sixteenth century through the lavish support of Ishmael da Rieti. In 1571 a ghetto was established and Jewish life deteriorated. The synagogue, located at Via delle Scotte 14 (tel. 284647) dates back to the Middle Ages, and is the proud possession of the local Jewish community. The interior marble columns were brought from Jerusalem, its walnut circumcision chair is elaborately carved, and its Ark doors bear the ax scars of eighteenth-century plunderings. (Unfortunately, the synagogue is open only on Saturdays and holidays.) The *hazan* is Dr. Guiseppe Lattes, and the community leader is Dr. Enzo Franco, Via Belvedere 28 (tel. 287590).

SPEZIA

The local synagogue is at Via Settembre 165, as is the Talmud Torah school.

TRIESTE

There are fewer than 1,200 Jews in Trieste where Chief Rabbi Elia Richetti (tel. 631898) and community president Dr. Mario Stock, Via Torino 34 (tel. 77573) are the leaders. (Community headquarters are at Via San Francesco 19; tel. 768171.) Before World War II there were 6,000 Jews in Trieste; by 1945 the Jewish population was only 780 persons. Trieste Jewry are proud of their beautiful Ashkenazi synagogue, Il Tempio Israelitico di Trieste, at Via Donizetti 2. In the center of town, it has a Moorish tower, a Byzantine interior, and Gothic windows. Erected between 1908 and 1912, the synagogue is essentially a Byzantine-style basilica with four marble pillars which hold up the central cupola. This truly magnificent edifice was the creation of the noted architects Ruggero and Arduino Berlam.

There is a small Ashkenazi synagogue at Via del Monte 7. Also see the old Jewish "quarters" at Piazza San Francisco d' Assisi. Visit Risiera di San Saba, site of the Nazi concentration camp and now a national monument to Italian Jews and Resistance fighters killed by the Nazis. Among the famous Jews of Trieste is the great Hebrew educator Samuel David Luzzatto (1800–1865). Trieste Jewry have distinguished records in the fields of medicine, law, and insurance.

TURIN

The two synagogues for the city's 1,600 Jews are at Via San Pio Quinto 12 (tel. 682387) and Via Pietro Giuria 26 (tel. 689781). The former, built in 1834, has a seating capacity of 1,500 men and 500 women; though substantially destroyed by World War II bombing, it was rebuilt by the Jewish community and the Italian government. Turin's Eiffel Tower, the Mole Antonelliana, was begun in 1863 as a synagogue, and then turned over to the municipality, which completed the 620-foot tower in 1897 and dedicated it to the memory of King Victor Emmanuel II. Cesare Lombroso (1835–1909), the famous Jewish professor of psychiatry and medical jurisprudence at the University of Turin, has a memorial and street named after him. Chief Rabbi of Turin is Sergio J. Sierra (tel. 682-387), and the president is Emilio Bacchi. There is a kosher butcher, Luigi Nada, Via XX Setiembre 2 (tel. 543312).

URBINO

Urbino, near the Adriatic coast of Italy, is an Italian hill town with interesting Jewish antecedents. The families of the Coens and the Moscatis keep Judaism alive today. The local synagogue is at Via Stretta.

VENICE

Although Jews have lived in the territories of the Republic of Venice since the first century, Jews did not come to Venice until 1090. When the city allowed Jews to change and lend money at a fixed interest rate in 1366, the basis for a flourishing community was established for approximately 1,300 Jews on the island of Giudecca. By the second half of the thirteenth century Jews had built two synagogues of which unfortunately there is no trace today. Later Jews were restricted in trade; they were forbidden to trade with Christians, and could practice no profession other than medicine. In the year 1288 Venetian Jews were banished to the town of Maestre on the mainland, and for the next 200 years Venice had no Jews. The term *ghetto,* however, was applied to the nearby villages of Mogliano and Chirignago where Jews dwelt. But Jews returned to Venice and settled in the central sections of Rialto, San Silvestro, and San Aponal. They were forced to wear identification badges: first, a yellow "O" on their chests, then a yellow cap, and finally a red cap. On March 20, 1516, all Jews were confined to Venice's first ghetto, an area near San Girolamo. Not until 1866, when Venice was united with Italy, did the gates of the ghetto truly open.

At the beginning of the sixteenth century, when a wave of persecution forced Jews all over Europe to seek refuge in areas that would tolerate them, Venice, then at the height of its splendor, proved to be such a place. Thomas Coryat, a sixteenth-century English traveler, wrote this description of the Venetian Jew: "I observed some few of those Jews, especially some of the Levantines, to be such goodly and proper men . . . most elegant and sweet-featured persons, which gave me occasion the more to lament their religion."

Since the fifteenth century, the Jewish community of Venice has been a melting pot. The first to arrive were those fleeing from the Spanish Inquisition. They were followed by others from Central Europe, and by Jews from other parts of Italy. From its glorious peak in the sixteenth century, when the arts and sciences blossomed and most of the financial activities of the republic were transacted there, the ghetto declined to an isolated area of extreme poverty, until all Italian ghettos were opened in the nineteenth century. The ghetto was built around three nuclei: the "New Ghetto," assigned in 1516 to Jews of German and Italian origin; the "Old Ghetto," assigned in 1541 to the Spanish and Levantine community; and the "Very New Ghetto," which was added in 1603.

Venice today has 770 Jews; its acting Chief Rabbi is Dr. Manahem Emanuele Artom. President of the community is Giorgio Voghera (tel. 715012). Only one synagogue, the Scuole Spagnola, or Spanish Synagogue, on Via Cannaregio, is open daily for religious services. The Scuole Spagnola was founded in 1555 by Marrano fugitives; the building was restored in 1635 by the famous Venetian architect Baldassare Longhena. Surviving are three other beautiful synagogues built between 1415 and 1700: two German, the Scuole Grande Tedesca and the Scuole Canton, which date back to 1529 and 1531, respectively, and are located in the Ghetto Nuovo area; and the Scuole Levantine, which was founded in 1575. Unlike synagogues elsewhere, synagogues in Venice are scarcely noticeable from the outside, but they are richly adorned on the inside. The true prayer hall is on the 2nd floor, never on the ground floor, which is reserved for meetings or as a waiting room; there is always a women's gallery, elliptical in shape.

Principal Jewish areas in Venice are still the Ghetto Vecchio and Ghetto Nuovo (not far from the railroad station) where, in addition to the synagogues, one will find a Jewish rest home, Casa Israelitico di Reposa, which also houses a kosher restaurant (tel. 716002). The Jewish Museum is located in the Old Tedesca Synagogue. There is a kosher butcher, De Sanzuane on S. Luca (tel. 24658).

Venice's Jewish cemetery at San Nicolo (Via Cipro and Riviera) on the Lido dates back to 1386, and its seventeenth-century vertical tombstones have particularly interesting Hebrew inscriptions. The earliest graves bear distinguishing symbols such as the blessing hands of the Cohen family, the jug and basin of the Levi family, candelabras, or animals. Also on the Lido is the New Cemetery dating from the eighteenth century.

Many fine paintings of Jewish themes may be found in the Academy of Fine Arts, Basilica of Santa Maria della Salvte, and in the Doges' Palace. Ca D'Oro, or Franchetti Gallery, was a gift to Venice by a prominent Jewish family.

VENOSA

In this southern town are located Jewish catacombs of great historical importance. The Venosa catacombs—both Jewish and Christian—lie abandoned on a hillside in open country. Sheep graze nearby and people can easily enter and pick up archaeological "treasures" to carry away. Recently the Union of Italian Jewish Communities lodged a protest with the local supervising agency for historical sites in Potenza, after swastika graffiti were discovered on the catacomb walls. Vandalism dates back centuries, ever since the tombstones were discovered behind the wall of an incomplete basilica in Venosa that stands roofless under the sky.

The Hebrew tombstone inscriptions show the different origins and lesser degree of assimilation of these Jews as compared to those who settled in Rome, where catacomb inscriptions are almost exclusively in Latin and Greek. The inscriptions also reveal that this southern community was well integrated in local society, producing a high percentage of doctors, writers, prominent landowners, and members of the city administration. Further proof of their having lived on excellent terms with their Christian and pagan neighbors is shown by the fact that the main entrances of the Jewish and Christian catacombs are only a few feet apart.

VIAREGGIO

At the end of a narrow dead-end street (behind a hospital) stands the local synagogue at Via degli Oleandri 30. The community leader is Attilio Orvieto, Via de Martiri Di S. Terenzio 18 (tel. 41844).

Kosher meals are available at Via Leopardi 4 on the Lido, and at the Plaza Hotel and Principe di Piemonte Hotel.

There are Jewish communities in the following other cities, towns, and villages of Italy:

Alessandria: Chief Rabbi Dr. Ruggero Coen; local synagogue at Via Milano 5–7 (tel. 62-224). President is Angelo Vitale.

Carmagnola: Local synagogue at Via Domenico Berti.

Cherasco: Local synagogue at Corso Marconi; community leader is Roberto Segre.

Cuneo: Local synagogue at Via Mondovi 21; community leader is Riccardo Cavaglion, Corso Dane 55 (tel. 2090).

Gorizia: The local synagogue is at Via Ascoli 13.

La Spezia: Synagogue at Via Settembre 165. The *hazan* is Adolfo Croccolo, Via 20 Settembre 200 (tel. 31728), and the community leader is Alberto Funaro, Via R. Migliari 32 (tel. 28-504).

Lucca: The Jewish community leader is Eugenio Gennazzani, Via dei Garofani B (tel. 56-766).

Merano: Local synagogue at Via Schiller 14 (tel. 23-127). President is Dr. Federico Steinhaus, Corso Liberta 14 (tel. 24520).

Mondovi: Local synagogue at Via Vico, Mondovi Piazza; community leader is Marco Levi, Corso Statuto 27 (tel. 2555).

Parma: Local synagogue at Vicolo Cervi 4; president is Fausto Levi, Via Fonderie 5.

Pescara: About 220 miles southeast of Rome is this seaside resort of 110,000 Italians. Here Gianpaolo Coen owns a large rug and fabric store, Coen and Pieroni, and is the only Jew in town.

Saluzzo: Local synagogue at Via Deportati Ebrei; the local leader is Vittorio Segre, Via Bodoni 59 (tel. 13026).

Senigallia: Local synagogue at Via Dei Commercianti. See Amos Zuares.

Udine: Local leader is Roberto Gentili, Via S. Martino 28 (tel. 24-502).

Vercelli: Local synagogue at Via Foa; office at Via Morosone 19.

Verona: Chief Rabbi Emanuele Weiss Levi; local synagogue at Via Rita Rosani, and community center at Via Protici 3 (tel. 21-112), headed by Carlo Rimini.

KOSHER RESTAURANTS

Florence: Restaurant Servi, first floor, Via L. C. Farini 2a (tel. 210670).

Milan: Eshel Israel, Via Benevenuto Cellini 2 (tel. 708877); Hotel Liberty, Traversa 14, in Milano-Marittima (tel. 991-281).

Naples: Grand Hotel, Rettifilo 55 (tel. 315-115).

Palermo: Villa Iglea has a kosher restaurant (tel. 29-1580).

Riccone: Lido-Mediterraneo Hotel.

Rimini: Grand Hotel and Residencia (operated by the Arspesella family).

Rome: In the old ghetto area of Rome are kosher restaurants Piperno a Monte Cenci, Giggetto, and Carciofi alla Giudia, which feature artichokes—Jewish style, fried in olive oil—a Roman cheesecake, and fried fish fillet. The Jews of Rome have lived in Italy for 2,000 years, and they are as genuinely Jewish as they are Italian, for they enjoy their *poppettone di tacchino* (stuffed turkey breast) to traditionally conclude the Yom Kippur fast, and *ruota di faraone* (a wheel of noodles and salami) to symbolize Pharaoh's sealed fate) at the Seder.
Other kosher restaurants include Luciano's Zion at Via Portico d'Ottavia 16 (tel. 6569809); Tenenbaum's at Via Cavour 226 (tel. 474-479); and Pension Carmel Bachbouth, Via Gioffredo Mameli 11 (tel. 580-9921).

Trieste: Casa Centilomo at Via Cologna 29 (tel. 95145).

Venice: Jewish Rest Home, Ghetto Nuovo 2874 (tel. 716002); Hotel Pigalle, Via Padova, Lido di Jesolo (tel. 91-617).

Viareggio: Ristorante, Via Leopardi 4 (also Principe di Piemonte Hotel).

USEFUL ADDRESSES

Rome: U.S. Embassy, Via Veneto 119 (tel. 4674).
Canadian Embassy, Via G. B. de Rossi 27, 00161 (tel. 855341).
Israeli Embassy, Via Michele Marcati 12 (tel. 874541).

JAMAICA

Portuguese Marranos (secret Jews) lived in Jamaica prior to 1655 when England invaded the island and took over from the Spanish. Some scholars even trace Jewish beginnings on Jamaica to the year 1530 and believe that Spanish Governor de Cordova, who ruled Jamaica in the 1590s, was a Marrano. History reports that a local Marrano pilot, Captain Campoe Sabbatha, guided the British fleet under Admiral Penn (and General Venables) into Kingston harbor on May 16, 1655. Another Marrano named Acosta superintended the commissary for British troops, having previously served as chief negotiator of the Spanish surrender in 1655.

The early Jewish settlers were joined in 1680 by other Jews who had fled Recife, Brazil, when the Portuguese captured that port. Jamaica had opened its doors to Jewish victims from the Spanish Inquisition at the end of the fifteenth century. Actually it was an Amsterdam Jew, Simon de Caceres, who advised Oliver Cromwell in his West Indian projects, and so after the British occupation, Jews were able to practice their religion openly in Jamaica. By 1735 there were 800 Jews on Jamaica, living in Port Royal, Spanish Town, Montego Bay, and Kingston, in all of which they built Sephardic synagogues. In the eighteenth century these Jews were joined by other Sephardic Jews and later by Ashkenazi Jews from England and Europe.

Jamaican Jews quickly integrated themselves into the life of the island, particularly in the field of commerce. Among the many Jews in the sugar and vanilla industry was Abraham Gomez Henriques (died 1673) who owned 3,000 acres of land.

The earliest Jamaican synagogue at Port Royal was buit in 1676 and destroyed during the earthquake of 1692. The rebuilt synagogue, as well as two other synagogues in Spanish Town, was later destroyed by a disastrous fire in 1815. These Spanish Town synagogues were again rebuilt and in 1844 were amalgamated into one synagogue which continued to operate in Spanish Town until 1884. Today there are about 350 Jamaican Jews.

KINGSTON

The only Jamaican synagogue now in existence, United Congregation of Israelites—Shaare Shalom—is in Kingston, at the corner of

Duke and Charles Streets. No rabbi serves the congregation today. The congregation is Progressive, being based on a Sephardic ritual with a number of its own individualistic traditions. In May 1971, the Ashkenazi and Sephardic congregations legally merged to form the United Congregation of Israelites in Jamaica. Shaare Shalom Synagogue seats 600 worshipers, and the edifice is made of reinforced concrete; the facade is in the Spanish Colonial style. The *hechal* (ark) and the *bima* (reader's platform) are in polished mahogany; both are adorned by eight magnificent brass candlesticks which were donated in 1793, and they have blue Wilton carpets with a yellow *Magen David* design on the floor. The Ark contains thirteen scrolls, some of which are more than 200 years old and were originally housed in other synagogues on the island. An unusual feature of the synagogue is the sand strewn over the floor. (Sephardic synagogues in Amsterdam, Curaçao, Panama, and the Virgin Islands also follow this practice.) Some explain this custom as a reminder of the sand which covered the floor of the original Tabernacle in the desert. To others, it represents the blessing of God to the Patriarchs that their descendants would be numerous "as the sand on the seashore." Less poetic is the fact that it deadens sounds on the wooden floor. The synagogue houses many relics of seventeenth-century Jewish life, including the lifetime work of Jacob Andrade whose Jamaican family goes back more than 300 years, and who wrote *A Record of the Jews in Jamaica from the English Conquest to the Present Time* (published in 1941). Andrade's monumental book also describes the lives of early Jewish plantation owners such as Alexandre Bravo (1797–1868), the first Jew elected to the Jamaican Assembly in 1837; Sir Alfred d'Costa, the first developer of Jamaican bauxite whose memory is preserved by a plaque erected by the Reynolds Aluminum Company near Crescent Park, twelve miles east of St. Ann's Bay; and Daniel Hart, the first Jamaican to free his slaves before slavery was outlawed in 1834.

In 1969, a private primary school, Hillel Academy (51 Upper Mark Way Ken 8) was established in Kingston, but only 10 percent of the pupils were Jewish. Among the students was the Prime Minister's daughter. The Jewish pupils receive full-time instruction in Hebrew and Jewish religion, but this is not compulsory for the other pupils; some of the teachers are Jewish, members of old Sephardic families who were among the early settlers on the island. (The old school building at 11A Oxford Road houses the Home for the Jewish Aged.)

Kingston also has a Jewish Institute at 31 Charles Street (tel. 25931), adjacent to the synagogue.

Streets in Kingston named after prominent Jamaican Jews include Ashenheim Avenue, Carvalho Drive, d'Aguilar Road, Fernandez

Avenue, Lindo Street, Hart Street, Levy Road, Lopez Street, Myers Road, Nathan Street, and Penso Street. Jewish businesses include House of Myers rum and the daily newspaper *Kingston Daily Gleaner* (founded in 1834). Ernest H. DeSouza, 2A Kings Drive in Kingston (tel. 927-7948) is the current leader of Jamaican Jewry.

There are five cemeteries in Kingston where Jewish dead have been buried: Church and North Streets, southeast and southwest corners (1716–1872 and 1788–1795); Elletsen Road near Windward Road (1798–1882); Orange Street and Calabar Road (1822 to the present); and Windward Road near Elletsen (1872–1913).

Jamaican Jewry have played an active role in government since their emancipation in 1831. As early as 1849, only eighteen years after Jews had achieved full civil rights, eight out of the forty-seven members of the Jamaica House of Assembly were Jews; in 1866 there were thirteen Jewish members. Indeed, Jamaica's Jews had the distinction of being the first British subjects of their faith to gain complete political equality, twenty-seven years before the same equality was granted in England. Jews and Catholics who had been barred from voting or holding public office—privileges reserved for Anglicans—also attained full rights of Jamaican citizenship in 1831. The prime mover in the effort to abolish the civil disabilities was Moses Delgado, a descendant of Jamaica's first Jewish settlers.

In August 1972 Jamaican Jews, together with all Jamaicans, celebrated the tenth anniversary of Jamaica's independence. But the Jews had a special reason to be proud, for presiding over the celebration was the Jewish mayor of Kingston and St. Andrew, Senator Eli Matalon. On October 20, 1975, Jamaica's Prime Minister, Michael Manley, awarded Hon. Eli Matalon, then Minister of National Security and Justice, the Order of Jamaica for outstanding public service to his country "beyond the call of duty." One of Kingston's most interesting Jewish personalities was Myer Lyon ("Leoni") who had been cantor in London's Ashkenazi Great Synagogue and a singer at Covent Garden Opera. In 1789 he came to Kingston to become the first cantor of the newly organized English and German Jews' Congregation. Leoni is remembered as the adapter of the Slavic melody to the ancient Hebrew hymn "Yigdal." In 1770 a Methodist minister, Rev. Thomas Olivers, attended a Sabbath service in London's Great Synagogue; moved by Leoni's chanting of "Yigdal," Olivers had him write down the melody, to which Olivers wrote the English text, "The God of Abraham Praise," which is in most Christian hymnals today.

The new Glynbourne Opera House in Kingston was officially opened in December 1970; its benefactor was the famous Jewish patroness of the arts Roma Presano Doyen-Fitchett.

MONTEGO BAY

Montego Bay on the north shore has a small Jewish community which meets in the homes of its members. (Rabbi Martin Pinto presides.) All that remains of an 1844 synagogue, Congregation Beth Ya'akob, destroyed by a 1912 hurricane, is the flight of stone steps at 36 Market Street, opposite the Presbyterian church. There are Jewish cemeteries in Montego Bay at Union Street (next to a Catholic Church) and at Falmouth Road (near the racecourse). Both Corinaldi Avenue and Hart Street are named after prominent Jamaican Jews. The Abraham Hart House (at Market and Harbour Streets) is the gabled clapboard office and residence of the noted Jewish merchant and founder of the Montego Bay Jewish community (1812–1875).

SPANISH TOWN

At Hunt's Bay in Spanish Town is the oldest Jewish cemetery on Jamaica with gravestones dating back more than 300 years. The earliest decipherable grave, of Abraham Gabay, goes back to 1672, and there are others dated 1677 and 1678. Many of the tombstones carry inscriptions in Hebrew, English, and Portuguese. Some have the rose and hourglass, others a tree being cut down by a hand bearing an ax, and others a skull and crossbones. Predominantly a Sephardic cemetery, nevertheless a few Ashkenazim were buried there, including a merchant born in Hamburg, Salomon Levy, who died in 1690.

There are a number of other Jewish cemeteries on the island, and the present synagogue gardens in Kingston contain a number of interesting gravestones which have been transferred from old cemetery sites.

USEFUL ADDRESSES

Kingston: U.S. Embassy, 2 Oxford Road (tel. 929-4850).
Israeli Embassy, 60 Knutsford Boulevard (tel. 926-8768 or 926-8875).

JAPAN

Although it is legendary to associate the Japanese people with the Lost Ten Tribes of Israel, Jewish settlement in Japan accurately dates back only to the middle of the nineteenth century. Jewish silk merchants probably crossed from Korea in the second century A.D. but did not stay. The first Jewish settlements in Japan were in Yokohama, Nagasaki, and Kobe in 1861, and included about fifty Jewish families, mostly Russian, all in trade and commerce. In 1894, a Jewish community was established in Nagasaki; a synagogue and cemetery came into existence, and within ten years the community numbered about 100 persons. After the Russo-Japanese War, Kobe became the center of Jewish life; many captured Czarist soldiers of the Jewish faith were released and settled in Japan, marrying Russian women who joined them. During the first decade of the twentieth century, Kobe Jewry helped one thousand Russian Jews migrate through Japan to the United States and other countries.

After World War I Russian Jewish refugees settled in Manchuria and other parts of China. Perhaps 5,000 came to Yokohama as transients on their way to the United States and other countries. Some Russian Jews settled in Tokyo. In the 1920s the presence of several thousand Jews in Japan prompted the Western-style of anti-Semitism: the infamous "Protocols of Zion" was distributed among the foreign population.

World War II brought refugees from Germany and Poland streaming into Japan from the Russian port of Vladivostok. More than 1,000 German Jews settled temporarily in Kobe, as did more than 3,500 Polish and Lithuanian Jews. Although 2,000 Jews remained in Japan during World War II (and were decently treated by the government), a similar number were moved by the Japanese government to Shanghai, where they joined other refugees from all over the world.

During American occupation of Japan (1945–1952), many American Jews settled in Japan. After the Communist take-over of China in 1949, Jews from Harbin, Tensiang, and Shanghai entered Japan. The Kobe Jewish community was reorganized, and in 1953 the Japanese government officially recognized the Jewish community of Tokyo. In the same year the Jewish Community Center in Tokyo was ceremoniously opened by the brother of the former Emperor of Japan. Today about 400 Jews reside in Japan, mostly Israelis.

The *New York Times* (May 19, 1979) carried a fascinating story describing Japanese plans (before the 1941 attack upon Pearl Harbor) for rescuing European Jews from the hands of the Nazis. According to secret documents of the Japanese Foreign Ministry the Japanese planned to enlist the skills and financial resources of persecuted Jews in Europe to establish in Manchuria an *Israel in Asia* to strengthen Japan's Greater East Asia Co-Prosperity Sphere. Devised in 1934 and known as the "Fugu Plan," it invited 50,000 German Jews as a vanguard for millions of other Jews. These Jews were to turn the Manchurian wilderness into a buffer state against the Soviet Union and to attract American sympathy and investments. The plan's name derived from the *fugu*—a blowfish containing a poison that must be removed before the fish can be eaten. In a book entitled *The Fugu Plan: The Untold Story of the Japanese and the Jews During World War II,* authors Rabbi Marvin Tokayer and Mary Sagmaster Swartz pointed out that advocates of the Fugu Plan had exaggerated ideas of Jewish wealth and influence. They refer to a ninety-page secret document, titled *The Study and Analysis of Introducing Jewish Capital,* which spoke of "a truly peaceful land so that the Jews may be comfortably settled to engage in business at ease forever." Secret documents disclosed that a top-level Japanese Cabinet meeting was held in December 1938 at which Finance and Commerce Minister Seishin Ikeda explained the broad aims of the Fugu Plan in these words: "Dangerous or not, we need the Jews. The settlers themselves will be an asset to Manchukuo and Japan. . . . Even more important, their settlement will encourage other Jews to release capital we cannot get any other way. By simply welcoming these beleaguered Europeans, we will gain the affection of the American Jews who control the press, the broadcast media, the film industry and possibly President Roosevelt himself. We cannot afford to alienate the Jews. If Japan imitates Germany's severe control of the Jews, discrimination will develop in connection with our foreign trade. On the other hand, if Japan goes in the opposite direction and befriends the Jews, entirely new economic possibilities will be open to us."

Early in 1940, Mitsuzo Tamura, a Japanese steel-container manufacturer and a strong advocate of the Fugu Plan, visited Rabbi Stephen S. Wise in New York at the request of Lew Zikman, a Jewish industrialist in Manchuria. But Rabbi Wise, president of the World Jewish Congress, offered him no encouragement, citing Japan's militarism and mistreatment of conquered people. Later, in June 1940, Rabbi Wise indicated to Jewish leaders in Tokyo that he might consider the Japanese settlement plan if the State Department approved. But the war in Europe and growing tensions between Japan and the United States ruled out such a possibility.

KOBE

In Kobe, Japan's largest port, there is a small Jewish community of twenty families, mostly refugees from India and Syria. In 1971, an ancient Persian torah was presented by the International Synagogue of New York's Kennedy Airport, to the Ohel Shlomo Synagogue of Kobe. For information on the Kobe Jewish community, call Victor Moche (tel. 222872 or 333730), or write to Jack Gotlieb, Box 841, Kobe, Japan. The Jewish community center is located at 66/1 Kitano-Cho 4-chome Ikuta-Ku (tel. 078-221-7236).

During World War II a Hassidic rebbe, loved and admired by the Jewish refugees in Kobe, was summoned for an interrogation by militaristic Japanese naval officers apparently greatly influenced by Hitlerian racial theories. Medals glistening, their uniforms sharply creased, the officers confronted the rebbe and posed one question: "Why do the Germans hate the Jews so much?" Stroking his beard, the rebbe replied: "Because we, like you, are Asians." He explained the Germans' idolatrous regard for blond, Nordic, blue-eyed people. The Japanese listened, pondered, and ended the interview, abandoning any thoughts about launching an anti-Jewish campaign.

NAGASAKI

While there are no Jews today in Nagasaki the old Jewish cemetery at Sakamoto Gaiijin Bochi should be visited. The Jewish community here was founded in 1900 by Russian emigrées, and prospered for several decades.

TOKYO

Approximately 400 Jews reside in Japan, mostly in Tokyo. In 1983 B'nai B'rith International announced that all Japanese Jewry had joined its organization. The Jewish community center is located directly opposite the Red Cross Hospital and at the opposite corner from the Tokyo Girls' School at 8-8 Hiroo, 3-chome, Shibuya-ku (tel. 400-2559). It has recreational rooms and social facilities as well as a synagogue and a library containing a Judaica collection of more than 1,000 volumes of Jewish history, religion, music, philosophy, literature, and art. There is a kosher kitchen and a *mikvah*. It is a three-story, modern red-brick structure with both a *Magen David* and a gigantic menorah on the entrance facade. Regular Sunday School and weekday Hebrew classes are given, including, until recently, a class in Judaism for Japanese wives. According to the rules of the Jewish community center, "Jewish visitors staying in Japan for less than fourteen days may use the facilities, other than the swimming pool and game rooms." President of the Jewish community is Walter Citron. A young American from Connecticut served as rabbi—Jonathan Z. Maltzman. The Jewish community itself maintains a Jewish section in the Yokohama cemetery as well as a commercial arbitration service.

Freedom of religion is guaranteed by the Japanese constitution. The three major religions are Buddhism (introduced in the sixth century from India), Shinto (indigenous and chiefly concerned with the worship of nature and ancestors), and Christianity (since 1549). There has never been any overt anti-Semitism in Japan, probably because the white Jew is indistinguishable from the white Christian. The Japanese also have a profound respect for old people regardless of race or religion. Japan maintains an embassy in Israel, and Israel maintains an embassy in Japan. In Japan there are thirty *kibbutzim* (modeled after Israeli *kibbutzim*), most of which have been established since 1959. Yamagishizumu Kibbutz on Hokkaido Island, for example, is called in Japanese a *shikenjo,* or experimental farm. Thirty-three members from industrial and professional backgrounds farm the 1,400 acres.

There is a Japanese fundamentalist Christian sect, the Makoyas, who claim descent from the Ten Lost Tribes and have a revivalist faith in the State of Israel. There are said to be over 10,000 Makoyas, who are based in Tokyo. Periodically some 200 Makoyas visit Jerusalem, and at the Western Wall pray, chant, and sway in Hebrew and Japanese. They wear conical hats and kimonos exotically embroidered with huge Stars of David and Japanese symbols. A number of Makoyas are enrolled as students at Hebrew University. Another Christian sect is Bet Sholom, whose 20,000 Japanese members are based in Kyoto. The Biblical Seminar sect numbering 10,000 has headquarters in Shiba. They do not missionize among Jews, preferring their membership to remain Japanese. Israel's ambassador to Japan is Amnon Ben-Yohanan (whose territory embraces Japan, Hong Kong, and Korea). Ambassador Ben-Yohanan served as chancellor at the Tokyo embassy and studied at Japan's Sophia University.

KOSHER RESTAURANTS

Since Dinken's Restaurant closed in March 1975, the only kosher food in Tokyo is obtainable at the Jewish Community Center (dairy).

USEFUL ADDRESSES

Fukuoka: U.S. Consulate, 5026 Ohori, 2-chome (tel. 75-9331/4).

Naha, Okinawa: U.S. Consulate General, Asahi Building, 664 Yamakushibaru, Aza Aja (tel. 68-0856/60).

Osaka/Kobe: U.S. Consulate General, Sankei Building, 9th floor (tel. 341-4250, -4258/9, -2756).

Sapporo: U.S. Consulate, North 1 West 13 (tel. 22-5121/3).

Tokyo: U.S. Embassy and Consulate, 10-5 Akasaka, 1-chome, Minato-ku (tel. 583-7141).
Canadian Embassy, 3-38 Akasaka, 7-chome, Minoto (tel. 408-2101).
Israeli Embassy, 3-Nibon-cho, Chiyoda-ku (tel. 264-0911).

KENYA

Since 1912 Jews have lived in Nairobi in an organized Jewish community. Kenya was once proposed as a Jewish commonwealth in place of Palestine; during the Hitler years, efforts were made to settle Jewish refugees in the Highlands of Kenya. Today air travel has made Nairobi's geographical position between the large South African Jewish community and the State of Israel exceptionally significant. The Israeli raid on Entebbe, Uganda, was made possible through the good offices of the Kenya government.

Jewish farmers from Eastern Europe first settled in Kenya and British East Africa shortly after 1900, and within seven years the fifteen Jewish families formed a congregation. In 1903 the British government had offered Zionists land for Jewish settlement, but the "Uganda Plan" never materialized. Also in 1903, a burial ground was granted the Jews by Uganda Railways, and in May 1908 the congregation was offered a plot of land for a synagogue. (The congregation had been meeting in Goldberg's store on Government Road, probably the first European-owned store in downtown Nairobi.) Four years later the first synagogue building in East Africa was built.

The small Jewish community of Nairobi has been active over the years, particulary the East African Jewish Guild, a social and cultural organization. Refugees from Nazi tyranny were welcomed by Kenya Jewry, and hundreds of refugees were relocated on farms all over the country. One farm, Upper Gilgil, covered 833 acres, and served to train German and Austrian Jews for agricultural occupations. In August 1938 the Jewish Cultural Society in Nairobi conducted classes in English for the benefit of these refugees.

By 1944 the Nairobi Hebrew Congregation membership had increased to 115, and in February 1946 a new Jewish cemetery was consecrated; the next year a new rabbinate residence was completed. The growth of the Nairobi Jewish community prompted the use for religious services of the larger Vermont Memorial Hall (built by Simon Vermont, one of Nairobi's earliest Jewish settlers). In September 1955 a new synagogue (the dream of the Hungarian-born Jewish architect and synagogue president, Imre Tozsa) was dedicated, and the Governor of Kenya, Sir Evelyn Baring, laid the foundation stone. Officiating at the ceremonies was the Hon. Israel Somen, the Jewish mayor of the City of Nairobi. Today there are 180 members of the synagogue, located at the corner of Uhuru Highway and University Way (tel. 21882). Nairobi even has a "flying mohel," Rabbi Jacob Ellituv, Jerusalem-born rabbi of the Nairobi Hebrew Congregation; he flies 15,000 miles annually to circumcise Jewish children.

Israelis in Kenya operate a popular Hebrew day school in Vermont Memorial Hall. El Al Airlines flies regularly into Nairobi, and the Israeli Embassy in Nairobi (tel. 22666) is a popular meeting center for transient Jews visiting Kenya. The New Stanley Hotel is owned by a Kenya-born Jew, Jack Block, son of Abraham L. Block, one of the founders of the Nairobi Jewish community. The Norfolk Hotel is also Jewish-owned.

Jews in Kenya have always enjoyed full civic rights and equality, despite periods of stress and strain and outbursts of anti-Semitism. Operating under the authority of the Chief Rabbinate of England, Nairobi's congregation has maintained ties with British Jewry and with the Western World.

Dominant among the Kenya tribes are the Masai, who may be related to the Jewish Falashim of Ethiopia. In particular, the Masai have a much lower circumcision age than that of other tribes in Kenya. The Masai drink mostly milk and prefer not to eat meat at the same time. At special gatherings they blow the horn or *shofar* to call the tribe together. A marriage cannot be dissolved unless done before a full hearing of the elders of the tribe. Hebrew-sounding names such as Labon, Mosiso, and Isaako, appear in the clans (subtribes) of the Masai.

USEFUL ADDRESSES

Nairobi: U.S. Embassy, Mol/Haile Selassie Avenue (tel. 334141). Office of the High Commissioner for Canada, Industrial Promotion Services Building, Kimathi Street (tel. 27426). Israeli Embassy, P.O. Box 30354 (tel. 22666).

LATVIA

In 1940 the life of Latvia as a nineteen-year old independent nation abruptly came to an end when Latvia was involuntarily incorporated into the Union of Soviet Socialist Republics. After Russian occupation in 1940, Jews became "politically unreliable" and many Jews were deported to Siberia. But the 100,000 Jewish inhabitants of Latvia still recall those pre-1940 days of independence when they had an influence far out of proportion to the nation's population. They helped to organize the banking system; controlled the export of timber and flax, the main staples of Latvia's economy; and dominated the brewing, tanning, flour-milling, textile, and fish-canning industries.

Latvian Jews once enjoyed a full cultural life. They had a network of schools, both religious and secular, teaching Yiddish, Russian, and German. There was a Jewish music academy, a Yiddish theater, and a newspaper. Latvian Jews later became the founders of many famous *kibbutzim* in Israel, including Kfar Blum, Kfar Giladi, Ein Harod, Ein Gev, and Afikim.

Today in Riga there is a small synagogue at 8 Paitavas Street; also one in Daugavpils.

LEBANON

Jews settled in Lebanon more than 3,000 years ago. In A.D. 500, Beirut was a flourishing Jewish community. In 1913 Beirut alone had 5,000 Jews, but today, after the 1982 Israeli invasion of Lebanon, there are fewer than 300 Jews, most of whom continue to reside within the old Jewish quarter of Beirut, Wadi Bou Jamil. Still open on occasion is one synagogue, a Jewish community infirmary, and a Jewish school. Since most of Lebanese Jewry have left, the majority of Jews are of Syrian origin, including the Chief Rabbi of Lebanon, Rabbi Sachud Chrem, who years ago left his native Syria to reside in Lebanon, which remains the only Arab country in which Jews have the semblance of a right to practice their religion. The president of the Beirut Jewish community is a practicing urologist, Dr. Joseph Attie. In the city of Sidon, Bhamdoun Synagogue is open.

One of the last remaining "foreign" influences in Beirut is the Alliance Israelite Universelle School at rue Georges Picot (tel. 237-14).

USEFUL ADDRESSES

Beirut: U.S. Embassy, Corniche at Rue Ain Mreisseh (tel. 361800).

LIBERIA

Several years ago, Israeli technicians established an eye clinic in the capital city of Monrovia. A comprehensive study of eye diseases in Liberia was led by the head of Jerusalem's Hadassah–Hebrew University Hospital Eye Department; concurrently, two Liberian nurses and a Liberian doctor received advanced training in ophthalmology in Jerusalem.

There is but one resident Jewish family, but there are at least thirty-five Jews working here from the United States, Israel, and France. There is an Israeli day school for Jewish youth in Monrovia.

USEFUL ADDRESSES

Monrovia: U.S. Embassy, United Nations Drive (tel. 222991). Israeli Embassy, P.O. Box 407 (tel. 226440).

LIBYA

For more than a thousand years before the Arab conquest of North Africa in the seventh century A.D., Jews lived in flourishing communities in coastal Libya. (In the Bible, Cyrenaica and Tripolitania are indirectly mentioned in connection with Egyptians who fought against Judah.) In A.D. 73, more than 3,000 Jews were executed following their revolt against Rome; and in 115, further Jewish revolts against oppression resulted in the killing of hundreds of thousands. In 1551 the Turks encouraged the settlement of Spanish Jews fleeing Spain, and for a short time Jewish life prospered. In 1588 there was a forcible conversion of many Jews to Islam. Ali Gurzi Pasha murdered hundreds of Jews in 1785, and by 1860 anti-Jewish measures were so harsh that Libyan Jewry paid heavy exit fines to leave that country.

In 1942 Libyan Jewry numbered 40,000 persons; by 1974, after the rioting and attacks against Jews in 1948 and in 1967, the Jewish population had dropped to 20. All Jewish property was seized without compensation upon Libya's independence in 1951, and all Jewish ties were severed; Jewish life in Libya came to an end years later. Recently, the city of Tripoli built a new highway and a harbor over and around a large Jewish cemetery. The desecrated land contained the graves of Tripolitanian Jews, as well as the bodies of Jewish soldiers who fell fighting with the Eighth Army's Jewish units in World War II.

In Israel, Libyan Jewry may now be found in Netanya and Bat Yam as well as on a number of *moshavim*. About 2,000 Libyan Jews reside in Rome where they have their own synagogue and fund a 1,500-pupil school with fifty-two teachers.

USEFUL ADDRESSES

Tripoli: U.S. Embassy, Shari Mohammad Thabit (tel. 34021).

LIECHTENSTEIN

This tiny principality wedged between Austria and Switzerland has no established Jewish community, although thirty Ashkenazi Jews are living in the cities of Vaduz and Schaan. The Jewish representative body is the Hilfsverein der Juden. In 1938 Liechtenstein had a reigning Jewish princess, Elsa Guttmann, and her portrait still decorates the postage stamps.

LUXEMBOURG

In this picture-book country, the independent Grand Duchy of Luxembourg, there are about 1,000 Jews in a predominantly Catholic country of 350,000 citizens. Jews first settled here in 1276. In 1343 the Holy Roman Emperor attempted to protect the local community from the massacres of Jews that followed the Black Death, but all was in vain. After other massacres of Jews in 1349, the Jewish community was depleted, but somehow continued to exist until 1391. During the Middle Ages, the Jews were expelled and readmitted; and in 1555 were banished again when Spain gained control of the duchy. In 1808 the community was reestablished and, with the Emancipation that followed the French Revolution, a synagogue was built in 1823. Because of Luxembourg's diplomatic neutrality, it was a haven for Jewish refugees throughout the nineteenth and early twentieth centuries, but with the occupation of the area by the Nazis, the entire community was deported to concentration camps. Before the Nazi conquest almost 5,000 Jews called Luxembourg their home.

Most Jews today live in the capital, Luxembourg City. The Great Synagogue at 45 Avenue Monterey, an impressive modern edifice, replaced the earlier Moorish sanctuary destroyed by the Nazis. The Luxembourg government aided the 1953 synagogue rebuilding project financially and appointed Chief Rabbi Emanuel Butz, 59 Route d'Arlon (tel. 25756) upon the recommendation of Jewish communal leaders.

There are about forty Jewish families residing in the village of Esch-sur-Alzette and a few families in Mondorf-les-Bains, where there is a one-room Jewish chapel, the only Luxembourg synagogue to survive the Nazi pillage.

In Esch-sur-Alzette the synagogue is on the Rue du Canal (opened in 1954) and is headed by Rev. M. Hofman, 120 rue de l'Alzette. A very active B'nai B'rith lodge of forty dedicated members has served the Jewish community for twenty years.

Living in Luxembourg City at 139 Avenue de la Faiencerie is Professor Dr. Charles Lehrmann, former Berlin rabbi and author of several books on the role of the French Jew in French literature.

At Ettelbruck another old synagogue has recently been restored.

KOSHER RESTAURANTS

Mondorf-les-Bains: Hotel Bristol, 4 Avenue Dr. Klein (tel. 681-15).
(Supervision: Orthodox community in Brussels; religious services
under Rabbi Chajkin are also held on the premises.)

USEFUL ADDRESSES

Luxembourg City: U.S. Embassy, 22 Boulevard Emmanuel-Servais
(tel. 40123).
Israeli Consulate, 11 Boulevard du Prince (tel. 41070).

MADEIRA

This island possession of Portugal, described as the "Pearl of the Atlantic," and lying 625 miles off the southwest Portuguese coast and about 360 miles off the African coast, is still the home of a few Jews who left Gibraltar during World War II and settled here. But there is no organized Jewish community; the Jewish tourist might greet Moshe Lew (tel. 20884) at Regina Ltd., next to the post office in Avenida Zarco in the capital city of Funchal.

Northeast of Madeira is the island of Porto Santo, twenty miles away. Here Christopher Columbus (believed by many to be a Marrano Jew) assembled his charts and plotted his course before setting out for the New World.

KOSHER RESTAURANTS

Kosher meals are available upon request from the Hotel Madeira Palacio, P.O. Box 614 (tel. 30001), and from the Madeira Sheraton Hotel (tel. 31031), both in Funchal.

MALAWI

In this young African nation, Israeli technicians have worked for the past twenty years, despite Arab political interference. At least ten training institutions and model farms have been established with Israeli help.

There is no established Jewish community in Malawi, but twelve Jews reside in the capital city of Blantyre, and in Zomba and Lilongwe. David R. Waiman, an economist, practices Judaism in the town of Mzuzu (tel. 332335). Religious services are held on the premises of the Israeli Embassy in Lilongwe.

During the ten-year period from 1953 to 1963, when Malawi, Zimbabwe, and Zambia were confederated, Jewish life prospered.

USEFUL ADDRESSES

Lilongwe: U.S. Embassy, P.O. Box 30016 (tel. 730166).
Israeli Embassy (tel. 731789).

MALAYSIA

One of the thirteen states of Malaysia is the lovely resort island of Pilau Pinang or Penang, and here in its capital city of Georgetown reside ten Jews. Before World War II when Penang was a British colony there were more than 200 Jews—mostly from India and Iraq. Today the first Jewish family of Penang consists of Abram Jacob, his wife, his mother, his brother, and his children, all Orthodox and Sephardic. Inside the Jacob home at 28 Nagore Road is a small synagogue with eight *sifrai Torahs,* three of which are housed in elaborate silver casings. Malaysian law requires that churches, mosques, and synagogues be open to the public, so one door of the Jacob residence is always left open. The old synagogue at 7 Abboo Sittee Lane has been closed for years.

On a street called Jalan Yahudi or "Jews' Road" in Georgetown is a Jewish cemetery established in 1835. Penang Jews help maintain their identity by selling off parts of the cemetery which the community acquired in 1835. Jews of that time had bought the tract with money found among the personal effects of a Jewish woman who died after arriving in Penang and who wanted to be buried in a Jewish grave. The cemetery is in Synagogue Street.

Today the few Penang Jews are seeking exit visas for Australia. One of those remaining is David Mordecai, manager of the Causaniva Hotel at Batu Ferringhi.

USEFUL ADDRESSES

Kuala Lampur: U.S. Embassy, A.I.A. Building, Jalan Ampang (tel. 226322).

MALTA

Since Roman times Jews have lived on the island of Malta in the Mediterranean, although newly discovered catacombs attest to a Jewish community on Malta as early as the third century B.C. Recent excavations have unearthed an ancient *menorah* and tombstones with Hebrew inscriptions, perhaps dating back to the days of the Second Temple. Intrepid Jewish seamen undoubtedly sailed with the Phoenicians in pre-Roman times and stopped off at Malta. One of the most notable early Jews who resided on Malta was Abraham Abulafia (born in 1240). He lived on the rock of Comino and was an extraordinary man by all accounts. A Spanish mystic, he cherished dreams of breaking down the barriers between Judaism, Christianity, and Mohammedanism, and he practiced *Kabbala.* In Italy, he tried to convert Pope Nicholas III to his ideas; he was sentenced to be burned and the pyre was prepared when the pontiff suddenly died and Abulafia escaped and fled to Sicily. There he was denounced as a false Messiah by Rabbi Solomon ibn Adret of Barcelona, and again the itinerant mystic moved on—this time to Malta. The Jewish community here were reluctant hosts, and eventually he sought sanctuary on the rock of Comino. There he composed his *Sefer Haot,* or Book of the Sign, about 1288. This writing is filled with invectives against his brethren in Malta. After another work—*Imre Shefer* (1291)—Abulafia faded from history.

During the Middle Ages there were Jews on Malta and on the neighboring island of Gozo. They came from Sicily, from Sardinia, from Spain, from Greece, and from the neighboring coast of North Africa. Most noteworthy in this assortment of Jewish families was the name Inglesi. Samuel Inglesi was the head of the Maltese community in 1484. (The surname Inglesi is unique in Italian Jewish history and his family's ancestors may have fled from England after the expulsion in 1290, or perhaps were shipwrecked English pilgrims on the way to the Holy Land.) On May 31, 1492, a secret order arrived on Malta for expulsion of the Jews. At this time there were 500 Jews living in Malta and some 350 on Gozo. As a result of this order, the Jewish history of 1,500 years came to an end.

In early 1493 the majority of Maltese Jews fled to North Africa, Turkey, and to Bulgaria. After 1550 Malta was controlled by the

Knights of St. John, and for nearly 300 years Jews were seized and captured as slaves or held for ransom on Malta. Among the noted Jewish slaves was Jacob Lebeth Levi, translator of the Koran into Hebrew from Latin who eventually died as Rabbi of Zante in 1634. It was not until 1800 that British occupation of Malta brought slavery to an end.

Today there are approximately thirty Jewish families on Malta, although the transient population may include as many as 200 Jews, mostly British and Israeli, who have villas on George Cross Island. A local synagogue built in 1912 was at 9 Spur Street, but in 1979 was demolished as part of Malta's development program. Sydney Berger, the proprietor of the Le Roy Hotel in Sliema (tel. 32447), is not only the leader of the small Jewish community but is a fascinating person in his own right and tells the story of Maltese Jewry with gusto. Secretary of the Jewish community is G. Tayar; tel. 22006.

There are Jewish catacombs in the St. Agata Cemetery in Valletta; the Jewish cemetery is still called Kibur el Lhud (Burial Place of the Jews), from Moslem times. The Jewish community maintains its office at 3/4b Mac Iver Flats in Sliema. Israel has close relations with Malta, and Israeli experts have helped with reforestation work on the island.

USEFUL ADDRESSES

U.S. Embassy, 2nd floor, Development House, St. Anne Street, Floriana (tel. 623653).

Israeli Embassy, Ta'X biex, Antonio Nani Street. (tel. 33259).

MEXICO

Several thousand Marrano Jews* came to Mexico with the Spanish conquerors at the beginning of the sixteenth century. Four Jews were among the *conquistadores* of Hernando Cortez who captured Mexico City in 1521. Hernando Alonso, a ship's carpenter, built the thirteen bridges Cortez required to attack Montezuma's palace in the middle of Lake Tenochtitlán; but in 1528 Alonso was the first Jew burned at the stake in Mexico City for practicing Judaism. In 1523 descendants of Jews and Moslems were ordered out of Mexico, but few obeyed the decree. The records of the Inquisition in Mexico reveal that more than 1,500 of the early Jewish settlers were brought to trial during the sixteenth and seventeenth centuries. The most noted of all Mexican Marranos was Luis de Carvajal y de la Cueva; in the 1560s King Philip II of Spain gave him the rights to explore and govern a huge expanse of land from San Antonio, Texas, to Tampico, Mexico. But accused of the secret practice of Judaism, he was tried and exiled from Mexico in 1590. Mexican Marranos practiced circumcision, and over the years converted many Indians to Judaism; they lived as "crypto Jews," even held high offices in the Catholic Church and in the Mexican administration. Marranos were doctors, silversmiths, tailors, shoemakers, merchants, and traders. Within the confines of their homes many practiced Judaism, but to the authorities, they were practicing Catholics. In 1821 the Mexican Inquisition was officially abolished, but not until 1910 did Jews feel secure enough to live openly as Jews.

The Marranos of Mexico (like the Xuetas of Mallorca, Spain, and the Marranos of northern Portugal) still live apart from the community, suspicious of their Catholic neighbors and the white Jewish community. Nevertheless, at least two presidents of Mexico were

---

*The Mexican anthropologist, Dr. Enrique Luis Tayabas, believes that the Mayans and Aztecs, the earliest inhabitants of Mexico, were descendants of ancient Hebrew tribes that landed on the coast of Mexico several thousand years ago. Dr. Tayabas based his theory upon a study of Mexican rock carvings which contain Hebrew characters.

Marranos: Porfirio Diaz (1876–1880; 1884–1910) and Francisco Madero (1910–1913). Diego Rivera, the famed artist and muralist, is descended from Marranos; in 1932 he revealed his Jewish ancestry. (Visit the Diego Rivera Museum [Anahuacali] at Calle de Museum, off the Calzada del Tlalpo in Mexico City.) There is one Marrano village, Nonoalco (near Mexico City), that is "open" about its Judaism: Rabbi Licenciado Ramirez leads the small congregation which eats only kosher foods, circumcises its sons, and observes the traditional Jewish holidays.

After Mexico won its independence in 1821, Jews from Europe found their way here. Shortly after 1900 as many as 1,000 Jews migrated to Mexico from the United States, England, and Germany. The first organized Jewish community in Mexico was founded in 1912 by Syrian Jews, and between 1918 and 1920 immigrants from Eastern Europe joined them. Most of these Jews had wanted to enter the United States, but quota laws kept them out. They waited in Mexico for an opportunity to emigrate into the States, and in the meantime tried their hand at all sorts of business ventures in a country which was only then emerging into the twentieth century. They began as peddlers, carrying their heavy packs (loaded also with matches and razor blades) over the mountains to remote Indian villages. Later they set up small shops, and then factories. In the process of contributing a vital economic service to Mexico, many of these Jews became wealthy but they never forgot they were Jews. They built synagogues, at first primitive, later princely, and founded Jewish schools. They spoke Yiddish, Arabic, and Ladino at home, the very languages they had brought with them from overseas. These languages served as a barrier against assimilation with Mexicans, but also separated the Jewish groups from each other. In the 1920s, the international organization of B'nai B'rith established a Mexican Bureau to help Jewish immigrants obtain loans for small business ventures, learn the Spanish language, and find housing. (B'nai B'rith offices in Mexico City are at Acapulco 70, fifth floor; tel. 511-2131.)

In 1910 President Francisco Madero permitted the Sephardim to build Mount Sinai Synagogue at Tennyson 134 in Mexico City; and in 1911 the first Jewish cemetery was established. In 1922 the Nidje Israel community representing the Ashkenazim was founded; their principal synagogue is at Acapulco 70 in Mexico City (tel. 5142085). Beth El Conservative Synagogue is at Horacio 1722, Polanco. Mexican Jews from Aleppo, Syria, organized Tsedaka Umarpe Synagogue at Cordoba 167, Mexico City. Jews from Austria and Hungary built Sociedad Emuna at Himalaya 630; and German Jews erected Sociedad Hatikvah-Menorah at Acapulco 80, all in Mexico City.

Agudas Achim Synagogue is at Montes de Oca 32 (tel. 5140426), and the Sephardic synagogue is at Monterey 359 (tel. 5641197). The first Jewish school, Colegio Israelita, at San Lorenzo 1 (tel. 5755010) was opened in 1924. The Central Committee of Mexican Jews meeting at Acapulco 70 (tel. 5140676) was formed in 1940, and the Jewish Sports Center (tel. 5573000) was built to serve all 40,000 Mexico City Jews. The English-speaking Beth Israel Community Center is located at Virreyes 1140 (tel. 5208515). The Union of Rabbis of Latin America meets at Campos Eliseos 199 in Mexico City (tel. 5453760).

Today the Mexican Jewish community is young and still growing—a prosperous minority, numbering about 40,000 persons. Almost 85 percent of Mexican Jewry reside in Mexico City; but Jews also reside in Acapulco (35); Apipilulco (10); Ciudad Juárez (75); Cocula (10); Cuernavaca (400); Guadalajara (750); Jalapa (25); Monterrey (750); Nogales (25); Nuevo Laredo (65); Oaxaca (10); Puebla (50); Tampico (100); Tijuana (350); Torréon (50); and Veracruz (50).

ACAPULCO

In the Pacific Ocean resort city of Acapulco there are perhaps thirty-five Jews. Religious services are held in Posada del Sol Hotel, and in the Holy Cross Episcopal Church, off Avenida Costera, M. Aleman Boulevard (directly behind Las Vegas Hotel).

COZUMEL

On the island of Cozumel (territory of Quintana Roo) Adolf Klinger and his brother are two Jewish bachelors of German descent.

CUERNAVACA

The synagogue is attached to the Eishel Old Age Home and Kosher Restaurant at Madero 402–404. Also visit the Children's Home of Dacem-OSE at Revolución 3.

GUADALAJARA

Patterning themselves after the highly successful Mexico City Jewish Community Sports Center, the 750 or more Jews of Guadalajara have succeeded in building a sports center complex at A.C. Yaquis 651 (tel. 15-04-01). Here are housed all the Mexican Jewish institutions and organizations including a synagogue. The completion of this magnificent modern edifice resulted from the merging of the Sephardic and Ashkenazi segments of the community, which for years had persisted in maintaining separate facilities.

Perhaps the 750 Guadalajara Jews feared a repetition of what happened to the Levy family. Almost a hundred years ago an itinerant Jewish peddler from Missouri named Levy arrived in the nearby town of Colima; he started a business and soon prospered. He married a beautiful Catholic woman and was converted to Catholicism. Today his sixty-five-year-old grandson owns and operates more than twenty-four drugstores under the family name. The Levy family is a leading patron of the Catholic church, and the present-day Levy family has no relation to Judaism. (Totally unrelated to them is Alberto Levy, the administrator of the Comunidad Israelita de Guadalajara. Of French-Jewish ancestry, his father had come to Guadalajara in the 1920s from Marseilles. It is to the credit of this Alberto Levy that the various elements of the sixty-year-old Jewish community have been brought together.)

Jews of Guadalajara are augmented by the 800 or more American Jewish students attending the University of Guadalajara (including its well-known medical school). In addition, there are more than 2,000 retired American Jews living in the area but they have not participated in Jewish community living to any extent.

The synagogue in the sports center is headed by thirty-three-year-old Rabbi Aaron Kopitis. The Sephardic synagogue is at Avenida Las Americas 957 (tel. 50401; Carlos Rabinovic, president), and the Ashkenazi synagogue is at Vallarta 2172 (tel. 50104). The Jewish school, called Colegio Israel, enjoys an excellent reputation. Classes extend through the ninth grade and its graduates are usually among the top students in the high schools of Guadalajara and later in the university. American Jewish students at the University of Guadalajara attend religious services at a center at José Maria Heredia 2647. The sixty-year-old cemetery for Guadalajaran Jewry is located in the neighboring town of Atemajac. President of the Guadalajara Jewish community is Ricardo Elias.

The Jewish sports center in Guadalajara is proud of its athletic facilities, which include an Olympic-size outdoor swimming pool, tennis and handball courts, and a putting course. There are meeting rooms, restaurants, and other social facilities. The local B'nai B'rith lodge sponsors an active BBYO, or youth group.

MÉRIDA

In the capital city of Mérida, Yucatán, there is but one Jew out of more than 300,000 residents. He is Theodoro Stolnicki (of Polish descent) who came to Mérida almost fifty years ago, opened up a small jewelry store, Joyeria Teodora, Calle 63-A, and has carried on the Jewish tradition in Mérida—observing at great difficulty *kashrut* and the Jewish holidays.

MEXICO CITY

Although there are only 33,000 members of the Jewish community in the capital of Mexico City, the population of eighty million seems convinced that there must be at least 1 million Jews. The influential Mexican community consists of both Sephardic and Ashkenazi Jews, the overwhelming majority of whom are relatively recent immigrants. The fact is simply that the Jews of Mexico City are wealthy, powerful, and have obtained this status during the past twenty or thirty years. A significant number have excelled in the sciences and the arts. (Approximately 3,000 came from Syria; 20,000 from Poland and Romania; 9,000 from Turkey, Greece, Lebanon, Bulgaria, and Yugoslavia; and about 1,000 from the United States.)

In Mexico City the Jewish tourist must visit the following places:

Banco Mercantil at V. Carranza 57. A commercial bank founded in 1929 by B'nai B'rith and the Mexican Jewish community.

Centro Deportivo Israelita, or Jewish Sports Center at Boulevard Manuel Avila Comacho 620 (tel. 5-57-30-00). Founded in 1950, this recreational complex, replete with an Olympic-size swimming pool, catering facilities, libraries, day camps, health clinics, theater, ballroom, Turkish baths, beauty salon, barber shop, volleyball and basketball courts, fourteen tennis courts, and some eight special courts for high tennis (a local sport which is a mixture of squash and tennis), serves as the focus of Mexico City's Jewish social life. There are also halls for judo and yoga, and laboratories for art and handicrafts, with emphasis on engraving, ceramics, and painting. There are classes in folk dancing, Israeli dancing, and modern Hebrew. Membership is 14,000—two out of every five Jewish men, women, and children in Mexico City. A 150-year-old fresco mural dominates one wall of the center: Moses, Isaiah, Freud, Einstein, Heine, Spinoza, Bialik, Sholem Aleichem, Theodor Herzl, and other figures in the panorama of Jewish history are featured. (The painter was Fanny Rabel, a student of Diego Rivera.)

Colegio Hebreo Tarbut at Lago Menu 55 (tel. 5312611). Tarbut is a private school with separate Hebrew and Spanish divisions. It has excellent facilities, stretching over a square block and accommodating almost 1,400 pupils. Although tuition fees are fairly high, each year there are more applicants than the school can accept. A fleet of ten buses transports students from all over the city to and from the school. Doran Moro, the principal, is Israeli. An unusual aspect of the Tarbut school is its "learn in Israel" program: the first study tour occurs at the end of the ninth grade. At the end of high school, Tarbut graduates spend an additional six months on a *kibbutz*.

Colegio Israelita at San Lorenzo 290 (tel. 5755010). The oldest Jewish day school in Mexico teaches Hebrew and Yiddish and also has a theater and sports facilities.

Kehilla. The duly elected body of representatives of the Jewish community is housed at Acapulco 70 (tel. 5140576). Founded in 1957, the Kehilla deals with Hebrew education, religion, *kashrut,* problems of senior citizens, and all other matters of concern to Jewish citizens of Mexico. (**Nidje Israel** is the religious arm, and its activities include an old-age home in Cuernavaca, schools, orphanages, a *mikvah,* kosher restaurants, a loan society, and even a fund providing dowries for poor girls.)

Ose Medical Center at Tuppan 63 (tel. 5643362).

Panteon Israelite, or Jewish cemetery, at Calle Sur 138.

There is a small synagogue, Kahal Kodesh Bene Elohim, at Caruso 254 in Colonia Vallego; Indian Jews worship here in a small stucco building, poorly lit and meagerly furnished. The Circulo Cultural A.C. holds services at Avenida 5 de Febrero 633 (tel. 5-30-24-35).

Mexico City has many kosher butchers. Jewish day schools are well attended, and over 1,000 Jewish students are enrolled at the University of Mexico. There is virtually no intermarriage outside the ghettolike Mexican Jewish community. (Many Israelis have married Mexican Jewesses.) Mexico has a Yiddish newspaper (with a Spanish supplement) and a Yiddish theater. Mexican Jews are proud of their Hazamir Choir, founded in 1957, which appears regularly on radio and television.

MONTERREY

In the mid-seventeenth century hundreds of Marranos fled Mexico City and settled here after changing their names to avoid detection. The Jewish community offices are at Centro Israelita de Monterrey at Canada 207. There is also a small synagogue at Vista Hermosa under the leadership of Rabbi Moises Kalman (Canada 202).

PUEBLA

The local synagogue is at 2 Norte 5, and the Jewish community of thirty-five families has only recently been organized.

TIJUANA

The local synagogue is at 18 Avenida 16 de Septiembre.

VENTA PRIETA

Sixty miles outside Mexico City is the village of Venta Prieta, an agricultural community of 400 Mexican Indians who claim their ancestors were Marranos or baptized Jews who secretly practiced their Judaism for the past 400 years. This tribe of Mexican Indians not only keeps the Ten Commandments, but maintains a synagogue, employs Hebrew teachers, and regularly uses *tfillin* and prayer books donated by the Mexico City Jewish community. These Jews of Venta Prieta practice circumcision and trace their parentage to Spanish and Portuguese Jews who fled the Inquisition in 1492. Many were also the victims of Mexico's Inquisition. Intermarriage with the native Indians assured their survival, and their descendants have proudly carried on their Jewish tradition.

Relations between Venta Prieta and the wealthy, Ashkenazi-dominated Jewish community of Mexico City have been far from good. The European immigrants, arriving as refugees in the 1920s and 1930s, viewed the people of Venta Prieta as being more like Mexican Indians than Jews and offered little help. The religious revitalization of Venta Prieta was carried out in the 1950s and 1960s with the help of foreign Jewry. Prayer books and funds were donated by Jews in the United States and Argentina, and in 1960 a "Mitzvah Corps" group of the Reform movement in the United States helped construct a new synagogue.

There are also small Jewish settlements at Toluca (State of Mexico), Cocula (State of Jalisco), and at Apipilulco (State of Guerrero), principally Mexican Indians of Marrano ancestry who converted to Judaism. They devoutly practice the Jewish religion as they know it: circumcision, kosher food, Sabbath, and holiday observances. One sect known as "Church of God," of approximately 7,000 persons, speaks Hebrew, observes all religious holidays, and has its own synagogue in the Peralvillo area of Mexico City.

KOSHER RESTAURANTS

Acapulco: Shalom, 2nd floor, Posada del Sol Hotel Zion, Costera M. Aleman Boulevard 253,

Cuernavaca: The Eishel, Madero 402–404 (tel. 20516) (synagogue also).

Mexico City: Carmel, Genova 70-A.
Jewish Sports Center, Avenida Avila Camacho 620.
Casa Amiga, Emilio Castelar 209B Col., Polanco.
Kinneret, corner Genova and Hamburgo Avenides.
Shalom, Acapulco 70 (above Ashkenazi synagogue).
Volovsky's, Montes de Oca 32 (in Agudas Achim Synagogue).

USEFUL ADDRESSES

Mexico City: U.S. Embassy, Paseo de la Reforma 305 (tel. 553-3333).
Canadian Embassy, Melchor Ocampo 463–7 (tel. 533-14-00).
Israeli Embassy, Sierra Madre 215 (tel. 5406340).

MONACO

This independent principality on the southern coast of France has perhaps 800 Jews but very little Jewish history. The Jewish community dates back only to World War II when Monaco refused to enact the anti-Jewish legislation demanded by the Nazi occupiers and Jewish refugees arrived in small numbers.

The information director of the Tourist Bureau of Monaco is a Polish Jew, Leon Rochtin. President of the Monaco Cultural Jewish Community is Michael Woolf, 27 Boulevard Albert I (tel. 309464). B'nai B'rith has offices at 17 Boulevard Princess Charlotte (president Guy Witrow; tel. 301739). A kosher butcher is Sam Amar at 2 Avenue St. Laurent (tel. 301173).

For years, Monte Carlo's synagogue was at 14 Quay Antoine in an apartment house. But the current synagogue is at 15 Avenue de la Costa (tel. 301646) opposite the Balmoral Hotel. Rabbi Isaac Amsellam, 4 Boulevard de Belgique (tel. 300476) presides. Nearby is the Loew's Monte Carlo Hotel owned by UJA leader Preston Robert Tisch of New York.

MOROCCO

The Jewish community of Morocco dates back to the fall of the First Temple in Jerusalem in 586 B.C. In the third century B.C., Jewish slaves accompanied their Phoenician masters, as indicated by the ruins of a synagogue found at the Roman colony of Volubilis. Jews fled from Roman persecution during the first century and settled in the Atlas Mountains.

When Morocco became independent in 1956, there were 300,000 Moroccan Jews. Today most of Moroccan Jewry are in Israel—about 500,000 persons. Fewer than 20,000 continue to live in Morocco under the protection of King Hassan II.

A visit to Morocco in the 1980s may not be a pleasant experience; an uneasy atmosphere pervades the entire country. The American Jewish traveler will feel that he is unwelcome both as an American and as a Jew. While there are few overt signs of anti-Israel propaganda in this Arab country, the fact remains that it is not prudent to display any sign of being an American, or of being Jewish. Indeed, the Jewish traveler may even forgo a visit to the *mellahs* where a large number of Moroccan Jews still dwell. (The entrance to the *mellah* in Marrakech humbles the visitor who must crawl on his or her knees to enter the area through a break in the ghetto wall.)

Morocco still has the largest Jewish community in the Arab world. A majority of the 20,000 Moroccan Jews are desperately poor as are their fellow Moroccans. Recent attempts on the life of King Hassan II make for economic and political instability, and the security of Jewish life in Morocco is gravely threatened. Interestingly, Moroccan Jews still venerate King Mohammed V, father of the present king, who prevented the Vichy French from introducing the Nuremberg race laws into Morocco and insisted that all his subjects were equal before the law. It is the rampant poverty that has put a damper on emigration of Jews from Morocco; almost half are direct beneficiaries of aid from the American Joint Distribution Committee.

There are no diplomatic relations nor other official contact with Israel. There is no mail service between the two countries, and there are no restrictions on Jewish emigration. Most of Moroccan Jewish leadership has already left the country, so Jewish life is grinding to a halt.

227

The dire poverty of all Moroccans accentuates life in this underdeveloped Arab nation. Jews live in slum areas even more primitive and deprived than the classic European ghetto. Years ago, many Moroccan Jews lived in mountain villages and were ill educated and isolated. These people were of Berber origin, converted to the Jewish faith in the time of the Queen of Sheba, wife of King Solomon. Many Berber tribes had converted to Judaism before the Arabs came. In the seventh century, the Berber Jews, led by a Jewish seeress-queen, Dahia el Kahina, defeated the invading Arab forces.

A survey of Jewish communities throughout Morocco presents the following particulars.

AGADIR

Contact David Moryoussef, president of the Jewish community of 800 persons, at Boulevard Moulay Abdallah.

BENI MELLAL

Contact Habib Harrosh, president of the Jewish community of 300 persons (tel. 174).

CASABLANCA

For the 15,000 Jews residing in Casablanca, at least forty-five synagogues are functioning daily, including Nehim Zemiroth Synagogue, 29 rue Jean-Jacques Rousseau; Temple Beth El, rue Verlet Hanus; Em Habanim Synagogue, 14 rue Lusitania; Benarroch Synagogue, 24 rue Lusitania; and Hazan Synagogue, rue Roger Farache. Chief Rabbi Chalom Messas resides at rue Adrienne Lecouvreur (near Place Verdun) (tel. 226952); the president of the Casablanca Jewish community is Dr. L. Benzaquen. A teacher-training college with an enrollment of over 100 Moroccan Jews and a few Arabs (men and women) is maintained by the Alliance Israelite here. A brilliant Moroccan Jew, Robert Banon, administratively heads the American Consulate in Casablanca.

EL JADIDA

The president of the Jewish community of 450 persons is Victor Corcos (tel. 2302). The community center is at Avenue Richard d'Ivry.

ESSAOUIRA

The president of the Jewish community of 500 persons is Nessim Levy-Bensoussan (tel. 312). The synagogue is at 2 rue Ziri Ben Atyah.

FEZ

Here is the home of Rambam (Maimonides), who came from Spain, lived in Fez (where he temporarily converted to Islam), and then went to Egypt where he was the vizier's doctor. (Enemies threatened his life but he was saved by the vizier.)

Maimonides lived here from 1160 to 1165 and wrote his famous *Letter on Conversion (Iggeret Hashemad)*, which decreed that Jews threatened with death could feign conversion to Islam and still remain loyal Jews if they practiced Judaism secretly. There is an ancient synagogue, Ruben Sadoun, at rue Frejus and well worth a visit.

Chief Rabbi of Morocco Yedidya Monsonego resides in the city of Fez. Dr. Jacques Ben Simon is president of the Fez Jewish community, with offices at 1 rue de Portugal. Beth El Synagogue is at rue de Beyrouth, and Sadoun Synagogue is at ruelle 1 Boulevard Mohammed V. There is an old cemetery, a Jewish home for the aged, and a Hebrew school still functioning. The cemetery houses the grave of Solica, a beautiful sixteen-year-old Jewess from Tangier who refused to convert to Islam in order to marry the sultan, centuries ago.

A clock bell installed in the twelfth century by Maimonides is on the upper floor of the Bou Anania Medersa. From the street there is a view of the thirteen bronze gongs resting on consoles, protected by a sculptured penthouse. According to a Moroccan legend, this clock was operated by a Jew living in the building: in the course of a riot he was murdered, but before dying, he cast a spell on the clock, which has never chimed since.

KENITRA

Here some 600 Jews continue to eke out a living amid a hostile Arab community. (In 1948 there were 7,500 Moroccan Jews in Kenitra.) Still Rabbi Yahia Benarroch makes his daily rounds. The Passover *Sedarim,* the *Mimouna* feast at the end of Passover, the "hiloula" pilgrimage on Lag b'Omer to the tomb of the venerated Rabbi Amram of Ouezzane, are events that still sparkle in the lives of Kenitra's remaining Jews. The ancient synagogue at rue de Lyon supplements the community center at 13 rue Benani. The American air force base in nearby Port Lyautey brings many American Jews into contact with Kenitra Jewry. Very few single American Jewish men leave Morocco without a Jewish wife.

MARRAKECH

Marrakech has at least four active synagogues: Bitton Synagogue at rue de Touareg; Lazama Synagogue at rue Talmud Tora; Attias

Synagogue at rue Saka; and Azoulay Synagogue at rue A. Azoulay. The president of the Jewish community center is Henri Kadosh (tel. 2265). The Alliance Israelite teacher-training school (40 percent of its costs defrayed by the government) is a prominent site in Marrakech. Jewish community offices are at 33 rue Carlos (tel. 22408).

Leaving Marrakech one enters the Ourika Valley where there is an old synagogue containing the tomb of the eighteenth-century Rabbi Solomon Ben Lahnech, who was commissioned by the rabbinate in Jerusalem and sent on a holy mission around the world. He reached Marrakech and the Ourika Valley, where he died. Another rabbi, Chaim Ben Diwan, is also buried in the Ourika Valley. He was famous and beloved by Jews and Muslims; barren women still pray on his tomb. Surrounding the tomb are prayer rooms where people come seeking miracles. Some Jewish women of the Ourika Valley wear a curious draped vermillion robe and a headdress covered with a fine white veil.

MEKNÈS

The Jewish community center and synagogue is at 4 rue de Ghana (tel. 21968). In 1931, out of 55,000 Meknès residents, 7,800 were Jews; by 1936 Jews numbered 10,000; in 1951, 13,000; in 1956, 15,000. After 1960 the Jewish population declined to approximately 3,000 by 1972 and today there are far fewer than that.

OUEZZANE

This Moslem holy village (167 miles from Casablanca) is also holy to Jews. Here is the tomb of the miracle-working Rabbi Amram, who came to Morocco from Hebron to collect money for Israel and died in this mountain village in 1782. His grave is the traditional site of the Lag Ba'omer *hiloula*. Local Jewish leaders include Henri Cadoch and David Amar.

OUJDA

The president of the Jewish community is Henri Cohen, rue Sidi-Brahim. There is also a synagogue at the same address.

RABAT

Here dwells the Chief Rabbi of Morocco, Eliyahu Zion. There is a synagogue in Rabat at 3 rue Moulay Ismail and the president of the Jewish community center is Albert Dhery, 3 rue Ibn Toumert, who also served as president of the Moroccan Jewish Community Council, located at 3 rue Moulay Ismail (tel. 24504). The Museum of Antiques at Rabat has a notable collection of Jewish bronze lamps, the reflectors of which have the form of a branched candlestick.

SAFI

The 700 Jews here attend services at Mursiand Synagogue, rue du Rabat, and at Beth El Synagogue on the same street. The president of the Jewish community center (1 rue Boussouni) is Meyer Ohayon.

SEFROU

The president of the Jewish community is Rahamim Tobaly. There are two synagogues: Em Habanim Synagogue at Route B'El Menzel (tel. 63), and Sla D'El Fouki Synagogue in the Mellah.

TANGIER

The coastal city of Tangier (population 150,000) is proud of the celebrated Caves of Hercules where the waters of the Atlantic merge with those of the Mediterranean. "Jews Beach," west of the city, marks the landing site of 20,000 Jews expelled from Spain in the fifteenth century.

In Tangier, there are more than thirty synagogues for its 800 Jews, including Temple Nahon at rue Moses Nahon; Yeshiva Etz Haim at 43 Avenue Sidi Amar; Shaar Raphael and Ephraim at 27 Boulevard Pasteur; Temple Cochron at rue du Mexique; and an old synagogue in rue des Synagogues, off rue Siaghines. The Chief Rabbi is Yamin Cohen, and the Jewish community center is at rue de la Liberté 1 (tel. 31633). Abraham Azancot is president of the community. There is a Jewish hospital at 78 rue Haim Benchimol. Visit the Rif Hotel to see Aime Serfati, manager and prominent Moroccan Jew.

TÉTOUAN

The local synagogues, Benoualid and Pintada, are in the old *Mellah,* and Yagdil Torah Synagogue adjoins the community center at 16 Calle Moulay Abbas (tel. 2195). The president of the Jewish community center is Jacob Serfati, 37 Calle Luneta (tel. 2839). The Jewish district here was constructed during the reign of Moulay Sliman (1807). Settled mainly by Portuguese Jews, the area has a central artery traversed by many small, covered streets.

TELIIT

This ancient Jewish village is in the Dades region of the High Atlas Mountains. Today it is inhabited by the Blue Berbers who have retained semblances of Jewish life. Moroccan folklore and mysticism attribute a certain magic power to a Jewish religious site, a special power called *baraka* which heals the sick and makes barren women bear children. Near the border of the Sahara Desert is the village of Er Rachidia whose Jewish population is twenty persons (Joseph Chetrit is president of the Jewish community).

KOSHER RESTAURANTS

Casablanca: Gan Eden, 10 rue Idriss Lahrizi; Cafe Rich Bar, 8 rue Idriss Lahuzi; Wichita, Boulevard de la Corniche.

Fez: Raphael Botbol, 2 rue de la Martiniere.

Rabat: Chez Michel, rue Patrice Lumumba.

Tangier: El Mebrouk, 1 rue Murillo Dorado; rue Jeanne d'Arc.

USEFUL ADDRESSES

Casablanca: U.S. Consulate General, 8 Boulevard Moulay Youssef (tel. 224149).

Rabat: U.S. Embassy, 2 Avenue de Marrakech (tel. 62265).

Tangier: U.S. Consulate General, Chemin des Amoureux (tel. 33025).

NAMIBIA

Namibia (previously South-West Africa) was a German protectorate from 1890 until 1915 when the country was "invaded" by the Union of South Africa. During this early period Jews first settled in South-West Africa and established a synagogue in 1910 at Keetmanshoop. Unfortunately, nothing remains today of these early beginnings, except for a cemetery at Swakopmund.

There is a synagogue in Windhoek, the capital city, at the corner of Post and Tal Streets. There is still a Jewish kindergarten and a Talmud Torah. The Sam Cohan Communal Hall is on Lewis Botha Avenue. In 1971 three Jews served on the Windhoek City Council.

In the 1920s and 1930s there were as many as 100 Jewish families residing in South-West Africa. In 1971 the Jewish population exceeded 550 persons. Today only fifty German Jewish families continue to reside here.

In 1978 an Israeli filmmaker made a documentary on this remote semidesert country. The film demonstrated that although Namibia Jewry have long lived in peace with their fellow black residents, the exodus of Jews has already begun, along with other white residents, as Namibia is caught in a bitter class and racial struggle.

NETHERLANDS
(HOLLAND)

Jews have lived in the region of what is now known as the Netherlands or Holland since the Middle Ages, but Dutch Jewry did not begin to flourish until the close of the sixteenth century when Marranos from Spain and Portugal began to settle in Amsterdam. In the early seventeenth century freedom of worship was granted simultaneously with the expansion of Dutch trade, and this event provided opportunities for Jewish traders. By 1616, when Amsterdam authorities officially sanctioned their community as "Members of the Hebrew Nation," there already were 200 to 300 Spanish-Portuguese Jewish families living freely in the Netherlands as Jews. As word of the miraculous tolerance of the Dutch spread throughout Europe, the Jewish population of Amsterdam expanded quickly. Ashkenazi Jews poured in following the outbreak of the Thirty Years War in Germany in the 1630s. Eastern European Jews followed when the Cossack Revolution broke out in Poland in 1648. Portuguese Jews who had gone to Brazil followed the Dutch home after the colony was lost to the Portuguese in the 1650s. The two communities, Sephardim (Portuguese-Spanish) and Ashkenazim (German–East European), developed simultaneously and back-to-back in the area between the Amstel River and Amsterdam harbor, southeast of the Centrum and just beyond what was then the textile manufacturing district established by their fellow refugees, the Huguenots. Before long this Jewish Quarter was overcrowded and plagued with pockets of poverty; communication was complicated by the use of four languages (Spanish, Portuguese, German, and Yiddish), a condition which obviously lasted beyond the first generation. The first Jewish newspaper to appear in Amsterdam in 1678 was in Spanish, and the first biweekly was in Yiddish. Conflicts were inevitable but the area had a special gaiety and appeal, and introduced the Dutch people to new foods and new customs. The young painter Rembrandt was so fascinated by the Jews and found such inspiration in their faces that once he achieved some success, he bought a house in the Jewish Quarter and lived there for nearly twenty years.

The Jewish communities of Amsterdam prospered, and in the 1670s the first permanent synagogues were built across from one another on what is known today as Jonas Daniel Meijer Plein in Amsterdam. Unfortunately, both the Ashkenazi Grand Synagogue of 1671 and its neighbor the Ashkenazi New Synagogue of 1752 were destroyed, but the magnificent, classically styled Portuguese Synagogue of 1675 (the prototype for congregations established throughout the West Indies and colonial America) still stands at Mr Visserplein 3, and still is in use for religious services. Religious schools were founded and quickly became models of scholarship for other Jewish communities; the first Jewish prayer book printed in the Netherlands was published in 1627. In 1632 Amsterdam's most famous Jew was born—Baruch Spinoza, mathematician and philosopher. Liberalism and the tradition of inquiry were strong elements of the Sephardic tradition, and this penchant sprang forth again in young Spinoza. He talked openly about his ideas which angered the leaders of the Jewish community; after several attempts to draw Spinoza back into the mainstream of the community's life and thought, the congregation found it necessary to have him expelled in 1656. Spinoza was then banished from Amsterdam by the authorities. Although this restriction was soon lifted, the young scholar preferred to spend the rest of his life elsewhere and died at the young age of forty-four in The Hague, unknown except to fellow scholars because he never dared attach his name to his writings. Although Spinoza wrote wisely on many subjects, it was more than 150 years after his death before anyone realized how brilliant he had been.

In 1796 Dutch Jewry was formally emancipated, and in 1797 Holland became the first country in the modern world to admit Jews to Parliament. In the eighteenth century Amsterdam had more than 10,000 Jews—the largest body of Jews in Western Europe—and was the nerve center of European Judaism with its academies, active printing presses, and learned rabbis. (In 1815 rabbis, like Christian ministers, were paid by the government.)

Dutch Jews also turned their minds to business and figured significantly in the successes of the West India Company, after the company was reorganized in the late seventeenth century. By developing trade through contact with relatives who had settled in the West Indies and North America, Dutch Jews became involved in everything from diamonds to beaver skins to slaves; and by the mideighteenth century, they controlled one-quarter of the shares in the powerful trading company. But no business pursuit that the Jews were involved in throughout their history in Amsterdam was more important nor of greater significance to Amsterdam than diamond-cutting. Traditionally, diamond-cutting and polishing had been a "cottage industry" with the artisan working in his house and the artisan's wife faithfully spending countless hours spinning the disks upon which her husband worked. In 1822 Amsterdam's first diamond factory was established with horses for power. Shortly thereafter, steam was employed to drive the polishing disks, and by the end of the nineteenth century Jewish diamond-cutters in Amsterdam were acknowledged to be the best in the world.

Many famous Dutch Jews have had streets named after them, including Jonas Meijer, distinguished lawyer who drew up the constitution for the Kingdom of the United Netherlands in 1815 (Jonas Daniel Meijerplein in Amsterdam is named for him); Herman Heijermans, greatest Dutch dramatist and writer of twenty-three plays including *Ahasuerus* about a Russian pogrom (Heijermansweg is named for him); Henri Polak, important labor leader (Henri Polakaan is named for him); Dr. Leonard S. Ornstein, great Dutch physicist (Ornsteinstraat is named for him); Josef Israels, Dutch artist (Joseph Israelskade is named for him); and Lodewijk Visser, distinguished jurist (Visserplein is named for him). Another interesting Dutch Jew was Michael Godefrol who, as a thirty-two year-old judge in northern Holland in 1946, developed a new judicial code which became the Code of the Nation. As a reward, he was the first Dutch Jew to be Minister of Justice. Because of his efforts, the Dutch government later refused to approve a commercial treaty with Switzerland until civic equality was granted to Swiss Jews.

In 1797 the first Reform congregation in Europe, Adath Jeshurun, was established in Amsterdam. At the outbreak of World War II, Holland had 150,000 Jews; under Nazi occupation more than 100,000 Dutch Jews perished. The 15 million people of the Netherlands are strong supporters of Israel. Much of the venom of the Arab oil boycott in 1975 was directed against the Netherlands for its support of Israel, but the Dutch government did not budge despite the fact that it has no petroleum resources of its own. The foreign minister of the Netherlands even refused to go to Saudi Arabia on invitation when the Saudis declined to give a visa to a Jewish journalist who was to accompany his party.

Today the Jews of Holland number only 30,000, half of whom are Orthodox, although no more than a few thousand are actively involved in Jewish life. Some 2,000 Jews are members of one of the three Liberal congregations, and only 750 belong to the single Portuguese congregation in Amsterdam; the relative inactivity of so large a proportion of Dutch Jewry is a serious problem.

AMSTERDAM

The first Jewish religious services in Amsterdam were probably held in the home of Rabbi Uri Halevy in 1602. The first congregation was the House of Jacob, followed by Neveh Shalom and Beth Israel; in 1639 the three congregations united under the name Talmud Torah for all Sephardim and built the synagogue in what is now called Waterloo Square. In 1670 at the site of St. Anthony's Gate a plot of land was purchased for a new synagogue, to be modeled on a reconstruction of King Solomon's Temple. The Great Sephardic or Portuguese Synagogue at Visserplein 3 has been a model of synagogue building for more than 300 years. This beautiful Ionic-style edifice by E. Bouman is built inside a courtyard of old houses which predate 1665; it was constructed during the years 1671 to 1675 at a cost of 186,000 guilders. This was an enormous sum in the seventeenth century but the Sephardic community wanted the finest synagogue possible after waiting more than 200 years to pray together openly. (The synagogue seats 900 men at ground-floor level and 400 women in the two galleries, but is always crowded with more than 1,000 worshipers and sightseers.) Although the building was restored during 1953 to 1959, it is basically the same as it has been for 300 years. Twelve columns representing the Twelve Tribes of Israel support the two galleries. The Ark is heavy, of the cupboard type, and its architectural order is Doric. This beautiful Portuguese synagogue, lit by 1,000 candles in large low-hanging brass chandeliers, has been an inspiration to writers and artists over the years, including the famous Dutch painter Emanuel de Witte, whose paintings are exhibited at the Rijksmuseum in Amsterdam. The Brazilian rosewood *bima* is especially magnificent; the adjoining library has 20,000 volumes and a collection of priceless old prints and rare manuscripts that date back to 1620. (Open Sunday through Friday, 11 A.M. to 2 P.M., and Saturday, 9 A.M. to 2 P.M.; apply to the sexton at 195 Rapenbergerstraat. The library is open Sundays, 9 A.M. to 1 P.M. An advance appointment is necessary to attend services or to visit the library; call 226188.)

The Portuguese Synagogue has also been the site of countless public demonstrations by the Dutch Government in appreciation of the contributions of Dutch Jewry. For three centuries members of the ruling family of the Netherlands, the House of Orange, have shown sympathetic and supportive interest in the Jews and their historic synagogue. In 1695, twenty years after its dedication, King William II visited the Portuguese Synagogue and attended religious services.

Today Amsterdam's 15,000 Jews have a large number of lesser known, yet distinguished synagogues to attend. There are Ashkenazi synagogues at Lekstrasse 61, Gerard Doustrasse 238, Linnaeustrasse 105, Veenstrasse 26, Nieuwe Kerkstrasse 149, Swammerdamstrasse 70, de Lairessestrasse 145, and Rooseveltlann 112. In January 1971 a new Ashkenazi Orthodox synagogue was opened in the Buitenveldert garden suburb of Amsterdam at Boechorststraat 26,

Amstelveen. A Liberal synagogue may be found at Graafschap-strasse 8. Chief Ashkenazi Rabbi is M. Just at Frans van Mierisstrasse 77 (tel. 734733), and the Sephardic rabbi is B. Drukarch, Plantage Badiaan 22 (tel. 55936). Rabbi David Lillienthal, Gorenhof 79 (tel. 12580) leads the Liberal congregation.

Dominating Amsterdam for the Jewish traveler is the **Anne Frank House** at Prinsengracht 263 (tel. 242837). It is open week-days from 9 A.M. to 4 P.M. and on Sundays from noon to 4 P.M. Here fifteen-year-old Anne Frank, her sister, and her parents hid for two years of the Nazi occupation, along with four other Dutch Jews; at the time that the Franks became *onderduikers* ("hiders") the building was used as the offices and warehouse of the spice-importing firm which Anne's father had headed until the German invasion of the Netherlands made it seem a wiser course to "hand over" the busi-ness to his Aryan partners. Built in 1635 this building followed the seventeenth-century style of a front house and back house with a courtyard in between to allow light to reach the middle rooms. While business continued without interruption in the front house and on the first two floors of the back house, the eight Jews lived day after day in fearful stillness on the top floors of the back house. For food they were dependent upon what Otto Frank's associates and two loyal secretaries could squeeze out of their own rations or obtain through one of the underground suppliers who were risking their lives to feed people in hiding. Everything was a problem: garbage had to be burned in the stove and the toilet left unflushed for hours at a time; privacy was impossible, yet emotions had to be contained and silence was an absolute necessity; even at night and on weekends, caution was paramount. There are pencil marks on the walls where the Franks and Van Daans measured the growth of their children, and there are writings showing how Otto Frank followed the Allied advances with colored pins on a map cut from a news-paper. The magazine pictures and the postcards that Anne pasted on the wall are still evident. The house has changed little over the cen-turies; the annex, which served the Frank family from 1942 to 1944 as a hiding place, had been rebuilt in 1740. The Documentation Section today on the second floor features a wall display giving the overall view of Nazi persecution of Jews. A display case contains photographs and various personal items of Anne Frank, as well as her diary. The Anne Frank House has bedrooms, bathroom, dining room, kitchen, and attic. Words, however, cannot describe the pathos of this edifice, maintained today by the Anne Frank Founda-tion as an international center for young people.

Spinoza Clinic on Spinozastraat is an ophthalmological hospital named for the great Jewish philosopher who earned his living as a lens grinder.

The great painter Rembrandt van Rijn was a friend and neighbor of the Jewish community. **Rembrandt House** (at Jodenbreestraat 4–6) is a large brown house with mullioned windows and brick-red shutters; Rembrandt and Saskia van Rijn bought it for 13,000 guilders in 1639. Rembrandt lived in this spacious house for nineteen years, until the painting now known as "The Night Watch" so angered the men portrayed that Amsterdam's rich burghers soon found someone else to paint their portraits, and Rembrandt was forced to declare bankruptcy. From the time he left the house in 1658 until 1906, when it became a museum, a series of prosperous Jewish families lived here. Rembrandt painted and sketched many scenes from Jewish life and did the portraits of many prominent Dutch Jews. Inside Rembrandt House today are Rembrandt's press and more than 250 of his etchings, including one from the year 1635 entitled "The Jewish Bride," for which his wife, Saskia, posed and which was an early indication of his fascination with the Jews among whom he chose to live.

Also of particular interest in Amsterdam is the **Hollandse Schouwburg,** an old theater which in 1942 and 1943 served as a way station for Jews escaping Nazi deportation. Before World War II there was a theater here at Plantage Middenlaan 24 where many Jewish artists performed for largely Jewish audiences until the 1941 occupation regulations forbade Jews to attend any entertainment. Then, after deportation was initiated the following year, the Nazis heartlessly selected the empty theater for use as a detention center, thus turning a place of joy into a source of pain and humiliation for thousands of Dutch Jews. Today only the facade of the playhouse and part of the stage walls are left, but the site has been made into a memorial garden, a place of peace and reverential quiet.

Also visit the **Portuguese Cemetery** at Ouderkerk-on-Amstel where Menasseh ben Israel is buried. The **Museum de Waag** (Nieuwmarkt 4), an old city "weigh-house" gate from the Middle Ages, houses the Jewish Historical Museum on the third floor. There is an impressive array of Jewish holy objects including a handwritten German prayer book from the thirteenth century; circumcision seats from 1820; and books, draperies, candlesticks, and other artifacts donated over the years by the Amsterdam Jewish communities. There also is a room where copies of Nazi bulletins and orders are shown along with the pen and watercolor drawings made in the Theresienstadt Camp by cartoonist Jo Spier. It is quite remarkable that the early objects are still here; although the valuable collection was carefully hidden when Holland was invaded in 1940, the Nazis found a large portion of the cache and took many of the items to Munich, where they were found after the war. Through the efforts of the Netherlands government and private donations, the Jewish Historical Museum was reassembled and reopened in 1955, with the addition of the documentation of the Occupation.

Also of interest is the **Gratitude Monument** at Weesperplein. Designed by the sculptor Wertheim and erected in 1947 by the Jews of Amsterdam, it gives "thanks to those who looked after the Dutch Jew during the Occupation years." Its panels depict the wartime sufferings of the Dutch people. The **Dockworker Statue** at J. D. Meijerplein is a roughly modeled man in work clothes, Mari Andriessen, commemorating the events of February 1941 when, after the Nazis had rounded up 400 young Jews for deportation, the Amsterdam dock workers staged a brave protest strike and stood up barehanded to meet the German soldiers. This work captures the bravery of the Dutch people and honors their willingness to stand up for the rights of their neighbors; its placement on the Jonas Daniel Meijer Square is significant as this was the religious heart of the old Jewish Quarter and ever since the seventeenth century had been the location of all of the principal synagogues of Amsterdam. The Amsterdam University Library houses the **Rosenthal Collection of Jewish Literature,** one of Europe's greatest collections of Hebraica and Judaica. At the **Amsterdam Historical Museum** (Kalverstraat) there are displays pertaining to the development of the Dutch Jewish community. At the **Biblical Museum** (Stadhouderskade 137) are nearly 500 religious objects and such exhibits as scale models of the Tabernacle in the Wilderness, Jerusalem in Roman times, and objects from early Palestine; there are also collections dealing with religious life in Israel today. Within a short walk are two plaques: one opposite Apollolaan 95 is a memorial to three young Jews who were shot there during a Nazi roundup; the other honors Gerhard Badrien, one of the many Jews who fought valiantly in the Dutch underground in World War II.

The significant role of Amsterdam in Dutch Jewish life is still evident today in some of the stores involving such Dutch Jewish family names as Soetendorp, Mouwes, and Cardozo. Mrs. Leenike Mouwes operates Amsterdam's kosher restaurant at De Lairessestraat 13 (tel. 736709); her brother runs a delicatessen in The Hague; and her parents operate a kosher sandwich shop and grocery store at Utrechtstraat 73 (tel. 235053). For more than 200 years the Mouwes family has been in the restaurant and grocery business.

The B'nai B'rith lodge, Loge Hillel No. 985, had as its past president S. A. Themanns (Ter Gouwstraat 10), and as its secretary Benno Durlacher (Stadionweg 38). Visitors may contact N. H. Wijnperle, Beethovenstraat 32, Amsterdam.

DELFT

The Hillel House on the Technical University campus should be visited (Koornmarkt 9; tel. 01730-20300).

GOUDA

In the home of the famous Gouda cheese, stands a lovely Jewish museum that was once a convent. There is a collection of fine old Jewish ceremonial objects in brass and silver, including a large Chanukah menorah and exquisite Torah ornaments. These priceless objects belonged to the Gouda Synagogue built in 1806.

HAARLEM

Haarlem is the center of Holland's bulb-growing industry and the birthplace of Frans Hals. The local synagogue is at Kenaupark 7 (tel. 14342). Rabbi I. Braniki, Kievesparkweg 75 (tel. 52144) presides.

THE HAGUE

The Sephardic synagogue is located at Wagenstraat 101 (tel. 18375A) under Chief Rabbi Menachem Fink; the Liberal or Reform synagogue is at Prinsessegracht (Rabbi Avraham Soetendorp; tel. 559486). The B'nai B'rith Lodge Hollandia No. 945 had as its president I. B. Van Creveld (Woudenbergstraat 141), and as its secretary J. L. Klein (Breitnersingel 52). The Baruch Spinoza House is at Paviljoensgracht 72–74, and the community center is at Bezuiden Houtseweg 361 (tel. 830705).

MAASTRICHT

There is a synagogue at Capucijnengang 2 (tel. 32320), serving the local Jewish community (the oldest one in all of the Netherlands). Erected in 1842, this synagogue was almost entirely destroyed by the Nazis, but was rebuilt with Dutch government funds. Contact Hans Landau at Karvellweg 18, or Rev. J. van Gelder (tel. 26117).

MADURODAM

Near The Hague is the miniature town of Madurodam, named for Captain George J. L. Maduro, a member of an old Dutch Jewish family. Madurodam was built as a fairy-tale town of 45,000 lights. It seems that Maduro was studying at the University of Leyden in Holland when World War II broke out, and he enlisted in the Dutch army soon afterward. Because of his outstanding bravery in action, Maduro was awarded the "Willemsorde" medal but he did not live to receive it. Unfortunately, he was captured by the Nazis who sent him to a concentration camp when they learned he was Jewish. Maduro managed a daring escape but was recaptured and died in Dachau in 1945. The money to build Madurodam was provided by Maduro's parents as a living memorial to their beloved son. All proceeds from admission charges help a great variety of youth-related projects in the Netherlands; Madurodam supports a summer camp for poor children, a riding academy for the handicapped, and a scholarship program for talented young musicians.

OUDERKERK

Just five miles south of Amsterdam is the famed Portuguese Jewish cemetery in which may be found the tombstone of Menasseh ben Israel, famed poet, historian, scholar, and the rabbi who persuaded Oliver Cromwell to readmit Jews to England. (He was also the teacher of Baruch Spinoza.)

ROTTERDAM

The Progressive synagogue is located at Bokellaan 21, and the Sephardic synagogue and communal center are at Davidsplein 4 (tel. 249765). The sandstone wall at the entrance to this modern center portrays the Western Wall in Jerusalem.

There are also synagogues in the following Dutch communities: Almelo (Molenkamppark 20); Amersfoort (Drieingensteeg 2); Apeldoorn (Zutphenestraat 76); Arnhem (Pastoorstraat 17); Breda (F. D. Rooseveltlaan 77); Bussum (Kromme Englaan 1a); Deventer (Lange Bisschopstraat 19); Dordrecht (Vrieseplein 17); Eindhoven (Casimirstraat 23); Enschede (Prinsenstraat 16, and Strausslaan 22); Groningen (Folkingedwarsstraat 16); Haarlem (Kenaupark 7); 's Hertogenbosch (Prinz Bernhardstraat 8); Hilversum (Laanstraat); Leeuwarden (Sacramenstraat 19); Leiden (Levendaal 8); Middelburg (Nijverheidsweg 24); Nijmegen (Gerard Nootstraat 25); Utrecht (Springweg 164); Westerbork (Memorial center, non-Jewish); Zandvoort (Haltestraat 75); and Zwolle (Schoutenstraat).

KOSHER RESTAURANTS

Amsterdam: Beit Hamazon, Anjelier Straat 57.
Mouwes Glat Kosher Counter Restaurant, De Lairessestraat 13 (tel. 736709) and Utrechtstraat 73 (tel. 235053).
Ufaratsta, Wouwermanstraat 27 (tel. 763759).
S. Meijer, Nieuwmarkt 13 (tel. 248225).

There is also a Yiddish Cabaret, Lila Lo, on de Clercqstraat 109 (tel. 180071).

Enschede: Mrs. Serphos, Prinsestraat 12 (tel. 05420-17228).
The Hague: Mouwes Kosher, Gedempte Graacht 85 (tel. 631108).

Rotterdam: Hotel Atlanta, Coolsingel 97 (tel. 110420).

Utrecht: A. Van Leeuwen, Springweg 168 (tel. 314742).

Scheveningen: Hotel Carmel, Bosschestraat 6 (tel. 541024).

USEFUL ADDRESSES

Amsterdam: U.S. Consulate General, Museumplein 19 (tel. 790321).
The Hague: U.S. Embassy, 102 Lange Voorhout (tel. 624911).
Canadian Embassy, 7 Sophialaan (tel. 614111).
Israeli Embassy, Buuitenhaf 47 (tel. 647850).

Rotterdam: U.S. Consulate General, Vlasmarkt 1 (tel. 11-75-60).

NEVIS

Nevis, one of the Leeward Islands of the West Indies, was settled in 1670 by five Jewish families, and about ten years later a synagogue was built. By 1724 Jews constituted one-fourth of the capital's white population. Surviving tombstones in the "Jews' Burying Ground" date from 1679 to 1768. A hurricane in 1772 probably drove out all Jewish residents—who, like other residents of Nevis, prospered from the slave trade. Best known of Nevis Jewry was Rowland Gideon (1654–1722), also known in the synagogue records as "Rohiel Abudiente." Born in England of a family originally from Lisbon, he lived in Boston and traded in tobacco and other commodities with the Caribbean islands. In 1680, he traveled to Nevis, where he met and married a woman named Bathsheba, who died in chilbirth in August 1684. Her mourning husband ordered a tombstone elaborately carved for her in Hebrew and English, the handsomest monument in the Nevis cemetery. Rowland Gideon then went to Barbados and eventually returned to England, where he remarried and died a wealthy man and leader of the Sephardic community in London.

Nevis was the birthplace of Alexander Hamilton (born 1757) who, having been denied admission to the local Anglican school, received his elementary education in the local synagogue near Charlestown. Nearby is a path still known as "The Jews' Walk."

In the city of Charlestown are the remains of the eighteenth-century Sephardic cemetery—just behind the Courthouse, patiently restored by Mr. and Mrs. Robert Abrahams of Philadelphia. The Abrahams' are today the only known Jews on Nevis—summer visitors; their plantation, "Morning Star," is three miles from Charlestown in Fig Tree Parish.

NEW ZEALAND

Jews began arriving in New Zealand long before the country attained nationhood in 1907. The first Jew was Joppe, quartermaster of a ship which landed at Murderers' Bay in 1814 with a group of English missionaries. The first Jewish settlement began in 1830 when Sir Moses Montefiore's cousin, John Barrow Montefiore, arrived from Australia. The next year, Joseph Israel Montefiore, the latter's cousin, built a trading station at the Bay of Islands in the northern part of New Zealand. The country's oldest business, Cooper and Levy, was established in 1829 in Sydney, Australia, and regularly sent trading schooners to New Zealand. The firm named two New Zealand harbors, one Port Cooper (now Lyttleton) and the other Port Levy on the South Island. During the gold rush of 1861, Jews operated many businesses, and provided monetary and legal services. Jews served in the Maori Wars of 1860 to 1871, and even received favorable treatment from the fanatically anti-Christian Hau Hau, who considered themselves an Old Testament sect.

There are today approximately 5,000 Jews among 3.5 million New Zealanders, and they reside principally in the cities: Auckland—2,000; Wellington (including Lower Hutt, ten miles away)—2,100; Christchurch—300; and in the smaller communities of Dunedin, Hastings, Palmerston North, and Hamilton. There are synagogues in Hastings, Wellington, Auckland, Christchurch, and Dunedin. Though their numbers are small, New Zealand Jews live a full and rich Jewish life and maintain close relationships with Israel.

In spite of its geographic distance from the principal centers of Jewish life, New Zealand Jewry maintain a life-style not dissimilar to that of American Jewry. As for all New Zealanders, their isolation makes them particularly hospitable to visitors who find them to be warm and considerate hosts, both in their synagogues and temples and in their homes. And like their non-Jewish neighbors, they are fiercely proud of their country and play an active role in its political, commercial, and academic life.

AUCKLAND

The founding father of the Jewish community in the principal city of Auckland was David Nathan of a Dutch Orthodox family, who arrived in 1841 and married Rosetta Aarons, the widow of the ship's captain. Nathan soon prospered in commerce, and founded the first Orthodox synagogue, Beth Israel Congregation, now located on Grays Avenue (tel. 372908) under the leadership today of Rabbi Ben Artzi (Nathan's great-grandson, Lawrence David Nathan, recently retired as head of the Auckland Jewish community). And just three years after the 1840 Treaty of Waitangi, which brought New Zealand under British rule, Abraham Hort, Sr., went to Wellington (now the capital city) with the intention of promoting planned Jewish immigration to relieve Jewish poverty in England. That objective was never reached, and the Jewish population of Wellington has always remained small. However, Jewish contributions to New Zealand life have been anything but small: the most eminent name in the history of New Zealand Jewry is that of Sir Julius Vogel who was twice Prime Minister during the 1870s. Another Jew, Sir Michael Myers, served as Chief Justice from 1931 to 1946. Phillip Phillips was mayor of Auckland from 1871 to 1875 and was succeeded by Henry Isaacs. In recent years, Auckland reelected Sir Dov-Meyer Robinson for six terms as that city's mayor. Colin Milton Kay is today the sixth Jewish mayor of Auckland; he prospered as the head of a large chain of retail fashion shops, and is also an athlete of national stature. Today New Zealand Jews are found in the vanguard of business and the professions, and are leaders in the garment, brewery, and hotel industries as well as in law, medicine, and communications.

In addition to Beth Israel Congregation synagogue which won an architectural award in 1969 (its architect, John Goldwater, is a cousin of U.S. Senator Barry Goldwater), Auckland has the Orthodox Hebrew Congregation as well as Temple Shalom at 180 Manakau Road, Epsom (tel. 544139) which is Liberal (designed by John Goldwater's father, Albert). The B'nai B'rith lodge's president is B. Meltzer (tel. 555506).

CHRISTCHURCH

The local synagogue, Canterbury Hebrew Congregation (Orthodox), is on Gloucester Street (tel. 78421). Jews settled here in the late 1830s, and by 1863 had received a government grant for a wooden synagogue. The present synagogue was built in 1881. Today there are approximately sixty Jewish families in Christchurch under the spiritual guidance of Rabbi Jeffrey Leverton, 313 Riccorton Road.

DUNEDIN

Dunedin is the most southern Jewish community in the world; twenty Jewish families reside here. Dunedin, located at the lower portion of South Island, was settled by Scotsmen. By 1880, following the gold rush, there were 200 Jews in Dunedin, making it the largest Jewish community in all of New Zealand; the local synagogue was built to accommodate 500 persons. But economic conditions were better in Wellington and Auckland and in Australia, so many of Dunedin's Jews soon migrated.

In 1966 the 500-seat synagogue was sold, and a modern 100-seat structure was built at 806 George Street. There is no rabbi, but the leader of the community is Ernest Hirsh, a refugee from Nazi Germany, who fled here because Dunedin was the farthest site from Nazism. President of the congregation is F. C. Salinger. The University Medical School of New Zealand is in Dunedin and includes both Jewish lecturers and Jewish students.

HASTINGS

The local synagogue is at 703 Avenue Road as is the local Jewish community center (tel. 82204). Services are conducted by lay members.

HOKITIKA

When gold was discovered in Greenstone in 1864 Jews also flocked to the west coast of the South Island—especially to Hokitika, a town that sprang up overnight with a population of 50,000 miners. There were over 100 hotels (the journey from Wellington took weeks). In 1865 hundreds of Jews set up business on Revell and Weld Streets, and everyone prospered. In September 1865, a traditional wooden synagogue seating 125 persons was opened on Tancred Street. Five years later mining around Hokitika waned, and the population soon departed. Families and Jewish businessmen dispersed, and the synagogue was seldom used except for funerals. By 1900 only one Jew remained in Hokitika—Arthur "Stonewall" Benjamin. At his death in 1962 at the age of ninety-two he had looked after the synagogue for the greater part of his life—he even risked his life rescuing the Torah scrolls during a fire. Although he was an active participant in the community, he also remained a devout Jew in a place far removed from the rest of New Zealand Jewry.

WELLINGTON

Wellington's first Jews arrived in 1840 (Benjamin and Solomon Levy), but it was Abraham Hort, from London, who organized the Jewish community in 1843. On their first Sabbath after landing in New Zealand, he gathered his family and the other Jews, and in a prayer composed especially for the occasion, expressed gratitude to the Almighty for their safe arrival. The same year Hort founded the

Wellington Jewish community, by authority of the Chief Rabbi of England.

More recently, the Jewish community has built a new Beth El Synagogue (Orthodox) and social club at 80 Webb Street (tel. 845081). Completed in 1977, it includes a 600-seat synagogue as well as a chapel accommodating 100 worshipers.

Temple Sinai is a Liberal congregation at 147 Ghuznee Street (tel. 848179).

In 1960, a B'nai B'rith lodge was established in Wellington, followed a year later by the opening of a sister lodge in Auckland. B'nai B'rith Young Adult units also flourish in both cities. In addition, a young-married group of B'nai B'rith is active in Wellington. In 1975, Israel opened an embassy in Wellington. The vice mayor of Wellington is a young Jewish attorney, Ian Lawrence.

It was at Wellington in 1978 that Israel's ambassador to New Zealand shook hands with the Egyptian ambassador before a service at the Anglican Cathedral to pray for peace in the Middle East. The service was part of a week of activities to mark Israel's thirtieth anniversary. It was opened by the Dean of Wellington, first in Arabic, then in Hebrew, and finally in English. A member of Wellington's Arab community read from the Koran in Arabic and English, and then Rabbi Shimon Bar-Noy, of the Wellington Hebrew Congregation, read a prayer in Hebrew.

USEFUL ADDRESSES

Wellington: U.S. Embassy, 29 Fitzherbert Terrace, Thorndon (tel. 722-068).

Israeli Embassy, 13th level, Williams City Centre, Plimmer Steps (tel. 722-362).

Canadian Embassy, I.CI. Building, Molesworth Street (tel. 739-577).

NICARAGUA

The only synagogue for the 200 Nicaraguan Jews, Beth El, in the capital city of Managua, was completely destroyed during the December 1972 earthquake. Built just fifteen years before, this one-story masonry building was distinguished by its beautiful Star of David windows. Most of Managua's Jews are of Polish and Romanian origin, settling here in the early 1940s. The Nicaraguan government has been friendly, and from 1948 to recent years Israel has been represented in Managua by an honorary consul selected from the local Jewish community. Recently Israel established a consulate in Managua (P.O. Box 583). (The Israeli ambassador in Costa Rica is also accredited to Nicaragua.) Nicaragua's U.N. representative has been a profound supporter of Israel.

In May 1979, Leonardo Hellenberg, former secretary of the Jewish community, reported that only sixty Jews had remained in Nicaragua after the civil war with the Somoza regime. The Sandinista rebels opposed Nicaraguan Jewry because Israel had sold weapons to Somoza. In February 1979 two of the rebels came to Beth El Synagogue in Managua and placed a bomb there. The guard said they told him they had no grievance against him, only against the Jews and only because Israel sold weapons to the Somoza regime; fortunately local police defused the bomb. Hellenberg noted that the Palestine Liberation Organization and the Sandinistas had signed a mutual aid pact in Mexico City in September 1978, and that such incidents against Jews came from the Sandinistas. He reported that a textile factory belonging to a Jew in Managua was partly burned and the arson was committed by a dozen men who identified themselves as Sandinistas. Again those rebels also said they had set fire to the factory because of Israeli sales of weapons to the Somoza regime. About half of all textile factories in Nicaragua were owned by Jews. By the end of 1983 the Nicaraguan Jewish community no longer existed.

USEFUL ADDRESSES

Managua: U.S. Embassy, Km 4½ Carretera Sur (tel. 23061).
Israeli Consulate, P.O. Box 583.

NORWAY

Jews first came to Norway in 1852, mostly from Russia and Lithuania, for Norway was the last of the Scandinavian countries to permit Jewish settlement. Despite the liberal tenor of the constitution of 1814 (framed when Norway broke away from the Danish crown) Norway specifically barred Jews and Jesuits from entering Norway. It was not until 1851 that the ban on Jewish immigration was lifted. Its repeal was largely due to the vigorous efforts of Henrik Wergeland, Norway's national poet, who devoted years of his life to that goal. He wrote and lectured extensively on the Jewish question; his book of essays and his collections of poems, *Joden* (The Jew) and *Jodinden* (The Jewess), contributed substantially toward creating a sentiment favorable to Jews in the country. He died in 1845, six years before the repeal of the ban on Jewish and Jesuit immigration, but his work has not been forgotten. Every year, on May 17, Norway's Constitution Day, the Jewish community of Oslo gathers at the Wergeland monument in the Var Frilser's Cemetery to honor his memory.

Norway's first Jewish cemetery was opened in Oslo in 1876, but until 1880 there were no more than fifty Jews in all of Norway. Immigration increased more rapidly after 1881 under the stimulus of the Russian pogroms, and in 1892 a Jewish Society was formed in Oslo, followed by a similar group in Trondheim in 1905. In 1939 the Jewish population peaked at 1,500 persons, and at present Norway has Europe's smallest Jewish community, with 900 Jews.

OSLO

It is in Oslo, the capital of Norway, that the Norwegian Jewish community has principally taken root. The Oslo Jewish community comprises approximately 700 persons out of a population of about 500,000; and, for the most part, Jewish life revolves about the Mosaic Religious Congregation, Grunnlagt 5, and the Jewish Communal Center, located at Bjergstien 13 (tel. 469418). Current president is Kai Fewberg (tel. 671686). The synagogue was founded in 1892, but not built until twenty-eight years later in 1920; it was reconsecrated in 1945 at a service attended by the king of Norway, Olav V. It is a large white stucco edifice with numerous wooden Magen Davids over its windows. (A second synagogue built in 1921 was destroyed by the Nazis during World War II.) The adjoining Jewish Communal Center focuses upon social and cultural activities, although the individual Norwegian home remains the prime site for Jewish gatherings. This Jewish Communal Center, opened in 1960, was financed almost entirely by the Conference on Jewish Material Claims from Germany.

When the Nazis invaded Norway in 1940, women and children were held hostage until all Jewish males were delivered to the Gestapo. Of the 625 Jews of all ages (almost 50 percent of the Jewish community) who were deported to concentration camps in Germany, only thirteen survived. With the help of the Jewish underground, including such stalwart Norwegian citizens as Markus Sender, former president of the Oslo B'nai B'rith lodge (Avenue Ewa, Lakkegaten 45), many Jews were transported into Sweden for safety. The bishops of Norway publicly denounced from the pulpit of every church the anti-Jewish acts undertaken by the Germans. Inspired by the courageous stand of their religous leaders, the Norwegian resistance movement organized an escape route for the remaining 600-odd Norwegian Jews, helping them across the heavily guarded frontier to safety in Sweden.

After liberation, the Norwegian government initiated a resettlement program for displaced persons and authorized the admission of more than 700 Jews into Norway. The Norwegian people also responded by offering refugees free transportation, housing, and the full benefits of Norway's social services. In 1948 in Oslo members of the royal family and cabinet ministers met at a special ceremony to express sympathy and understanding for the tragedy which had befallen Norwegian Jews during the war, and a Norwegian-Israeli Association was formed to promote relationships between the two countries. When a Dutch aircraft crashed near Oslo in 1949 carrying twenty-eight impoverished Jewish children on an eight-month vacation in Norway, the association offered immediate aid; unfortunately the only survivor was a twelve-year-old boy, Isaac Allal. Again the people of Norway responded by contributing $40,000 to establish in Israel a "Kibbutz Norway." And as a gesture of heartfelt appreciation, the Histadrut in Israel sent 1,000 cases of Jaffa oranges to Norwegian schoolchildren. In 1960 when Isaac Allal at the age of twenty-three visited Norway from Israel, he encouraged the Norwegian Boy Scouts to plant Norwegian spruce trees at the scene of the airplane disaster.

Norway is justly proud of Max Tau, the Jewish writer and humorist who received the valued Sonnin Prize for his contribution to peace and reconciliation. Pro-Israel sentiment in Norway has been strong since the establishment of the Jewish state. Trygve Lie of Norway, the U.N.'s first secretary-general, used all his diplomatic skills to secure passage of the U.N. resolution which brought the State of Israel into being.

Of the places of interest for the Jewish traveler, the following should not be overlooked in Oslo:

Jewish Memorial Park, inaugurated in 1961, is located on the Kjerregrav Hill in Hurum. (For the motorist, follow Route 40 from Oslo, past Sandvika to Nesbru, and then Route 231 to the Elgton bus stop near Storsand. Leave the car at this thirty-mile point and follow the footpath uphill to the park.) The park is situated at an altitude of 1,500 feet and affords one of the finest views of the Oslo Fjord. The thirty-fourth tree, which was planted by the Israeli consul in Oslo, bears a copper plate with the following inscription in Norwegian: "This place is dedicated to the memory of the 27 Jewish children, 3 social workers, and 4 air crew who died in the air disaster here in 1949. Erected by Boy Scouts from Romerike County at the request of the sole survivor, Isaac Allal."

Jewish Cemetery (Stroensveien 105) is an enclave in the Oslo Municipal Cemetery. It was opened in 1875, and there are many old tombstones inscribed with Hebrew texts. A small chapel equipped with facilities for funerals is located at the far end of the cemetery. Of perhaps the greatest interest is a Jewish War Victims Memorial Monument, shaped like the Star of David. On the stone panels of the monument are inscribed the names of the 612 Norwegian Jews killed by the Nazis during World War II. From the center of the Star of David rises a column in the shape of a truncated tree trunk on which a memorial plaque is affixed. The unveiling ceremony was attended by King Olav V and the royal family.

Jewish Rest Home is located ten miles west of Oslo at Skui in Baerum. (There is also a Jewish old age home in Oslo at Hilbergsgate 21.)

Henrik Wergeland's Monument is located in the Var Frilser's Cemetery and was erected by the Jews of Denmark and Sweden to honor Norway's national poet.

Resistance Museum, a short walk from the city hall, is a part of Akershus Castle, the stone fortress built by the Viking King Haakon in 1300. The exhibit is an impressive display of photographs, documents, and other artifacts of the period of German occupation and Norwegian resistance to it. Included is a section on the persecution of the Norwegian Jews, on the deportation of some and the escape of others, aided by the resistance movement.

TRONDHEIM

In Trondheim (3 degrees below the Arctic Circle) is located the most northern synagogue in the world, the Mosaic Religious Congregation at Arkitekt Christiesgate I (near the Nidaros Cathedral). Organized in 1905 the synagogue notes that Sabbath candlelighting time varies by many hours as the seasons change: i.e. in the winter, the candles are lit as early as 2 P.M., when the sun has already set; and during the long days of midsummer, the candles are lit as late as 11 P.M., when the rays of the sun, still high in the sky, shine on polished brass candlesticks. The synagogue building was originally built as a railroad station and was purchased in 1923 by the Jewish community, and opened in 1925. The premises were taken over by the Nazis as a warehouse and barracks during World War II. In 1955 the edifice was enlarged by adding a Jewish Communal Center, which also includes a Hebrew School (tel. 29434).

In December 1975 Trondheim Jewry celebrated the seventieth anniversary of the founding of the Jewish community, and the fiftieth anniversary of the opening of the synagogue.

Of special interest to the Jewish traveler in Trondheim is the **Jewish War Victims Memorial,** consisting of three granite slabs on which are inscribed the names of the sixty Jews of Trondheim murdered by the Nazis. In a suburb of Trondheim is the **Ringve Museum,** which has a unique section devoted to musical instruments from Israel, including *shofars*, which were brought by the original Trondheim settlers from Lithuania.

President of the 150-person Trondheim Jewish community is Jakov Komissar, a third-generation Trondheimer, residing at Tunveien 12a.

There are also a few Jews in the cities of Narvik and Bergen.

KOSHER RESTAURANTS

There are none in Oslo, but there are vegetarian restaurants: Kurbadet, Akersgate 74 (tel. 20-64-14); and Frisksportrestauranten, Grensen 18 (tel. 33-35-30).

USEFUL ADDRESSES

Oslo: U.S. Embassy, Drammensveien 18 (tel. 448550).
Canadian Embassy, Oscars Gate 20 (tel. 466955).
Israeli Embassy, Drammensveien 82c (tel. 447924).

PAKISTAN

In this Moslem country, 250 Jews still practice their religion. During the Middle Ages isolated Jewish families lived here, but organized Jewish life did not begin until the nineteenth century under British rule. Before the partition of India in 1947, more than 2,500 Jews lived in this area.

In the city of Karachi, Magain Shalom Synagogue at the corner of Jamila Street and Nishtar Road is unfortunately the only center of Jewish activity. President of the Karachi community is M. Solomon (tel. 78528). There is no rabbi nor Jewish school; a cantor conducts services. A few Bene Israel Jews from India still reside in Peshawar.

USEFUL ADDRESSES

Islamabad: U.S. Embassy, AID/UN Building (tel. 24701).

Karachi: U.S. Consulate General, 8 Abdullah Haroon Road (tel. 515081).

PANAMA

The Jewish community of Panama is unique because in this predominantly Catholic country of 2 million people, approximately 1,000 Jewish families play a very significant role in Panamanian life. For example, a government-supported Jewish school, Estado de Israel in Panama City, is attended by over 1,000 Catholic children from low-income families. Even Panama's former leader, the late General Omar Torrijos, sent his children to the Jewish day school. There is a portrait of Israel's president in each classroom, and Israel's Independence Day is annually observed in the school. Scores of Israeli technicians advise Panamanians in their occupations and businesses, and government relations with Israel are good.

In the sixteenth century the first Spanish colonial governor of Panama was a Marrano, Pedro Arias Davila. While a Catholic, Davila was widely regarded in Central America as a Jew, and was one of many Jews who were sent to the isthmus in those years to help colonize Spain's new territories. At the end of the colonial period (1821) Panama became a province of Colombia and was settled by Sephardic Jews from Jamaica and Ashkenazi Jews from Central Europe. A new wave of Sephardic Jews came to Panama in 1867 from Curaçao, and in 1876 they established the first Jewish community, Kol Shearith Israel.

At the end of the nineteenth century, the idea of a Panama canal which would change geography was an exciting concept. A Jewish youngster in Vienna, whose hero was Ferdinand de Lesseps, builder of the Suez Canal, was especially charmed with the idea of a canal, and he studied mathematics to become a canal engineer. But when this young man reached Paris his interests changed; he was Theodor Herzl, father of Zionism.

In the late 1800s the Jews of Panama were principally descendants of Spanish Jews from Holland and Portugal who had originally settled in Brazil and later went to the West Indies, but because of floods and earthquakes they finally settled in Panama. In time their rabbis died, and the group was left with Hebrew books which were incomprehensible to the new generations. When a rabbi from Cincinnati visited Panama in the 1930s he suggested that they use the

Union of Hebrew Congregations prayer book. As a result, this group of Sephardic Jews identifies itself with the Reform movement and is quite fluent in the English language. It presently has a Reform rabbi from Israel and plays an active part in the Jewish community.

In 1967 Max Del Valle became Panama's president for a brief time. In a political upsurge that year, the president was deposed and Del Valle as vice-president assumed his duties until a new government took charge. Del Valle was one of two Jews, outside of Israel, who have served as president of a country. (The other is the late Moses Pijada who was Yugoslavia's president after World War II.)

The Jews of Panama are 90 percent Sephardim, and the majority hail originally from North Africa, Syria, and Turkey. While Panama City Jewry, numbering in excess of 1,500 persons, is today generally Reformed (Kol Shearith Israel Synagogue), there are ultra-Orthodox Jews among the Syrian group (Sheveth Achim Synagogue). Beth El Synagogue is Ashkenazi. All in all, there are seven Panamanian synagogues, three in Panama City, two in Colón (about 200 Jews), one in David, and one in Balboa, Canal Zone. Jewish institutions range from an Albert Einstein Institute (located on Israel Street) with an enrollment of 350 students, to a JWB-operated Jewish USO, to a Hebrew cultural center. (Rabbi Heschel Klepfisch heads both the school at Via Israel Paitilla (tel. 262869) and the Ashkenazi congregation.) American Jews, numbering perhaps 300, also reside in the Panama Canal Zone, but unfortunately have little contact with Panamanian Jewry.

Among the leaders of Panamanian Jewry are Ricardo Holzer, an architect and international B'nai B'rith leader, and Carlos Zelenka, also a B'nai B'rith leader and owner of ten department stores.

The different divisions of the Jewish community are brought together under one umbrella organization called Consejo Central Comunotario Hebrea de Panama with a rotating presidency. This organization is affiliated with the Federation of Jewish Communities of Central America.

The chief economic adviser to the Panama Government is Moshe Glicksberg, a prominent Panamanian Jew. In fall 1977, General Omar Torrijos, then head of Panama's government, visited Israel.

USEFUL ADDRESSES

Panama City: U.S. Embassy, Avenida Balboa y Calle 38, Apartado 6959 (tel. 271777).

Israeli Embassy, Edificio Grobman, Calle Manuel Maria Icassa, 5th floor (tel. 648257).

PARAGUAY

Jews from Poland first entered Paraguay in 1912. Subsequent migrations between 1933 and 1947 brought both Sephardim and German Jews. Today there are about 1,200 Paraguayan Jews, 90 percent of whom are Ashkenazim, a fairly constant figure. Paraguayan Jews keep a very low profile.

In the capital city of Asunción the leading Ashkenazi synagogue is at General Diaz 657. At the same address is the Alianza Israelita representing the entire Jewish community; secretary-general is Isaac Goldenberg (tel. 41744). Practically all Paraguayan Jewry reside in Asunción. Asunción's Hotel Guarani houses the Jewish-owned store of precious and semi-precious stones, H. Stern.

Ira Levin's novel *The Boys from Brazil* and the motion picture of the same name portray in realistic terms the archvillain SS Hauptsturmführer Dr. Josef Mengele (the man who ran Auschwitz), the infamous Angel of Death. But Mengele is real and very much alive in Paraguay where he lives under the protection of the half-German Paraguayan president and dictator, Alfredo Stroessner. As a Paraguayan citizen, Mengele cannot be extradited, despite the request by the West German Embassy in Paraguay. Isser Harel, former head of Israel's intelligence service, has revealed that when Eichmann was captured, he refused to disclose Mengele's hideout because he feared Mengele more than the Israelis. A Danish physician, Dr. Bjarne Berbom, met Mengele in 1974 in the border town of Foz Do Iguacu between Paraguay and Brazil. Mengele told Dr. Berbom that he regretted nothing, for his "scientific experiments" were worthwhile. Twenty bodyguards watch Mengele at all times. He is frequently seen in the streets of San Bernardino and is believed to control the Estrella Nazi organization in Paraguay which possesses an enormous fortune from the sale of art looted by the Nazis. Mengele's escape in 1949 from West Germany to Argentina was organized by the Odessa organization.

USEFUL ADDRESSES

Asunción: U.S. Embassy, 1776 Mariscal Lopez Avenue (tel. 201-041).

Israeli Embassy, Edificio Lider 2, 3 er Piso (tel. 95097).

PERU

How many Jewish communities excite 20 percent of their membership (or more than 1,000 persons) to watch a Bar Mitzvah on a Friday night? Young Rabbi Naftali Rothenberg has good reason to be proud of his active following in Lima, Peru. Israeli-born, he is the youngest of only thirty rabbis serving the nearly 1 million Jews throughout Latin and South America. He is the official rabbi of the Union Israelita del Peru, Valle Riestra 807, San Isidro, Lima, Peru.

The first Jews settled in Peru after the 1848 revolution in Germany. By 1870 these German Jews had established the Sociedad de Beneficencia Israelita de 1870, which exists to this day at José Galvez 282, Miraflores. They acquired land for a cemetery which is also being used today. However, because of a low birthrate and intermarriage, these original settlers have disappeared, and the organization has been kept alive by a new wave of German immigrants. Toward the end of the nineteenth century a few Sephardic families from North Africa established a community in Iquitos, where a rubber boom attracted them. Because of adverse living and economic conditions many left or intermarried. Before World War I Sephardic Jews came from Turkey and Syria, and between World War I and World War II Jews from Eastern Europe, particularly Romania and Poland, emigrated to Lima. They started as peddlers and later branched out into other businesses throughout the country; and they established Jewish communities in provincial capitals. But, as before, these communities died out, and the early settlers returned to Lima, where there were greater opportunities for education. Between 1933 and 1943, a large group of German Jews came to the country in spite of the strict Peruvian immigration laws. Today more than 5,000 Peruvian Jews are divided into three communities of Sephardim, Germans, and Ashkenazim, the last group being the largest.

Lima has many synagogues, including the Union Israelita–Le Gran Sinagoga (Avenue Brazil, block 15; tel. 241412), an austere, gray building with services regularly attracting more than 100 persons. Others include:

Sharon Sinagoga, Avenue Dos de Mayo 1815, San Isidro.

Adath Israel Sinagoga, Iquique 360, Brena.

Knesseth Israel Sinagoga, Pasaje Malvas 135.

Sociedad de Beneficencia Israelita Sefardi Sinagoga, Enrique Villar 581 (tel. 717230).

Gran Sinagoga, Husares de Junin 163 (tel. 241-412).

Organized Jewish activities include a B'nai B'rith group (José Quinones 290, Miraflores; tel. 413461), a Zionist group, a very active Maccabee group, and a Yiddish newspaper. At the third Annual Inter-American Maccabee Games, the Lima community entertained hundreds of Jews from abroad. The Jewish Club has a full-size soccer field and basketball court seating 500, and an Olympic-size pool. Peruvian Jews are thirsty for involvement with Jewish life; more than 600 subscribe to Jewish Telegraphic Agency reports in Spanish directly from Israel.

The Peruvian government first guaranteed freedom of religion in 1933, and since then Peruvian Jews have organized excellent facilities, including a network of Jewish schools and the beautiful Great Synagogue at Husares de Junin 163. In 1946 a Jewish school named after a Marrano, Leon de Pineto, was opened; there are approximately 800 children enrolled, representing 95 percent of the Jewish children in Lima. The Hebraica Sports Club was founded in 1956; Nosotros (We) has been published monthly since 1931.

The Asociación Judia del Peru is an effective umbrella organization; the Chief Rabbi of Peru is Rabbi Abraham Benhamu (tel. 406896).

Places of Jewish interest in Lima include the **Colegio Leon Pineto** on Avenue Juan Peset y Los Munganes; **Cemetario Israelita; Club Hebraica;** and **Museo de la Inquisitzia.**

Peru today is a military dictatorship intent upon creating an entirely new society. Such basic industries as fishing, banking, and insurance have been nationalized since 1968. The small Jewish community has dwindled because of the limited economic opportunities. Anti-Semitism is increasing, and the leftist government press is anti-Israel and sometimes anti-Jewish. There is also the growing influence of the Arabs and even the Soviets who have made Peru a major base. On the other hand, the opportunities created by social and economic reform, far from crowding Jews out, have provided a new fluidity to Peruvian Jewish life. Jews have slipped rather comfortably into this layer of nouveaux riches in Lima, where the old barriers of race and class seem to have disappeared. For the first time, young Jews can look beyond business to careers in the professions, in government, in management, in the universities, and in the arts.

The acknowledged spokesman for Lima's Jews is a tall, bald man in his late forties named Yaacov Hasson. He is currently a professor of humanistic studies and philosophy at the university and is considered one of Peru's leading intellectuals. He carries the title of Executive Director of the Office of Human Relations of the Jewish Community of Peru, for which he receives a modest salary paid jointly by the various congregations. Hasson admits to considerable concern about the long-term future of Peru's Jewish community.

USEFUL ADDRESSES

Lima: U.S. Embassy, southwest corner Avenidas Inca Garcilaso de la Vega and Espana (tel. 286000).
Israeli Embassy, Natalio Sanchez 125, Santa Beatriz (tel. 321005).

PHILIPPINE ISLANDS

Marrano Jews and/or *conversos* came with the Spanish conquerors to the Philippines in the sixteenth century, but openly practiced Judaism only after 1872. Following the Spanish-American War in 1898 Jews from Turkey, Lebanon, Syria, and Egypt arrived; after 1917 Jews from the United States joined Russian Jewish refugees, and in 1919 the first synagogue was built, followed by a second synagogue in 1924. By the 1930s there were 500 Jews in Manila, soon to be augmented by German Jews and by Jews from Shanghai in 1937. The 1,200 Philippine Jews in 1939 enjoyed the services of a rabbi and a *hazan*. But Japanese occupation of the Philippines in 1942 resulted in the jailing of many Jews, except German Jews who were treated as German citizens.

Jews returned in numbers to the Philippines, but following Philippine independence in 1946, many found the going rough, and departed for the United States. Temple Emil in Manila had been turned into an ammunition dump by the Japanese, and the building itself exploded in February 1945, leaving only the walls standing. Nevertheless, the synagogue was rededicated in August 1947, and the following year Bachrach Hall Community Center (tel. 593431) was built at 1963 Taft Avenue in Manila. Services are conducted today at Temple Emil by Ezra Toeg, 14 Taurus Street, Bel Air Village Makati, Rizal (tel. 868576). The religious leader of the Filipino Jewish community is an Israeli, Amnon Wallenstein. Religious services are also held by the Jewish chaplain at Clark air base outside Angeles City.

It is interesting to note that in the late 1930s thousands of Central European Jews were offered government land on the island of Mindanao. A few came, but the remnants of these Jewish communities have long since disappeared.

USEFUL ADDRESSES

Cebu: U.S. Consulate (tel. 4661).

Manila: U.S. Embassy, 1201 Roxas Boulevard (tel. 598011).
Israeli Embassy, Metropolitan Bank Bldg. 5th floor, 6813 Ayala Avenue, Makati, Metro-Manila (tel. 88-53-20).
Israeli Consulate General, 24 Cambridge Circle, North Forbes Park.

POLAND

Jews first settled in Poland in the ninth century, and during the twelfth century found themselves in charge of Polish coinage because Polish nobility cared very little for commerce. (Many of these coins bore Hebrew inscriptions.) The relative freedom then enjoyed by Polish Jewry had resulted from the Kalisch Statutes of 1264. But within a century anti-Semitism appeared; Polish nobles and peasants joined forces against the Jews. Yet, in adversity, Jewish learning and scholarship flourished, particularly during the sixteenth century. Poland produced the greatest talmudic scholars, codifiers of ritual, founders of mystic Hassidism, and eminent Jews of learning. Yiddish was their language, their culture, and their life, and the secular Yiddish school system was developed. One of Poland's most famous Jewish scholars was Lazarus Zamenhof, father of Esperanto, the international language. He was an ophthalmic surgeon by profession, and invented Esperanto in 1887 to help establish universal peace.

From a total of 3 million Polish Jews just before World War II, the population has dwindled to fewer than 6,000 Jews today—90 percent of Polish Jewry were murdered by the Nazis. There is today no rabbi, no Jewish school, and no functioning Jewish organization in all of Poland. Jewish community life barely exists; the remaining Jews are either elderly, not interested in Judaism, or simply too poor to travel. Their protector is the American Federation of Polish Jews, which has filed claims with the Polish government to restore and preserve Jewish places of interest. The AFPJ has asked the Polish government for full payment of pensions to survivors of the Holocaust living outside Poland, and also for indemnification for Jewish property seized by Polish authorities.

The Polish government for obvious reasons has sanctioned a limited amount of cultural activity by its Jewish citizens. The Jewish Historical Institute (located in a wing of the Great Synagogue at Tlomacki Place in Warsaw) functions as part of the Polish Academy of Science, and its Judaica collection contains 60,000 books, 1,200 rare manuscripts, and 100,000 art objects, as well as the famous Emanuel Ringelblum Archives (tel. 271530) from the Warsaw Ghetto. Warsaw's Yiddish Theater on Grazybowski Square with its huge revolving stage and lighting consoles still holds performances three times a week, and has a reputation that fills it almost entirely with non-Jews. (Earphones provide simultaneous translation in Polish.) The theater is funded by the government which sees it as a useful point of interest for the many Jewish tourists who visit the city. Szymon Szurmiej is the director. Housed in the Jewish community center (tel. 121416), the theater seats only 110 and supports thirty-five actors. Also in the same building is the office of *Volk Stimme* (People's Voice), a pro-government Yiddish-language newspaper. Abraham Kwaterko is the editor.

The Warsaw Ghetto Fighters' Memorial at 18 Mila Street is in a local park: the word "Jew," however is not to be found in the inscription, although the rear portion depicts men, women, and children with Star of David armbands, holding sticks and stones in clenched hands, following a man holding the Torah aloft.

The Great Synagogue of Warsaw is in deplorable condition; only the presence of scaffolding reveals the government's desire to renovate it as a cultural attraction.

Jewish cooking is available at Amica Restaurant (6 Kredytowa Street) and at Samson Restaurant (3 Freta Street).

BIALYSTOK

Once a major Jewish city, it has no Jews today. The Bialystok Jewish Cemetery at Zabia and Proletariacks Streets is a public park; graves have been desecrated and simply covered over. The synagogues are either warehouses or public clubs. There are two plaques in Yiddish in the city, one noting the site of a synagogue burned down by the Nazis after hundreds of Jews had been herded inside; and the other describing the bravery of one Isaac Malmeda in leading the Jewish uprising against the Nazis. The notorious Nazi concentration camp Treblinka is halfway between Bialystok and Warsaw; 750,000 Jews perished there. Nearby, the village of Chelm has no Jews, but there is an old synagogue at 8 Copernicus Street.

Two kilometers west of Bialystok is the village of Tykocin. Here is a remarkable synagogue, a large round building that the Polish Ministry of Culture is busily restoring. Its *bima* and polychromed interior are resplendent with photographs.

CRACOW

Most of Cracow's Jews are between sixty-five and eighty-five years of age. Yet the Jewish community recently fought a legal battle for 130 buildings including synagogues (one dating back to the fourteenth century) that had been seized by the government. The Jewish community claimed that in the absence of heirs to these properties, the community was the legal heir, and so the community sued and won the symbolic sum of one zloty per year. But the government still kept the buildings. The old Jewish quarter of Casimir Town is crowded with cemeteries, abandoned synagogues, and apartment houses with Hebrew inscriptions. Not one of the thirty-three synagogues in Cracow is open for prayer, though the Remuh Synagogue of Moses Isserles at Ul. Szeroka 40, is permitted to open on certain occasions (call A. Jackobowitz). In order to preserve a Jewish cemetery in Cracow during World War II the community "buried" it by covering with earth the monuments and grave markers. After the Holocaust an attempt was made to unearth the monuments and markers, and in the process the rescuers discovered another Jewish cemetery that had met the same result. That cemetery had been buried in the early eighteenth century when a Swedish army was expected to invade Poland.

The Auschwitz death camp is about forty miles from Cracow.

The Old Synagogue at Ul. Szeroka 2, built in the fourteenth century, is a Jewish museum, part of the Cracow History Museum. The Kuppa Synagogue, built in 1595 at Ul. Miodowa, is a factory today; Poper Synagogue, built in 1620 at Ul. Szeroka, is a non-Jewish young men's social club; and the High Synagogue, built in 1620 at Ul. Jozefa, is the home of a Polish architect. The Izzaka Synagogue is an artists' studio. The cemetery is at Ul. Miodowa 55 (tel. 54566).

LODZ

The synagogue is at Zachodnia 78.

LUBLIN

There is no synagogue and no sign of Jewish life except for the eighteenth-century cemetery, a four-square-block area.

SIEMIATYCE

There is a small museum housing paintings of ghetto scenes under the Nazis. The painter is a non-Jew, Joseph Charyton, who lived here until his death in 1972.

WLODAWA

On the Soviet border is the magnificent "Fortress Synagogue," preserved as a Polish government cultural attraction. But nowhere is the story of Jewish contributions to Polish history recalled.

WROCLAW (formerly Breslau)

There are perhaps 100 Jews, none of whom were living here

before World War II. The Grand Synagogue is crumbling from neglect and has been replaced by a room for the dozen worshipers who gather on the Sabbath. The present Jewish population knows little of the history of this famous community: the world-renowned rabbinical seminary is today a kindergarten for the children of Polish policemen; the Great Cemetery is visited only by thieves who remove marble tombstones.

The tragedy of Poland is evident from the current use made of Jewish property by the government: at Wlodawa the Jewish cemetery on the Soviet border is submerged under the municipal garbage dump; in Zamosc the synagogues are used as municipal offices and as a youth club; at Gora Kalwarja the synagogue is a storage warehouse for old furniture and used agricultural implements; and in Tarnow, the *bima* of the old synagogue is in the center of a public park. On the other hand, the Polish government has repaired and maintained selected synagogue edifices as tourist attractions. In April 1983, upon the fortieth anniversary of the Warsaw Ghetto Uprising, the Great Synagogue in Warsaw was permitted to open. Blown up by the Nazis in 1943, the building had been reconstructed at the cost of more than 1 million dollars.

Historic stone synagogues in a number of Polish towns survived the ravages of Nazism only to have their priceless frescoes and murals destroyed by Polish officials who converted the buildings into commercial warehouses. Physically there are still synagogues in Lodz (at Zachodnia 78); in Cracow (at Ul. Szeroka 40); in Warsaw (at Ul. Krajowej/Rady Narodowej 6); and in small Polish towns (Bielsko, Biala, Bytom, Czestochowa, Dzierzoniow, Gliwice, Katowice, Legnica, Sosnowiec, Swidnica, Szczecin, Tarnow, Walbrzych, Wroclaw, among others), but attendance is nil, and the atmosphere is sterile.

Jews no longer live in such Hassidic centers as Gora Kalwarja, Kock, Bobowa, Nowry Sancz, Rymanow, Radomsko, and Biala. Most of the towns have empty synagogue buildings standing, either abandoned or used as public buildings. In Chelm (the town of so many Jewish fables), the cemetery is in ruins, and the only synagogue is now a warehouse.

The Polish government has preserved the death camp sites. At Treblinka, where 800,000 Jews perished, signs in six languages, including Yiddish, tell exactly what happened. Similar is the case in Chelmno, Sobibor, Belzec, Auschwitz, and Trawiniki concentration camps. At the Majdanek death camp near Lublin, a huge museum has been established, giving prominent place to the suffering of the Jews.

Poland today, at least for the Jew, is a graveyard of the past, for nowhere is there any sign of Jewish religion or even Jewish culture. In every *shtetl* there are too many bitter memories of Poland's historic maltreatment of its Jews.

USEFUL ADDRESSES

Warsaw: U.S. Embassy, Aleje Ujazdowskie 29/31 (tel. 283041-9). Canadian Embassy, Ulica Matejki 1/5 Srodmiescie (tel. 29-80-51).

PORTUGAL

Jews settled in Portugal prior to the thirteenth century, while the country was under Arab domination. In 1143, when the first king came to power, there were already synagogues in the towns of Santarém and Beja. In 1260 in Lisbon, King Alfonso III appointed a Chief Rabbi and made him responsible for Portuguese Jewry. The Jewish royal treasurer Joseph Ibn Yichia had secured permission for Jews to be governed by their own laws. Notwithstanding anti-Jewish outbreaks in 1373, 1449, and 1482, Jews achieved prominence at court as physicians, astronomers, and royal treasurers. The most famous Portuguese astronomer was Abraham Zacuto, a Jew from Salamanca, Spain.

After the expulsion of Jews from Spain in 1492, large numbers of Jews entered Portugal, some freed upon payment of a poll tax, and others as virtual slaves. But in 1496, Jews were forced to accept either conversion or expulsion from Portugal by King Manoel I. Most Jews were forcefully converted, but many Portuguese Jews fled, principally to London, Amsterdam, and New York, establishing "Portuguese" synagogues in their new countries. After the revolution of 1820 Jews from North Africa and Gibraltar reentered Faro and Lisbon, and 120 years later Ashkenazi immigrants came from Central and Eastern Europe to increase the Jewish population of Portugal to a few thousand. During World War II, the capital city of Lisbon was a stopover for thousands of Jewish refugees from Nazism, but very few remained within the country or applied for Portuguese citizenship.

Today about 600 Jews reside in all of Portugal; but only in Lisbon, Oporto, and in the Algarve and Azores are there signs of Jewish life. The decline came largely in the 1960s when the younger people opposed Salazar's African war and left for Israel, the United States, and Brazil. But Lisbon's Jewish institutions are structured to serve a large number: there are synagogues, a hospital, a cemetery, and even a Jewish community center. The hospital, which once supplied excellent health services, has been converted into an old age home. The community of Lisbon has a rabbi, as well as Hebrew teachers supplied by the Jewish Agency. But only 10 percent of the population is under twenty; Dr. Joshua Ruah, president of the Lisbon community, contributes a major share of that himself, being the father of five.

The central Jewish community facilities in downtown Lisbon compare favorably with those in larger European Jewish communities. The community center is at Rua do Monte Olivete 16; tel. 664436. The Lisbon Sephardic synagogue, Shaare Tikva, at Rua Alexandre Herculano 59 (tel. 681592) houses many historical documents and religious objects dating back to the fourteenth and fifteenth centuries. Rabbi Avraham Assor, Rua Rodrigo da Fonseca 38, serves the congregation. A Moorish-type structure, the synagogue is hidden behind an iron gate that encloses a courtyard in the center of which stands the synagogue. (Synagogues were not permitted to face the street.)

The Ashkenazi synagogue in Lisbon is at Rua Elias Garcia 110 (tel. 775283), and serves a small congregation, as does the Jewish Club at Rua Rosa Aranjo 10, which opened in 1943 to link the older Sephardim and the newer Ashkenazim (tel. 572041).

In the city of Oporto, the synagogue is at Rua Guerra Junqueiro 340. Only three Jewish families remain; an elderly gentleman, Paulo Presman, S. Joao Da Madeira, serves as president. There is a small synagogue at Rua Do Brum 16 in Ponta Delgada, capital city of the Portuguese island of San Miguel in the Azores, a group of islands in the Atlantic Ocean.

Marranos or Secret Jews: The *London Jewish Chronicle* of November 29, 1974, carried an interesting story of Crypto-Jews, Secret Jews, New Christians, or Marranos (as they are variously called) who continue to live in northern Portugal about 200 miles from Lisbon. The forced conversion of 1497 had converted the entire body of Portuguese Jewry into titular but insincere Christians. Since the Church in Portugal simply did not tolerate anyone who was not Catholic, mass baptisms were the order of the day. The forced conversion was so successful that the Portuguese Inquisition did not begin until the year 1540, sixty years after Spain's Inquisition began. The existence of Portuguese Marranos in the twentieth century was not generally known until 1917 when a Polish Jewish engineer, Samuel Schwartz, discovered them in various towns of northeast Portugal. Captain Arturo Carlos de Barros Basto, a Portuguese officer, in 1920 publicly declared himself to be a Marrano, taught himself Hebrew, and announced that he would return to Judaism by establishing a Marrano synagogue in Oporto. He died in 1961 after a futile effort to return his fellow Marranos to a full Jewish life.

Today, in 1984, there are a few thousand Marranos still living in small communities of northern and central Portugal: Argozelo, Belmonte, Braganca, Carzao, Covilha, Escalhao, Fundao, Lagoaza,

Mogadouro, Mosanto, Moncorvo, Oporto, Pinhel, Rebordelo, and Vilarinho. One scholar estimates that there are 1 million Marranos out of a Portuguese population of 10 million. Despite forced conversions to Catholicism some 400 years ago, these remnants of Jewry still practice their Judaic religion secretly—generally not with understanding but with sincerity from memory. One town, Belmonte, in the Serra da Estrela mountains, is the abode of several hundreds of these "Jews" who still hide their Jewishness from their fellow Portuguese. These modern-day Marranos know only those rituals of Judaism that were secretly taught generations earlier at the risk of their lives. For example, some of the criteria of Judaism among the Secret Jews include: possession of Hebrew prayer writings; possession of Jewish religious objects; possession of Jewish art; speaking Hebrew in prayers; circumcision (though very rare today); Friday night ceremony for lighting the candles; not mixing meat and milk foods. On the Sabbath they refrain from cooking food; meat and poultry are soaked and salted; after a funeral they sit on special low benches in their homes for seven days and burn a special oil lamp; the wedding ceremony includes a blessing in the name of the god of Abraham, Isaac and Jacob; and there are observances of some Jewish holidays: ten days after the new moon in September, a day of fasting is observed, and everyone dresses in white clothing; eight days after the new moon in February a fast is observed (probably Purim and the Fast of Queen Esther); on the fourteenth day of the new moon in March Passover is observed—for two days no bread is eaten, but on the third day they eat an unleavened bread, and a whole lamb is roasted.

Although these Marranos are in fact free to become full-fledged Jews, the powerful effect of religion in hiding has forged these ancient practices under persecution into their *modus vivendi,* and they continue to live as practicing Catholics.

ALBUFEIRA

Perched on a cliff above a delightful, secluded harbor in the Algarve resort area is the village of Albufeira. Here the only practicing Jew appears to be Alf Worth, an Englishman who owns and operates the Hotel Boa Vista and the Esplanade Restaurant. Mr. Worth has preserved relics of the old synagogue at Faro, and hopes to renovate it as well as Faro's medieval Jewish cemetery.

The Esplanade Restaurant on Rua B has Jewish-style cooking (tel. 175183).

BELMONTE

The "hidden Jews" who inhabit this remote community in northeast Portugal (a little town perched high on the hills of Serra Da

Estrela; the highest point, Torre, is 6,500 feet high) did not know for nearly five centuries that they were not the last remnants of the Jewish people on earth. Approximately 200 homes of the 4,000 inhabitants of Belmonte belong to known Marranos. A stone inscription from the arch of the ancient synagogue here, dating back to the thirteenth century, was recently found and reads, "And the Lord in His holy temple, let all the earth be hushed in His presence (Habakkuk 2.20)." The stone inscription is preserved in the Abraham Zacuto Museum in the city of Tomar. The "synagogue" of Belmonte is in the Rua Das Lages, but is simply a convenient gathering place for these Marranos. Jewish surnames include Henriques, Vas, Morao, Nunes, Diogo, and Caetano, while first names include Moises, Ester, Sara, and Daniel. One of the most delightful "practicing" Jews is a forty-three-year-old woman, Ana; she and her husband, Rafael, are itinerant peddlers of wearing apparel. Their extreme poverty does not dilute their profound faith in Judaism. Suca, a charming middle-aged woman, spoke only within the confines of her small house; she first checked the windows to make sure no Christians were watching.

The "dean" of Marrano scholars is Amilcar Paulo, Rua do Covelo, 349, in Oporto. He also heads the Instituto de Relacoes Culturais Portugal-Israel, Rua de Guerra Junqueiro, 340 (tel. 60220) and has personally researched hundreds of ancient tomes, spent months in the company of Marranos in many mountainous communities, and written countless articles on the Marranos. (Unfortunately, his knowledge of English is very limited.)

BRAGANCA

In the mountainous northeast, the poorest and most backward region of Portugal, reside other Jews—many are shoemakers. Braganca was granted a royal charter in 1187 and is still an ancient stronghold with many fine treasures. Professor Eduardo Augusto de Carvalho, Rue Alexandre Herculano, 229 (tel. 22166) is a distinguished non-Jewish scholar who has studied the life-styles of the Marranos throughout Portugal.

The Braganca shoemaker Joao Baptista Dos Santos (Rua Combatentes Da Grande Guerra 99) recalls how during Passover a few Jewish women would gather on the sandy shore of the Sabor River and lead each other in prayer. He was more fortunate than his brother Marranos because he spent one year in the 1940s in Oporto attending Rosh Pinna Yeshiva. Today he recites in Hebrew daily prayers which he learned from his parents. He was married in the church where he was baptized, and his children by his Christian wife have the biblical names of Rachel and Leah.

CASTELO BRANCO

In the municipal museum is the cornerstone of a thirteenth-century synagogue famed as the "Belmonte Synagogue."

CASTELO DE VIDE

There is a picturesque Jewish quarter, Judiaria, where houses in the narrow street are all white and many have Gothic doors. Below the Jewish quarter is Fonte da Vila, a Baroque granite fountain, and nearby is the local castle.

COIMBRA

This university city was where Jews faced the Inquisition: they had to renounce Judaism or be burned at the stake.

FARO

This prominent Algarve resort town has a medieval fourteenth-century Jewish cemetery of interest. The city was a famed center of Hebrew printing in the fifteenth century.

LISBON

Lisbon has been a place of refuge for Jews since the fifteenth century, and the sights of Jewish interest attest to this history. The Cemeterio Israelita on Avenida Alfonso III is hidden by a stone wall with no visible markings on the wooden gate. Beyond the wall are terraced rows of man-sized horizontal tombstones, and Rua De Judiaria (Jews' Street) is the only remnant of what was once an important Jewish community. At one time there were four Jewish quarters in Lisbon: the largest was located in the Da Madelena quarter; a second was in the old Pedreira section outside the city walls; the third was in the Alfama area; and the fourth, known as the Petite Juiverie, was in the block of houses that now extends between the Church of San Juliao and the Bank of Portugal Building.

OPORTO

Portugal's second largest city has a synagogue—Sinagoga Kadoorie or Mekor Haim at Rua de Guerra Junqueiro 340 (tel. 60220). Here Captain Carlos De Barros Basto lived and was chiefly responsible for the building of the synagogue. A *converso,* he had entered the Jewish faith in Tangiers, Morocco, and in the 1920s launched his futile effort to revive Judaism among other *conversos.* (Call upon Eteline Rasas Ramos Pinto, a delightful woman who speaks English. Also, Professor Amilcar Paulo, Rue do Covelo 349 [tel. 484458], the renowned Marrano scholar.)

REBORDELO

A few homes here show a Star of David on their doorposts, revealing the presence of Marranos. The home of Moises Abraao is one example—the *magen* was carved by his father.

SILVES

Near the Spanish border, not far from Evora, are the remains of a small Jewish quarter.

TOMAR

There is an ancient synagogue (completed in 1497) on the Rua d'Joaquim Jacinto; it is very small and has a Gothic ceiling. For many years the premises were used as a wine cellar, but today the building is a national monument. The Abraham Zacuto Museum, filled with early nautical devices, is located in Tomar.

KOSHER RESTAURANTS

Lisbon: Mrs. R. Querub, Rua Rodrigo de Fonseca 38 (tel. 530396).
Rev. L. Toledano, Avenida Albarea Cabral 5-5 (tel. 640906).
Mrs. E. Pariénte, Rua Sociedade Farmaceutica 7-3° (tel. 556378).

USEFUL ADDRESSES

Lisbon: U.S. Embassy, Avenida Duque de Loule 39 (tel. 570102).
Israeli Embassy, Rua Antonio Enes 16-4° (tel. 570251).
Canadian Embassy, Rua Rosa Araujo 2 (tel. 562547).

PUERTO RICO

Unfortunately, Puerto Rico has no venerable synagogue, no ancient cemetery, and no early Jewish settlement, but its 2,000 Jews constitute the largest Jewish community in the Caribbean. History records that Marrano Jews from the Balearic Islands may have settled here in 1520. Until recent years some of their Marrano Catholic descendants observed such Jewish traditions as lighting candles on Friday evening. Probably the first Jewish congregation was organized in 1898 in the city of Ponce, by Rabbi Adolph Spiegel, who conducted Rosh Hashanah services for the American military forces when they first arrived that year in Puerto Rico.

From 1900 to the early 1920s there were individual Jews in Puerto Rico but no community nor congregation. The family of Charles Gans had come from Connecticut and established a cigar factory on the island in 1899. Milton Farber and Nathaniel Nemerow were also early settlers. A number of Eastern European Jews, unable to gain admittance to the United States after the 1924 immigration quota law became operative, took up temporary residence in Cuba while awaiting entry to the mainland; others, after learning Spanish, arrived in Puerto Rico and settled their families here. Among these arrivals were Simon Benus and Aron Levin, who developed a chain of department stores throughout the island.

The present Jewish community in Puerto Rico truly dates back to the 1920s, when a number of Eastern European and American Jews settled here, principally in San Juan and neighboring Santurce. More came during World War II, and after the Castro revolution in 1959, about 250 Cuban Jewish families arrived. The first religious school was opened in 1952. In 1953, the community purchased an old mansion once owned by a Nazi sympathizer and converted it into the Jewish Community Center and Shaare Tzedek Synagogue at 903 Ponce de Leon Avenue in Santurce (tel. 724-4157).

Today this Conservative synagogue has a membership of about 225 families; Rabbi Martin T. Sandberg leads the congregation. The Jewish Community Center is in the same building, as is the magnificent Morris Rothenberg Memorial Library. The president of the Puerto Rican Jewish Community Center is Henry Reinhold.

273

There is also a small Reform congregation, Temple Beth Shalom, founded in 1967, at Loiza and San Jorge Streets in Santurce. The local B'nai B'rith Lodge was founded in 1964; and, before his death, Nathan Leopold (of the Leopold and Loeb murder case) was a member. Among places of Jewish interest in Puerto Rico is La Casa del Libro (House of the Book) at 225 Cristo Street in Old San Juan; this government-sponsored library of rare books and fine printing was founded in 1955 by the late Dr. Elber Adler, an American Jew who was a noted book collector and typographical expert. His bequest of $100,000 to the library in 1963 remains the largest single gift ever made to a Puerto Rican cultural institution.

KOSHER RESTAURANTS

Kosher food can be purchased at Pueblo supermarkets in addition to the following restaurants:

The Red Rooster (in the Condado area).
Lindy's Excelsior Hotel, 802 Ponce de Leon Avenue.
Condado Holiday Inn.
Palace Hotel (Hirsh's Kosher Restaurant).

ROMANIA

More than 90 percent of Romanian Jewry have emigrated to Israel since the end of World War II, and in Israel today there are 350,000 Romanian Jews. Fewer than 45,000 Romanian Jews manage to survive under the protection of Dr. Moses Rosen, who is not only the Chief Rabbi, but also a member of the Romanian Parliament. Rabbi Rosen is a gifted speaker in several languages, a television personality, and a world traveler; for more than twenty-five years, he has also headed the Federation of Jewish Communities (located at Strada Sf. Vineri 9–11). His father preceded him as Chief Rabbi and as president. Of all the Balkan countries only Romania maintains relations with Israel; in 1971 a joint Romanian-Israeli committee for scientific relations was established, and El Al has regular flights to Bucharest.

Rabbi Rosen's Federation of Jewish Communities (tel. 155090 or 138927) has helped subsidize eleven kosher restaurants, given monthly income allowances to 10,000 Romanian Jews, and built and maintained homes for the aged, 24 Talmud Torahs, and 150 synagogues throughout the country. Jewish community services (supported by JDC and other international Jewish organizations) are still active in Bucharest, Timisoara, and Arad. The severe earthquake that hit Romania in 1977 caused the collapse of many buildings and resulted in heavy loss of life. In Bucharest, scene of the worst destruction, at least eleven Jews died and several synagogues were hard hit. The JDC rushed emergency aid to the thousands of Jews who lost their homes and possessions, and helped the Federation of Jewish Communities of Romania to distribute food and clothing to those in need. Israel sent a planeload of medicines and other emergency supplies. The federation controls the 150 Romanian synagogues, seventeen of which are in Bucharest: for example, Choral Temple at Strada Vineri 9–11 (tel. 141924); Great Synagogue, Strada Vasile Adamache 11 (tel. 215947); Malbim Synagogue, Strada Bravilor 4; and Sephardic Synagogue, Strada Nikos Beloianis 9. The Choral Temple, opened in 1866, can accommodate 4,000 worshipers. The Synagoga Mare a Croitorilor (the Great Synagogue of the Little Tailors), located at Strada Mamoulian 8, has recently been converted into a museum on the 2,000-year history of the Jewish people in this country. Their presence is recorded by thousands of artifacts, manuscripts, scrolls, and tablets dating from the Roman conquest of Romania in the first century up to the German occupation in 1940. The Synagogue of the Little Tailors was in the once-flourishing Jewish Quarter of Bucharest, where as many as seventy houses of worship were active before Hitler. In Bucharest there are kosher restaurants serving Romanian foods such as *flanken, kishke,* noodle soup, and *strudel.*

In 1971 a sociomedical center was opened in Bucharest to provide medical assistance for aged and handicapped Romanian Jews. A bimonthly trilingual newspaper (Romanian, Yiddish, and Hebrew) reports on general Jewish world concerns. The Jewish Library (Strada Popa Russu 28), adjoining the editorial offices of the newspaper, has a rich depository of Jewish memorabilia.

The Jewish cemetery on Giorgiu Road, Bucharest, has a concrete model of the ill-fated SS *Struma,* a tiny ship (carrying 769 Jewish refugees) which hit a mine off the Romanian coast in 1942 and sank with the loss of all lives except one. The Yiddish State Theater of Bucharest is housed in its own edifice at Strada Dr. J. Barasch 15. The theater has 600 seats, each equipped with simultaneous-translation earphones. A school for drama is also housed in the building; its costs are underwritten by the government as an official cultural enterprise. President of the Bucharest Jewish Community is Professor Lechter Emil.

Outside of Bucharest, there are many sights of Jewish interest. At **Jassy** in Moldavia there is a remarkable fifteenth-century synagogue at Sinagogilor Strada 7, probably Romania's oldest existing synagogue. The white stucco synagogue in **Brasov** (Poarta Scheiulni 27) is currently undergoing repairs; the synagogue in **Constanta** (Strada C. A. Rosetti 2, off Boulevard Tomis) is also worth visiting. In **Arad** the synagogue on Bela Farsa Strada accommodates 2,500 Jews. There are four synagogues in **Bacau** at Jerni Strada 15, Alexander Celbin Strada 15, Stefan Celmari Strada 20, and Aurel Marcus Strada 18.

CLUJ

In 1972 the Federation of Jewish Communities of Romania dedicated a restored synagogue in Cluj, Romania's second largest city, to the memory of the 180,000 Jews who were deported in 1944 by the Nazis from northern Transylvania to Auschwitz where they died. Near the center of town on the highway north of Cluj is an abandoned synagogue.

In 1980 the 340 Jewish families in Cluj inducted Rabbi Dr. Carol Iolesz, a survivor of Hungarian-German persecution. Cluj, capital of Transylvania, had more than 16,000 Jews until 1944, when the entire population was deported to Auschwitz. During World War II,

Cluj was occupied by Hungary. Local synagogues are at Strada David Francisc 16, Strada Baritiu 16, Strada Croritoilor 13, and Strada Horea 21. The community center is at Strada Tipografici 25 (tel. 95123162).

JASSY

At one time Romania's third largest city had a 65 percent Jewish population. Dr. Simion Caufman, a pharmacist, heads the local Jewish community which before World War II had most of the Romanian synagogues. Jassy is no longer a center of Jewish learning and Jewish culture; the lure of emigration to Israel and Western democracies decimated the Jewish community following World War II.

In 1976 leaders of the Romanian Communist Party, members of the Federation of Jewish Communities, and members of the public paid homage to the 12,000 Jews murdered by the Nazis and their agents in Jassy thirty-five years earlier. At the unveiling of the memorial built by the Jassy Council in the square of the 300-year-old Great Synagogue, Mayor Ion Manciuc said that the memorial also served to remind people that such atrocities should never be repeated. Romanian Jewish leaders also paid homage to the victims of the "Death Train" organized by the Nazis to deport Romanian Jews the day after the pogrom of June 29, 1941. Some 1,200 men and women who died in the grossly overcrowded train are buried in a common grave at the Jewish cemetery in Podul Iliaiei, near Jassy, and another 650 at Tirgu Frumos, twenty-eight miles from Jassy. The Federation of Jewish Communities of Romania has built memorials in each cemetery. Jassy synagogues are at Strada Stefancel Mare 38, Strada Dimitrov 17, and Strada Sinagogilor 7.

In **Oradea** (near the Hungarian border) is an interesting Jewish community center and synagogue at Strada Mihai Viteazu 4. Small groups of Hungarian Jews still reside in Timisoara. Visit the House of the Federation of Jewish Communities in Eforie Nord.

Romania is the only Communist country in Eastern Europe that refused to sever relations with Israel after the Six Days' War, and the Romanian government continues to expand economic and cultural ties with the Jewish state. Recently, a postage stamp was issued in Romania in honor of Sholem Aleichem, the author of many of the plays performed by the Yiddish State Theater.

KOSHER RESTAURANTS

(Supervision: Chief Rabbi Dr. D. M. Rosen, Bucharest)

Arad: Strada 7 Noembrie Nr. 22 (tel. 960-13245).

Bacau: Strada Alexandru cel Bun Nr. 11 (tel. 931-14714).

Borsec: Strada Jokai (tel. 15).

Botosani: Strada 7 Aprilie Nr. 81 (tel. 12489).

Bucharest: Jewish Community Restaurant, Strada Popa Soare 18 (tel. 220-398).

Cluj: Strada Paris 5–7 (tel. 951-111026).

Cristian: (near Brasov): Strada Garii 3 (tel. 11).

Dorohoi: Strada 6 Martie 48 (tel. 324).

Eforie Nord: Vila Mira, Strada A. Miureseanu 3 (tel. 917-411-38).

Galati: Strada Dornei Nr. 7 (tel. 93013662).

Jassy: Community Center Restaurant, Strada Elena Doamna 9 (tel. 980-138-83).

Oradea: Strada Mihai Viteazu 5 (tel. 991-114-56).

Timisoara: Strada Gh Lazar Nr. 5 (tel. 961-328-13).

USEFUL ADDRESSES

Bucharest: U.S. Embassy, Strada Tudor Arghezi 7–9 (tel. 124040). Israeli Embassy, St. Dr. Burghelea 5 (tel. 132636).

ST. EUSTATIUS

In the Netherlands Antilles on the island of St. Eustatius (southeast of Puerto Rico) stand the solemn remains of a yellow brick synagogue, Honen Dalim (Kind to the Poor), built around 1738 by a once-thriving Jewish community. Jews first came to the island as early as 1660, but a French raid in November 1709 drove out these early settlers, most of whom returned years later to continue the prosperous trade with English, Dutch, French, and Spanish ships. Sephardic Jews from Spain, Portugal, and South America prospered here until the end of the eighteenth century when other havens opened up for oppressed Jewry. Trade winds made St. Eustatius an easy destination for sailing ships to and from Europe.

In the capital city of Oranjestad are the offices of the St. Eustatius Tourist Bureau headed by a very pleasant and able young man, James Maduro, who bears the name of one of the most prominent Sephardic families in the Caribbean. But James Maduro is not Jewish: his name was probably adopted by his ancestors who were slaves before emancipation.

St. Eustatius is a cello-shaped island with a spacious harbor and a dominant, 1,968-foot volcanic crater called "the Quill." It was in the shadow of the Quill that the first synagogue, Honen Dalim, was built in 1738 by five Jewish families then numbering twenty-two persons. Curaçao's congregation generously contributed, as did the Amsterdam synagogue, with Torah scrolls. In August 1772, when a hurricane devastated the island and damaged the synagogue, the Jewish community of New York City sent money to repair it. By 1778 there were 150 Jewish families and during the American Revolution the warehouses of Jewish merchants supplied much of America's needs. One Jewish settler from New York, Isaac Naftali, was influential in getting the local government to decree that freedom of religion and freedom of trade go together. Jews served guard duty except on the Sabbath.

However, in November 1776 the peaceful serenity and prosperity of St. Eustatius was disturbed as it became the first foreign community to salute a warship of the newly emergent United States. Dutch Governor Johannes de Groot ordered a 21-gun salute from Ft. Oranje to the American flag aboard the U.S. Navy frigate *Andrew*

Doria. But, in 1781, British Admiral Sir George Rodney captured St. Eustatius and allowed his men to loot the prosperous Jewish-owned warehouses because they had supplied munitions and food for the Americans in defiance of British orders. Admiral Rodney sold much of the booty at auction on the island of St. Kitts, and he personally faced lawsuits in England by merchants whose ships and goods had been seized. St. Eustatius was then a Dutch possession and supposedly neutral in the American Revolutionary War. Admiral Rodney also exiled 250 male Jews to the neighboring British-held islands of St. Kitts and Antigua, leaving their women and children destitute. St. Eustatius never recovered from the 1781 British attack and the looting of the island by Rodney's men. However, nine months later the French captured the island and permitted the Jews to return; but the Jewish community lasted only until 1850. Today there is but one Jewish family on the island.

The capital and only city of Oranjestad looks like an old engraving of an English village of 1795. The poignant, ruined stone churches, the crumbling, aboveground burial vaults, and the rubble of wrecked Jewish warehouses in the bayside Lower Town give little indication that this island was a great center of world trade (slaves, sugar, and munitions) in the days of sailing ships.

In 1973 some Jewish students and their teachers from Berkeley, California, under the leadership of Rabbi Leo Abrami and his wife, Susan, devoted their efforts to restoring the ancient synagogue, Honen Dalim. Near the synagogue, at the end of a hilly cobbled street, is a Jewish cemetery where gravestones date back to 1680.

ST. MARTIN

What was once a proud and prosperous eighteenth-century Jewish community is today but a shadow of its former self. There are a dozen Jewish families on St. Martin, all dependent for their livelihood upon the tourist trade. The eighteenth-century synagogue no longer exists, although part of its walls may be found at 6 Front Street in the village of Philipsburg. Today this site is occupied by the West Indian Tavern whose menu presents these interesting facts:

> Many centuries ago, in the days of the Pirates' spices, Spanish galleons and Peter Stuyvesant, when the Great European maritime nations repeatedly fought for, lost and recovered all the Leeward Islands . . . Sint Maarten was a thriving community. Plantation life flourished and much of the business was transacted by three large Jewish families. These people built what is thought to be the island's own synagogue at the top end of the narrow strip of land later to be named Philipsburg after a Scotsman called John Philips. But the tide of prosperity turned on the island, trade dropped almost to nothing, the plantation fell to waste; the menfolk found employment elsewhere and the Jewish families left. 150 years passed; the synagogue fell to its foundations but upstreet Philipsburg once again became a fashionable place to live. Built on the very ruins of this old synagogue by an old and famous island family now over 100 years ago, one of the old cedar houses has been restored to become the first pub in St. Maarten where you can enjoy the warm homely atmosphere of an original and unspoiled Dutch homestead.

The synagogue had been built under the authority of the Amsterdam Jewish community and the local Dutch government. But a hurricane in the early 1830s severely damaged the edifice, and soon thereafter the Jewish community began to decline.

Today the unofficial head of the local Jewish community is A. Horovicz, who owns and operates the Windmill stores. Claire E. Peterson (P.O. Box 186) is the moving spirit behind the effort to organize the small Jewish community. She recently enlisted the help of Mikva Israel–Emanuel Synagogue on the island of Curaçao, but her efforts proved futile for a variety of reasons including the diverse ages and the various religious persuasions of the Jewish residents. Among the prominent Jewish businessmen (other than world-famous Spritzer & Fuhrmann with stores throughout the Dutch Caribbean) is Julio Meit, who owns Julio's Smoke 'N' Booze and Tasting House on Front Street. E. Belilos owns the New Amsterdam stores with branches on Aruba and Curaçao. A Yemenite Jew, Ezra Amram, operates a unique Sabra jewelry and dress shop. The Summit Hotel on Simson Bay lagoon is owned by a New York Jewish businessman. Max Donner of the Bronx, New York, owns Pelican Key Villas, and R. Shapiro owns Vacation Villa on Simson Bay. For a truly memorable experience, spend the day aboard the *Maison Maru,* a sixty-foot catamaran, owned and operated by Captain Larry Berkowitz, a New York City psychologist.

SCOTLAND*

The Scottish Jew has an independent approach to the problems of Jewish life. This is particularly true in the lovely university city of Edinburgh where calm self-confidence is evident among the 3,000 Jews there. Jews first applied in 1691 for permission to live and trade in Edinburgh, but not until 1780 was there an organized Jewish community. In 1795, the town council sold a plot of ground to a local Jewish dentist for burial purposes, and in 1816 the cemetery was acquired by the Jewish community when the synagogue was opened at 4 Salisbury Road. In 1932, two small congregations united to form the Edinburgh Hebrew Congregation with a 1,000-seat synagogue. After extensive alterations in 1980, the building serves also as the local Jewish community center (tel. 6673144). It is especially noted for its original musical productions with Israeli themes. The B'nai B'rith lodge in Edinburgh has for almost a quarter of a century served the Jewish community; during the annual International Music Festival week, the lodge hosts out-of-town Jewish visitors. Edinburgh's educational atmosphere and relatively quiet business life (compared to Glasgow and most of England) are most conducive to pleasant residential living.

ABERDEEN

Scotland's third largest city is a seaside resort and also the site of a university. The local synagogue is at 74 Dee Street (tel. 22135).

AYR

At 52 Racecourse Road in the Inverclay Hotel is the only synagogue in town. Kosher food is served here.

DUNDEE

The synagogue on St. Mary Place was founded in 1874, and is still attended by Jews of German origin (tel. 28140).

---

* NOTE: Wales and Northern Ireland are included under "England."

GLASGOW

The industrial city of Glasgow, with a population of slightly over 1 million, has about 12,000 Jews, most of whom came from Eastern Europe during the past sixty years. Although the first synagogue in Glasgow was opened in 1823, Glasgow has today at least eight synagogues including Crosshill at 20 Belleisle Street (tel. 4237033); Giffnock & Newlands at Maryville Avenue (tel. 6386600); Langside at 125 Niddrie Road (tel. 4234062); Netherleen Clarkston on Clarkson Road at Randolph Drive (tel. 6393396); New Reform at 147 Ayr Road; Newton Mearns on Beech Avenue (tel. 6392442); Orthodox at 85 South Portland Street; Queens Park on Fallach Road (tel. 6326579); and the Garnethill Hebrew Congregation (dating from 1879) at 29 Garnet Street (tel. 3324151).

Major events recently organized in the city are the "Jewish Way of Life" exhibition, and an exhibition of Jewish art in Kelvingrove Art Gallery, one of Britain's major civic galleries. Among the present members of the community are Dr. Benno Schotz, the Queen's Sculptor in Scotland, and Dr. Jack E. Miller, national treasurer of the British Medical Association and past president of Glasgow Jewish Representative Council, the "parliament" of Scotland's estimated 15,000 Jews. Another member is Dr. Sidney Naftalin, who was medical officer to forty refugee children from Nazi Germany who were given sanctuary in the synagogue buildings from 1938 to until they were evacuated in 1942.

Glasgow is justly proud of its Jewish pipe-band, the only one in the entire world. In recent years the city has had a Jewish Lord Provost (mayor), and two Glasgow Jews are members of Parliament. Sir Isaac Wolfson, international business tycoon, came from Glasgow.

ST. ANDREWS

The historic birthplace of golf and site of the oldest university in Scotland (1412) also has a home for Jewish students at the university (the Jewish Students' Society).

SHETLAND ISLANDS

There is a single Jewish family which has been living for more than forty years on these remote islands, visited annually by the Edinburgh rabbi.

KOSHER RESTAURANTS

Ayr: Inverclay Private Hotel, 52 Racecourse Road (tel. 0290 64393).

Edinburgh: Mrs. D. Leigh, 6 St. Catherine's Place (tel. 031-667-4254).

Glasgow: Freed's, 49 Coplaw Street (tel. 041-423-8911).
Hillel House, Glasgow University (tel. 041-423 0942).
Whyn Kosher Guest House, 38 Regent's Park Square (tel. 041-423-1435).
Wolfe's, 35 Overdale Street (tel. 041-623 4986).
Cohen's, 2 Burnfield Road (tel. 041-638 4383).

Prestwick: North Beach Hotel, Links Road (tel. 0292-79069).

USEFUL ADDRESSES

Edinburgh: U.S. Consulate General, 3 Regent Terrace (tel. 556-8315).

SENEGAL

Only a handful of Jews reside here; there are perhaps twenty Jewish families from Lebanon and Morocco representing foreign business firms.

All Jews reside in Dakar, the capital. Israel maintains an embassy at 57 Avenue Albert Sarraut (tel. 224-04). Local leader of the Jewish community is Clement Politis, 42 rue Vincens (tel. 212784).

The U.S. Embassy is in Dakar at 49, Avenue Jean XXIII (tel. 214296).

SINGAPORE*

Adventurous Jews seeking their fortunes in trade settled in Singapore more than 175 years ago. After the British conquest in 1819, Jews from Baghdad arrived, and by 1841 Singapore had twenty-two Jews. Shortly thereafter, the government provided land, and the first synagogue was erected on Synagogue Street. By 1858 there were twenty Jewish families, mostly English, who became exceptionally wealthy in the opium trade with India and China permitted by the British until 1910. Singapore Jews then switched to textiles, carpets, and rubber manufacturing, and acquired ownership of vast quantities of real estate. By 1870 there were fifty wealthy Jewish familes, all highly respected. By 1890 there were 190 families, mostly Sephardic.

Jewish migration to Singapore after 1939 increased the population to 1,500 Jews. During World War II 350 Jews were jailed or put into forced labor camps by the Japanese; several died in prison. In 1947 the number of Singapore Jews fell to 877; today out of a population of 3 million there are only 450 Jews.

The original synagogue property purchased in 1842 was sold in 1870, and a new community group was organized. Maghain Avoth Synagogue was opened in April 1878, and is still located appropriately on Synagogue Street (recently renamed Waterloo Street). Rev. Isaac Benzakin leads the congregation (tel. 3360-692). The building is set back from the street with a circular driveway. It is Sephardic in design and in practice. The synagogue was rebuilt and enlarged in 1925 and has been maintained in excellent condition. Daily and Sabbath services are held here, and also at the other Sephardic-Ashkenazi synagogue, Chased-El (at 2 Oxley Rise), built in 1905. Chased-El was the personal edifice of a fascinating man, Sir Manasseh Meyer, an extremely wealthy Jew who was knighted for his public service. His name leads the list of benefactors on a marble slab at Raffles College, now the University of Singapore. Meyer's Chambers, a prominent building on Raffles Square, bears his name below a *Magen David* on the keystone over its main doorway. On majestic

---

* NOTE: In nearby Sarawak, Borneo, the only Jew is native-born Dr. Yawha Cohen, whose mother was killed by the Japanese while she was helping prisoners of war.

grounds in Singapore where he lived with his wife and seven children, he built this magnificent synagogue, a permanent *succah,* a Jewish community center, and the Sir Manasseh Meyer Talmud Torah Hebrew School at 71 Oxley Rise (tel. 7379746). It seems that after a dispute with the leaders of the Maghain Avoth Synagogue, he decided to set up his own private synagogue; it has been continuously maintained since his death by the philanthropy of his daughter, Mrs. Nissim.

Singapore has a Jewish community Sunday School for about 30 students under the youthful leadership of Rabbi Isaac Ben Zakin, a native of Spanish Morocco. The school occupies the lower floor of the Menora Club premises on Oxley Rise.

One of the more recent presidents of the Singapore Jewish community was an Indonesian-born Jewess, Mrs. Felice Kate Isaacs, who runs an optical store with her husband. President of the Jewish Welfare Board in Singapore is Frank Benjamin (P.O. Box 474; tel. 2350155) and the vice-president is S. Khafi, Afghan Malaya Trading Co., 10 Oxley Road (tel. 2356264).

Another prominent Singapore Jew is David Marshall, Singapore's prime minister in 1955. Among Marshall's services to the Jewish community was his effort to save Singapore's first Jewish cemetery, which marked the first traces of Jews in Singapore: "My beloved forefathers in their wisdom went into the jungle where tigers roamed to rent a parcel of land for one dollar a year. They took a lease for ninety-nine years forgetting that the dead live much longer than the living. This was in 1838, twenty years after the founding of Singapore." In 1939 the government of Singapore sought to reclaim the land; as president of Singapore's Jewish Welfare Board, Marshall resisted and continued to resist for more than three decades, although in 1983 the Jewish Welfare Board agreed to close the old Orchard Road cemetery as well as the cemetery on Thomson Road, after the government decided to use the land for an underground railway. The government did agree to pay the expenses of transfering the remains to another cemetery.

USEFUL ADDRESSES

U.S. Consulate, 30 Hill Street (tel. 3380251).
Israeli Embassy, 9 Faber House (10th floor), 230/k Orchard Road (tel. 2350966).

REPUBLIC OF SOUTH AFRICA

It is a curious fact that whereas the history of the children of Israel began in North Africa, in Egypt, their descendants did not lay a cornerstone in South Africa until 3,500 years later. In 1652, Jews arrived and settled in the Cape Town area. After the British occupation in 1795 Jews from England came in large numbers. In 1841, the entire European population of South Africa was but 9,359. Benjamin Norden, one of the early settlers in South Africa and founder of the city of Durban, assembled seventeen male Jews on Yom Kippur at his Cape Town home. The *hazan* was an American merchant, Samuel Rudolf, who settled here and subsequently served the Jewish community for many years as its president. Later that year Simeon Marcus, a Dutch Jew from Amsterdam, organized the community of twenty Jews under the name of Tikvath Israel, or "Hope of Israel." Later a burial ground, the "House of Life," was the gift of John Norton; it served the community until 1887.

In 1846 R. J. Joseph arrived from England, joined the Hope of Israel Society as the honorary secretary, and became Cape Town's first *mohel.* In 1849 a plot of land was purchased, and a synagogue was established in a house there. In August 1849 Rev. Isaac Pulver arrived from London as the first rabbi for the Cape Town Hebrew Congregation serving twenty-eight persons. Problems arose, and he returned to England. Not until 1859 did the Jewish community in Cape Town have another rabbi, Joel Rabinowitz, from Birmingham, England. He held the post for twenty-three years, and the Jewish community grew from its original sixty families. Rabbi Rabinowitz visited Jews in every part of the colony and was truly the first head of South African Jewry. He encouraged the building of a new synagogue on St. John's Street in Cape Town—dedicated in September 1862. In the early 1880s Jews from Eastern Europe began to arrive in great numbers—40,000 entered in all. After 1912, another 30,000 Jews came from Lithuania, Latvia, Poland, Germany, and England.

In 1884 the Cape Town Hebrew Congregation became the site for the 100th birthday celebration of Sir Moses Montefiore, the most eminent Jew in the world and the donor of a considerable sum of money to the congregation in 1849. A special stained-glass window was erected in his honor. In 1904 a new synagogue building, the Great Synagogue, was constructed, due to the efforts of Cape

Town's mayor, Hyman Liberman, whose generosity was only equaled by his unceasing efforts on behalf of the Jewish community. Today there are 28,000 Jews in Cape Town, proud of the twin towers of their Great Synagogue on Government Avenue. These towers are among Cape Town's most prominent landmarks, standing out across the botanic gardens with Table Mountain in the background. Adjoining the synagogue is a Jewish museum.

Of the 120,000 Jews presently residing in the Republic of South Africa (population 30 million), Jews constitute about 4 percent of the total white population. A majority of South African Jews are native-born. The largest proportion of Jews, about 60,000, are in Johannesburg, the richest city in Africa; and at least 10 percent of this number are Israeli citizens who have flocked here. Johannesburg Jews, for the most part, came from Amsterdam where they were in the diamond-cutting business, and they continued their business interests in diamonds here. Jewish population in the Transvaal (including Johannesburg) today is about 75,000; Cape Province (including Cape Town and Port Elizabeth), 35,000; Natal (including Durban), 7,000; and about 4,000 in the Orange Free State. South African Jewry is represented by the Jewish Board of Deputies, officially recognized as the spokesman for South African Jews. Jews play a prominent part in South African public life: in recent years there were one Jewish senator, five members of the House of Assembly, three judges of the Supreme Court, and a large number of mayors, deputy mayors, and members of provincial and city councils. In Johannesburg, for example, one-third of the members of a recent Johannesburg City Council were Jews. In recent municipal elections the Progressive Reform Party won nineteen seats, fourteen of which went to Jews. In Johannesburg the thirteenth Jewish mayor, Alan Gadd, was recently elected. There appears to be no mass exodus of Jews from the Republic of South Africa, despite the restrictive racial policies of its government.

Among the many Jewish places of interest the following should not be overlooked: Herman Wald's magnificent memorial to the Holocaust victims, Westpark Cemetery, Johannesburg; statue of President Paul Kruger in Church Square, Pretoria, presented to the city in 1899 by Sammy Marks, prominent Pretoria Jew; Beth Din, Yeoville, Johannesburg; Durban Jewish Club; Gardens Synagogue of Cape Town (with its famed turrets); Jewish Museum of Cape Town, housed in South Africa's oldest synagogue; and the C. P. Nel Museum, Oudtshoorn, housing Jewish memorabilia. The South African Jewish community maintains one of the finest networks of Jewish day schools in the world. Seven thousand five hundred students attend such schools in Johannesburg, Pretoria, Cape Town, Port Elizabeth, Durban, and Benoni. Another 4,000 attend afternoon Hebrew schools, and about 3,000 are in Jewish nursery schools. South

Africa has four weekly Jewish newspapers, all published in Johannesburg.

The following is a partial listing of South African synagogues:

Bloemfontein (Orange Free State): United Hebrew Institutions* Community Center, 2 Fairview (tel. 745972).

Cape Town (Cape Province): Great Synagogue, Government Avenue; Tefereth Israel, Schoonder Street, Gardens; Cape Town Orthodox, 16 Vredehoek Avenue; Green and Sea Point, Marias Road; Claremont, Grove St.; Bellville, Rhos Street; Rondebosch, corner Avenue de Mist and Stuart Road; Goodwood, Dirkie-Uys Street; Maitland-Milnerton, Station Road; Beth Hamedrash de Ponevesz, Maynard Street; Chabaad, 31 Arthur's Road; Observatory and Mowbray, William Street; Temple Israel Reform, Upper Portwood Road; Temple Israel Reform, Salisbury Road; Muizenberg and Kalk Bay, Camp Road.

Durban (Natal): Great Synagogue, Essenwood Road and Silverton Road; Temple David, 369 Ridge Road.

East London (Cape Province): Shar Hashomayim, 56 Park Avenue; Temple Hillel, Belgravia Crescent.

Johannesburg (Transvaal): Orthodox Great Synagogue, Wolmarans Street; Yeoville, Hunter Street and Kenmere Road; Oxford, 20 North Avenue; Berea, Tudhope Avenue; Parkview-Greenside, Chester Road; Emmarentia, 129 Barry Hertzog Avenue; Adath Jeshurun, 41 Hunter Street; Cyrildene Observatory Hebrew Congregation, 32 Aida Avenue; Northeastern Hebrew Congregation, Orchards; Orange Grove Hebrew Congregation, Sydenham Highlands; Northern Hebrew Congregation, Birnam Park; Etz Hayim, 20 Barnato Street; Valley Observatory, 11 The Curve; United Progressive Hebrew Congregation, Hillbrow; Temple Israel, Paul Nel and Claim Streets; Beth Emanuel, 38 Oxford Road; Temple Shalom, Louis Botha Avenue.

Kimberley (Cape Province): Griqualand West Hebrew Congregation, Memorial Road; Community Hall, Voortrekker Street; Beth Hamedrash, Baronial Street.

Oudtshoorn: Baron von Rheede Street. A handsome Ark from the John Street Synagogue has been given to the C. P. Nel Museum which has installed it in a large gallery of the museum's eastern wall, and the museum now claims it is the only museum in the world of which a diminutive synagogue is an integral part.

---

*It should be noted that there are United Hebrew Institutions with synagogues and community centers in Benoni, Boksburg, Brakpan, Germiston, Springs, Randfontein, Krugersdorp, and Kempton Park, all in Transvaal.

Port Elizabeth: The Port Elizabeth Hebrew Congregation, Glendinningvale; Summerstrand, Brighton Drive; Progressive Temple Israel, Upper Dickens Street.

Pretoria: Pretoria United Hebrew Congregation Great Synagogue, 717 Pretorius Street; Adath Israel, 551 Sibelius Street; Progressive Temple, 315 Bronkhorst Street.

KOSHER RESTAURANTS

Cape Town: *Approved by the Beth Din:* Heerengracht Hotel, St. George Street (tel. 413151).
Mustard Seed (vegetarian), Regent Road, Sea Point; and
South West House, Greenmarket Square.
Norton (vegetarian), Albow Centre, Hatfield Street.
Not approved by Beth Din, but serving only kosher food: King David Hotel, 369 Main Road, Sea Point (tel. 44-8741).
Rio Grande Hotel, Muizenberg (tel. 44-81151).
Imperial Hotel, Muizenberg.
Sharon Hotel, Alexander Road, Muizenberg (tel. 885225).
(Muizenberg is a seaside resort about sixteen miles from the center of Cape Town, and facilities are available in the season only, November to March.)

Johannesburg: Connoisseur Hotel, Leyds and Nugget Streets (tel. 7245211).
Carmel Hotel, 22 Muller Street, Yeoville (tel. 43-2250).
Mirkin-Seeff Hotel, 25 O'Reilly Road (tel. 6424981).
WyntonJoy, Catherine Avenue and Kapstein Street, Hillbrow (tel. 6424881).
Jerusalem, 126 Louis Botha Avenue (tel. 4322212).

USEFUL ADDRESSES

Cape Town: U.S. Consulate General, Broadway Industries Center, Heerengracht, Foreshore (tel. 214280).
Israeli Embassy, 812 Regis House, Adderley Street (tel. 431779).

Durban: U.S. Consulate General, 29th floor, Durban Bay House (tel. 324737).

Johannesburg: U.S. Consulate General, 11th floor, Kine Center (tel. 211684).

Pretoria: U.S. Embassy, Thibault House, 225 Pretorious Street (tel. 284266).
Israeli Embassy, Apolo Center, 9th floor, 405 Church Street (tel. 269008).
Canadian Embassy, NBSA Centre, Church and Beatrix Streets (tel. 24718).

SOUTH KOREA

There are twenty-five Jewish families residing in the capital city of Seoul. Religious services are held in homes such as the residence of A. Muzati, Cosmos Apartment 301, Riverside (tel. 792-9231) and at the U.S. Army Base (Rabbi Aviv Weiss, tel. 79045024).

USEFUL ADDRESSES

Seoul: U.S. Embassy, 82 Sejong-Ro, Chongro-ku (tel. 722-2601).

SPAIN

Legend has it that Jews first settled in Spain after the destruction of the First Temple. Indeed the first Israelite colony was probably established in 586 B.C., after the destruction of Solomon's Temple. *Sfarad,* the Hebrew word for Spain, is mentioned in the Bible. Jews arrived with the Phoenicians and established towns with Hebrew-sounding names; they set to "work" and founded Málaga (*melacha,* work); other towns with Hebrew-sounding names are Toledo (*toledot,* generations) and Seville (*shefelah,* the plain). Granada and Tarragona were once called "Jews' Town" because of the large numbers of Jews living there. The Jews of Spain are mentioned in the canons of the Church Council at Elvira in the year 312. After the fall of the Roman Empire, Spanish Jews were favorably treated by the Visigoths, but by 612, relentless persecution of Jews was the order of the day. Freedom returned in 711 with the invasion of the Arabs, and for the next two centuries Judaism and Jewish life flourished in Spain. Many Jews rose to positions of great influence, as evidenced by the careers of Hasdai Ibn Shaprut and Samuel Ibn Nagrela (who was vizier to the king of Granada). But in 1136 the practice of Judaism was forbidden in the province of Andalusia, though in northern Spain Jews continued to succeed as diplomats and financiers. With the end of the Moslem domination at the close of the fourteenth century anti-Jewish propaganda and persecutions took hold. In 1391 a wave of massacres of Jews, beginning at Seville, swept through all of southern Spain. In 1478 the Inquisition brought about the wholesale expulsion of all Jews from Spain; the final blow was the edict of Ferdinand and Isabella in 1492. More than 150,000 Spanish Jews found refuge in North Africa and in the Turkish Empire. Left behind were perhaps an equal number of Marranos (fervently Jewish at heart) who became victims of the Inquisition. Jews did not set foot in Spain again until the twentieth century.

Today there are approximately 12,000 Jews in all of Spain: 3,000 in Barcelona, 3,500 in Madrid, 1,500 in Málaga and the Costa del Sol, and the remainder scattered in Valencia, Seville, Alicante, Majorca, Tenerife, Córdoba, San Sebastian, Marbella, and Bilbao. The arrival of Moroccan Jews and Jews from South America has strengthened Spanish Jewish life today. Jewish schools in Madrid and Barcelona have been enlarged, and new Jewish communities have been formed in Granada and Seville. There are many Jewish students and lecturers at Madrid University and the Madrid Jewish community has established a type of Hillel House on the campus. In all parts of Spain there has been a dramatic resurgence of Jewish life.

It was not until 1948 and 1949 that the government of Spain determined that Jewish tourists should have the opportunity to view the sites of the ancient synagogues which, for the most part, had been closed to worship for almost 500 years. In 1939 Eastern European Jews fleeing from Hitler's persecution established a synagogue in a Madrid basement on Calle Cardenal Cisneros, and ten years later a model apartment in the building became the synagogue, but only after 1956 Spanish legislation legally recognized the Jewish community of Madrid as a public corporation for social, educational, and welfare purposes. In 1966 the Spanish constitution granted religious freedom to all religious minorities. In 1968 a Jewish community center at Calle Balmes 3 in Madrid was officially opened; the center has a 550-seat synagogue (Rabbi Yudah Benasuly officiates), chapel for youth, auditorium, lounge, *mikvah,* library, classrooms, recreation room, and office facilities (tel. 4459843). A new synagogue was opened in 1954 in Barcelona; Camp Masada for Jewish youngsters was established in 1965; and the formation of the Council of Jewish Communities of Spain followed.

AGUILAR DE CAMPÓO

Hanging from the altar of the sixteenth-century Church of San Miguel in Aguilar de Campóo is a lamp taken from the local medieval synagogue. The silver inscription in Hebrew stated that Rabbi Samuel Ben Pinhas Caro was the founder of the synagogue. There is also a plaque in Hebrew on the Puerta da Reinosa in this town. Near the Puerta de Reinosa, not far from the Church of San Miguel, there are the remains of shops owned by Jewish merchants during the Middle Ages.

ALICANTE

In 1972 a new Jewish community was founded in Alicante on the Mediterranean, where Jews had lived centuries earlier. Some fifty families, headed by Jaime Bentolila Garzon, built a synagogue, making Alicante the eighth city in which a Jewish community has been re-established.

AVILA

In this ancient walled city is the Chapel of Moses Rubi (at the corner of Calle Bracamonte and Calle Lopez Nunez). Originally built in 1462 as a synagogue it has served as a church for the past 500 or more years.

BALEARIC ISLANDS (MAJORCA)

Majorca, one of the five Balearic Islands (Balearic has the Hebrew meaning of *baal-yoreh* or master at throwing or shooting), has about 300 Jews who were officially recognized as a Jewish community by the Spanish government in 1971, although Jews had first settled here during the reign of Roman Emperor Claudius in the first century B.C., and the Jewish community had grown to become the dominant class in trade and industry by the fifth century A.D. When the Moors later occupied Majorca, the Jews remained in trade and contributed to the island's increasing prosperity. Indeed, the late 1300s were known as the "Golden Age of the Jews in Majorca." Largely owing to the fame of the Jewish cartographers Abraham and Jahuda Cresques, Majorca became the center of commercial activity and her ports attracted ships from all parts of the world. There is a street in Palma named in memory of Jahuda Cresques. Majorca was also noted for its unexcelled Jewish scholars and men of learning.

But this "Golden Age in Majorca" did not last long: a terrible pogrom broke out in 1391 (as it did in Spain). Many Jews were killed and the Jewish quarter was almost destroyed. This was the prelude to the official ending of Jewish life on the island in 1435. With the reconquest of Spain by Christian Europe, culminating in the marriage of Isabella of Castile and Ferdinand of Aragon, Majorca became subject to the edict of 1492 which gave Jews four months in which to either convert to Catholicism or leave Spanish territory. Many Jews in Majorca converted, but a number continued to practice their religion in secret. In Majorca these Jews became known as the Xuetas.

The Xuetas or secret Jews led difficult lives from the very beginning. But as the years passed, the Spanish regime gradually became more liberal, and in 1773, the enlightened Charles III issued an edict allowing the Xuetas complete equality with other Majorcans. However, the edict was ignored both by the island's authorities and by the Xuetas themselves, who by this time had become a sect apart from Majorcans.

Descendants of the Xuetas still exist today, but they consider themselves different from other Majorcans and do not mix freely. Among themselves they are divided into two groups—artisans and businessmen—which have little to do with each other and rarely intermarry. The Xuetas are proud of their Jewish ancestry; some even claim that the greatest figures of the Inquisition period, such as Cortes and Columbus, were "secret Jews" like themselves. It is, however, highly unlikely that any of the Xuetas still practice the

Jewish religion. Most of them tend to be ultra-orthodox Catholics and even more conservative than their fellow islanders. Some of their religious rites, however, are said to hark back to their Jewish ancestry. In the 1940s, Jewish refugees from Nazism arrived on Majorca, but the Xuetas found themselves unable to identify with these Ashkenazim. Since the rebirth of Israel in 1948, however, many Xuetas from Majorca have gone to Israel and accepted conversion back to Judaism. Today the small Jewish community of Ashkenazim is headed by Dr. Arnold Spicer (tel. 686311). The Comunidad Israelita de Mallorca is at Apartado Correos 389 in Palma (tel. 680898).

The cathedral in Palma contains many Jewish relics including a synagogue candelabra with 365 lights. In its Tesoro Room are two silver maces over six feet long—relics of the early days of Jewish life on the island. The Church of Santa Clara stands on the site of a pre-Inquisition synagogue, and the Montezion Church occupied in the fourteenth century the Great Synagogue of Palma or Mt. Zion Synagogue. The Bank of España in Calle San Bartolomé stands on the site of another synagogue from which Majorcan Jews marched to greet King James I. Some historians claim that the Church of San Miguel in Calle San Miguel was also a synagogue. The Church of El Temple, near which the Jewish cemetery had been situated, is also recorded as having been first a synagogue. The old ghetto of Palma is found on the Calle de la Platería.

Early in 1976 the Jewish community of Majorca bought more than an acre of ground at Santa Eugenia, twelve miles from Palma, for a cemetery. The community holds religious services at the Santa-Ana Hotel at Cala Mayor, on the western outskirts of Palma, and has social gatherings there on Wednesdays and Sundays. The community is run on traditional lines. Unfortunately, most of the Jews in Majorca are not well off, and the community is seeking funds from abroad.

Today kosher wine (known as *pinario*) is again being produced on Majorca. According to the producers, the last recorded occasion when there were Jewish-owned vineyards and kosher wine production on the island was in the fifteenth century near the town of Binisalem.

BARCELONA

About 3,000 Jews live in the thriving business community of Barcelona. (President of the Jewish community is Aquiba Benarroch.) At Calle Porvenir 24 is the first synagogue built in Spain since the Inquisition, nearly 500 years ago. The synagogue is dedicated to the memory of Moses Maimonides. The white stone building, five stories high, has a Sephardic synagogue on the first floor (with a women's balcony, *bima* in the center, and Ark decorated with rich hangings), and an Ashkenazi synagogue on the third floor. The windows on the lower floors have wrought-iron decorations bearing the menorah and Star of David. (Rabbi Saloman Bensabat is the spiritual leader; tel. 2006148.) The offices of the Jewish community are also housed in the new building (tel. 2008513), together with classrooms, a youth lounge, and a gymnasium. The old ghetto area in Barcelona is located at Calle del Call. The Hall of Archives in the Provincial Archaeological Museum was built from tombstones taken from abandoned Jewish cemeteries, the Hebrew inscriptions being still visible.

The Gran Plaza de Toros in Barcelona is a huge structure on the Avenida José Antonio Primo de Rivera. Its facade is beautiful blue-and-white mosaic. In the middle of the mosaic is a decorative motif: the Star of David. (No one seems to know why.) In shops along the Ramblas, the promenade running down to the sea from the Plaza Cataluna, the merchants sell tiny pillboxes, combs, and scissors. Each has a gold Star of David; to the merchants it is a traditional decoration.

Overlooking the western section of Barcelona is Montjuich, or "Mountain of the Jews," so named for the extensive Jewish property holdings here in the eleventh and twelfth centuries. Along the slope is an ancient Jewish cemetery.

In the famous Benedictine monastery of Montserrat, about eighteen miles northwest of Barcelona, there is a library with some 500,000 volumes and nearly 100 Hebrew manuscripts, six ancient *Sifrei Torat,* eight *megilot* (Scrolls of Esther), biblical fragments, seventeen illuminated marriage contracts, rabbinical responsa, and two copies of the *Shevat Yehudah* of Solomon Ibn Verga, an important fifteenth-century account of events prior to the expulsion from Spain.

BÉJAR

During the Middle Ages the city of Béjar had a large Jewish population. The local synagogue was at Calle de 29 de Agosta; today the exact spot of the synagogue is marked by house No. 5 with its wooden sidings. The Jewish quarter was directly behind the Ducal Palace; inside the palace, on the right side of the entrance, is a copy of a stone tablet in Hebrew, the original of which is in the Sephardic Museum of Toledo.

BESALÚ

In this Costa Brava village, a fourteenth-century *mikvah* was recently unearthed, along with other remnants of the ancient Jewish quarter.

BURGOS

This Castilian community has had a long history of Jewish involvement. The Jewish quarter of Burgos was across the bridge from the castle in the Campeador section of the city in the area of Calle Fernan Gonzalez. Under the reign of King Fernando III (1217–1252) as well as that of King Alfonso X (1252–1284), Jews were especially favored citizens. King Alfonso X protected them under laws granting them equality with other Spanish citizens and giving validity to Jewish transactions.

CÁCERES

On the outskirts is the Chapel of San Antonio, formerly a thirteenth-century synagogue. Part of the old Jewish quarter still exists in that neighborhood.

CANARY ISLANDS

In 1972 the fifteen Jewish families in the city of Tenerife organized the Comunidad Israelita and met at Calle San José 18–20 (tel. 247781) under the leadership of Jacques Benchetrit, who resided at Calle Castillo 53 (tel. 241331). The president of the Tenerife Jewish community is Pinhas Abecassis (tel. 247296).

There is also a small Jewish community at Las Palmas; Solomon L. Zrihen serves as president (Calle Nestor de la Torre 34; tel. 248497). Religious services are held on the top floor at 10 Calle Remadios.

CEUTA

The Spanish enclave city of Ceuta is physically in north Morocco. In 1971 a new synagogue was inaugurated; it seats 350 people and includes a library, banquet hall, kitchen, and classrooms.

CÓRDOBA

Córdoba is one of the ancient centers of Jewish learning. The foundation of its gigantic mosque was laid in 785. The ancient Rambam Synagogue with arches and stucco work is near the venerated home of Moses Maimonides (born 1135) on Calle de los Judios 20. The Rambam Synagogue is a small Moorish edifice with its east wall having a vacant spot which the Ark once occupied; on the west wall is the outline of a cross hung when the premises were occupied by the Church of St. Crispin, after the Jews were expelled from Spain.

In the old ghetto is Calle Juda Levi, named for Judah Halevi, famed medieval poet (1085–1140). In Plazuela Maimonides there is a statue of Moses Maimonides. The Puerta de Almodovar on the

Calle de los Judios was one part of the Moorish fortifications and served as the entrance to the Jewish quarter.

GERONA

The old Jewish quarter occupied the northwest section of the city, and is currently being reconstructed by private investors who are building a Jewish community center.

GRANADA

The Alhambra exhibits a Star of David over one of its prominent windows in a room off the Courtyard of the Lions. Here King Ferdinand and Queen Isabella, on March 30, 1492, signed the order expelling all Jews from Spain. The oldest sections of the Alhambra were built by Joseph Ibn-Naghdela, the Jewish prime minister of a Moorish caliph. The twelve lions supporting the alabaster basins in the Fountain of Lions are modeled after the twelve oxen of King Solomon's Temple.

HERVÁS

The Calle de la Sinagaga marks the site of the old Jewish quarter. In 1971, for the first time in 500 years, a rabbi was welcomed to this ancient town; Rabbi Baruch Garzon of Madrid was invited to participate in the naming of the street which used to be a main street of the Jewish ghetto; it was named Calle de la Amistad Judeo Cristiana.

LÉRIDA

The Star of David is prominently featured in the windows of the cathedral, though it is called King Solomon's Seal.

MADRID

In 1959 Bet Zion Synagogue was organized at Calle Pizarro 19 in Madrid, a departure from Spanish tradition which had not permitted public worship apart from Catholicism. In December 1968, the first *formal* synagogue, Beth Yaacov, since 1492, was opened at Calle Balmes 3. Today Madrid Jewry is headed by Philip Halioua, Conde de Cartagena 3 (tel. 2514149).

The new Sephardic Museum (Calle Zorilla 18, one block from American Express offices) exhibits historical memorabilia of Spanish Jewish community life. Nearby is the Arias-Montana Institute (Calle del Duque de Medinaceli 4) whose library contains more than 16,000 volumes on Sephardic Jewish history. The world-famous Prado Museum of painting and sculpture has much of Jewish interest, such as Murillo's *Rebecca and Eliezar* and Titian's *Moses Saved from the Waters.* And at the Museo Arqueologico (Calle de Serrano 13) there is an upper pillar from a thirteenth-century Toledo synagogue, inscribed in Hebrew. Gabirol College at Nicaragua 1 educates 100 Jewish youngsters and teenagers in Judaism. There are Zionist summer camps, ladies' auxiliaries staging Israeli bazaars to raise funds for Israel, and even tours to Israel sponsored by the Madrid Jewish community. Today most of the Jews in Madrid are refugees from Morocco, although there is a sizable number of Ashkenazim from Hungary. The ancient ghetto area of Madrid was Calle de la Fe, facing San Lorenzo Church.

On the outskirts of Madrid at El Escorial one may view in the cathedral's library an open volume of Genesis in Hebrew. Jewish history is preserved not only in the medieval Hebrew manuscripts, but in the 16,000-volume library of the Aria Montana Institute, a scholarly organization funded by the Spanish government for the express purpose of Judaic research. The Monastery of San Lorenzo houses many medieval Hebrew Bibles and illuminated manuscripts. On the walls of the Patio of Kings in the palace of Philip II are sculpted effigies of the six Kings of Judah. The palace also has many oil paintings of such Jewish figures as Solomon, Elijah, and David.

In 1978 Queen Sofia of Spain, who took a course in Judaism at Madrid University, was the first Spanish monarch ever to visit a synagogue for Sabbath services (which she did as part of the course). She sat upstairs in the women's gallery, for Jewish observance in Spain is strictly Orthodox.

MÁLAGA

The synagogue and Jewish community center (tel. 214041), established in 1965, is located on the third floor of the building at Calle Duquesa de Parcent Calle, No. 8 (Rabbi Joseph Cohen). The British Consulate is in the same building. In 1970 a statue was unveiled of the Spanish Jewish poet-philosopher Shlomo Ben Yehuda Ibn Gabirol, who was born in Málaga in 1021. The sculpture is the work of an American living in Spain, Reed Armstrong. Today Málaga has approximately 350 Jews, principally emigrés from North Africa. President of the Jewish community is Andres Bohbot, Calle Alhondiga 4 (tel. 381170).

MARBELLA

A Jewish community was established here with the completion of the synagogue in 1977. (Contact Alberto Verdugo Toledano, c/o Meyer, Urbanizacion Panorama, tel. 823702.) Most of the funds and materials for the building were provided by Simon O'Hayon and his family, who settled at 20 Real Villas in Marbella after leaving

Morocco. The synagogue accommodates 100 people, and the building contains a *mikvah* and four apartments. Decoration of the synagogue was carried out by members of the Pinto family, who contributed to the restoration and redecoration of the El Transito Synagogue in Toledo.

MEDINACELI

An ancient synagogue, known after 1492 as the Convent of Jeronimos, has been restored as a synagogue by the Spanish government.

MIRANDA DE EBRO

Jews lived comfortably in this small community until 1492 when their synagogue was converted to a church. The old synagogue has been located in Calle del Puente, close to the Puerta del Puente.

ORENSE

At the beginning of the fifteenth century the Jews of Orense paid the highest taxes because they were the most prosperous. But, beginning in 1442, the rulers of Cadorniga commenced frequent persecution of Jews including the ransacking of the synagogue (located behind the Jesuit school); the Inquisitor Gamarra also confiscated Jewish property, and the end of Orense Jewry was in sight. Earlier, the Jews of Orense had held public office, were silver makers who monopolized the sale of religious objects to the Church, textile weavers, and moneylenders.

The Jewish community formerly lived between Rua Nova and the Calle de Instituto and Calle del Obispo Cesareo. House No. 13 on the Calle del Obispo Cesareo is called the "House of the Jews" in memory of one Gorina Perez who practiced sorcery under the name of Countess de Formesta.

PONTEVEDRA

During the Middle Ages, Pontevedra was a great port and commercial center where Jewish wealth was particularly noted. The Jewish quarter was located between Casa de Baron (today occupied by a Parador Nacional) and the Church of St. Mary. Today one can see small Jewish medieval houses with their little porches, on such streets as Calles de San Pablo, Plateria Vellas, Amargura, and Tristan de Montenegro; at the point where Rua Alta becomes Calle de San Telmo there is a well-preserved Jewish house. Some say that Pontevedra has the best preserved medieval Jewish quarter in all of Europe.

Pontevedra's Jewish cemetery in the Middle Ages was located in the triangular Plaza Santa Maria, also known as Campa Do Xudeus.

SALAMANCA

The oldest Spanish university is in Salamanca; it proudly displays the name of Abraham Zacuto on its list of "Illustrious Professors of This University." Abraham Zacuto, who taught astronomy at the University of Salamanca, is famous for his astronomical charts and tables which were used by Christopher Columbus and other explorers. Above the door of the oldest classroom of the university is a Hebrew inscription: "Happy are thy men, happy are these thy servants, that stand continually before thee, and that hear thy widsom" (I Kings 10:8).

SAN SEBASTIÁN

In this Basque town contact Mosche Othaitz, Calle Hermanos Iturrino 27, 2nd floor (tel. 413199).

SANTIAGO DE COMPOSTELA

The Christian pilgrimages of the Middle Ages to this famed site prompted Jewish artisans and Jewish merchants to journey here. Jews earned their living from the pilgrimage trade by designing and selling Christian amulets, mementos, silver icons, and other religious objects. The Jewish quarter was close to the cathedral; many shops and homes were in the Calle Azabacheria which led to the Plaza de Cervantes; others were on the Calle de la Troya, Calle de las Algalias Arriba and Calle de las Algalias Abajo, Calle de Jerusalem, and Calle de las Truques.

The Cathedral of St. James possesses many biblical artifacts created by Jewish artisans. Medieval symbolism is resplendent in the Portico de La Gloria, the massive door or entranceway of biblical design from the twelfth century. Here are figures representing the Jewish people, the prophet Isaiah, Adam and Eve, Abraham, Jacob, Judah, Aaron, Samuel, David, and Moses with his index finger raised. The figure of Isaiah predominates for there are many illustrations taken from the Book of Isaiah. In another section of the Portico de La Gloria are representations of Moses with the Laws, Daniel, Jeremiah, and such minor prophets as Osias, Joel, and Amos, and also Queen Esther. La Puerta de Platerias features Romanesque sculpture depicting Isaiah, Micah, Moses, Aaron, the sepulcher of Abraham, and the famed statue of King David.

SEGOVIA

The sites of medieval Jewish life in Segovia were Calle de la Juderia Vieja and Calle de la Juderia Nueva. The former starts from the Plaza del Corpus, where there is today a convent whose facade was part of a thirteenth-century synagogue. After several blocks, including a passageway through a tunnel (constructed only twenty years ago), the street empties into the Plaza del Socorro, the heart of the old Jewish quarter. From here, climbing upward, the visitor comes to Calle de la Juderia Nueva, graded in steps and flanked by simple buildings. On this street stands an ancient house where the Jewish doctor Don Mayr may have lived. Across a slope above the stream bed is a pine forest covering ground that was once a Jewish cemetery (tombs have been discovered here). Here also is the Convent of Corpus Christi whose interior is actually that of a fifteenth-century synagogue. Outside the cloister walls is the tomb of Maria del Salto, the Jewess who flung herself over the wall in 1410 rather than accept conversion. The Alcazar here contains the sixteenth-century "Tower of the Jews."

SEVILLE

Seville has many streets named after legends involving Jews: for example, the Calle de la Pimienta, recalling the miracle which converted a Jewish grocer, and the Calle de la Susona de la Muerta, referring to the loves of a beautiful Jewess and the death of her noble brothers. There is a Jewish section in an ancient burial ground in the Macarena district. An old synagogue is found at Calle Torres 5 in the Barrio de Santa Cruz and serves twenty Jewish families today. (Call Dr. Elias Botebol, Calle Tomas de Ibarra 20; tel. 225703.) Services are also held at Calle Peral 10, and at Calle Escudero 5. Simon Hassan (tel. 275517) heads the Seville Jewish community.

Among the treasures in Seville Cathedral are two keys to the city presented by the Jewish community to King Ferdinand III centuries ago. The Columbus Archives at Avenida Queipo de Llano 5 have fascinating Hebrew records, including astronomical writings, cartographic materials, and the *Almanac Perpetuum,* used by Columbus on his later voyages to America.

TARRAGONA

The cathedral has many relics inscribed in Hebrew, including Jewish tombstones and old Jewish coins. Portella de Judeus, or "Little Gate of the Jews," stands at the entrance to Calle de Talavera.

TOLEDO

Although Toledo today has no established Jewish community, this city remains the historical center of Spanish Judaism. There are two ancient synagogues which have been opened by the Spanish government. Santa Maria la Blanca Synagogue, or the Great Synagogue, was built in the thirteenth century and is located on Calle de los Reyes Catolicos near the Tagus River; it stands today in a quiet garden, once the heart of the ancient ghetto. It resembles a mosque and was probably built by Arabs; next to it is the Plaza de la Juderia in the heart of the old ghetto. Unfortunately the synagogue has not been properly maintained by the Spanish government; it is damp and large parts of its walls are falling away, destroying segments of carved and painted Hebrew inscriptions. The roof is in a state of decay.

The El Transito Synagogue in the Calle de Samuel Levi was built of brick and founded by Samuel Levi Abulafia who was the treasurer of King Pedro I in the fourteenth century. Built in 1357, its beauty is unmarred by the passage of time. The builder was Rabbi Meyer Abdeli from Granada, the most renowned architect of the period, assisted by Moorish craftsmen; the synagogue was patterned after the magnificent Alhambra. The El Transito Synagogue served as a Benedictine monastery after 1492, and today it is not only a national monument, but a museum for Sephardic culture. Its interior is rectangular, 69 feet by 52 feet and 40 feet high; its bare walls are carved with Hebrew verses from the Psalms and enriched with golden silk handwoven tapestries. The carved ceiling, 40 feet above the tiled floor of the main sanctuary, is an intricate mosaic of wood and mother-of-pearl. The wood is Lebanon cedar, the same wood with which the Temple of Solomon in Jerusalem was built more than two thousand years earlier. The four walls are covered, literally, with incredibly detailed filigree work—embroidery in stone, representing grape leaves, palmettos, lilies-of-the-valley and twisted vine shoots. Imposed on these traceries of biblical fruits and flowers are Hebrew verses from the Psalms, also carved in stone. One of them reads: "Happy are they who dwell in Your house." Abulafia did not long survive the completion of his masterpiece. His lavish expenditures incited the hatred of his enemies, who had long sought to oust him from his position of favor at court. They accused him of disloyalty to the king. Pedro, administering justice in the manner of that age, subjected Abulafia to the rack. Abulafia died under the torture, still proclaiming his innocence.

Like the Sephardic Museum, the El Transito Synagogue has a fine collection of Jewish tombstones, amulets, ornaments, and pictorial reproductions of Jewish sites throughout Spain. Some of the newly found tombstones (from Valencia, León, Seville, and Mérida, in particular) date from the Arab conquest of Spain and bear inscriptions in Arabic. A magnificent washbasin inscribed in Greek, Latin, and Hebrew is one of the museum's masterpieces.

Nearby in the Calle San Juan de Dios in the Jewish quarter of Aljama is the ancient home of Samuel Levi Abulafia, truly a palace, in which the painter El Greco resided many years later. Across the narrow street from Abulafia's palace and connected to it by an underground passage is the synagogue.

Posada de la Hermandad, a local church, was formerly a small synagogue. The Provincial Museum in the Hospice de Santa Cruz preserves many relics of fourteenth-century Jewry.

Recently the city of Toledo acquired its first Jewish resident since the Inquisition. Abe Zuckerman formerly operated a kosher restaurant in Madrid; here in Toledo, he has opened a nonkosher restaurant opposite Toledo's two ancient synagogues.

TUDELA

Benjamin of Tudela (see Introduction) is remembered here with a memorial plaque erected in 1960. The plaque is adjacent to the local cathedral which has a chapel that was once part of a synagogue. The mosaic floor features several Stars of David.

VALENCIA

The local synagogue is at Calle Asturias 7 (tel. 339901).

VILLADIEGO

The ancient Jewish quarter in Villadiego is fairly well preserved because the Augustinian monks constructed a monastery within the Jewish quarter and retained much of the ancient wall and many of the buildings. In the Church of San Lorenzo are many Jewish stone tablets, which include the names of hundreds of *conversos*.

VITORIA

At the end of the two streets of Olaguibel and Carlos VII, in the northern part of the city, is a public park called Judizmendi. It was not made into a park until 1952, exactly 460 years late. It seems that in the year 1492, particularly during the four-month period following the expulsion of Jews from Spain, a severe epidemic raged throughout the city and Jewish doctors fought the epidemic along with non-Jewish doctors. The city was very grateful for this help but could not halt the expulsion of Jews; so, in return for the fine treatment at the hands of their fellow citizens, the heads of the Jewish community deeded the ancient Jewish cemetery and the surrounding grounds to Vitoria with the understanding that no building would ever be erected and that the land would be kept free. Nevertheless, a public school was built on the property in the early part of the twentieth century. Finally, in 1952, Judizmendi Park was established. In the northern section of the park a monument commemorates the fact that the Jews of Vitoria in 1492 gave the land to the city.

KOSHER RESTAURANTS

Barcelona: Kosher Vegetarian, Calle Canuda 41.

Fuengirola: Torreblanca Hotel (Robert and Françoise Aknin, owners; there is also a synagogue and *mikvah*).

Madrid: Sinai, Avenida Jose Antonio 29 (tel. 2318252).
Jewish Center, Calle Balmes 3 (tel. 2573877).
Moise Benzion, Rodriquez San Pedro 8.

Palma de Majorca: Hotel de Mar de Illetas (tel. 231-846).

USEFUL ADDRESSES

Barcelona: U.S. Consulate General, Via Layetana 33 (tel. 319-9550).

Bilbao: U.S. Consulate General, Avenida del Ejercito 11, 3rd floor (tel. 4358308).

Madrid: U.S. Embassy, Serrano 75 (tel. 2763400).
Canadian Embassy, Edificio Espana, Plaza de Espana 2 (tel. 2475400).

Seville: U.S. Consulate General, Paseo de las Delicias 7 (tel. 231885).

SURINAM

In Surinam (formerly Dutch Guiana) is probably the oldest Jewish community in America, dating from 1639. Jews settled in the first capital city, Toranica (or Torah Rica), now abandoned. The original Jewish settlers in Dutch Guiana had first settled in a Dutch colony in northern Brazil following the expulsion from Spain. But in the seventeenth century the colony collapsed, leaving the Jews at the mercy of the Portuguese. They moved to French Guyana where they were not welcomed. Finally, they wandered into Surinam and settled in the savannah lands, building the first South American synagogue in 1668. They soon became prosperous plantation owners and were granted full religious freedom by the early British rulers. Other Jews soon came from Recife, Brazil, with capital, energy, and know-how, and were given land for a cemetery, school, and synagogue in Joden Savanna, where they achieved a form of autonomous state under the Dutch. The first synagogue survived until the great fire of 1832, when all of Joden Savanna was razed. Today only the tower sections of the synagogue walls remain; and these ruins have been declared an official historical site.

For a century Surinam Jews owned some of the largest plantations of Surinam, until labor shortages and frequent raids from hostile Bush Negroes made their property unprofitable. By the eighteenth century most of the Sephardim had abandoned their plantations and moved to Paramaribo to make their living as merchants. They were joined by the Northern European Ashkenazi Jews who had come over with the English. The two groups have remained distinct through the centuries, with very little intermarriage.

In 1719, Surinam Jewry built a synagogue in Paramaribo at Gravenstraat 186. Fifteen years later the Ashkenazim took over the Sephardic synagogue and in 1835 rebuilt it on a much larger scale to accommodate the increasing Jewish populace. It is an old building with polished dark hardwood and shiny brass candelabra, simple yet elegant. The floor of the synagogue is covered with clean white sand, symbolizing the journey of Moses across the desert.

The Ashkenazi Synagogue is located on Keizerstrasse. In the late 1700s Jewish life in Surinam declined as the economic life of the country deteriorated.

There are approximately 500 Jews in Surinam out of a population of 450,000. Many Surinam Jews are merchants, while others work for the government. President of the Sephardic community is E. J. Robles, Van Roseveltkade 34 (tel. 4770), and president of the Ashkenazi community is D. H. Emanuels, Albergastraat 23 (tel. 99901). There are four Jewish cemeteries, all of great historic interest.

The racial breakdown of Surinam is interesting; Creole, 35 percent; Hindustani, 35 percent; Indonesian, 15 percent; Bush Negroes, 9 percent; Chinese, 2 percent; and Europeans and others, 2 percent, including 0.53 percent Jewish.

A unique tour involves a jungle trip into the area around Joden Savanna, a worthwhile pilgrimage for Jews because it is a reminder that Jews have gone everywhere, endured all hardships, and conquered all difficulties to avoid persecution.

USEFUL ADDRESSES:

Paramaribo: U.S. Embassy, Dr. Sophie Redmondstraat 129 (tel. 76459).

SWEDEN

Jews first came to Sweden in 1775 when King Gustavus III revoked the anti-Jewish ordinances of his predecessors. Before that time, only Jews who accepted baptism were admitted. Nevertheless, there were Jewish paymasters in the army of King Charles XII (1697–1718); until recently, on the island of Marstrand, in the Kattegat, the remains of a synagogue hewn out of a cave dating back to the Middle Ages were visible. King Frederick I invited Portuguese Jews from Amsterdam and London to come to Stockholm in 1745, but none of them would agree to conversion.

Aron Isaac, a German Jewish engraver, received permission in 1775 to build a synagogue and to have other Jews join him in Stockholm. Similar rights were accorded in 1779 to Jews in Gothenburg and Norrkoping. In 1782 Jews were granted the right to live anywhere in Sweden, though they could not yet own land, vote, or hold office. In 1838, full civil rights were granted. In 1870, Sweden's Jews achieved complete political emancipation and basic acceptance as citizens and members of the community. Stockholm, Gothenburg, Norrkoping, Lund, Malmo, Uppsala, and Karlskrona were the sites of these early settlements of Jews.

The greatest Jewish influx from Germany occurred at the beginning of the nineteenth century; a century later, Eastern European Jews poured into Sweden. During World War II Jews from Norway and Denmark, together with escapees from German concentration camps, settled in Sweden which, though officially neutral during the war, provided sanctuary—and hospitality—for both Danish Jews and Norwegian Jews fleeing persecution and the threat of deportation in their German-held homelands. In September 1942, 900 Jews escaped across the snowy northern frontier between Norway and Sweden; the following year the Swedish government settled 8,000 Danish Jews—openly defying Hitler with an official proclamation of asylum for the refugees. Sweden also opened its borders to Danish freedom fighters fleeing from the Nazi occupation, permitted the establishment of secret resistance organizations, and provided the communications link between the Danish resistance movement and the Allied armies.

Today approximately 17,000 Jews live in Sweden (compared with

6,000 in 1933). Of this number approximately 6,000 reside in Stockholm and neighboring towns, some 2,000 in Gothenburg, 2,000 in Malmo, 250 in Norrkoping, and perhaps 350 in Boras. Jews also reside in Karlstad, Kalmar, Halsingborg, Landskrona, Kristianstad, Vasterars, and Sundsvall. In 1969 and 1970 some two thousand Polish Jews readily found acceptance in Sweden. Sweden is the only country in the world where the Jewish population has *doubled* since World War II.

GOTHENBURG (GOTEBORG)

The small local orthodox synagogue is located at Storgatan 5; the Conservative-Liberal synagogue, Mosaiska Forsamligens, is at Ostra Larmgatan 12 (tel. 136778). The Orthodox synagogue, facing a picturesque canal, is the oldest existing synagogue building in the country, having been dedicated in 1855. Rabbi Jacob Soethendorp, who leads the Conservative-Liberal congregation, is a former American schoolteacher who married a Swedish physician.

The Jewish community center at Ostra Larmgatan 12 (tel. 177245) is a modern three-story structure adjoining the Conservative-Liberal Synagogue, and contains the community's offices (headed by Elias Bentow), a kosher restaurant, a religious school, and a small chapel. Organizations housed at the center include the Jewish Youth Organization and B'nai B'rith Lodge, Logen Gothia No. 1929, whose secretary is Th. Lillienthal (Box 12, Gothenburg 1).

HALSINGBORG

The local synagogue is at Springpostgrander 4.

KRISTIANSTAD

The local synagogue is at 18 Ostra Storgatan.

LANDSKRONA

The local synagogue is at 9 Skolallen.

LUND

This small Swedish village has a synagogue at Lilla Sodergatan 3, and an active Jewish student organization for university students, housed in a Jewish center at Ostia Maartensgatan 10 (tel. 148052).

MALMO

The 2,000 Jews here maintain several synagogues including the Orthodox synagogue at Foreningsgatan 6 (corner of Betaniaplan).

One of the dramatic events of the rescue of the Danish Jews took place here on Yom Kippur Eve in 1943. During the night a large group of Jewish refugees had been conveyed by fishing boats from Copenhagen; and as many of them as could, filled the synagogue to join Cantor Israel Isaac Gordon in the traditional Kol Nidre service.

In Malmo there is a B'nai B'rith lodge, Malmo-Logen No. 1909, whose secretary is Holmer Davo Fischbein (Ronneholmsvagen 13). Another Orthodox synagogue is located at Kamregatan 11 (tel. 040-118460). This building includes the Jewish community center (tel. 11-8860) and also contains a home for the aged, a *mikvah*, library, kindergarten, and offices for a number of organizations including a youth club, B'nai B'rith, and a group of Polish refugees who publish a mimeographed Polish newspaper.

Visit the Jewish cemetery to see the "Flight with the Torah Scroll," a memorial monument in bronze and granite dedicated to the refugees from Denmark and to the victims of Nazism. The work is by Willy Gordon, one of Scandinavia's leading sculptors.

NORRKOPING

The synagogue on Braddgatan is the second oldest in Sweden, having been opened in 1858. The Jewish community is so small that the synagogue is used only on Rosh Hashana and Yom Kippur.

SKARA

Jacobowsky Library of Judaica, a great private collection, at Harlungdagatan 1, is owned by Dr. C. V. Jacobowsky, librarian of the Skara Municipal Library.

STOCKHOLM

The Great Synagogue of the central community of Stockholm (Wahrendorffsgatan 3) was built in 1870 and accommodates 830 people (tel. 08-639524). Although Conservative, men and women sit separately, and there is organ music with a ladies' choir. American-born Chief Rabbi Morton H. Narrowe, Torstenssonsgatan 4, officiates; he attended Yeshiva University and Jewish Theological Seminary in New York City. Both he and his wife, Judi, grew up in Philadelphia, Pennsylvania.

There are two small Orthodox congregations in Stockholm: Adas Jisrael at St. Paulsgatan 13 (tel. 08-441995) and Adas Jeshurun at Nybrogatan 12 (tel. 08-618282). The Orthodox leader is Rabbi Aron Katz. The central Conservative synagogue maintains religious schools, cemeteries, and various institutions, including a summer camp, an old age home, a nursing home for the chronically ill, and several housing developments.

The Jewish cemetery, at Hagaparken, in the suburb of Solna, is the newest of the city's four Jewish cemeteries. At Igeldammsgatan, Alstromergatan, and Kronobergsgatan, all in the Kungsholm section of the city, are the three oldest Jewish cemeteries in Sweden, both dating from the late eighteenth century. A Hagaparken cemetery feature is the T-shaped granite memorial to Jewish victims of Nazism; the Hebrew lettering on the sculpture is copied from that on the oldest grave in the Sephardic cemetery outside Amsterdam, Holland.

Judaica House, at Nybrogatan 19 (tel. 636566), was inaugurated in September 1963 and is equipped with modern recreational facilities for youths and adults; it includes a Jewish kindergarten and a Hillel day school. Eric Erickson, a non-Jew, has been the director of Stockholm's Jewish community center since 1963. (The director of the Hillel school also is a non-Jew; at least 200 Jewish children attend; tel. 621611).

UPPSALA

Uppsala University's Caroline Library collection of more than 1 million volumes and manuscripts has a famous collection of Hebrew manuscripts. The Jewish Students Club is at Dalgatan 15 (tel. 125453).

VASTERAS

The local synagogue is at 1 Svardsliljegatan.

KOSHER RESTAURANTS

Gothenburg: Restaurant, Stampgatan 68 (tel. 155549).

Malmo: For kosher food there is a vegetarian restaurant in the nearby town of Hoor (tel. 0413/25332), or meat restaurants in Malmo: AB Koscher Kott at Carl Herslowsgatan 7 (tel. 35515) and Koscher Livs, Skolgatan 2 (tel. 976800).

Stockholm: Stockholm Kosher Jarnhovsgatan 5 (tel. 428030) offers kosher canned meat, ready-prepared foods, and other products. Community Center, Nybrogaten 19 (tel. 636566).

USEFUL ADDRESSES

Stockholm: U.S. Embassy, Strandvagen 101 (tel. 630520).
Canadian Embassy, Kungsgatan 24 (tel. 23-79-20).
Israeli Embassy, Torstenssonsgatan 4 (tel. 630435).

SWITZERLAND

Jews have inhabited Switzerland since the Middle Ages, under the most trying conditions. In 1294 a ritual murder accusation resulted in the expulsion of all Jews from Berne; gruesome massacres of Jews at Basel and Zurich occurred in 1349 during the period of the Black Death. In 1622 Jews were excluded from the entire country in perpetuity, although Jewish communities somehow existed until 1803 in the villages of Lengnau, Klingnau, and Edingen. Not until 1861, after international protests, were restrictions removed; the federal constitution of Switzerland in 1874 officially abolished all restrictions against Jews. World Zionist Congresses were held in Switzerland in 1897, 1929, and 1937. During World War II Switzerland gave shelter to many Jewish refugees. Today there are approximately 21,000 Jews in Switzerland, mostly in Zurich, Basel, Geneva, Berne, Waadt, and St. Gall.

BADEN

There is a small synagogue at Parkstrasse 7 (tel. 261707).

BASEL (or BASLE)

There are Orthodox synagogues at Leimenstrasse 45, Leimenstrasse 24, Ahornstrasse 14, and Rudolfstrasse 28. At Steinenberg 14 (Barfusserplatz) is the Stadtcasino where Theodor Herzl convened the first World Zionist Congress. The University of Basel Library at Schonbeinstrasse 20 has an important collection of sixteenth-century Hebrew manuscripts. The B'nai B'rith lodge, Basel-Loge No. 595, had as its president Dr. Herbert Kaufmann (Feierabendstrasse 47). The Jewish Museum at Kornhausgasse 8 is open for a few hours in the late afternoon on weekdays, and on Sunday mornings.

BERNE

The Jewish community in Berne is small and scattered, but there is a synagogue at Kapellenstrasse 2 (tel. 254992). Community president is Dr. Rolf Bloch (tel. 524239). In Munsterplatz is a fine statue of Moses holding the Torah, erected in 1791.

BIEL

The local synagogue is at Ruschlistrasse 3 (tel. 237267).

GENEVA

There are about 3,300 Jews in this international city. Synagogues are located at Place de la Synagogue (Chief Rabbi Dr. Alexandre Safran, 11 rue Marignac; tel. 204686), and at 54 route de Malagnou (tel. 466697). The Jewish community center is located at 10 rue Saint Leger (tel. 204686). Geneva is also international headquarters for countless world Jewish organizations, including American Joint Distribution Committee, B'nai B'rith International Council (U.N. liaison office), Consultative Council of Jewish Organizations, Jewish Agency for Israel, Women's International Zionist Organization (WIZO), International Institute for Technical Training at Anieres (ORT), the World Jewish Congress (rue de Varembe 1; tel. 341325), and the World Organization for Rehabilitation and Training Federation (rue de Varembe 1; tel. 341434). One of those individuals responsible for the continuity of Jewish life in Geneva is Nissim Gaon, who is an exceptionally wealthy builder, having made his money by raising peanuts in the Sudan. Gaon single-handedly built a beautiful synagogue, Hechol Haness, at 54 Malagnou Avenue in Geneva. The Orthodox Ashkenazi Synagogue is at 11 Place de la Synagogue, and Machsike Hadass is at 2 Place des Eaux Vives. The Liberal congregation meets at 2 Chemin de Bedex.

A boat trip up Lake Leman to Vevey enables the visitor to see the many homes for the Jewish aged built by JDC and Claims Conference funds. These JDC homes have given shelter to Jewish refugees from as far away as Egypt and even Hong Kong.

GRINDELWALD

High up on the way to Jungfraujoch, Grindelwald offers kosher meals at Wagner-Kahn's Hotel Silberhorn (tel. 532822); there is even a *mikvah* here.

LAUSANNE

The local synagogue is located at Avenue Juste Olivier 1, and commands a magnificent view of the city from its elevated site. A large *Magen David* graces its outer facade. The Jewish community center is located at 17 Avenue de la Gare (tel. 226733).

LUCERNE

The synagogue, built in 1912, is at Bruchstrasse 51 (tel. 223054). Here also is the world-famous Yeshivat Lucerne, one of the great

Jewish religious scholastic centers (tel. 422685). Beth Jacob Seminary is at Schlossweg 1 (tel. 422479).

LUGANO

The synagogue is located at Via C. Maderno 11 not far from the center of town. (The Hebrew school is also at Via Maderno 11.) It has simple but graceful lines. The Conservative synagogue of the Associazione Ebraica de Canton Ticino is at Via E. Bosia 15–17 in Lugano-Paradiso. There are 400 Jews in Lugano.

MONTREUX

The local synagogues are located at Avenue des Alpes 25 (tel. 615839) and at Villa Quisisana (tel. 613230), which also houses a *yeshiva*.

ST. GALL

The local synagogue is at Frongartenstrasse 18 (tel. 235923), and the Jewish community center is next door (tel. 227155).

ZURICH

There are Orthodox synagogues at Freigutstrasse 37 and Lowenstrasse 10; the Polish Orthodox synagogue is at Erikastrasse 8. At the Swiss Institute of Technology Professor Albert Einstein taught theoretical physics from 1912 until his departure in the 1930s for the United States; there is a bust of him in the main lobby. The Federation of Swiss Jewish Communities is located at Helenastrasse 3 (tel. 329404).

There are also synagogues in the following Swiss communities: Davos (Etania Sanatorium); Delemont (route de Porrentrury); Fribourg (Avenue de Rome 9); Kreuzlingen (Hafenstrasse 42); La Chaux-de-Fonds (rue du Parc 63); Winterthur (Rosenstrasse 5); and Yverdun (rue Valentin 26). Switzerland is also the home of seven Jewish schools: Bex-les-Bains: Institut Ascher; Celerina: Hochalpine Jued, Schule; Heiden: Kinderheim Wartheim; Lucerne: Yeshiva, Brambergstrasse 20; and Beth Jakob Seminar, Saelistrasse 33; Mont-Pelerin: Home d'Enfants "Le Colibri"; Montreux: Yeshiva Ez-Chajim, Villa Quisisana.

KOSHER RESTAURANTS

Arosa: Hotel Metropol (tel. 311058).

Basel: Community Topas Restaurant, Leimenstrasse 24 (tel. 228700).

Berne: Bellevue-Palace Hotel, Kochergasse 3 (tel. 224581).

Crans-Montana: Bristol/Richelieu Hotel (tel. 413712).

Davos: Etania Kosher Hotel (tel. 36318).

Geneva: The kosher restaurant, Galil, has been closed, but a new kosher restaurant, Shalom, opened at 78 rue du Rhone (1st floor); tel. 289093. (Downtown Geneva has a fascinating shop, La Boutique Shalom, at 30 rue du Coutance, which features many imports from Israel.)

Grindelwald: Hotel Silberhorn (Kahn-Wagner) (tel. [036] 53-28-22).

Lausanne: Kolbo Kasher, 2 Avenue Juste Olivier (tel. 221265).

Locarno: Hotel Astoria (tel. 33 67 61).

Lucerne: Drei Konige, Bruchstrasse 35.

Lugano: Hotel Kempler, Via Cattori 14–16 (tel. 54 28 22). Hotel Dan, Via Fontana 1 (tel. 54 10 61).

Montreux: Pension Wajngort, 8 rue du Lac (tel. 71 25 02).

St. Moritz: Hotel Edelweiss (tel. 35533).

Zurich: Restaurant Hadar, Lowenstrasse 12 (tel. 2115210). Cafe Shalom, Lavaterstrasse 33 (tel. 2011476).

USEFUL ADDRESSES:

Berne: U.S. Embassy, Jubilaeumstrasse 93 (tel. 437011). Israeli Embassy, Marienstrasse 27 (tel. 431042).

SYRIA

For more than 3,000 years Jews have lived in the principal towns of the Eastern Mediterranean in the area of Syria. In Antioch where Jews had settled before Roman times they were granted equal citizenship rights with the Greeks. In A.D. 600 these Jews, after attempts at forcible conversion, rebelled and many were killed. In 1171 only ten Jewish families remained in Antioch. In Tripoli Jewish soldiers were part of a garrison established by the Arab governor to guard against Byzantine attack. Early in the eleventh century Tripoli Jews were persecuted and their synagogue was turned into a mosque. In the sixteenth century Jewish refugees from Spain resettled in Tripoli and prospered. Jews have lived in Aleppo since biblical times; in A.D. 1173 there were 1,500 Aleppo Jews, and in the year 1900 the Jewish population exceeded 10,000. Damascus contained 10,000 Jews in Roman times, and more than 3,000 when Damascus was visited by Benjamin of Tudela in A.D. 1173. In 1900 Damascus had 20,000 Jews and eight synagogues. Jews also lived, before and after the Arab conquest in the seventh century A.D., in such other Syrian towns as Latakia, Baniyas, Hama, Masyaf, and Homs.

It is unknown whether the estimated 4,500 Jews in Syria—mainly in Damascus (2,500), Aleppo (1,200), and Kamishli or El Qamishliye (300)—are still alive. According to Syrian government sources, there are fourteen synagogues in Damascus, all open for worship. But between 1948 and 1967 over 20,000 Syrian Jews left the country. The Grand Rabbi of Syria would be ninety-five years old and may have died. Selim Toteh heads the Jewish community and maintains an office in Haret El Yahud, the ancient Jewish quarter.

The Damascus Jewish community, according to government sources, runs two schools with an attendance of 900 pupils. One school is financed by the Alliance Israelite Universelle of Paris and the other, Ben Maimoun School (500 enrolled students), is maintained by contributions from American Jews. Damascus University has thirty-four Jewish students, studying medicine, dentistry, agriculture, literature, and engineering, according to government sources.

However, in truth, the country's Jews have long been subjected to brutal conditions, and after the Yom Kippur War of June 1967, their suffering greatly intensified. Syria has a Special Committee for Jewish affairs, composed of representatives of Internal Security, General Intelligence, the Ministry of Justice, the Ministry of Finance, and the Council of Palestinian Refugees. This committee is responsible for numerous stringent anti-Jewish measures: Jews are not permitted to travel or leave the country; may not work for the government, the banks, or Arab employers. Most Jewish schools have been closed and Jews must carry marked identity cards at all times.

A dozen Syrian Jewesses were recently allowed to marry American Jews by proxy and leave the country, but Syrian Jewry are still captives of their Arab government. All Jews must carry identity cards marked *Musawi* (belonging to the Mosaic faith); no religious identification is made on the cards of Moslems or Christians.

USEFUL ADDRESSES

Damascus: U.S. Embassy, Abu Rumaneb, Al Manour Street (tel. 333052).

TAHITI

While there has never been an established Jewish community in Tahiti, there have been many Jewish residents over the years. One of the most fascinating was Alexander Salmon. Born in 1819, he was the son of a London rabbi, and came to Tahiti in 1841. Here he became enamored of a native princess, Ariitaimai, an accomplished author and scholar, and they fell madly in love. Their marriage resulted in the birth of nine children. Alexander Salmon died in 1866, and his seventh child, Marau Salmon, married Pomare V, the king of Tahiti, and became Queen Marau. The Tahitian monarchy came to an end in 1880, when the French took over.

Alexander Salmon's widow died in 1897, and her grandson Alexander Salmon served as Honorary American Consul in Papeete.

TAIWAN

Taiwan, or Formosa, the Nationalist Chinese island republic, today has a sixty-family community of Jews. Indeed, Taiwan, since 1949, has served as a place of refuge for Jews escaping tyranny.

The Jewish community in the capital city of Taipei is under the leadership of Y. S. Liberman, Eisenberg Group of Companies, P.O. Box 17-82 (tel. 5519111). Mr. Liberman was previously a vice-president of the Jewish community of Tokyo.

The Jewish community center in Taipei at 335 Shih Pai Road, Sec. 2, Pei Tou (tel. 8714814) houses a synagogue, two function halls, a kosher kitchen, and two classrooms. The recreational areas have a pool table, table tennis, billiards facilities as well as a large swimming pool.

Unfortunately the Taipei Jewish community is totally transient in that all Jews represent major Israeli or Western businesses and are simply serving a short term in Taiwan. (Treasurer of the community is Richard Chitayat who represents Zim Lines; and the social director is Nahum Dishon who represents the Israeli electronics firm Tadiran.) Religious services are conducted in a Conservative manner with mixed seating. Services are also held at the President Hotel where the *chazen* is Harry Lipkowitz who resides permanently in the hotel.

TANZANIA

Several years ago Israeli technicians trained a team of local citizens to build the eleven-story Kilimanjaro Hotel in Dar es Salaam. The result was that the building was completed far ahead of schedule. Israel's aid to the Kilimanjaro Hotel went even further: an Israeli hotel staff was sent for the first year's operation and, concurrently, a group of Tanzanians attended a special course at Israel's own government-run hotel school in Herzliya.

There is no Jewish community in Tanzania, although there are four Jewish families in Dar es Salaam and one Jewish family in Moshi. Before 1960 there were about 100 Jews in Dar es Salaam, Moshi, Arusha, and Tanga.

USEFUL ADDRESSES

Dar es Salaam: U.S. Embassy, 36 Laibon Road (off Bagamoyo Road) (tel. 68894).
Canadian High Commissioner, Gailey and Roberts Building, Independence Avenue (tel. 20-651).
Israeli Embassy (tel. 67-281).

Zanzibar: U.S. Consulate, 83A Tuzungumzeni Square (tel. 2118).

THAILAND

Although there was no formally established Jewish community in Thailand until just a few years ago, approximately 100 Jewish families now have a community center and synagogue at Soi Sainamthip 121, just off Sukhumvit Road (tel. 391338). A Lebanese Jew, Isaac Djemal, Russian-born Haim Gerson (tel. 56657), and Bangkok-born Mrs. Elisabeth Zerner helped to found the Jewish Association of Thailand, which is housed in the Jewish Community Center and meets regularly. At least another 250 Jews including American servicemen are known to be residents in Bangkok. Of this number, Americans are in the minority: English, Swedish, Spanish, and Israeli Jews have larger representation. Four ladies of the community teach Jewish history, singing, and dancing every Friday afternoon. The Bangkok Jewish community holds an annual Chanukah party, a Purim bazaar and carnival, a traditional break-fast on Yom Kippur, and a community Seder on Pesach.

Thai Jewry also include Mrs. Myra Borisute (P.O. Box 4-180, Bangkok 4) who with six children still manages to take an active role in Jewish community life. Her husband, Dr. Sungkas Thongborisute, owns and directs Paolo Memorial Hospital and Clinic, Span Kwai Square, in Bangkok. Mrs. Elisabeth Zerner donated the local synagogue building. An American lawyer, Albert Lyman (tel. 32083), and his wife, Freda, are very active too. Robert Golden, a New York–born Jew, has authored a popular Thai–English dictionary. Selim Eubbani imports kosher food from the United States and still serves as Bangkok's honorary rabbi. Jewish visitors are also welcomed to Bangkok by N. H. Baum of the House of Siam Ltd., 8 Sathorn Nua (tel. 31797).

Thai Jewry are proud of the fact that in 1977 two daughters of the king of Thailand paid a formal visit to Israel. Good relations continue between Israel and Thailand. However, the Libyan government has been supporting a separatist Moslem movement in the four southern provinces of Thailand where there is a majority Moslem population. The Thai government is watching these developments because Thailand is proud of its absolute religious tolerance.

USEFUL ADDRESSES

Bangkok: U.S. Embassy, 95 Wireless Road (tel. 2525040 or 2525171).
Canadian Embassy, 138 Silom Road (tel. 2341561).
Israeli Embassy, 31 Soi Lung Suan, Ploenchit Road (tel. 2523131).

Chiang Mai: U.S. Consulate, Vidhayanond Road (tel. 234566-7).

Songkhla: U.S. Consulate, 9 Sadao Road (tel. 311-589).

Udon: U.S. Consulate, 35/6 Supakitjanya Road (tel. 22158).

TRINIDAD AND TOBAGO

These two Caribbean islands, independent members of the British Commonwealth, received their first Jewish settlers in the 1660s while the islands were under Spanish rule. When the British took over in 1797 and 1818, there were no Sephardic Jews, for they had left with their countrymen. In 1900 the thirty-one Jews in Trinidad were all English civil servants or representatives of British firms. One, Sir Nathaniel Nathan, served as Chief Justice of the Trinidad Supreme Court.

After World War I a handful of Jewish families from Syria and from the Balkans settled in Port-of-Spain. Then in the mid-1930s Trinidad became a temporary haven for nearly 2,000 Jews from Nazi Germany and Austria. With the outbreak of World War II, these German and Austrian Jews were unfortunately interned as enemy aliens, and further immigration was halted. At the end of 1940 Jews who had obtained visas for other countries were released and some 100 Jewish families left. Today about 300 Jews live on Trinidad and Tobago.

Among those Jews who stayed on after 1945 were Mr. and Mrs. Hans Stecher and Mr. and Mrs. Chimon Ber Averboukh. Stecher had arrived penniless in 1938; today he and his wife operate a flourishing chain of retail stores on Trinidad. All Stecher stores display the flag of Israel. The Averboukhs, who came in 1933, began with a small clothing store, and later expanded into real estate. In Averboukh's housing development, New Yalta, most of the streets are named for famous Zionists and scientists. The local Zionist organization which Averboukh led for many years is now headed by his widow. She and Mrs. Stecher maintain close contact with the Israeli ambassador in nearby Venezuela.

The first and only Jewish congregation, the Jewish Religious Society, was organized in 1938 and opened a synagogue a dozen years later in a remodeled house in Port-of-Spain. At one time the congregation planned to erect a house of worship. But the Jewish population steadily declined, from 800 in 1939 to 120 in 1959. By 1971 only fifteen families remained and all ideas of building a synagogue were abandoned. Even the makeshift synagogue was closed. A trust fund was established to provide perpetual care for the Jewish dead. It is the Mucurapo Cemetery in Port-of-Spain where there is a special section, Bet Olam, reserved for Jewish burials.

Religious services are held in the homes of the few remaining Jewish leaders, including Louis Grinberg, Gandelman and Grinberg Novelty Store, 30 Frederick Street, Port-of-Spain (tel. 62-32245 and 62-52155); and Mrs. Hans Stecher, owner of Stecher Ltd., 61 Independent Square, Port-of-Spain (tel. 62-51591, 62-53201, and 62-54746).

Just before Trinidad and Tobago gained independence in 1962, the islands' first prime minister, Dr. Eric Williams, visited Israel seeking advice and technical assistance. Indeed, as the story goes, Trinidad policemen today wear six-pointed Stars of David on their badges because the first police chief was a Jew.

USEFUL ADDRESSES

Port-of-Spain: U.S. Embassy, 15 Queen's Park West (tel. 6226371).

TUNISIA

Jewish settlement in Tunisa goes back to Roman times. In the responsa of the Gaonic Period the city of Kairouan is identified as the greatest center of rabbinic scholarship in the West. But after 1146 many Jews accepted Islam, and Jewish culture waned. Spanish refugees after 1492 founded separate communities in Tunisia, but under Spanish rule (1535–1574), Tunisia massacred or sold into slavery hundreds of Jews. Under French protection, Jews acquired French citizenship in 1910. During World War II, the Jewish community suffered again from Nazi occupation and the Vichy laws. Over 100,000 Jews lived in Tunisia before the Holocaust.

In recent times Jews were employed as merchants, office workers, and skilled craftsmen. Although the majority of the Tunisian Jewish community has departed for Israel and Western Europe, there still remain some 7,000 Sephardic Jews who manage to eke out a living. In the city of Tunis there is no outward manifestation of anti-Israel or even anti-Jewish propaganda. Indeed, this North African country seems bent upon minding its own business.

DJERBA

Djerba is an island off the southeastern coast of Tunisia, and here Jews from ancient Palestine first settled in the seventh century B.C. Jews came as traders; during Roman times the Jews of Djerba were prosperous traders in grain. Today less than 1,000 Tunisian Jews live here.

The Jewish community of Djerba is centered in two villages, Hara El-Seghira and Hara Khebira. In Hara El-Seghira the famed Ghriba Synagogue embraces within its walls a door from the Second Temple of Jerusalem which, according to ancient tradition, was carried in 70 B.C. by priests escaping from Roman rule in Jerusalem. The Ghriba Synagogue also is proud of its ancient Torah scroll, dating back to the days of the Babylonian Exile. The philosopher Maimonides once lived here.

In the village of Hara Khebira life has changed very little over the centuries. It still centers about the synagogue, and there are a surprising number of synagogues. There are five schools with approximately 300 pupils; Hebrew grammar, geography, Bible, Commentaries, Mishna, and Talmud are part of the curriculum. Women still bake their *challah* in the communal oven, and Hebrew booksellers still thrive. The chief occupations of Jews are traditional—jewelry-making and tailoring. Many Jews are merchants supplying the tourist trade in the island's main town, Houmt Sook. Djerba's male Jews still wear black piping on the bottom of their trousers as a sign of mourning for the loss of the First Temple of Jerusalem.

MAHDIA

In the former Tunisian capital city of Mahdia stands an old synagogue, with wooden benches, worn religious relics strewn over the wooden floor, and an old velvet curtain over the dilapidated Holy Ark (whose Arab inscription is illegible).

SFAX

The local synagogue Azriah is located at 71 rue Habib Mazoun, near the town hall.

SOUSSE

There are two local synagogues, one at 38 rue de France and the other on rue Amilcar. President of the Jewish community is Jean Hayat, Av Habib Thameur (tel. 20443).

TUNIS

The Grande Synagogue de la Hara is at 43 Avenue de la Liberté; there is a smaller synagogue at 107 Avenue de Paris which is in fair condition; other synagogues are located at rue Eve Nohelle, rue de la Loire, rue des Djerbiens, and rue Sidi Sridek 16. Chief Rabbi for Tunisia is Rabbi Fradgi Uzan, 26 rue de Palestine (tel. 282-409). There is also a Lubavitcher Yeshiva where 130 Tunisian Jewish students are taught by Rabbi Nissan Pinson. Community center offices are at 10 rue Cap de Vent (tel. 280571).

KOSHER RESTAURANTS

Tunis: Brasserie Suisse, 43 Avenue Bourguiba.
Le Robinson, 14 Avenue de Madrid (tel. 249051).

USEFUL ADDRESSES

Tunis: U.S. Embassy, Avenue de la Liberté 144 (tel. 282566).
Canadian Embassy, 3, rue Didon, Notre-Dame de Tunis (tel. 284950).

TURKEY

Jews have lived in Turkey since biblical days. Here Abraham and Jacob sojourned at Haran, and Noah landed his Ark at Mount Ararat. Haran is today a village on the Syrian frontier—a veritable beehive of mud huts and wheat fields. Mount Ararat is a sightseer's mecca.

Today Turkish Jews are Sephardic, descending from Spanish Jews who entered Turkey after 1492 upon the invitation of the Turkish sultan as allies to fight Christendom. In fact, Bayezid II, sultan of Turkey, sent "mercy ships" to pick up Spanish Jews who he believed could contribute to the culture, science, and commerce of his nation. The religious tolerance of the Ottoman Empire allowed the Jewish community to flourish in trade. Before and during World War II, the young Republic of Turkey sent for leading Jewish and anti-Nazi scholars and awarded them professorships in Turkish universities. However, since 1948 (when Turkey recognized the State of Israel) some 37,000 Turkish Jews have migrated to Israel. Today there are about 24,000 Jews in Turkey.

ANKARA

Ankara, the drab capital of the Republic of Turkey, has been the home of Jews for over 2,000 years. Ankara Jewry, totaling perhaps 600 persons and led by Avraham Cohen, live with a sense of insecurity, for bitter anti-Semitic attacks have frequently occurred. In Saman Pazari there is an old Jewish ghetto with many mementos of the past, including an ancient synagogue, Birlik Sokak (tel. 116200), located behind a wall on Birlik Sokhagi, off Anafartalar Street.

BURSA

Jews have lived here for 2,000 years, although the greatest influx was at the end of the fifteenth century when Spanish Jews arrived. They built the Mayor Synagogue, an architectural beauty with crystal chandeliers, arched windows, and twenty-four ancient *sifrai torat,* and the Gerush Synagogue (or Synagogue of the Expulsion). Bursa's eighty Jewish families are remnants of the glorious past. Adjoining the Mayor Synagogue are communal buildings and little shops. Izak Beyo is the religious leader of Bursa.

EDIRNE

Edirne, Turkey's capital city from 1365 to 1453, is 140 miles northwest of Istanbul, and was the home of many famous Jews including Solomon Alkabetz (composer of the Sabbath hymn "L'khah Dodi"), Joseph Karo (codifier of the Shulchan Arukh), Joseph Halevy (famed Sorbonne professor), and Abraham Danon (editor of the Jewish Encyclopedia). Today 600 Jews reside here, although 10,000 Jews left after 1948 for Israel. The Great Synagogue (constructed after the 1905 fire which destroyed Edirne's synagogues) seats 600, and has many chandeliers and a silver-embroidered Ark curtain. Yuda Romano is the religious leader of Edirne; Dr. Sami Haras has a well-earned reputation as the best medical doctor in the area.

EPHESUS

Ephesus is exciting for the tourist because it has the finest remains of a Roman city, including the site of an ancient synagogue.

ISTANBUL

More than three-quarters of Istanbul's 22,000 Jewish citizens live in the Galata Bridge district, which bridges the East and West. The largest and most important of the twenty-four synagogues is the Sephardic Neve Shalom, at 67 Buyuk Hendek Caddesi in the Galata Bridge district. The only Ashkenazi synagogue (serving about 1,500 worshipers) is at 37 Yuksek Kaldirim (tel. 442975), also in the Galata Bridge area, although the bulk of its Ashkenazi members live in the northern suburbs of Istanbul. There is a unique Italian synagogue at 29 Okcu Musa Caddesi. The Mahazikei Hatorah Synagogue in Shishli was organized by young Turkish Jews; and Knesseth Israel Synagogue at 79 Buyuk Hendek Caddessi is Istanbul's famed all-children's congregation. Other synagogues include Beth Israel Synagogue at 41 Effesok, Osmanbey (whose origin goes back to 1453), a modern Sephardic synagogue in the newer Shisli residential area in northern Istanbul; Etz Haim Synagogue at 38 Muallim Naci Caddessi, in the Ortakoy section; and the Mayer Synagogue at 4/2 Aziz Sodak. The Merkez Synagogue at 8 Icadiye Caddesi, and Virane Synagogue at 8 Yakup Sodak, are both in Kuzguncuk on the Asian shore of the Bosporus; Hemdath Israel Synagogue, 35 Izzettin Pass Sodak, is in the Haydarpassa, also on the Asian side of the Bosporus. The Janea Synagogue, 184 Vodina Caddesi, is a 300-year-old synagogue organized first by Greek Jews; and Ochrida Synagogue, 15 Kurtci Cesmi Sokak, in the Balat quarter, is one of four Istanbul synagogues over 300 years old whose congregations existed in Byzantine times. Sabbatai Zevi, the false Messiah, preached here in 1655. The Ochrida Synagogue takes its name from an ancient Macedonian town now in Yugoslavia. But the most fascinating Turkish synagogue is in the Haskoy suburb of Istanbul at 3 Mahlul Sodak. It is a small, jewellike synagogue built below ground level where 200 or more Karaite Jews worship; Jews here followed the biblical injunction, "Out of the depths have I called thee." Karaite Jews are predominately goldsmiths, jewelers, and money-changers, and their ancestors came to Istanbul during Byzantine times. Another synagogue was founded by Bulgarian Jews, the Yambol Synagogue at 1 Ayan Cadessi; it also is over 300 years old.

The Grand Rabbi of Turkey is Rabbi David Asseo, 23 Yemenici Sodak (tel. 440472). The community center is at Buyuk Hendek Sokak 61 (tel. 441576).

Istanbul also has many other places of Jewish interest. The Or Hayim Jewish Hospital, located on the Golden Horn at 162–54 Dibbek Caddesi Karabas Mahalesi, is a 120-bed hospital staffed by Jewish physicians. There are numerous Jewish institutions including a Jewish high school at Mektep Sodak; a rabbinical academy in Haskoy at 10B Kececi Peri Mahalesi Mehtep Sodak; and the most famous Beoglu Private Jewish School, started many years ago by the local B'nai B'rith lodge.

Other places of Jewish interest include the Balat Quarter in the old city on the southern shore of the Golden Horn where the historic Jewish ghetto was located. Haskoy Cemetery, at the northern tip of the Golden Horn, is the oldest burial ground in European Turkey, and has tombstones from the fifteenth century. The Museum of Antiquities in Gulhare Parki Caddesi has original inscriptions from the Siloam reservoir built by King Hezekiah of Judah in the eighth century B.C. to provide water during the Assyrian siege of Jerusalem. The Grand Bazaar, the huge roofed city within a city in the old town near University Square, contains one of the most fascinating shopping complexes in the world. It has many Jewish merchants from all parts of the Balkans and Middle East who sell a variety of wares and who speak Ladino, a Spanish-Hebrew dialect. On Buyuk Ada, the largest island off Istanbul, the country club is Jewish.

IZMIR

Izmir, or old Smyrna, is today Turkey's second largest port and third largest city. Perhaps as many as 1,500 Jews live within its confines. Beit Israel Synagogue in the Karatas District near Asarsor, erected more than fifty years ago, serves the community, along with Bikur Holim Synagogue on Esrefpasa Caddesi.

Most of the wealthy Izmir Jews live in the Alsancak District where there is also a "secret" new synagogue in a residence—secret because the Turkish government prohibits the erection of any new synagogues. The false Messiah Sabbatai Zevi was born and lived in Izmir, and his home in Lambat Sokhagi, near the Ergat Bazaar, has been made into a monument by Izmir Jewry. (Sabbatai Zevi converted to Islam.) The community center is at Azizier Sokak 920/44, Guzelyurt (tel. 23708).

SARDIS

At Sardis (ancient capital of King Croesus) in a fertile river valley of western Turkey, an ancient synagogue was unearthed in 1970 by a joint Harvard and Cornell University expedition. An altar carved from limestone and fitted together in curving lines, apparently built between 547 and 334 B.C., was found. The outer stones were joined by iron clamps leaded into careful cuttings, and the blocks formed a six-step altar. The mosaic floors and the columns of the main entrance have been rebuilt, as was a two-story building that was apparently the Jewish community's center for baths, sports, and public meetings. The archaeologists also found a bronze container, thought to be a poor box, containing 400 tiny Roman coins; the container had been wrenched from its moorings on a wall. Nearby 1,000 graves were cut in rock.

Small Jewish communities exist in Adana, Mersin, Iskenderun, Milas, Tekirdag, Canakkale, and Gelibolu (Gallipoli), where there are also small ancient synagogues. There are also the abandoned Jewish communities of Tokat (in north central Turkey) and Diyarbakir (in southeastern Turkey) where the local museum features an ancient Torah scroll.

USEFUL ADDRESSES

Ankara: U.S. Embassy, 110 Ataturk Boulevard (tel. 265470).
Canadian Embassy, Vali Dr. Resit, Cadessi 52 Cankaya (tel. 12-24-48).
Israeli Legation, Cinnah Cad, Farabi, Sokak 43 (tel. 263904).

Istanbul: U.S. Consulate General, 104–108 Mesrutlyet Caddesi, Tepebasi (tel. 436200).
Israeli Consulate, Buyuk Ciftlik Sokak 10/1, Nisantas (tel. 464125).

URUGUAY

Approximately 50,000 of the 3 million Uruguayans are Jewish—mostly merchants. Uruguay was an ardent supporter of Israel at the U.N. in 1947 and 1948, but since 1973 Uruguay has changed to a pro-Arab position. Indeed, the life of Uruguayan Jews has become insecure and fearful, although Jewish-Catholic relations are good. There is no overt anti-Semitism according to Yosef Yerosalimski, who edits a Jewish weekly in Spanish, *Semanario Hebreo,* Lorenzo Latorre 1165 (tel. 982550); he also runs a daily two-hour Yiddish radio program in Montevideo. There are two Yiddish daily newspapers—one is *Haint* at Andes 1158 (tel. 81567)—two Yiddish weeklies, and one Yiddish monthly. The Jewish community also supports a German Jewish daily newspaper.

Most Jews came to Uruguay during the past forty years, and are organized into four distinct communities: East European, with headquarters at Durazno 1118 (tel. 981172); German (or Central European), with headquarters at Rio Branco 1168 (tel. 80969); Hungarian, with headquarters at Durazno 972 (tel. 88456); and Sephardic (Turkey, Greece, and Arab countries), with headquarters at Buenos Aires 234 (tel. 86021). All four Montevideo communities maintain their own religious, educational, and social institutions. In all, Uruguay has twenty-four synagogues headed by six rabbis. All four communities unite under the banner of *Comité Central Israelita,* with headquarters at Rio Negro 1308 (tel. 916057) in the capital city of Montevideo.

The principal synagogues of Montevideo are Adat Israel at Democracia 2370; Anshei Jeshurun at Durazno 972; Bet Meir (Mizrachi) at Andes 1180; Harishona at Inca 287; Talmud Torah Majazikei Hadat at Defensa 2356; and Vaad Ha'ir at Canelones 828. There is a Hebraica-Maccabi Sports Club in Montevideo at Camacua 623 (tel. 910792).

USEFUL ADDRESSES

Montevideo: U.S. Embassy, Calle Lauro Muller 1776 (tel. 409051). Israeli Embassy, Boulevar Artigas 1585/89 (tel. 404164).

UNION OF SOVIET SOCIALIST REPUBLICS*

Approximately 2.6 million Jews live in the USSR, all suffering from the stifling restrictions of Soviet policy prohibiting the practice of religion and emigration. Despite such governmental restraints, perhaps 100,000 Soviet Jews departed for Israel from 1971 to 1974, but since then emigration has trickled down to those few brave souls who have withstood Soviet oppression.

There are at least fifty-six synagogues in the Soviet Union, but whether they are open for prayer or for exhibition is another question. What is unquestionable, however, is the plight of Russian Jews, whose destiny merits world concern. Prohibited from the free exercise of their religious and cultural traditions, Russian Jews are clearly second-class citizens. The largest Jewish centers are Moscow (250,000), Leningrad (180,000), Kiev (175,000), Odessa (125,000), Kharkov (100,000), Kishinev (60,000), Lvov (40,000), Czernowitz (40,000), and Minsk (40,000).

BIROBIDJAN

In 1928 the Soviet government established in Birobidjan a Jewish National District (OKRUG), and six years later an Autonomous Region (OBLAST). By 1941 there were 30,000 Jews residing here, and by 1966 the Jewish population had stabilized to that figure, one Jew out of every eight citizens. In 1941, at the height of Jewish activity, there were 128 elementary schools in Yiddish, a Museum of Jewish Culture, a daily Yiddish newspaper, a medical school, a school of music, and twenty-seven Jewish collective and state farms. The synagogue is at 9 Chapayev Street, Khabarovsk Krai.

---

*The author has not visited the USSR for one reason: permission cannot be obtained for the individual to travel at will throughout this vast country. Accordingly, this chapter is derived from the author's notes in research and from personal interviews with travelers who have been to the Soviet Union.

BYELORUSSIA

Minsk is the birthplace of so many leaders of modern Israel, yet the local synagogue at 109 Leninskaya Street has been closed down since 1966.

DAGHESTAN

For some 2,000 years, in the mountains 250 miles north of Baku, have lived an isolated community of Russian Jews, the Tat Jews. They practice Judaism without *cohanim* or *leviim*—indicating that perhaps these lost souls were part of the Lost Ten Tribes of Israel. Today there are fewer than 25,000 Tat Jews, many having left the mountains because of poverty to live on the Caspian Sea where they cultivate grapes. Their language is not Russian, but a combination of Persian and old scriptural Hebrew. When visited by a representative of the Israeli Embassy, these Tat Jews expressed in no uncertain terms their intense longing to return to Eretz Yisrael.

There is a synagogue in the Daghestani Republic in Derbent at 94 Tagi Zade Street.

GEORGIA

In Tiflis (or Tbilisi) the synagogues are located at Lesilidze 71 and at Kozhevni Tupik 65 (the two-level red-brick synagogue at Lesilidze 71 has separate services, upstairs and downstairs). The 55,000 Jews in the Georgia Republic are allegedly served by sixteen houses of prayer, three of which are in Kutaisi (including one at 47 Shaumian Street). In Batumi the synagogue is at 6 March 9 Street, and in Sukhumi at 56 Kmarksa Street. The Surami synagogue is on Internatsionalya Street.

LITHUANIA

Lithuania achieved independence after World War I; but by 1940 it was incorporated into the Soviet Union as one of the republics of the USSR.

Lithuanian Jewry closely resembled Polish Jewry organizationally and institutionally. They adopted the educational methods of talmudic study, although in the seventeenth century Lituanian talmudic scholarship came into its own. The Gaon of Vilna developed his own method of study, and in the nineteenth century the great Lithuanian *yeshivot* of Mir, Telz, and Slobodka were the most important centers of learning. The great poet Chaim Nachman Bialik received his early education in Lithuania . . . hence a *Litvak*. Before World War II there were 260,000 Jews in Lithuania; during the Nazi occupation,

136,000 Lithuanian Jews were killed, and by 1960, the numbers had dwindled to 24,000.

There is a small synagogue in Vilna at 39 Ulitsa Komyannimo Street, and in Kaunas at Krasnoarmaiskaya Street.

What is poignantly missing in Vilna today is the evidence of the greatness of the former "Jewish City" which Ludwig Lewisohn described in his 1925 book *Israel:* "All men of all races who love liberty and peace have a special relation to the Jews of Vilna." Isaac N. Steinberg, Russian Minister of Justice under Kerensky, in his 1950 book *Reconstructionist,* described it best: "Is Jerusalem ready . . . to become the Vilna of Israel as Vilna has been the Jerusalem of Lithuania?"

RUSSIA

In the capital city of Moscow where 250,000 Jews dwell, is the famed Central Synagogue, 8 Arkipova Street (tel. 2942901), not far from Red Square. It has recently been repainted and refurbished; there is even a new blue velvet curtain over the Holy Ark. Unfortunately there are but two other prayer houses in all of Moscow: the small wooden synagogue Marina Roshcha at Viacheslavsky Perevlok 3/5, and the Tsherkizovo Synagogue at Ulitsa Lermontova 70. Visitors to Moscow are officially welcomed by Rabbi Yaacov Fishman of the Moskovskaya Yevreiskaya Relighioznaya Obschchina; Rabbi Fishman is also the rabbi of the Central Synagogue.

In sharp contrast to these government-maintained synagogues is the magnificent large synagogue in Leningrad at 2 Lermontov Prospect which desperately needs rebuilding; it has an amplifying system and a neon *Magen David* over the Holy Ark.

Other synagogues in Russia are in Sverdlovsk (14 Kuibyshev Street); Klintsy (84 Lermontov Street); Kuibyshev (14 Chapayev Street); Briansk (29 Uritsky Street); Irkutsk (17 Liebkñecht Street); Kalinin (21 Solodovaya Street); Kazan (Pravokabannaya Tatarskya); Malakhovka (20 Lermontov Street); Astrakhan (30 Babushkina Street); Novosibirsk (104b Lomonosova Street); Rostov (18 Gazetny Street); and Rybnitsa (Voikova Street).

UKRAINE

The Kiev Synagogue at 29 Ulitsa Shchekovitskaya is shabby and in need of care, as is the predominantly Jewish Podol area in which it is situated.

Outside of Kiev, the capital city of the Ukraine, is the sinister ravine Babi Yar, where on September 29 and 30, 1941, 33,771 Jews were machine-gunned by the Nazis and thrown into the ravine, some still alive. Two years later in 1943, before retreating from Kiev, the Nazis forced the inmates of the concentration camp at Babi Yar to burn all corpses which had "disappeared" after successive Nazi bestialities. The concentration camp's inmates were then murdered by the Nazis, bringing the total of those killed by the Nazis at this site to more than 70,000 Jews and almost a quarter of a million non-Jews. In 1959 the Kiev City Council, following Kremlin orders to erase the memory of Babi Yar, decided to flood the ravine and turn the area into a public park and a sports stadium. Protest came from decent people everywhere who grieved that 300,000 human beings had no proper memorial. Yevgeni Yevtushenko, the distinguished Russian poet, wrote his famous poem *Babi Yar* which inspired Russia's greatest living composer, Shostakovich, to compose his *Symphony No. 13*. But the Soviet leaders did not listen and in early 1961 decided to dam the ravine. However, heavy rain burst the dam, engulfing the whole area. For two years construction was halted, but Soviet leaders persisted and finally filled the ravine. Today the Babi Yar area has a main highway built across it with a housing estate and a television center. No monument marks the grave sites at Babi Yar.

Other synagogues in the Ukraine are in Bar (37 March 8 Street); Berdichev (4 Sverdlov Street); Bershad (Narodnaya Street); Chernovtsky (53 Kobylitsy Street); Dniepropetrovsk (Kotsiubinsky Street 9); Odessa (5 Peresyp Lesnaya Street); Slavuta (Shkolnaya Street); Uzhgorod (47 Mukachevskaya Street); Vershad (Narodnaya Street); and Zhitomir (78 Dombrovskaya Street)

UZBEKISTAN

Here, not too far from the Afghanistan border is the ancient city of Samarkand. On Khudzumskaya Street (a dirt road), behind a locked blue gate, is the ancient synagogue. The walls are draped with velvet cloth bearing Hebrew letters embroidered in gold filigree. At least thirty beautifully decorated Torah scrolls grace the Ark. In recent years more than 8,000 of these Bukharan Jews have migrated to Israel.

Other synagogues in Uzbekistan are at Andizhan (7 Sovietskaya Street); Bokhara (18 Tsentrainaya Street); Kokand (45 Marshal Govorova Street); Margelan (7 Shakirdzhanova Street); Namangan (Frunze Street); and Tashkent (24 Sagban Street and 9 Chekalova Street).

Other synagogues in the Soviet Union may be found in the Republic of Kazakhstan (the city of Alma-Ata at 48 Tashkentskaya Street; and the town of Chimkent at 7 Svoboda Street); in the Republic of Azerbaijan (the city of Baku at 171 Pervomaiskaya Street and at 39 Dimitrova Street); in the Republic of Khirgizia (the town of Frunze at 20 Karpinsky Street); in the Republic of Moldavia (the city of Kishinev at 8 Yakimovsky Street); and in the Republic of Estonia (the city of Tallin at 9 Lasteaya Street).

USEFUL ADDRESSES

Leningrad: U.S. Consulate General, Ulitsa Petra Lavrova Street (tel. 274-8235).

Moscow: U.S. Embassy, Ulitsa Chaykovskogo 19/21/23 (tel. 2522451).
Canadian Embassy, 23 Strarokonyushenny Pereulok (tel. 241-90-34; night tel. 241-54-42).

VENEZUELA

The earliest Jewish settlers in Venezuela came from the island of Curaçao, and settled near the colonial coastal town of Coro in the early nineteenth century. In Coro an old Sephardic cemetery is still in use with more than 150 graves of Venezuelan Jewry. Recently the cemetery was restored under the supervision of José Curiel, Venezuelan Minister of Public Works, whose great-great grandfather was the first Jew to settle in Coro, and who bought the cemetery land in 1832. The Asociación Israelita de Venezuela, founded in 1922 by Sephardim from North Africa, raised funds for the project. Although Coro experienced pogroms in 1831 and 1855, there are still a few Jewish families living here.

CARACAS

The 19,000 Jews of Caracas support every Jewish institution and organization. The Herzl-Bialik Jewish School on Avenida Codazzi, San Bernardino, was built more than thirty years ago and now includes sports facilities of the finest kind as well as an impressive social center called La Hebraica. The Ashkenazi Synagogue of Union Israelita de Caraca is located on Avenida Marques del Toro, San Bernardino (tel. 515253) in a magnificent edifice and courtyard (Rabbi Pinhas Brener). The Sephardic synagogue, Tiferet Israel, is on Avenida Mariperez Los Caobos (tel. 7811942), and is headed by Rabbis Amram Anselem and Moises Binia. The Great Synagogue is at Avenida Francisco Javier Ustariz, San Bernardino (tel. 511869); Rabbi Yehuda Gertner and Rabbi Isaac Sananes preside. The B'nai B'rith Center and Hillel House is at 9a Transversal (entre 7a Avenue Avila, Altamira [tel. 326596]) in a beautiful residential area.

MARACAIBO

More than 800 Jews reside here; the Jewish community center is at Calle 74 No. 13–26 (tel. 70333), and the Chief Rabbi is Dr. Isaac Gabai.

There are more than eighty Jews in Maracay, Venezuela's fifth largest city; and some thirty Jews reside in Valencia. In Puerto La

Cruz, a busy oil port ringed by green hills, palm trees, and a cluster of islands, perhaps ten or fifteen Jews reside; the same number dwells in San Cristóbal, a 400-year-old city just thirty-five miles from the Colombian border on a lower slope of the Andes.

The wealth of the Jewish community of Venezuela is considerable. It should be noted that the great Venezuelan patriot, Simón Bolívar, in his struggle against Spanish rule at the beginning of the nineteenth century, was aided by Jewish wealth and notably by Mordechay Ricardo, a Jew living in Curaçao. Jews are active in industry and trade and there are many professionals among the younger generation.

USEFUL ADDRESSES

Caracas: U.S. Embassy, Avenida Francisco de Miranda and Avenida Principal de la Floresta (tel. 2847111).
Canadian Embassy, Avenida La Estancia No. 10, 16° piso Ciudad Commercial Tamanaco (tel. 913277).
Israeli Embassy, Centro Empresarial Miranda, Avenida Francisco de Miranda, Los Ruices (tel. 364511).

VIRGIN ISLANDS
(UNITED STATES)

European Jews first came to St. Thomas in 1665, a year before Denmark claimed the islands. A great number of Jews came from the island of St. Eustatius, a Dutch free port, after it was devastated by the British fleet in 1776. Gabriel Milan, a German Jew from Hamburg, served as governor of St. Thomas from 1684 to 1687. He was a soldier of fortune, and his brutality led to his hanging years later in Copenhagen. A Sephardic community was founded in the 1850s but their numbers soon dwindled. During World War I in 1917 the islands became American territory, and there followed an influx of Jews. Today about 475 Jews reside here.

Jews from St. Thomas have indeed made history. Judah P. Benjamin, the Jewish Secretary of State for the Confederacy, was born here. So was Camille Pissarro, the father of French Impressionism (1830–1903); Pissarro was born at 14 Main Street in Charlotte Amalie. David Levy Yulee, first Jew elected to the U.S. Senate (in 1845 from Florida) also came from St. Thomas. Among the famous Jewish citizens of the U.S. Virgin Islands was Morris Fidanque de Castro, named to the post of governor in 1950 by President Harry S. Truman. Another is the distinguished novelist Herman Wouk. Top laurels probably go to the past governor, Ralph M. Paiewonsky—the first native son to fill the office.

At the top of Synagogue Hill in the city of Charlotte Amalie on St. Thomas is the historic synagogue of Spanish-Portuguese origin, Beracha V'Sholom V'Gemilath Chasidim. It was built in 1796 and is the third oldest synagogue in the Western Hemisphere. The synagogue is remarkable for its age and beauty; some 5,000 visitors a year are received, according to Elaine Sonne, synagogue secretary. The synagogue was destroyed by fire in 1804, rebuilt in 1812, and then remodeled in 1833 and in 1973, but it is still distinguished by the interior woodwork, the central chandelier with eighteen hurricane lamps, and by the one-inch-thick layer of clean sand which covers the marble floor and commemorates the wanderings of the Israelites in the desert after the Exodus from Egypt. The Synagogue of Blessing and Peace and Acts of Piety (as it was first known) stands atop

Synagogue Hill with all its majesty. The congregation has only had four rabbis in the past 112 years. Today Rabbi Stanley T. Relkin serves this Reform congregation, although traditions of Orthodox Sephardim are still observed.

There are two Jewish cemeteries on St. Thomas: Savan (in a low-lying peninsula off Waterfront Drive, west of the shopping area; epitaphs date from 1792); and Altona (below the Virgin Isle Hilton Hotel; epitaphs date from 1837).

ST. CROIX

As early as 1784 there was a synagogue on the island of St. Croix, just forty miles southeast of St. Thomas. But by 1800 the congregation had disbanded—although one Moses Benjamin, a St. Croix merchant, still had kosher meat shipped to him from New York. The Jewish cemetery is in the western suburb of Christiansted adjoining the Morovian cemetery (epitaphs date back to 1779).

YEMEN

Jews have lived in Yemen since the earliest of times. Between A.D. 390 and 420 the ruler, Abu Karib Asad, became a Jew and propagated his new faith among his people. In 750, the citizens of Zabid and Mocha had large Jewish populations. Between the years 800 and 900, Jewish traders from Europe stopped off in Yemen on their way to the Orient. Maimonides wrote his "Epistle to Yemen" in 1172 to exhort Yemeni Jewry to abide by the faith of their fathers. Benjamin of Tudela visited Yemen Jewry in the twelfth century and reported that "the Jews take spoil and booty and retreat to the mountains, and no man can prevail against them."

Jews have lived in Yemen continuously since then, and in 1948 there were 55,000 Jews in Yemen. Principal Jewish settlements were in Sapa, Kaukaban, Sana, and Dhamar. But Jewish population has since decreased to about 500 persons, after 46,000 Yemenites arrived in Israel on the "magic carpet" of the 1950s. In 1980 the North Yemen government reported a community of 300 Jews, most of whom lived close to the Saudi Arabian border in the town of Sadah and the neighboring villages of Raidah, Haidan, and Khaulan. The Jews are silversmiths, leatherworkers, and metalworkers.

USEFUL ADDRESSES:
Sana: U.S. Embassy, P.O. Box 1088 (tel. 72790).

YUGOSLAVIA

Jews first settled in Yugoslavia (Dalmatia and Macedonia) in Roman times, as evidenced by synagogue inscriptions found in Stobi and by relics at Salona. The Stobi Synagogue, founded by Claudius Tiberius Polycharmus, is most remarkable as evidence of geographic expansion of Jewish communities about the year 165 A.D. Earliest communities sprang up in the fourteenth century at Ragusa (now Dubrovnik) and Spalato (now Split). Refugees from Spain began to settle after 1492 in Belgrade and Sarajevo where Sephardic traditions are still preserved. The great earthquake of 1667, which nearly destroyed Dubrovnik, left the ghetto and ancient synagogue intact. When the French seized Dubrovnik in 1806, Jews were given complete civil equality. Religious liberty was granted by legislation after 1878, and thousands of Ashkenazim migrated into Yugoslavia. Nazi occupation in World War II brought massacres and deportation on a vast scale. During World War II under the Nazi regime, 80 percent of Yugoslav Jews—60,000 people—lost their lives.

Today there are fewer than 6,000 elderly Jews living in Yugoslavia. Yet the Federation of Jewish Communities in Belgrade maintains contact with more than thirty Jewish communities scattered about the country. (Its offices are at St. 7 Juli 71a/III, tel. 624-359, and its president is Dr. Lavoslav Kadelburg.) The federation supports an ambitious social welfare program, including the maintenance of an old age home, summer camps for youngsters, youth clubs, and other institutions.

BELGRADE

The capital city of Yugoslavia has a large synagogue near its center at Kosmajska (Birjuzova 19), serving the Jewish community of fewer than 1,500 persons. It is a tall white-stone structure built in 1933, and was badly damaged by the Nazis who used it as a brothel. The synagogue was reconsecrated and rebuilt with funds from many sources including the Yugoslav government. There is another synagogue at Marsala Birjuzova 19. At the Jewish cemetery there are monuments to the Fallen Fighters and Martyrs of Fascism. Of outstanding interest for the Jewish tourist is the Jewish Historical Museum of the Federation of Jewish Communities in Yugoslavia. The museum's varied collection includes a tombstone of a Jew from Tiberias from the fourth century; sketches of ancient Yugoslav synagogues; embroidered curtains, *tallithim* and *tfillin;* and other synagogue art from the eighteenth century, and even old Sephardic costumes from Bosnia. One interesting exhibit points up the friendship of Mosa Pijade, a Jew, with Marshal Tito. President of the Jewish community is Stevan Levi.

DUBROVNIK

The Jewish community of Dubrovnik dates back to the year 1352 when Spanish Jews escaping persecution arrived here on the shores of the Adriatic Sea. From the very beginning the position of Jews was favorable. In 1407 Jews were given legal recognition as a community living within a small ghetto, Via del Ghetto. Jews played an important role in trade and commerce, although they were subjected to medieval discrimination such as wearing yellow badges, paying special taxes, and even being charged with ritual murder. In 1420 one of the important water fountains in Dubrovnik was given the name of "Fontana per Gli Ebrei" or "Fontana Kosher." It still stands today at the Pile (Brsalje), the water flowing from a lion's head.

Today only a half dozen elderly Jews reside in Dubrovnik. The synagogue at Zudioska Ulica 3 (or Jewish Street) dates back to the thirteenth century. Tucked away on the third floor of a typical medieval residence the synagogue comes back to life once a week for the brief Kabbalat Shabbas service. The "benefactor" is a wonderful, elderly gentleman, Emilio Tolentino, who "guards" the synagogue. Its windows are in Gothic style and the interior is Baroque. The synagogue is an oblong-shaped room divided by three arches and paneled in dark wood; from the ceiling hangs a beautiful antique Florentine candelabra. The Torah scrolls were brought from Spain in 1325, along with an irreplaceable Moorish carpet of floral design in brilliant colors, a gift from Queen Isabella of Spain to her Jewish doctor. Among other priceless relics in the synagogue are superbly embroidered tapestries and silver pieces for synagogue use. One prized possession is a letter to Dubrovnik Jews from Sir Moses Montefiore in England.

Outside of the walled city is a Jewish cemetery over 300 years old. On many of the old tombstones there are five-pointed crowns, a symbol granted in 711 to the Chief Rabbi of Córdoba, Spain, by the Moorish conqueror; this symbol was worn as a badge of freedom by Jewish exiles from Spain.

LJUBLJANA

The Street of the Jews on the right bank of the river marks the site of a fourteenth-century Jewish community.

NOVI SAD

Forty-five miles northwest of Belgrade, this city has about 400 Jews, about one-tenth its 1941 Jewish population. The stained-glass dome of its synagogue at Jna Ulica 35 (tel. 43022) reflects the fact that this synagogue, built in 1906, is not only one of the most beautiful Byzantine synagogues in the world but also the fourth largest in Europe, seating almost 1,000 persons. Unfortunately, today the synagogue is closed. There is a Jewish cemetery at the end of Doze Dizkoja Street. President of the local community is Egon Stark (tel. 43022).

OSIJEK

At Braca Radica 13 is a small synagogue which has a huge sculpture of an unknown Jewish mother and her child as a memorial to Jewish victims of the Nazis.

RIJEKA

The local synagogue is at Ivan Filipovitch 9. President of the local community is Josip Engl.

SARAJEVO

Sarajevo is today the third largest Yugoslav city and proud of its synagogue, its Jewish Museum, and the old Jewish cemetery—although the Jewish population of Sarajevo had dwindled in recent years to fewer than 200 persons. During World War II the Nazis massacred 11,000 Sarajevo Jews. The synagogue (tel. 22023) is located at Dobrovolijacka Street 83, which parallels the canal near the Princip Bridge. Erected in 1902, the Sephardic synagogue is Moorish in style, with four towers and domes topped by Stars of David. President of the Sarajevo Jewish community is Dr. Isak Levi, a professor of veterinary medicine at the local university.

The Jewish Museum is near the old Jewish quarter, Bjelave on the northwest slopes of the city, on Marsala Tito Avenue. Founded in 1966 on the occasion of the 400th anniversary of the arrival of Jews in Sarajevo, the Jewish Museum is actually located within an old synagogue. At the entrance to the museum is an 800-year-old brass candelabra brought to Sarajevo by Spanish Jews from Córdoba, Spain. Also at the entrance is an enlarged color photograph of the famous Sarajevo Haggadah of 1352. The original Haggadah is in the

National Yugoslav Museum in Belgrade under lock and key. The Haggadah has been ascribed to fourteenth-century Jewish artists in Spain, Catalonia, Provence, and Venice; Spanish Jews from Catalonia brought it here from Italy. Inside the Jewish Museum is a 200-year-old Ark curtain, hidden by local Moslems from the Nazis. There are displays of centuries-old prayer shawls, a *shofar,* circumcision tools, and other ritual objects. On the second floor is a replica of a Jewish tinsmith's shop, complete with doorway, sign, workbench, tools, raw materials, and finished products, Suspended from the ceiling on the third floor of the museum is a five-foot-long red book listing all of the 11,000 Sarajevo Jewish victims of the Holocaust. On Nevesinjska Street is an old cemetery with interesting grave markers.

SENTA

The Jewish cemetery at Dubrovacka Street 18 has a memorial to the thousands of Jews killed here by the Nazis.

SKOPLJE

The Albert Vajs Jewish Community Center (tel. 2432) at March 11th Street 46 is named after a past president of the Federation of Jewish Communities. On March 11, 1943, some 7,000 Skoplje Jews were deported to the Nazi concentration camp at Treblinka. The 1963 earthquake disaster left only ninety Jews. President of the community is Benjamin Samokovlija; his office is at Borko Talevski Street 24.

SPLIT

The small synagogue is located near the ruins of the ancient Diocletian Palace. The Jewish community center for 120 Jews is at Zidovski Prolaz 1 (tel. 45672).

SUBOTICA

The synagogue and community offices at Dimitrija Tucovica 13 (tel. 21705) were rededicated in 1963, after near destruction by the Nazis. The Jewish cemetery has an impressive memorial to the Jewish victims of Nazi atrocities.

ZAGREB

This capital of Slovenia has fewer than 1,200 Jews, although before World War II there were 12,000. The Jewish community center at Palmoticeva Street 16 (tel. 35369) is active, and its choir, which specializes in Yugoslav, Hebrew, and Israeli music, is well known. Dr. Dragan Volner heads the community. In the Central Cemetery of

Zagreb (Mirogoj) there is a monument to Jewish victims of World War II. The Jewish Old Folks Home at Bukovacka Cesta 55 was opened in 1957, and still looks after the aged.

USEFUL ADDRESSES

Belgrade: U.S. Embassy, Kneza Milosa 50 (tel. 645655). Canadian Embassy, Proleterskih Brigada 69 (tel. 434524).

Zagreb: U.S. Consulate, Zrinjevac 13 (tel. 440800).

ZAIRE

A small community of Sephardic Jews from the Greek island of Rhodes migrated to Zaire, previously known as the Belgian Congo, more than fifty years ago. The new African environment was conducive to farming, and prosperity ensued. But when the Belgian Congo became Zaire, the new government nationalized the farms, and many Jews left for Europe and the United States. Today, about 200 Jews still live in Zaire. In 1984 Zaire and Israel are on friendly terms.

USEFUL ADDRESSES

Kinshasa: U.S. Embassy, 310 Avenue des Aviateurs (tel. 25881). Israeli Embassy, Residence Les Flamboyants, Avenida Lumpangu 201-Gombe (tel. 25215).

ZAMBIA

This African republic is home to about 400 Jews living in such cities and towns as Chingola, Kitwe, Luanshya, Mufulira, Lusaka, and Ndola. The United Hebrew Congregation of the Copperbelt under the presidency of D. Messerer (Freedom Way, Mufulira) is the active leader of the Jewish communities of Zambia. There are synagogues in Kitwe on Regent Avenue; in Mufulira on Livingston Avenue; in Lusaka on Livingstone Road; and in Chingola (Moss Dobkins, 61 Princes Street [tel. 2275] heads the community). Among the Jewish leaders of Zambia are M. Bernstein of Kitwe (13 Essex Avenue); A. D. Figov of Luanshya (35 Wales Avenue); R. E. Yesder of Ndola; and A. Galaun and M. Prins of Lusaka (9 Lilyan Place).

USEFUL ADDRESSES
Lusaka: U.S. Embassy, P.O. Box 31617 (tel. 214911).

ZIMBABWE

This African nation, which gained its independence in 1980, has a Jewish population of perhaps 2,000 persons, living in such communities as Bulawayo, Gatooma, Gwelo, Que Que, and Harare (formerly Salisbury). Although there has been a mass exodus of Jews (from a high of 7,000 in 1961 to a low of 3,000 in 1977) Zimbabwe Jewry have expanded their communal institutions. The Harare Hebrew Congregation has built a new synagogue, and a new wing has been opened at the Home for the Jewish Aged in Bulawayo. Unfortunately, local Jewry is aging—30 percent are sixty years or older.

The Jewish community, like the rest of Zimbabwe, has been torn apart by the extremes of liberalism and by apartheid. More Jews would have emigrated in recent years were it not for the fact that Zimbabwe exchange control regulations forbade the transfer of capital out of the country.

The recorded Jewish connection with Zimbabwe goes back to the mid-nineteenth century when Daniel Montague Kisch of a well-known Anglo-Jewish family became one of the chief advisers to King Lobengula. But the founders of the modern Jewish community were mainly of Eastern European descent, who came to Zimbabwe via South Africa. A small number of Jews of German origin followed in the middle of this century.

In the capital city of Harare there are three synagogues: the Hebrew Congregation and the Milton Park Jewish Center on Lezard Avenue (tel. 27576); the Shaare Shalom Sephardic Synagogue, under Rabbi Shimon Assaraf, at 54 Montagu Avenue (tel. 22899); and the Progressive Jewish Congregation (tel. 26434). Approximately 1,000 Jews dwell in Harare.

In Bulawayo, where fewer than 600 Jews reside, there have been five Jewish mayors since 1965. The Central African Jewish Board of Deputies meets at Abercorn House, 12th Avenue and Abercorn Street (tel. 65188). The Bulawayo Hebrew Congregation (tel. 60829) is also on Abercorn Street, over which Rabbi M. Z. Cotten presides. There is a Progressive Jewish Congregation at the corner of Coghlan and Bailey Avenues, Kumalo (tel. 70443).

USEFUL ADDRESSES

Harare: U.S. Embassy, 78 Enterprise Road, Highlands (tel. 791586).

GLOSSARY

aron kodesh	cabinet or ark where Torah scrolls are kept
Ashkenazim	Jews who originated in Western Europe
Beth Din	"house of judgment" or rabbinical court of law
bima	dais or platform in synagogue
bris	circumcision of the male child
challah	braided bread eaten on Sabbath and during holidays
chazan	cantor or leader in synagogue prayer
halacha	the rabbinical law of the Talmud and of later Hebrew literature
Hassidim	religious and social movement founded by Israel Shem Tov (1699–1761) as a result of the depressed state of East European Jewry in the eighteenth century after the Chmielnicki Massacres and Church persecution; the movement embraces purity of heart as being superior to study, because all persons are equal.
Hechal Shlomo	the seat of the Chief Rabbinate and rabbinical headquarters in Jerusalem
Kabbala	"tradition" or the mystical religious part of Judaism
kashrut	regulations determining Jewish dietary laws
kibbutz	collective enterprise in Israel
Magen David	six-pointed star or shield of David
matzoh	unleavened bread
mezzuza	parchment scroll placed in a container which is nailed to the doorposts of places occupied by Jews
mikvah	ritual bath
minyan	ten male persons sufficient to conduct religious services
mitzvah	"commandment" or injunction of the Torah (613 in number), hence a good deed
oneg shabbat	"delight in the Sabbath," Friday evening or Saturday afternoon prayer and collation
Sephardim	Jews who originated in Spain, Portugal, North Africa, and the Orient

shabbat	Saturday, or the seventh day of the week, a day of rest
shofar	ram's horn which is blown on ceremonial occasions in the synagogue
shtetl	Jewish small town or village in Eastern Europe
shuchan aruch	"the prepared table," the codification of Orthodox Jewish law by Joseph Caro (1488–1575)
sifrai torot	"books of the Torah" or the five books of Moses, the Pentateuch
tallit	four-cornered cloth with fringes worn as a prayer shawl
tfillin	phylacteries worn during weekday services by Jewish males over the age of thirteen
Torah	scroll containing the five books of Moses, i.e., the Old Testament
yeshivah	Jewish parochial school

JEWISH HOLIDAYS

1984

Purim		Sun.	Mar. 18
Passover		Tue.	Apr. 17
	through	Mon.	Apr. 23
Holocaust Memorial Day		Sun.	Apr. 29
Independence Day		Mon.	May 7
Shavuot		Wed.	June 6
Tisha B'av		Tue.	Aug. 7
Rosh Hashana		Thu.	Sep. 27
		Fri.	Sep. 28
Yom Kippur		Sat.	Oct. 6
Sukkot		Thu.	Oct. 11
Hoshana Raba		Wed.	Oct. 17
Simchat Torah		Thu.	Oct. 18
Chanukah		Wed.	Dec. 19

1985

Purim		Thu.	Mar. 7
Passover		Sat.	Apr. 6
	through	Fri.	Apr. 12
Holocaust Memorial Day		Thu.	Apr. 18
Independence Day		Thu.	Apr. 25
Shavuot		Sun.	May 26
Tisha B'av		Sun.	July 28
Rosh Hashana		Mon.	Sep. 16
		Tue.	Sep. 17
Yom Kippur		Wed.	Sep. 25
Sukkot		Mon.	Sep. 30
Hoshana Raba		Sun.	Oct. 6
Simchat Torah		Mon.	Oct. 7
Chanukah		Sun.	Dec. 8

1986

Purim	Tue.	Mar.	25
Passover	Thu.	Apr.	24
through	Wed.	Apr.	30
Holocaust Memorial Day	Tue.	May	6
Independence Day	Wed.	May	14
Shavuot	Fri.	June	13
Tisha B'av	Thu.	Aug.	14
Rosh Hashana	Sat.	Oct.	4
	Sun.	Oct.	5
Yom Kippur	Mon.	Oct.	13
Sukkot	Sat.	Oct.	18
Hoshana Raba	Fri.	Oct.	24
Simchat Torah	Sat.	Oct.	25
Chanukah	Sat.	Dec.	27

1987

Purim	Sun.	Mar.	15
Passover	Tue.	Apr.	14
through	Mon.	Apr.	20
Holocaust Memorial Day	Sun.	Apr.	26
Independence Day	Mon.	May	4
Shavuot	Wed.	June	3
Tisha B'av	Tue.	Aug.	4
Rosh Hashana	Thu.	Sep.	24
	Fri.	Sep.	25
Yom Kippur	Sat.	Oct.	3
Sukkot	Thu.	Oct.	8
Hoshana Raba	Wed.	Oct.	14
Simchat Torah	Thu.	Oct.	15
Chanukah	Wed.	Dec.	16

1988

Purim	Thu.	Mar.	3
Passover	Sat.	Apr.	2
through	Fri.	Apr.	8
Holocaust Memorial Day	Thu.	Apr.	14
Independence Day	Fri.	Apr.	22
Shavuot	Sun.	May	22
Tisha B'Av	Sun.	Jul.	24
Rosh Hashana	Mon.	Sep.	12
	Tue.	Sep.	13
Yom Kippur	Wed.	Sep.	21
Sukkot	Mon.	Sep.	26
Hoshana Raba	Sun.	Oct.	2
Simchat Torah	Mon.	Oct.	3
Chanukah	Sun.	Dec.	4